From Douglas H. Paal,
President of the Asia Pacific Policy Center

*"[This book] is the most informative and well-told story available of
the creation of the Asia Pacific Economic Cooperation (APEC) forum.
Anyone seeking to make sense of the rise of Asia as the economic
center of global economic activity in the 21st century should start with
this volume.*

*Yoichi Funabashi has used his unrivaled access to key policymakers
on both sides of the Pacific to probe the motives, suspicions and
dreams of APEC's progenitors. Views about APEC among its members
and outside observers are almost as diverse as the nations themselves.
Funabashi's book puts the readers on a common footing with even the
most inside players.*

*Moreover, anyone who holds an opinion about Japan and its
emerging role in the world will find Funabashi's book a font of insight
and wisdom. His analysis challenges fashionable theories with a rarely
seen common sense. No author does a better job of helping the West
understand Japan."*

YOICHI FUNABASHI

ASIA PACIFIC FUSION
Japan's Role in APEC

Institute for International Economics
Washington, DC
October 1995

Yoichi Funabashi, *Visiting Fellow* (1987) is the Bureau Chief of the Japanese newspaper *Asahi Shimbun*. He is the author of several prize-winning books including *Neibu—Inside China* (1983). He was awarded the 1994 Japan Press Award—often called Japan's Pulitzer Prize—for his coverage of foreign policy and was granted the Yoshino Sakuzo award for the Japanese version of *Managing the Dollar: From the Plaza to the Louvre* (revised edition 1989).

INSTITUTE FOR INTERNATIONAL ECONOMICS
11 Dupont Circle, NW
Washington, DC 20036-1207
(202) 328-9000 FAX: (202) 328-0900

C. Fred Bergsten, *Director*
Christine F. Lowry, *Director of Publications*

Typesetting by Automated Graphic Systems
Printing by Automated Graphic Systems

Printed in the United States of America
97 96 95 5 4 3 2 1

Library of Congress Cataloging-in-Publication Data

Funabashi, Yōichi, 1944–
    Asia Pacific Fusion: Japan's Role in APEC / Yoichi Funabashi.
        p.   cm.
    Includes index.
        1. Japan—Foreign economic relations—Asia.   2. Asia—Foreign economic relations—Japan.   3. Japan—Foreign economic relations—Pacific Area.   4. Pacific Area—Foreign economic relations—Japan.   I. Institute for International Economics (U.S.)   II. Title.   III. Series.
HF1602.15.A74F86   1995
337.5205—dc20   95-24858
                                                                CIP

ISBN 0-88132-224-5

Marketed and Distributed outside the USA and Canada by Longman Group UK Limited, London

For Reiko, one and only

Contents

Foreword

The Japanese have a saying, "Don't try to chase two rabbits simultaneously." The Western way is to "kill two birds with one stone." I've tried to kill three with my old-fashioned Oasys word processor.

The first is an analysis of the trends and developments of the Asia Pacific region in the new international environment. The growing confluence of civilizations and shifting power political balance will work to reshape the future structure of the Asia Pacific. Asia's emergence has fostered new aspirations and new institutions, but it also contains many dangers and pitfalls. The growing pride and self-confidence has enabled Asia to move beyond the ideology of North–South divide and look optimistically to a future of prosperity. At the same time, the emergence of new political and economic powers has the potential to upset the existing order and undermine the secure environment that has fueled the region's economic growth.

The second dynamic that I explore is the growing movement toward regionalism and multilateralism in the Asia Pacific. As a case study, I examine the evolution of the Asia Pacific Economic Cooperation (APEC) forum, the most ambitious and important regional organization that has ever arisen in the region. Within this context I focus especially closely on APEC's attempts to facilitate economic liberalization in the Asia Pacific. The liberalization issue will be salient for APEC and each of its members for at least the next decade. I try to look behind the scenes and examine the agendas, and hidden motivations, of each major player in the debate.

My final task will be to explain the dilemmas Japan faces in the new Asia Pacific environment and outline Japan's options. Japan's chairmanship of APEC presents an invaluable opportunity for Japan to fulfill a role commensurate with its abilities and constraints. Through an active APEC policy, Japan can for the first time assume regional leadership without raising the ire and suspicion of either its Asian neighbors or its American friends. The time has come for Japan to move beyond just bridging East and West and toward the creation of a new, Asia Pacific community.

Writing in 1942 in his book *Inside Asia,* the ubiquitous and prolific author John Gunther noted that Asia, a "land of illiteracy and disease," was burdened by "a sense of looking backward, not forward" and inhabited by people who "by and large . . . are less generally competent than Europeans." After several months of traveling through the region, he finally concluded that "one can speak of Europe, but not Asia."

In this book, I am speaking of Asia, and of the Asia Pacific. Today the region is the most exciting and dynamic area of the world. It is the Asia Pacific peoples, through hard work and perseverance, who have been the main protagonists of the Asian "miracle." The cross-fertilized seeds of an Asia Pacific civilization have been sown. APEC has been an endeavor to refute each of the points Gunther made fifty years ago.

It was Fred Bergsten who encouraged me to write a book on Japan's role in APEC to coincide with its chairing of the Osaka meeting. Like I did in my previous work for the Institute, *Managing the Dollar: From the Plaza to the Louvre,* I found the process journalistically thrilling and intellectually stimulating. We originally had conceived of a policy-oriented monograph, focusing narrowly on the issues that needed to be addressed at the Osaka meeting. As I began to review the literature on the subject, however, I found a dearth of journalistic material on APEC's history and character. For this reason I decided to approach APEC from a more journalistic, historical angle. The study of APEC was challenging in many ways. An analysis of APEC requires one to go beyond economics to focus on the political, cultural, and civilizational factors that are at work in the region today. In the past I have traveled extensively throughout Asia, particularly for my research on the Asianization of Asia. This book provides me with the long-sought-after opportunity to explore how the growing Asianization trend under way in East Asia can integrate into the emerging sense of an Asia Pacific community.

As an institution, APEC remains a young and largely undeveloped forum of 18 diverse and disparate economies. Yet it is its youth and informality that has made it such an interesting and dynamic topic of study. I hope that this book will provide a basis for further analysis of the forum, and the question of Asia Pacific regionalism in general.

Throughout the process, Fred has remained an invaluable resource for me through our exchange of views, thoughts, and comments. As Chairman of the APEC Eminent Persons Group (EPG), Fred has already established a strong and thorough intellectual framework for considering APEC and its mission. As a journalist, I often find it difficult to compete with Fred's ability to relate poignant stories in such interesting and amusing ways.

Central to my research have been interviews with the dozens of leaders, ministers, officials, and intellectuals who have been instrumental in APEC's evolution. I would be remiss if I did not mention those national leaders and cabinet members who assisted me in putting APEC into a political perspective. Those leaders and former leaders with whom I had the pleasure of speaking with on the issue of APEC and the Asia Pacific include Anand Panyarachun, James Bolger, Goh Chok Tong, Tsutomu Hata, Robert Hawke, Morihiro Hosokawa, Paul Keating, Lee Kuan Yew, Mahathir bin Mohamad, Yasuhiro Nakasone, Fidel Ramos, and Noboru Takeshita. I must also mention those cabinet ministers with whom I had the pleasure of interviewing, some more than twice: Rafidah Aziz, James Baker, Jesus Estanislao, Gareth Evans, Han Sung-Joo, Han Seung-Soo, Sastrosurarto Hartarto, Ryutaro Hashimoto, Yohei Kono, Mickey Kantor, Raul Manglapus, Hiroshi Mitsuzuka, Vincent Siew, and Arifin Siregar. I am also grateful to the five officials who played the sherpa roles during the most critical stages of APEC's development: Richard Woolcott, Lee See-Young, Robert Fauver, Bintoro Tjokroamidjojo, and Hidehiro Konno. The depictions of their odysseys through the entire Asia Pacific area were genuinely insightful and thought provoking. In addition to these leaders, ministers, and officials, I am indebted to the many other EPG members, SOM delegates, and government officials whose insights provided invaluable information on the APEC process. I would also like to express my sincere appreciation to the four senior officials and diplomats from the United States, Japan, Indonesia, and China and one Australian scholar who read the manuscript of the book. Their important and insightful comments were invaluable. However, I take full responsibility, of course, for any omissions or mistakes.

Finally, I was fortunate to have two excellent, Japanese-speaking research assistants, Molly O'Meara and Raymond Greene, without whose dedication and hard work I could not have completed this book. I am also deeply appreciative of the work of my diligent and committed intern, Natsuo Nishio. It was my great pleasure to work with this intellectually expansive group.

YOICHI FUNABASHI
September 1995

Preface

The Asia Pacific Economic Cooperation (APEC) forum decided at its second summit meeting, in Indonesia in November 1994, to achieve "free and open trade and investment in the region by 2020." Since APEC member countries account for about one half the world economy, this was potentially the most far-reaching trade agreement in history. In November 1995, the third APEC summit in Japan will begin implementing the program. This book analyzes the prospects from the standpoints of both APEC as a whole and especially of host-country Japan.

The Institute has undertaken a series of studies on the economic effects of, and the outlook for, trade and investment liberalization and facilitation in the Asia Pacific. Analyses are under way on the costs of existing protection, and thus the potential gains from liberalization, in Australia, Canada, China, and Indonesia (and have already been published for Japan and the United States). Sectoral projects are in train on civil aviation, financial services, and telecommunications. This study addresses the crucial issue of the role of Japan in APEC, and especially its chairmanship of the organization in this pivotal year of its evolution.

The present study does much more, however. It provides a comprehensive and innovative analysis of the potential role of Japan in forging a "fusion" between the two sides of the Pacific, due to its deep engagement with both the United States and Asia. The book offers an in-depth analysis of both APEC itself and Japan's role in the region. It links the economics, politics, and security aspects of the Asia Pacific into a comprehensive mosaic of the forces that will shape the region's future for many years to come.

Yoichi Funabashi is uniquely placed to write this book. Now chief of the Washington bureau of the *Asahi Shimbun*, Japan's leading newspaper, he has received numerous awards—including Japan's equivalent of the Pulitzer Prize—for his five previous books on economic and foreign policy topics. One of those, *Managing the Dollar: From the Plaza to the Louvre*, was written in 1987 while Funabashi was a Visiting Fellow at the Institute and subsequently became the leading nonfiction best-seller in Japan.

The Institute for International Economics is a private nonprofit institution for the study and discussion of international economic policy. Its purpose is to analyze important issues in that area and to develop and communicate practical new approaches for dealing with them. The Institute is completely nonpartisan.

The Institute is funded largely by philanthropic foundations. Major institutional grants are now being received from the German Marshall Fund of the United States, which created the Institute with a generous commitment of funds in 1981, and from the Ford Foundation, the William M. Keck, Jr. Foundation, the Korea Foundation, the Andrew Mellon Foundation, and the C. V. Starr Foundation. A number of other foundations and private corporations also contribute to the highly diversified financial resources of the Institute. About 12 percent of the Institute's resources in our latest fiscal year were provided by contributors outside the United States, including about 5 percent from Japan. The Institute's project on Asia Pacific economic cooperation is receiving generous support from the Rockefeller Brothers Fund; the AT&T, GE, Pew, and Sasakawa Peace Foundations; and the IBM Corporation.

The Board of Directors bears overall responsibility for the Institute and gives general guidance and approval to its research program—including identification of topics that are likely to become important to international economic policymakers over the medium run (generally, one to three years) and which thus should be addressed by the Institute. The Director, working closely with the staff and outside Advisory Committee, is responsible for the development of particular projects and makes the final decision to publish an individual study.

The Institute hopes that its studies and other activities will contribute to building a stronger foundation for international economic policy around the world. We invite readers of these publications to let us know how they think we can best accomplish this objective.

C. FRED BERGSTEN
Director
September 1995

Introduction

Diverse but Not Divided

It all revolved around the word "community." Everyone in the room
agreed that their historic Vision Statement should call for the creation of
a Pacific community. Everyone but the Chinese delegate, Huang Wenjun.
He was adamant: the Asia Pacific Economic Cooperation forum, or APEC,
is not the European Community, he insisted, and China would endorse
nothing that would turn the 17-member body into one. No one disputed
his point that their historic November 1993 meeting in Seattle was fundamentally different from Maastricht, but what, they wondered, would be
the problem in setting forth a spirit of cooperation that reflected their
vision of the future of the Asia Pacific? Some tried to assuage the Chinese
delegate's fears that they were signing a legal document, but he held firm.
That night, Eminent Persons Group (EPG) Chairman C. Fred Bergsten
arrived in Seattle and was informed of the impasse on the word "community." The next morning at an EPG breakfast, Bergsten informed his
colleagues of the problem and urged them to come up with a solution.
In response, the three EPG delegates from Hong Kong, Taiwan, and
China huddled together in a corner. Two minutes later, they announced
a solution: they substituted the Chinese character for "family" for the
offending one that connoted a highly institutionalized group. Huang
Wenjun then talked hurriedly with Chinese Trade Minister Wu Yi and
Foreign Minister Qian Qichen. Upon seeing the less-controversial version
of the word, the Chinese ministers acquiesced, less than an hour before
the ministerial meeting was set to begin.[1] With this last-minute breakthrough, yet another barrier toward building an Asia Pacific civilization
was breached. APEC enthusiasts, however, soon found another potential

1

snag when Malaysian Trade Minister Rafidah Aziz quipped that what they had agreed to was "a community with a small 'c.' "[2]

The word "family" apparently appealed to the Asian leaders at the Blake Island, Washington, meeting. "The term 'APEC community,' if used, should only mean it like how families and relatives discuss their common matters," said Thai Prime Minister Chuan Leekpai during the meeting. "Members should utilize their diversity and complement each other." Singaporean Prime Minister Goh Chok Tong echoed this sentiment: "An APEC community should be perceived as something like a 'big family' where the countries and areas in the region can maintain a sense of unity and seek common perspectives."

These small episodes illustrate the grand dilemmas that have faced APEC in forging a sense of cooperation among its many diverse and dynamic members. Since its inception, APEC has struggled constantly to find its identity. APEC's evolution has resembled Zen discourse: loose, flowing, and hard to define in a legalistic, dogmatic way. APEC's chimeric nature has led one observer to remark that APEC is "four adjectives in search of a noun."[3] Even the naming was "a child of the circumstances" according to Bob Hawke, the former Australian prime minister who initiated the meeting. He explained that although "cooperation" was not a particularly elegant final word, it served to assure ASEAN that APEC would be a loosely organized group.[4] Ever since, optimistic expectations for APEC have been tempered. APEC's birth in Canberra in 1989 and the Bogor Declaration in 1994 were each described as potentially historic by US Secretary of State James Baker and US President Bill Clinton, respectively.

The concept of Asia Pacific economic cooperation is so young that there has even been a debate on how to write the term "Asia Pacific." Sandra Kristoff, the US ambassador to APEC, said she was so frustrated that "Asia Pacific was hyphenated haphazardly by so many people" that in the Seattle APEC literature she deliberately omitted the hyphen in an attempt to create a standard usage.[5] The following year at the Bogor meeting, the stubborn hyphen again found its way into the official text. The inability to decide on the small detail of hyphenation illustrates the transitory state of the region's institution building. The reluctance to drop the hyphen perhaps also highlights a lingering resistance in Asia to fully merge with the Pacific.

Despite the problems APEC has encountered defining itself, there is no doubt about its potential. Today APEC incorporates 18 economies that together marshal 40 percent of the world's population, more than half of the world's GDP, and over 40 percent of its exports.[6] APEC's size will only grow as the region's economy continues to expand and more nations, such as Vietnam and India, press for membership. By some estimates, APEC already includes the world's three largest economies: the United States, Japan, and China. It also encompasses the most dynamic economies in the world. In the last decade, more than half of the globe's increased production was in East Asia, and Japan alone added output equivalent to the entire economy of France.[7] The Asia Pacific will clearly be the locomotive for the world's growth well into the next century.

In its efforts to define itself, APEC has given rise to an entirely new vocabulary that has attempted to capture the essence of its unique activities. At the core of the APEC philosophy is the idea of "open regionalism." From its inception, APEC was not to be an economic bloc or legally bound free trade area like the European Community or the North American Free Trade Agreement (NAFTA). Instead, APEC has sought to realize a vision of global free trade, driven by the liberalization of the Asia Pacific region's dynamic economies.

As set forth at the founding meeting in Canberra, APEC decisions require a consensus from its diverse membership, not just a majority vote as do multilateral organizations such as the United Nations. On major issues such as the Bogor Declaration and the founding of the APEC Secretariat, APEC has used so-called "soft negotiations" to achieve what Indonesian President Suharto has dubbed "flexible consensus." In an effort to forge agreement on the Bogor Declaration at the 1994 APEC leaders' meeting in Indonesia, Suharto said, "Some of you perhaps have dissatisfaction, but we need your cooperation, as a flexible consensus is necessary."[8]

Another example of "APEC speak" is concerted unilateral action (CUA). Unlike NAFTA or the General Agreement on Tariffs and Trade (GATT), which rely on a bargaining process, APEC has encouraged nations to make concessions voluntarily, based on the theory that economic liberalization is a benefit unto itself, not just a card to play in order to achieve reciprocity. While CUA has shown itself to be useful rhetorically, so far there is scant evidence it is effective in practice. To make CUA more palatable to members wary of free riding, APEC has revamped CUA by including coordinated but informal actions—in other words, emphasizing "concerted" rather than "unilateral." This compromise was incorporated into the draft of the action agenda for the 1995 leaders' meeting in Osaka, Japan, during the preparatory senior officials' meeting (SOM) held in Sapporo, and it was yet another example of the "APEC way" of pursuing consensus.[9]

One of the most striking characteristics of APEC is the variety of cultures, religions, population sizes, and political ideologies that it incorporates. This diversity makes it radically different from the European Union, which encompasses a comparatively homogeneous region. APEC countries represent nearly every major religion in the world: Indonesia is the largest Islamic country on the globe, Thailand is perhaps the world's most devout Buddhist country, and the Philippines is Asia's largest Catholic country.

The range of incomes is even more impressive. The largest gap in terms of per capita income within the European Union lies between Germany and Greece—a ratio of 5:1, close to that between Japan and rapidly modernizing South Korea. In APEC, the largest per capita difference is nearly 40:1, from Japan's $25,000 to Indonesia's $570 in 1991.[10]

APEC countries also span the spectrum of ethnic diversity, from the nearly homogenous Japan and Korea to nations that contain dozens of ethnic groups, such as Indonesia and the United States. Added to this dynamic is the presence of 50 million expatriate Chinese spread out from Medan to Melbourne.

APEC also includes representatives of vastly different kinds of governments. Some, like Japan and Thailand, are limited monarchies. The British Commonwealth counts Australia, Malaysia, Singapore, Brunei, New Zealand, Papua New Guinea, and Canada among APEC members. The United States, South Korea, Taiwan, and soon perhaps Australia are all democratic republics. Indonesia remains an autocratic state, despite its recent moves toward economic liberalization. Two Latin American nations, Mexico and Chile, are in transition from one-party authoritarianism to multiparty democracy. Lastly, APEC includes communist China. China's politics are a relic of a bygone era, but the party in Beijing has managed to survive through ambitious economic expansion and market-opening measures that bear little resemblance to the economic doctrines of Marx and Mao.

It is widely accepted today that APEC's diversity in fact gives it an edge over more homogenized regions of the world. "We will not seek—and we do not seek—the cohesion of the smaller, more homogeneous Europe," US Assistant Secretary of State for East Asian and Pacific Affairs Winston Lord said. "The diversity of the Asia Pacific region is a reality we recognize and respect. Its distinctions will be a major source for the region's future dynamism."[11]

Skyscrapers

Economies in the Asia Pacific are growing faster than those in any other part of the world. Over the past 20 years, the annual economic expansion in most Asian countries has been well over 6 percent, sometimes reaching double digits.[12] Trade within the region has also skyrocketed. From 1960 to 1990, for instance, the bilateral flow of goods between Australia and South Korea has increased more than 600 times. Bilateral trade between China and South Korea increased by more than $10 billion since relations were normalized in 1992.[13] The International Monetary Fund estimates that China imports more from tiny Taiwan than it does from the United States.[14]

US trade with Asia surpassed that with Europe in 1978; today it is 1.5 times greater, and it is expected to double in the year 2003.[15] Today, for instance, the United States exports more to Japan than to France and Germany combined. It exports more to Indonesia than to the whole of Eastern Europe. In addition, 171,000 jobs in the United States depend on American exports to China, many in high-wage sectors such as aviation and telecommunications.[16] Trade within APEC has approached 70 percent, much higher than intra-European commerce.[17]

A sign of the growing self-confidence of the Asia Pacific economies is the skyscraper boom that is reverberating around the region. Just as American cities competed at the turn of the century to outdo one another in building monuments to their growing economic prowess, the race is on within Asia to construct the tallest, most splendid towers in the world. Of the 10 tallest buildings finished or under construction in the 1990s, as of August 1995, nine are in Asia.[18] In May 1995 Shanghai completed its largest building, the 1,535-foot Oriental Pearl Television Tower, a structure 150 feet taller than New York's World Trade Center that will include a five-star hotel and multiple conference centers.[19] Malaysian Prime Minister Mahathir bin Mohamad personally ordered the Petronas Towers, under construction in Kuala Lumpur, to be extended by 25 feet for the sole purpose of surpassing the Sears Tower in Chicago, currently the world's tallest.[20] Not to be outdone by the upstart Malaysians, China has announced that it will build an even higher building in Chonqing the following year. The major Japanese realtor Mori Building Co. is heading up a group to construct an even taller building in Shanghai that will reach nearly 100 stories.[21] Japan has announced initial plans for its Millennium Tower, which would rise 1,100 feet higher than the Chinese one.

The skyscraper boom is another instance of the cultural cross-fertilization of Asia and Pacific. While the financing for these massive projects comes from Asian firms flush with capital, the architectural concepts and designs are almost exclusively American. The combination has led to developments that provide colorful examples of the cross-fertilization under way between East and West. After the big architectural firms in Chicago and New York finish drawing up floor plans and building designs, Chinese *feng shui* masters review the blueprints for structural elements that could upset the Taoist balance. American architect Adrian Smith, for instance, has designed the Jin Mao building in downtown Shanghai, which incorporates the style of old Chinese pagodas. The building will also contain 88 floors, a fortuitous number in Chinese superstition.[22]

The rapid economic growth in the region is giving rise to a new global power center, one on track to become the world's largest. In 1960, East Asia, including Japan, represented 4 percent of the world's GNP while North America commanded 37 percent. Today, their shares are nearly equal (between 23 and 24 percent each).[23] If present trends continue, East Asia's share could exceed half of the total by the year 2040. On the basis of recent growth rates, East Asia's GNP would overtake that of North America in 2003 and that of Western Europe in 2011.[24] Using purchasing power parity (PPP) terms, China may well become the world's second largest economy within the next decade and surpass even the United States by the early part of the next century.[25] By several estimates, China already accounts for about 6 percent of the world's GDP, well above the share of every G-7 country except Japan and the United States.

The Asianization of the world's trade structure is the most significant economic development since the creation of the Bretton Woods system. This sea change has challenged the basic assumptions of business people, politicians, and diplomats about the world economic system and their roles in it.

APEC: Form Follows Content

APEC is not the first attempt at regional institution building in the Asia Pacific. Over the past century, numerous organizations have brought together scholars, journalists, and business leaders from around the Asia Pacific. Groups such as the Pacific Economic Cooperation Council (PECC) provided a intellectual framework for regional integration but had little impact on government policies; official coordination was hindered by ideological and colonial legacies.

The first attempts at forming a trans-Pacific forum date back as far as 70 years to the creation of the Institute of Pacific Relations (IPR). The IPR brought together scholars, merchants, and bureaucrats with an interest in expanding contacts across the Pacific. One of the early and ardent supporters of the effort was Japan's Inazo Nitobe, famous for his passion to become a "bridge across the Pacific." Nitobe's internationalist dreams were crushed when Japan invaded Manchuria in 1931, sending the Asia Pacific region down the road to all-out war. The IPR lingered on until it fell victim in the 1950s to US Senator Joseph McCarthy's "red-baiting" committee, which labeled the private organization a communist front.[26]

On an official level, there were three major attempts at creating regional organizations, all of which ended in failure. In 1921, in parallel with the League of Nations, representatives from Asia Pacific powers (including colonial European nations) met in Washington to enact naval disarmament measures meant to reduce the threat of war. Despite relative gains that Japan won because it had only a one-ocean navy, the agreement to limit its naval forces below those of the United States and Great Britain at the ratio of 5:5:3—the so-called "Rolls Royce Rolls Royce Ford" pact—undermined the legitimacy of the democratic government in Tokyo and provided an impetus to those seeking Japan's militarization.[27] China, considered an inferior power by the United States, was vexed that Japan was awarded control over much of Manchuria.[28] The uncertain international environment, with the rise of Chinese nationalism and Russian Bolshevism along with the economic chaos of the Great Depression years, also undermined the Washington system.

The second regional meeting was more representative in that it excluded European colonizers, but it was almost suicidal. The 1943 Greater East Asia Conference in Tokyo was a thinly veiled plot to cloak Japan's imperial aggression as a quest to protect self-determination. The assembled Asian delegates could claim that they were free of Western control but not foreign domination, and the fall of Japan three years later would put an end to any dreams Tokyo officials had of an Asian bloc led by a paternal *Pax Nipponica*. All these plans vanished as Japan lay demolished in 1945. Japan's military challenge to the West, which began with the defeat of Russia 40 years earlier, was finally put to rest.

The most recent attempt at official coordination in the region came in 1955 with the Bandung conference, which launched the Non-Aligned Movement. Meant as a forum for "Afro-Asian" unity, the movement was a political attempt by the South to resist control by the North (or more aptly, the West). One American newspaper claimed that the meeting meant "that at last the destiny of Asia is being determined in Asia, and not in Geneva, or Paris, or London, or Washington. Hands off is the word. Asia is free." Nationalism was the common thread running through these countries, most of which were newly independent. However, the United States and numerous European countries did not view it that way. US Secretary of State John Foster Dulles harshly condemned the body as a communist front. The exclusion of Western powers from the conference engendered the consternation and hostility of some. Columnist Walter Lippmann termed the conference "the most formidable and ambitious move yet made in this generation to apply the principle of Asia for the Asians."[29] Forty years later, the Non-Aligned Movement still exists, but its effectiveness is negligible. The dynamic economies of East Asia have little in common with their African "brothers," and several of the founding members in Asia have or will soon reach "Northern" status.

While it is easy to see the difference between APEC and earlier incarnations of Asia Pacific cooperation, it is hard to define the organization because it represents such a new model in international cooperation. APEC's unique character results not from any grand plan or strategy but from a steady progression. When the region's foreign and trade ministers met for the first time in Canberra in 1989, they had no solid vision for how to build an Asia Pacific organization. All of the assembled ministers realized that there were historic changes under way—increasing economic and social integration, decreasing political and military tensions—but none was confident that the group could collectively harness these trends.

Asia Pacific governments felt that official cooperation was needed, not to lay the groundwork for a new regionalism, but to facilitate what was already happening. They were inspired to invent a new brand of Pacific surfing to ride the immense wave already beneath them.

APEC has sought to build a free trade area in the Asia Pacific, or more accurately, free trade in the area. In so doing, it has repeatedly stressed that it represents "open regionalism" rather than a preferential trading bloc as in Europe. The theory of open regionalism allows for the granting of APEC concessions to nonmember economies in order to increase the level of international trade and encourages other regions to undertake their own unilateral liberalization. This commitment makes APEC more open than any other trade liberalization body thus far, including the GATT, which restricts its most-favored nation (MFN) status only to member countries.[30]

APEC has actively engaged the interests and opinions of the private sector. Industry experts join government delegations at APEC sectoral working group meetings and advise governments of areas that need the attention of the multilateral body. To exploit this public-private partnership, APEC has turned to private groups not only for advice, but also for data and analyses. Rather than creating a large in-house bureaucracy like the one in Brussels, APEC has used nongovernmental groups such as PECC, the Pacific Business Forum (PBF), and the APEC Eminent Persons Group. EPG Chairman Bergsten has explained that although the EPG and PBF are not controlled by governments, they are not exactly nongovernmental organizations (NGOs), because APEC created them. Thus Bergsten has described these organizations aptly as "kind of a hybrid."[31]

From the beginning, APEC has stressed the importance of process over structures, for both cultural and political reasons. Some East Asian governments worried that their "Anglo-Saxon" partners, given their legalistic histories, would attempt to codify APEC. The contrast in styles is revealed by a comparison between the facilitating documentation for the ASEAN Free Trade Area (AFTA), which contained a grand total of eight pages, and NAFTA, with over 2,000.[32] Some Asians have expected the United States and other Western members of APEC to try to establish a European-style organization in the region, but there are few signs that Washington has encouraged such a development. Some outside observers, particularly in Europe, have been wary of APEC because it has not completed substantive agreements like those of NAFTA and the European Union.[33]

APEC's 18 members may each have different goals for the forum, yet nearly all agree that providing a framework for regional interaction is important unto itself. The United States and Japan, for example, believe APEC can help to integrate China into the world economy. Southeast Asian nations see in APEC the value of integrating not only China, but also Japan and the United States, particularly investment from both countries, into the regional economic framework. After the fall of the Berlin Wall, ASEAN leaders began to fret over the possible diversion of trade and investment from their region to the emerging markets of Eastern Europe. These leaders also saw the potential for APEC to "lock in" the US security presence in order to balance Chinese or Japanese military might. APEC eventually will nurture political dialogue, because as economic integration progresses, politics will always follow economics.

Fusion

APEC's impressive development is only part of a larger experiment in civilization building in the Asia Pacific. After hundreds of years of conflict resulting from colonialism and ideological warfare, the Asia Pacific is finally emerging as a center of global commerce and civilization, and a melting pot of civilizations. Underlying this cross-fertilization have been the connections across the region—between Northeast Asia and Southeast Asia, continental Asia and maritime Asia, the Eurasian heartland and the Eurasian rim land, and Asia and the Pacific. The emergence of a unified economic entity among the so-called "Three Chinas"—China, Taiwan, and Hong Kong—is a clear example of economic linkages erected as the Cold War has receded. Singapore's influence and role in the arrangement have led some to describe a "Four Chinas" model as well, especially as Chinese cities such as Suzhou and Wuxi seek to emulate the Singaporean model. There are also growing ties among the three Asia Pacific giants— Japan, China, and the United States—as the triangular flow of investment, trade, students, and tourists has increased their interdependence and interchange.

This web of economic links around the Asia Pacific is paving the way for a fusion of ideas. The success of countries in East Asia that have wedded indigenous work ethics, emphasis on education, and communal cohesion with Western markets and democracy exemplifies the dynamic combination that an Asia Pacific civilization can embody. Newly confident Asian countries will be increasingly able to stimulate the economies of their North American and Oceanian partners and share their experiences to reinvigorate the entire Asia Pacific region.

This fusion will not only build bridges between economies, as a free trade agreement or customs union does, but liberalize them, by opening them up to the natural flow of goods, capital, people, information, and ideas. It is also not limited to international cooperation in the usual sense, but will transnationally engage local governments, businesses, and individuals, not just central governments and diplomats. In the end it will not only facilitate transactions but also effect a transformation in the way peoples, economies, and governments interact.

The Asia Pacific experiment to bring the greatest civilizations of the world into one dynamic sphere of confluence will lead to a new era of prosperity into the next century. Today, however, the region finds itself at a critical juncture, with forces from above and below pulling nations and peoples apart. Whether this dream will be fulfilled depends on the collective will of the peoples of the region to shape their future. A resurgence in ethnic conflict threatens to sabotage the global movement toward liberal trade and democracy. Harvard scholar Samuel Huntington has argued that the world is splitting into competing blocs based on culture and race.[34] The economic and cultural dynamics in the Asia Pacific, however, suggest that in at least this region, economic interdependence and cross-fertilization among civilizations can perhaps transcend the barriers of race and ideology.[35]

The next decade presents a historic window of opportunity for the Asia Pacific. The Cold War's cessation has freed most of the region from ideological warfare, and the region is free, at least temporarily, of major conflict and ruthless hegemony. The countries of the region must take advantage of the benevolent international environment to pool their wisdom and resources to build a framework of cooperation—APEC is such an enterprise.

Japan

Japan will play a critical role in the Asia Pacific's evolution. Since the Meiji era, Japan has been "in Asia" but not fully "of Asia." Its own self-perception and its image in the region have always been somewhat exceptionalist and separate. Unlike the rest of Asia, Japan has remained for the most part sovereign. In the League of Nations, Japan, along with China and Siam (Thailand), represented East Asia. Japan's self-perception of uniqueness was strengthened by the nation's spectacular reconstruction and ascendance to global power status in the past half-century but was eventually challenged by the mid-1980s as the economies of other Asian nations began to take off and globalize.

Asia is now facing the same challenges Japan has confronted. More than in any previous era, Japan can now share its experiences with Asia. As Japan has challenged the world trading system, Asia is just beginning to challenge it. Today, Asia's economic development presents theoretical and policy horizons of development that vary from the Chicago School model, just as Japan took a different trajectory from that model. Japan has already realigned the world power balance, but Asia will seek its alignment. Finally, Asia is confronted with a conflict between tradition and modernization similar to the one that Japan has suffered. Japan can and should share its experience and perspectives on liberalization and offer its markets to the region. Simultaneously, Japan can and should learn from the new liberalization experiences of its neighbors. Japan needs to redefine its role in the region and in the world. To accomplish this, it must become an integral part of Asia, of a globalizing Asia, and of a global Asia.

It is also critical for Japan to stabilize its relations with its largest strategic and economic partner, the United States. The close economic interdependence of the two economies has led to friction and mutual recriminations as the Cold War "glue" of a mutual threat has begun to dissolve. It is imperative that these disputes be managed in a more dispassionate and balanced way. The greatest threat is the potential for bilateral tensions to lead to a rupture in the US-Japan security alliance that is the foundation of the region's prosperity. The US-Japan partnership guarantees freedom of commerce and navigation and lessens the threat of an arms race. Recently, however, there have been calls in the United States to reconsider this relationship in light of existing economic strains. Yet America can ill afford to turn inward either economically or militarily. Japan, and for that matter Asia as a whole, is too important for the United States to neglect; reciprocally, the United States is of vital value to Japan.

Japan today stands at a crossroads. For nearly one and a half centuries, the nation has struggled with an apparent choice between East and West. Today, it ranks as a thoroughly modern member of the advanced nations, but at the same time, it feels a powerful pull toward its Asian roots culturally. Japan is not alone. Korea, the Philippines, and other Asian nations are facing a similar situation. In China, this issue has been divisive politically, philosophically, culturally, and ideologically, ever since the debate over *zhong ti xi yong* (Chinese substance and Western utility) in the late 19th century. Yet the growing fusion of the Asia Pacific is offering Japan and these other nations more room to harness elements of both East and West.

APEC presents Japan with an epochal opportunity to use the economic, political, and "civilizational" potentials that are emerging in the Asia Pacific. For the first time in this century, there is an organization that is truly regional and multilateral, based on shared interests and aspirations. Japan must look at APEC in a new light and jettison the methods and processes of the past. Time and again Japan has demonstrated that it has a unique capacity to adapt and learn as circumstances dictate. The new order in the Asia Pacific is just that kind of moment.

Plan of the Book

This book will first examine the cultural, economic, and political trends in the Asia Pacific over the past 30 years and the opportunities that these trends present for the region. Chapter 1 will pay special attention to the cross-fertilization of ideas, cultures, and economies that is rapidly binding the region. It will also trace the development of transportation, communications, and computer linkages that have facilitated the unprecedented interaction between the peoples of the Asia Pacific.

The next chapter will provide an overview of the leaders, intellectuals, and diplomats who have shaped the concept and framework of Asia Pacific cooperation. Since its founding, APEC has been a personality-led organization and has become even more so since the first leaders' summit in 1993. The human interaction that occurs during APEC meetings has been one of the strongest bonds of the forum, and the personal dynamics of each of the Asia Pacific leaders will play a critical part in the success or failure of Asia Pacific cooperation.

Chapters 3, 4, and 5 will chronicle three stages in APEC's development from a little-noticed meeting of ministers to a forum for Asia Pacific interaction at all levels and will pay special attention to the defining moments of the institution from the perspective of the participants. Chapter 3 will explore new evidence on the factors that went into the creation of APEC in 1989, shedding light on the important roles played by both Japan and Australia. Chapter 4 will offer an inside look into the decisions and debates that shaped the landmark 1991 Seoul ministerial and 1993 Seattle summit. Chapter 5 will examine the steps toward liberalization that began with the 1994 Bogor Declaration and that will proceed through 1995 and 1996 in Osaka and Manila, respectively.

Chapters 6, 7, and 8 will analyze the progress of the APEC process to date and rate its probability of success. These chapters will look especially closely at the main action areas of trade and investment liberalization and economic development and will also examine the interests, motives, and constraints each nation faces in realizing APEC's vision.

Chapter 9 will analyze the new international environment in which APEC has been formed and how this ever-changing situation will affect APEC's future. It also looks at the power dynamics behind APEC and how APEC will affect the overall balance in the Asia Pacific region. Emerging markets may develop into emerging powers and complicate regional interaction. The rise of Japan and China and the relative decline of American power could have a significant effect on the long-run balance of power in the region. Triangular relationships among these three major powers will be pivotal. ASEAN's arrival on the scene as a potential "fourth leg" could also add a complex dynamic to the balance of power politics within APEC. Europe's role as a partner, or spoiler, could also have a significant impact on the region's political and economic dynamics.

Chapters 10 and 11 will respectively examine Japan's interests and dilemmas in APEC. Japan was an early and ardent supporter of APEC, which provides Japan the opportunity to pursue its interests on both sides of the Pacific. However, current domestic and international factors complicate Japan's ability to play a leadership role.

Chapter 12 will review Japan's overall role within the Asia Pacific region. From hermit to hegemon to economic superpower, Japan has had a long, prominent, and complicated history within the region. How Japan will respond to conflicting pressures either to remain in the "Western club" or to accept its "Asianization" is of critical importance to every member of the Asia Pacific community. This dilemma has historically plagued Japan, and each decision has had serious consequences, both good and bad, for Japan and its Asia Pacific neighbors.

The final chapter will suggest a direction for Japan's role within both APEC and the broader Asia Pacific community. APEC presents a monumental opportunity for Japan to overcome the burdens of the past and chart a new course for its future. With the realignment of political, economic, and social forces occurring today, it is critical that Japan chooses its future policies wisely. APEC allows Japan to avoid the uncomfortable choice between East and West, and it provides a forum for Japan to lead without reverting to military force and conflict. APEC also keeps Japan engaged in the vital investment and export markets in Asia and North America. How Japan acts in Osaka will be seen as representative of its attitudes toward the region in the future.

Notes

1. Personal interview with C. Fred Bergsten, 31 July 1995.

2. *Far Eastern Economic Review*, 2 December 1993.

3. Jonathan Clarke, "The United States and Asia Pacific Economic Cooperation," working paper of the Asia Society, 1994, p. 4.

4. Personal interview with Robert Hawke, 28 June 1995.

5. Personal interview, 27 April 1995.

6. APEC comprises Australia, Brunei, Canada, Chile, China, Hong Kong, Indonesia, Japan, Korea, Malaysia, Mexico, New Zealand, Papua New Guinea, Philippines, Singapore, Taiwan, Thailand, and the United States.

7. Janadas Devan, *Southeast Asia: Challenges of the 21st Century* (Singapore: Institute of Southeast Asian Studies, 1994), p. 3.

8. Personal interview with participant.

9. Personal interview, 21 July 1995.

10. James Abegglen, *Sea Change: Pacific Asia as the New World Industrial Center* (New York: The Free Press, 1994), p. 132.

11. "Building a Pacific Community," address by Winston Lord before the Commonwealth Club, San Francisco, 12 January 1995.

12. Gautam Jaggi, *Association of Southeast Asian Nations (ASEAN) and ASEAN Free Trade Area (AFTA) Chronology and Statistics*, APEC Working Paper Series, no. 95-4, Institute for International Economics, 1995, p. 19.

13. *Direction of Trade Statistics Quarterly* (Washington: International Monetary Fund, June 1995); *Direction of Trade Statistics Yearbook* (Washington: International Monetary Fund, 1994).

14. *Direction of Trade Statistics Yearbook* (Washington: International Monetary Fund, 1994).

15. Marcus Noland, "Implications of Asian Economic Growth," APEC Working Paper Series, no. 94-5, Institute for International Economics, 1994, p. 2.

16. Devan, p. 57.

17. C. Fred Bergsten and Marcus Noland, eds., *Pacific Dynamism and the International Economic System* (Washington: Institute for International Economics, 1993), p. 50.

18. *New York Times*, 25 June 1995.

19. *New York Times*, 26 July 1995.

20. *Toronto Star*, 16 July 1994.

21. *Kyodo News Service*, 7 August 1995.

22. *Chicago Tribune*, 5 September 1993.

23. Kishore Mahbubani, "The Pacific Way," *Survival* 37, no. 1 (Spring 1995): 105.

24. Joseph Camilleri, "Asia Pacific in the Post Hegemonic World," in Andrew Mack and John Ravenhill, eds., *Pacific Cooperation: Building Economic and Security Regimes in the Asia-Pacific Region* (Boulder, CO: Westview Press, 1995), p. 182.

25. Nicholas Lardy, *China in the World Economy* (Washington: Institute for International Economics, 1994), pp. 116–19.

26. Lawrence Woods, *Asia-Pacific Diplomacy: Nongovernmental Organizations and International Relations* (Vancouver: UBC Press), pp. 29–40.

27. Walter A. McDougall, *Let the Sea Make a Noise: A History of the North Pacific from Magellan to MacArthur* (New York: Basic Books, 1993), pp. 521–30.

28. Walter LaFeber, *The American Age* (New York: W.W. Norton, 1994), pp. 340–41.

29. Richard Wright, *The Color Curtain: A Report on the Bandung Conference,* rev. ed. (Jackson, MS: University Press of Mississippi, 1993).

30. Vinod K. Aggarwal, "Comparing Regional Cooperation Efforts in Asia-Pacific and North America," in *Pacific Cooperation*, p. 47.

31. Personal interview, 26 May 1995.

32. Devan, p. 20.

33. *The Economist*, 13 November 1993.

34. Samuel Huntington, "The Clash of Civilizations," *Foreign Affairs* 72, no. 3 (Summer 1993): 22–49.

35. Kishore Mahbubani, "The Pacific Way," *Foreign Affairs* 74, no. 1 (January/February 1995): 100–111.

1

"He Who Gives, Dominates"

The Asia Pacific region invites a new type of fusion. Just as high temperature and pressure can join atomic nuclei to fuel the stars, the common interests of the peoples of the Asia Pacific can eventually meld Asian and Pacific civilizations to lend energy to the 21st century. The prospect is awe-inspiring, as nearly all of the great civilizations of the past 5,000 years—Confucian, Islamic, Buddhist, and Judeo-Christian—have the potential to unite on a grand scale. A shared stake in economic advancement has already helped to catalyze this reaction, as indicated by the cross-fertilization apparent among East Asia, the Americas, and Indochina. Rather than suddenly combusting, Asia Pacific civilizations will fuse gradually, slowed by resistance from managers and workers in protected industries, citizens fearful of losing their national and ethnic identities, people still mistrustful of the neighbors they fought in wars of ideology, imperialism, and liberation, and government leaders and bureaucrats reluctant to loosen the reins of power and realize the benefits of the global economy.

While such concerns resonate throughout the region, the Asia Pacific is likely to cohere at the civilizational level, allowing ample room for autonomy and diversity of individual cultures. Singaporean diplomat Kishore Mahbubani has written about "a fusion of Western and East Asian cultures" in the Asia Pacific.[1] Although it may seem to be a small semantic point, it is more accurate to assess the phenomenon as a fusion of civilizations rather than cultures. According to definitions crafted by anthropologists, cultures comprise the most basic systems of belief and behavior used by humans to adapt to their environments, whereas civiliza-

15

tions are ordered at the much higher level of structured, urbanized societies with symbiotic economies and formal political organizations.[2] The varied religions, traditions, and beliefs of the entire Asia Pacific are unlikely to amalgamate, but trends such as the rise of the nation-state, secularization, urbanization, industrialization, and economic interdependence will inexorably move the region's civilizations closer together.[3]

Highly structured civilizations will not merge into a homogenous entity, but will incorporate and overlap, in the same fashion as musical styles converge in jazz fusion. Music also demonstrates the great potential for the release of energy that accompanies fusion. Just as the combination of distinct musical traditions gives jazz fusion its flavor and excitement, the encompassing of unique societies and cultures will ensure the brilliance of the Asia Pacific civilization.

Before the arrival of European explorers and traders in the 16th century, relations among Pacific Rim countries were long governed under a broad *Pax Sinica* that was marked by thriving trade and economic interdependence. The Chinese influence in Asia was intertwined with the two other great Indian Ocean civilizations, Indian and Muslim, which were introduced to Southeast Asia between the 7th and 12th centuries.[4] The civilizational superstructure of ancient India, founded on the pluralistic concepts of Sanskrit texts, was selectively adapted by the peoples of the Malayan-Javanese archipelago and Indochinese peninsula to order their religion, state system, and arts. Muslim civilization was based on the tenets of the Islamic faith, which rose in the Middle East in the 7th century and spread across the Arabian Sea and Bay of Bengal to reach the islands of the Java Sea. Although it never crossed the Gulf of Siam, Islam had become a major ideological and social force in the Malayan-Javanese archipelago by the beginning of the 17th century.

Trans-Pacific trade flourished from the late 16th century into the 17th century via sea routes such as those, between Manila and Acapulco, which brought some Latin American influences to Asia. The Ming dynasty, for example, relied on South American–mined silver to finance its 2,500-mile expansion of the Great Wall in the late 16th century.[5]

The United States entered the scene in the 19th century, followed several decades later by Japan. In "one of the most remarkable coincidences in modern history," as an eminent historian noted, "the US and Japan challenged European supremacy at about the same time" in the early 20th century.[6] Asia Pacific civilizations were prevented from free interchange by the struggle between these two emerging powers over China and were later constrained by Cold War ideology. Today, the situation is entirely different. The old Chinese, Indian, and Muslim civilizations are combining with those of the United States and Japan in a new type of civilizational symbiosis.

The Pacific Rim is undergoing a transformation. Economics commands more than politics does, and the region can now refocus on trade and development, this time enriched by modern technology and transportation. Nearly a century ago, US Secretary of State John Hays made the oft-quoted observation: "The Mediterranean is the ocean of the past, the Atlantic the ocean of the present, and the Pacific the ocean of the future."[7]

Whether the Pacific Ocean itself will provide the link to the region's future is unclear. Hays, like many of his contemporaries, was likely drawn westward by intellectual curiosity, an awe of the size and grandeur of the sea, and a passion to conquer and move on to a new world. Peoples in the region are once again drawn to the ocean by interest in the new discoveries of their neighbors, awe of so many technological breakthroughs, and a passion to seek new opportunities. Both Americans and Asians have come to realize how the Pacific region will shape and define their future destinies.

Yet the role of the Pacific Ocean is a matter of perspective: it can either separate or connect its inhabitants, inhibit or ignite interaction and fusion. For the first time in history, it binds and ignites much faster and deeper than it separates and inhibits. Culturally the Asia Pacific region is combining the best of East and West (some would say the worst), coupling Asian virtues of social organization with Western political and intellectual freedoms. Han Sung-Joo, Korea's former foreign minister, opined that "[f]or the first time in human history, Western civilization stressing preeminence of the individual entity is encountering Sinic civilization emphasizing social harmony."[8] The old Sino-centered Asian trading world has been extended across the entire Pacific from Australia to Canada, Korea to Chile, linked by vast air, sea, and telecommunication networks, sharing a common tongue, English, and an intellectual belief in free trade.

The Asianization of Asia

With the end of the Cold War, the physical, technological, and psychological barriers that divided Asia have been largely overcome. After more than 400 years, Asians are finally beginning to shake off the burdens of historical conflict and mistrust. The rapid rise of transnational interdependence has allowed Asians to experience a sense of neighborliness and awakened interest in common traditions, cultures, and mores. Singapore Minister of Information and Culture George Yeo has described an emerging "chopsticks culture" encompassing China, Japan, South Korea, and Vietnam. "As Europeans and Americans seek a spiritual homeland in the Greco-Roman and Judeo-Christian traditions," he said, "the chopstick civilization nations also share a common bond."[9] Confucian influence is perhaps the shared element to which he referred. Increasingly, the Philippines has sought membership in this common cultural area, as is symbolized by the growing popularity of chopsticks in a nation where use of forks and knives has been more common. As Philippine President

Fidel Ramos put it, "Our Christian roots date back only four centuries, but well before that we were already being strongly influenced by Chinese, Japanese, even Indian and Malay migration."[10] Ramos reminded his APEC colleagues in Seattle of the Philippines' long-standing economic and cultural ties with East Asia.[11]

The Philippines, long derided for its attempts to mimic the United States that earned it the nickname "Amboy" from its neighbors, has begun to gradually Asianize over the past two decades.[12] The Philippines' first departure from its strict dependence on American economic and political control came with its founding membership in the Association of Southeast Asian Nations (ASEAN) in 1967. Since then, the Philippines has experienced the "soft authoritarianism" of the Marcos regime, closed the large US bases under Corazon Aquino, and sought closer relations with its major aid donor, Japan. As Philippine Ambassador Raul Rabe explained, the Philippines has gone "from a single focus to a regional and global focus."[13]

The Philippines' tricultural traditions especially qualify it to help unite the American, Asian, and Hispanic cultures that inhabit APEC. At the first APEC ministerial meeting, for instance, Philippine delegate Jesus Estanislao was instructed to advocate the inclusion of Latin America countries as soon as possible.[14] Philippine officials have come to see their role in bridging Asia and Latin America as the "Philippines' mission." Manila has strongly promoted these ties through forums such as the Hispano-Asian conference, which included Pacific island republics as well as Latin America and Spain. Former Foreign Secretary Raul Manglapus noted that the 1996 Manila APEC summit would provide an opportunity to remind the world of its position as a "strategic center" dating back to the days of the silk trade between China and Mexico in the 17th century.[15]

Korea has experienced a similar trend toward Asianization over the past several years. Among young Korean students it has become fashionable to study Japanese and Chinese languages in addition to English. As Korea's foreign direct investment to Indochina and Southeast Asia has impressively increased, it has also striven to improve its economic and cultural links with those areas. Since establishing an official dialogue with ASEAN in 1989, Korean trade with the region has increased by 30 percent to make the Southeast Asian grouping Korea's fourth largest trading partner. In Southeast Asia, Korean companies now rival their Japanese counterparts in investment and sales. In 1991 Seoul was accorded full dialogue partner status at the ASEAN Post-Ministerial Conference (PMC) in recognition of its growing status as an Asia Pacific as well as a global political and economic power. To nurture these ties, Seoul has created an ASEAN-Korea Special Cooperation Fund (SCF) that has undertaken, among other projects, the installation of an "ASEAN e-mail" system to connect ASEAN foreign ministries to the regional secretariat in Jakarta.[16]

Mexico, too, has become increasingly aware of its modern ties to Asia, which date back more than 100 years. In 1888, Mexico became the first foreign nation to grant Japan MFN trade status and more importantly, relinquish its rights to extraterritorial jurisdiction over its citizens in Japan, a symbolic move that endeared the Latin American country to the Japanese people.[17] More recently, economic ties with Japan and the rest of Asia have been a primary focus of the Mexican government. Former President Carlos Salinas de Gortari is known to have insisted that his children learn Japanese. One senior Mexican diplomat has noted that in 1985, Mexico had only 150 students in Japan. Today that number has reached 1,000 and is likely to increase.[18] Mexico also has growing ties with other Asian nations as well, particularly the Philippines but also China. Like most nations in the Asia Pacific, Mexico is home to a number of overseas Chinese, providing a potential link between the two nations.

Recently, even Canada has shown its willingness to bridge the divide between Asia and North America. Prior to the 1995 Halifax summit of the G-7 leaders, Ottawa invited the foreign ministers of the six ASEAN nations to Canada to present their position on G-7 coordination. During the meeting of the industrialized nations, Canada relayed ASEAN's concerns over exchange rate disequilibrium and the lack of an International Monetary Fund (IMF) early warning system for developing economies' financial markets.[19] Canada also hosts a large overseas Chinese community, especially in Vancouver, furthering its ties across the Pacific.

The growing strength of East Asia has also effected a change in attitudes and attention in the United States. In a speech just prior to the Seattle APEC summit meeting, US Secretary of State Warren Christopher said, "As we approach the next century, America must once again look west—west to Asia, and west towards a Pacific future."[20] Even discounting some inevitable degree of lip service to the host city Seattle, the "West of the West," this call to "Go West" once again, this time reaching out beyond America's western shores to Asia, is a radical departure from the traditional Eurocentric view of Asia as the "East."

Australia has served a similar role in uniting East and West within the Pacific community. Recent Australian governments have sought to cast their country's identity as that of a cross-fertilized Asia Pacific nation. Foreign Minister Gareth Evans has characterized Australia as "a distinctive blend of our European antecedents of individual liberty, social equity and openness, overlaid by strong multiculturalism, with an increasing recognition of our 'East Asianness.'"[21]

In 1973 Canberra officially abandoned its "White Australia" policy in recognition of its destiny with its dynamic neighbors to the north. As Australian trade has become increasingly dependent on Asian markets, Canberra has attempted to shift the basic orientation and outlook of both its policies and people. In 1995 slightly less than 5 percent of the population was ethnically Asian, but the government expects that number to more than double by the year 2020. As in the United States and Canada, immigration from Asia has strengthened personal and cultural ties across the Pacific.

In order to compete in the new economic environment, the Australian government has boosted the number of students enrolled in Asian language classes from 15 percent in 1980 to more than 30 percent by 1990.[22] Today, Australian junior and senior high school students can choose from among six East Asian languages, and the government has set a national goal of having 60 percent of its population fluent in at least one Asian language.

New Zealand has embarked on a similar course toward the region. In 1994 Wellington established the Asia 2000 Foundation to spearhead its efforts to sensitize the country economically and culturally to the Asia Pacific.[23] New Zealand has also strongly pushed its students to study Asian languages, and today there are more New Zealand pupils studying Japanese per capita than in any other nation except Japan.[24]

The Asia Pacific region, more than any other area of the globe, has seen the rapid development of transnational networking, as local regions in Asia find that they have more in common with their neighbors across national boundaries than with those within their own borders.[25] China's southern Guangdong Province, for instance, with a per capita income of over $5,500, finds itself closer economically to neighboring Hong Kong, whose residents average $12,000 per annum, than to the rest of China, where incomes average only $317.[26] This regional economic autonomy has led Guangdong to shrug off Beijing's authority. In 1992, when Beijing tried to rein in the province by cutting off its oil supplies, Guangdong circumvented the central government, buying oil off the international spot market.[27] The province has even gone so far as to use military force to ensure the supply of cheap rice from neighboring Hunan Province.

The growing independence of China's regions has sparked a debate over the prospects for a unified China or even a national vision of China. This quandary goes beyond policymakers and academics and has become the subject of considerable discussions among Chinese people in general, both in China and among its diaspora. The question of national identity, or *rentong*, scarcely appeared throughout China's long history until recently.[28] The debate began in earnest with the release of a series of television documentaries entitled the *River Elegy*. Originally run on Chinese Central Television in 1988, official and pirated editions sent the entire Chinese-speaking world into a frenzy of self-analysis and soul searching. The series asked one basic question: was China to remain a "Yellow River" civilization, mired in the backward-looking, land-locked culture of its past, or would it become an "azure blue" civilization, a maritime nation embracing the Asia Pacific and casting off the burdens of its past?[29]

Following the Tiananmen incident, the Chinese Communist Party banned the television series, denouncing it as foreign bourgeois propaganda. This spotlights the delicate nature of contemporary politics in China. Intellectuals follow the implications of being an "azure blue" nation to its natural conclusion. The Communist Party in Beijing, however, has realized the dangers of radical reform, especially after the breakdown of authority in Russia and Eastern Europe since 1989. The near-term problems of the Beijing regime have complicated the debate over *rentong*. "We love our country, but we hate our government" is a common refrain heard among Chinese people.[30]

Linkages at the Local Level

The growth of local autonomy has led to a further Asianization of Japan as well. The west coast cities of Fukuoka and Kita-Kyushu have begun to look toward neighboring cities in Asia. Fukuoka Airport, which is almost equidistant from Tokyo, Seoul, and Shanghai, is a natural hub for Asian air travel. The city government of Kita-Kyushu has created an Asian Affairs Bureau, the first of its kind among local governments in Japan. Designated as a "foreign access zone" by the central government, the city has constructed an "Asian Import Mart" to promote goods from the region. Kita-Kyushu is also home to a research center, cosponsored by the University of Pennsylvania, devoted to the study of the "Yellow Sea Rim Economic Area."[31] In nearby Oita, Prefectural Governor Morihiko Hiramatsu, winner of the prestigious Magsaysay Award for Asian humanitarianism in 1995 and famous for his "one village, one specialty" idea, recently invited local leaders from around the Pacific Rim to attend the Kyushu Asian Regional Exchange Summit to explore the future of Asianization at the grass-roots level. The next meeting is scheduled to be held in Manila.

The current development of a market-oriented, decentralized Asia Pacific harks back to the premodern days of trade along the Pacific Rim. Even under the Chinese tribute system, there were dynamic, free, and decentralized trade networks. In a similar fashion to the Hanseatic League in Northern Europe, the pre-modern *Negara* systems, centered on Indonesia's Batavia, provided networks between the cities of East Asia in the 15th and 16th centuries. These systems perhaps ran into the hundreds or even thousands before they were extinguished by Dutch colonial rule.[32]

Some have speculated that rather than moving toward a traditional regional trading bloc, a new type of Hanseatic League could arise, linking trading ports and economic areas without the benefits or impediments of official integration.[33] Around the Sea of Japan, Pusan, Niigata, Vladivostok, Fukuoka, and Yinchen are seeing an unprecedented increase in intraregional trade. Further south, Japanese, Indonesian, and Australian cities such as Naha, Denpassar, and Perth are flourishing through commercial links. Soon Vietnam will reenter the regional order, and towns such as Hue and Saigon, once centers of seaborne trade, will reestablish themselves as entrepôts for the region.

In fact, it is the great cities of Asia, not its nations, that are the locomotives of economic growth. As manufacturing and services overtake agriculture, especially in Southeast Asia and coastal China, cities are becoming not only larger but also more independent of the political entity that they inhabit. The economic and political importance of Asia's cities is enhanced by the information and telecommunications revolution and global communications. Following the success of Hong Kong and Singapore, Shanghai, Osaka, and Bangkok are beginning to develop indigenous economic zones, and frequently urban economic areas are linking with their counterparts across borders and water, as has occurred between Hong Kong and Shenzhen, Fukuoka and Pusan, and Singapore and Johore. Hong Kong entrepreneur Peter Woo compared the current development of Asia's cities to dynamic parts of the United States. "In the future, Guangdong province will become a California, Hong Kong a Los Angeles," he said. "China will develop based on the three pillars of Guangdong, Shanghai, and Wuhan."[34]

The emergence of Shanghai, Asia's largest city with an estimated 16.3 million residents, as a center of commerce and finance harks back to its heyday in the early 20th century, when it was known as the "Paris of the East," and its booming culture and sophistication pulsated with Jazz Age energy.[35] An American-trained Chinese economist marvels at Shanghai's promise: "It is the city of the best managers. . . . And you get feedback, which is rare in Chinese cities." Moreover, "civil service is still the best among all Chinese local governments and cities."[36] Despite the fact that Deng passed over Shanghai when selecting special economic zones, the city has created its own commercial area in Pudong that it expects to become Wall Street and Otemachi combined. "Shanghai is going to be the center of finance, of trade, of the entire economy by 2010," said Zhang Chi Gang, a Shanghai official.[37]

Asia Pacific Globalism

Driving the cultural and societal interaction of the Asia Pacific is economics. US Commerce Undersecretary Jeffrey Garten underlined the difference between Europe and the Asia Pacific: "While the European Union was the product of great triumphs of diplomacy and their creation of new legislative mechanisms, Asian integration has been driven by business."[38] Indeed, private businesses were the first to organize into transregional groups such as the Pacific Economic Cooperation Council (PECC) and the Pacific Basin Economic Council (PBEC).

These organizations have led the push to establish an effective APEC because they understand the benefits of official coordination in trade liberalization and international standards. According to the 1994 report of the Pacific Business Forum (PBF): "Businesses will go where bureaucracy is minimal and procedures straightforward and transparent. Therefore APEC must achieve pragmatic results."[39]

In 1586, Spanish navigator Fray Andres de Urdaneta discovered the first sea lane across the Pacific.[40] His journey from Manila to Acapulco took 130 days. Today, that distance can be, and is with increasing frequency, covered in a number of hours.

New airports are being constructed or opened in Osaka, Macao, Seoul, Kuala Lumpur, Hong Kong, Taipei, and Shenzhen, all in hopes of facilitating increasing economic activity. Singapore's Changi International Airport is regarded as the most modern and comfortable in the world and boasts amenities such as a science museum, business center, banks, hospital, hotel, and even a children's room that offers young passengers awaiting their flights high-tech toys such as holograms and a knob-operated dancing laser.[41] Not to be outshined, Kuala Lumpur and Hong Kong have sent observers to Singapore in preparation for building their own ultramodern airports in the coming years. The United States, Japan, and China are emerging as the three largest markets for commercial aircraft in the world, and the growth of air travel in the region surpasses every other area of the globe. Efforts are under way among aerospace companies in Singapore, Korea, Japan, China, and the United States to explore options for a future "Asian Airbus" to meet the growing demand for aircraft. American companies such as McDonnell Douglas Corp. and Boeing Co. are rapidly establishing a manufacturing presence in Asia and turning to the region for R&D investment capital. Twenty percent of the components that go into the newly unveiled Boeing 777 were made in Japan with major capital for the project coming from Japanese corporate groups.[42]

The free flow of information and ideas has also been important in financing the region's integration. News and financial data are available around the clock via satellite, allowing stock markets in Tokyo, Sydney, and Hong Kong to react instantaneously to activities in New York or Singapore. Information technology also provides scientists and engineers access to important technical data. Boeing has created an innovative computer network, for example, that allows Japanese and American designers thousands of miles apart to work simultaneously on one graphically displayed component. Asian nations have also hooked up to the Internet system to rapidly exchange ideas across a dozen time zones and an ocean.

Cellular telephones are increasingly ubiquitous in fast-moving Pacific markets. The average businessman in Hong Kong is as likely to have a cellular phone as a watch. In recent years China has seen a 200 percent annual increase in the demand for such devices, which are affectionately (or sarcastically) known as *da ge da*, "big brother."[43] The importance of telephone communications for the future of China's economy is so clear to the leadership in Beijing that they have decided that extending telephone lines should be given priority over developing road networks.[44]

In May 1993 in Thailand, when popular protests erupted against the military-backed government that had taken power in a coup the previous year, students, laborers, and businessmen turned out to demonstrate for the restoration of democratic rule. Led by protestors wielding portable phones, the movement was dubbed by the press *mob mue thue*, "the cellular phone revolution."

The development of information and communications systems has also outpaced attempts by the few remaining authoritarian regimes in the region to control negative press. China recently abandoned attempts to restrict Internet access and invested $11 million in a new system that will link Chinese academic institutions to the World Wide Web.[45] "It [the Internet] opens a wide window for Chinese people, especially educated people," said Qinghua University student Lu Ming. "They own the future of China. Internet will give them new information and new ideas about the world."[46] Paradoxically, Singapore is leasing Internet lines to its citizens while banning satellite dishes and restricting foreign publications.[47]

Investment

The Pacific economies are also linked by growing flows of foreign direct investment in all directions. The United States has used FDI to make up for stagnant levels of domestic investment, China to privatize its economy, and ASEAN to acquire technology. Corporations based in North America, Japan, and the newly industrializing economies (NIEs) have found it increasingly attractive to move large-scale production and R&D offshore because of lower labor costs, high productivity and educational levels, and damaging foreign exchange rates. China and the ASEAN nations have been quick to welcome this investment. FDI has been especially important to these developing economies as a means to acquire advanced technology and gain international competitiveness. Leaders of second-generation NIEs—Thailand, Malaysia, Indonesia, and China—have taken a much more open approach to FDI than their Japanese, Korean, and Taiwanese colleagues, who used FDI more selectively to decrease foreign penetration and protect domestic industries.[48]

Chinese and ASEAN nations have welcomed the presence of multinational corporations (MNCs), most from Japan and the United States, as a source of economic growth and investment. The impact of FDI can already be seen in the increased competitiveness among developing Asian economies. The establishment of 300 foreign-owned toy makers in China, for example, forced domestic competitors to increase efficiency and productivity. Today China has become one of the world's leading toy exporters.[49]

China and Southeast Asian workers also offer a strong combination of entrepreneurial instincts, education, and productivity. Literacy rates in APEC member countries are almost uniformly high. Only China and Indonesia, with large agricultural sectors, fall below 80 percent literacy.[50] The strength of local manufacturing is illustrated by the fact that Japanese MNCs now procure more materials and components locally in Asia than they do in any other area of the world.[51]

Foreign investment is not limited to Japanese and American MNCs. More than half of Asia's FDI has come from Asian countries (excluding Japan).[52] Investments by Korea, Taiwan, and Hong Kong in other Asian nations have increased tenfold since 1986. NIEs have followed Japan and the United States in moving production in many sectors to their lower wage neighbors in Asia, and have also entered the foreign-aid arena, providing technical and financial assistance to less-developed countries in Asia and elsewhere.

One interesting development in the Pacific investment picture has been the increase in FDI by the ASEAN countries and NIEs in Japan and the United States. Taiwan, Malaysia, and Singapore have led the trend in purchasing high-tech American and Japanese subsidiaries, sold off by cost-cutting MNCs.[53] This has allowed these countries to set their own pace for technology transfer rather than wait for foreign companies to invest in high-tech areas. Taiwan's Microtek International Inc., which makes laser printers and image scanners, employs 120 Americans in Los Angeles and Portland, Oregon, to perform high-tech, high-wage research and development.[54] In one of the highest-profile international mergers in recent years, South Korea's Goldstar company recently purchased Zenith, America's last television manufacturer.[55]

Members of the Chinese diaspora have provided considerable FDI to their homeland. Overseas Chinese corporate networks command over $500 billion in assets and have been influential players in developing both the Chinese and ASEAN economies.[56] Over 80 percent of total investment in China is made by Chinese living abroad.[57] Hong Kong companies alone employ over 3 million workers on the mainland and provide up to 90 percent of FDI in neighboring Guangdong Province.[58] Recently Singapore has begun to build an entire city near Suzhou, China, that will house up to 600,000 people.[59] Many cities in China see Singapore as a model for their own future. Clean, clear, and orderly with well-developed infrastructure, Singapore offers an alternative to the growing chaos accompanying the rapid urbanization that is sweeping their country.

Ethnic Chinese living abroad provide not only monetary investments but important entrepreneurial expertise to nascent industries in China and Southeast Asia. Senior Singaporean statesman Lee Kuan Yew ascribed the beginnings of Guangdong's economic boom to such investors: "Hong Kong people were able, because of proximity and talking the same dialect, [to] go back often to their villages or little towns and bring their machinery and work with the village authorities and establish very good relationships. Not based on any law, but based on trust."[60]

Similar links are being established between Taiwan and the mainland, despite the necessity of using third-country transit sites. Taiwanese investment is especially focused in Fujian Province, whose linguistic and cultural affinities with Taiwan make it a natural target for Taiwanese investors. More than 5,000 Taiwanese companies have established subsidiaries on the mainland over the past several years, many in the Special Economic Zone of Xiamen across the Taiwan Straits. Eight years ago, telephone calls between Xiamen and Taiwan averaged only 10 per month. Today direct calls have exceeded 60,000 per month.[61]

Trade

Even without normal diplomatic relations, commerce within the informal Chinese Economic Area grew three and a half times from 1978 to 1990.[62] It is the fastest-growing and most explicit illustration of a free trade area that has emerged without a free trade agreement. The nexus of the CEA has been Hong Kong, both because of its advanced service economy and its ability to serve as a conduit for trade between China and Taiwan. The CEA matches Taiwan's technical expertise and capital reserves with China's cheap labor and abundant resources in one of the world's most dynamic examples of the use of comparative advantage. If current OECD projections hold, total exports from the CEA will surpass those from Japan by the end of the decade, and by 2030, the CEA's GDP is expected to be the world's largest, although with its huge population, its per capita income will only resemble that of Mexico.[63]

A commitment to free trade is at the root of a new philosophy of Asia Pacific globalism. Asia Pacific nations have espoused free and open trade as a matter of both principle and policy as demonstrated by lobbying efforts for passage of the Uruguay Round of the GATT. To maintain their record levels of economic growth, Pacific nations depend on open markets for both goods and services. Asian nations are almost exclusively export-oriented; exports have outpaced domestic demand in the United States over the past several years. Ideas of comparative advantage and international division of labor are also widely accepted around the region. One country's sunset industry is the next's new opportunity.

Interest in economic globalism is illustrated by Singapore's bid to host the first WTO ministerial conference and in the campaign of former Korean Trade Minister Kim Chul-su to become its first director general.[64] In a show of regional unity, his bid won widespread Asian support, although it fell short in the global competition.[65] In the end, however, US support won Kim the post as one of the four WTO deputy directors in a compromise worked out with the European Union.[66]

Cross-Fertilization

The proliferation of televisions and satellite dishes will help fuel the civilization fusion of the Asia Pacific. For instance, Star TV, a satellite television network owned jointly by US and Hong Kong companies, broadcasts to more than 220 million people throughout Asia, bringing a mix of American, Japanese, and Chinese entertainment into 53 million homes each night.[67] The Japanese soap opera *Tokyo Love Story*, dubbed in Chinese for satellite broadcasts, has produced a number of comic-book spinoffs in Hong Kong.[68] Trans-Pacific satellite news programs are also enjoying increasing success. CNN and Asia Business News (ABN) broadcast throughout the region.[69] Local and national stations are increasingly airing programs from neighboring countries. The Japanese serial drama *Oshin*, for instance, which chronicles family life in a developing Japan, is on the air in more than 30 countries, mostly in Asia.[70] The Indonesian First Lady even called the series' producer, NHK, to request that the program be dubbed in English. Indonesian audiences were eventually able to watch the program not only dubbed in English, but with Bahasa Indonesian subtitles as well.[71]

Over the past several years, there has been a transformation in the Pacific's popular music scene as well. Michael Jackson still fills stadiums in Tokyo and Bangkok, but he must now compete with Japanese, Hong Kong, and Taiwanese pop singers. Japanese groups such as Hikaru Genji and Kome Kome Club have attracted millions of fans throughout Asia. Nationality is becoming increasingly irrelevant. Mika Chiba, whose songs in Mandarin and Malay have hit the charts across Southeast Asia, China, and Taiwan, is hardly known in her native Japan. Star TV launched its Channel V, which broadcasts Asian as well as American music videos.

Japanese *Manga* comic books and animation films have been another manifestation of cross-cultural mass consumption. These books and movies have been translated or dubbed into dozens of languages and are enjoyed by young people from Toronto to Taipei. The comic strip *Doraemon*, about a robot cat from the future, has become a cultural icon among young Thai and Vietnamese children who know the program from the pirated editions that circulate around the region. While *Doraemon* has not been consciously promoted by its Japanese inventors, it has been transformed in each market to meet the tastes and culture of the local environment: in China, characters originally dressed in traditional Japanese clothing are drawn adorned in Chinese fashion; in Hong Kong, characters are shown sitting in chairs rather than their original Japanese *seiza* position on a *tatami* mat.[72] In North America, Japanese *Manga* and animation have attracted more than 2 million fans, and films such as *Akira* and *Dragon Ball* have become cult classics.

Intra-Asian tourism is on the rise among the region's growing middle class. The World Tourism Organization has estimated that international arrivals in East Asia will top 101 million by 2000 and 190 million by 2010. Seventy-six percent of the trips originate in the region. Every week, plane loads of Thai tourists from Bangkok and Chaingmai arrive in Kunming, the capital of China's Yunnan Province, as part of "searching for roots" tours that explore the ancestral origins of the Thai people. Korea liberalized foreign tours after the 1988 Seoul Olympics. According to some estimates, tourism could replace oil as Indonesia's largest foreign exchange earner soon after the turn of the century.[73] Malaysian EPG member Noordin Sopiee noted that by the year 2000 the most lucrative tourists in Malaysia will be Chinese.[74] Years ago, Japanese tourists in Southeast Asia were usually businessmen on sex or golf tours, but today those much-resented travelers have been replaced by throngs of school groups and families. Many Japanese travelers have been deciding to go independently, in order to gain a much better appreciation of local cultures than their package-tour compatriots get. Some even opt for eco-tours to Southeast Asia and Australia, where sightseeing is combined with work to protect the rain forest or endangered koalas.

The Disney boom is another phenomenon that exemplifies the growing interaction and immersion of mass culture. With more than 16 million visitors per year, Tokyo Disneyland has become a magnet for the new Asian middle class and has surpassed its American counterparts in profits.[75] In the 1984 Taiwanese film *Summer at Grandpa's*, directed by Hou Hsiao-Hsieu, for instance, a young boy boasts to his friends about his cousin's trip to Tokyo Disneyland. Disney has accordingly tried to widen its market: the Disney Channel has taken to the air waves in Taiwan, and "Mickey's Corner" merchandise outlets have proliferated across mainland China.[76]

Nothing illustrates the region's cultural cross-fertilization more colorfully than its adoption and adaptation of baseball. In a twist on the normal flow of players across the Pacific, Japanese Hideo "Tornado" Nomo, a pitcher for the Los Angeles Dodgers, made a flawless debut at the 1995 American professional all-star game.[77] The movie *Mr. Baseball*, one of President Clinton's favorites, chronicles the life of an American playing for Japan's Chunichi Dragons and good-heartedly dramatizes the overcoming of differences that have evolved between Japanese and US versions of America's favorite pastime. Baseball is also popular in other nations such as Taiwan whose Little League teams are well known in America for their prowess in the annual international competitions. "The American kids think it's a game!" exclaimed one Taiwanese father after a US-Taiwanese match that went in Taiwan's favor.[78]

While Japan borrowed baseball from the United States, it has given back to the world a number of popular sports, including judo and sumo. Some of today's top-ranked sumo wrestlers hail from the United States, especially Hawaii. In 1993, Hawaiian Chad Rowan, better known as "Akebono," became the first foreign-born wrestler to achieve the highest sumo rank of *yokozuna* in the sports nearly 1,300-year history.[79] Another transplant from Hawaii was Akebono's stablemaster, Jesse Kuhaulua, who used to wrestle under the name Takamiyama, and in 1972 became the first foreigner to win a sumo tournament. Former University of Hawaii football player Salevaa Atisanoe, recognized by sumo fans as the gargantuan Konishiki, was the first foreigner to attain the sport's second-highest rank of *ozeki*. The success of such wrestlers has attracted many young American understudies to Japan. There are now sumo stables in the United States, like those certified by the Oahu Sumo Association in Hawaii, where youths can be introduced to the sport and groomed for professional careers.[80]

The English language, which helps to unite the Asia Pacific, has been embraced by business people, academics, and computer programmers out of pragmatism rather than government-imposed policies. A young member of Indonesia's Widjaja family, which owns a $2 billion stake in the Sinar Mas Group Conglomerate, said that their bibles were Kenichi Ohmae and Alvin Toffler. He added: " My father speaks both Fujian and Mandarin but cannot speak English. That's why he always tries to associate himself with overseas Chinese. I was lucky enough to study abroad, so I have made more friends all over the world through English."[81] Nations such as Taiwan and Japan have launched ambitious projects to improve spoken English among their citizens. The Japanese government initiated in 1987 the Japan Exchange and Teaching (JET) Program, to bring young people from 15 countries in North America, Europe, and the Asia Pacific to Japan to assist in teaching foreign languages, predominantly English.

In a recent meeting, Vietnam's Communist Party General Secretary Do Muoi asked Japanese Prime Minister Tomiichi Murayama for economic assistance to develop Vietnam's English education. "As Vietnam plans its membership in ASEAN, we urgently need more English-speaking officials," Do said.[82]

In Cambodia, another formerly francophone country, students recently protested government efforts to teach French and demanded they be taught English instead.[83] "American technology is superior to French technology, so we do not need the French to help us," exclaimed one Cambodian student. "We are the new Khmer generation. We don't need French; we need English," explained another during the 1993 demonstration in front of the Ministry of Higher Education in Phnom Penh.[84] In a more recent disturbance, students threatened to burn French flags in protest of language classes funded by foreign aid from Paris.[85]

Former Philippine Foreign Minister Raul Manglapus related the story of a French businessman who had commented that the Philippines was a good place to invest "because you have people who are free, you're well-educated, and besides that, you all speak English."[86] Manglapus also recalled a meeting he attended in Paris on Cambodian peace with a mixture of sympathy and amusement: "former French Foreign Minister Roland Dumas was our host, of course, in the French Quai d'Orsay," Manglapus recounted. "And the poor man had to make a speech in English, because otherwise he would not have been understood."

Unlike in other regions, in the Asia Pacific English is the undisputed lingua franca. As the official language of APEC since 1989, English was the base from which all the other six APEC languages were translated at the first leaders meeting at Blake Island in Washington in 1993.

Asian societies have traditionally put a high premium on advanced education. Education abroad profoundly shapes students' worldviews, engenders two-way education, and leaves the legacy of intellectual bonds. Education has thus strengthened bonds between peoples, particularly elites, within APEC, harmonizing the philosophies of Pacific business and political leaders. Australia has recently become a magnet for Asian students, particularly those from Indonesia, Hong Kong, and Singapore. Japan, too, is attracting increasing numbers of students, including more than 20,000 from China, 6,000 from Taiwan, and 11,000 from Korea, but also from Southeast Asia and Mexico, who come to study technical fields in particular. Yet the most prized, and popular, education is still found in American universities.

Many Asian business and government elites have had the common experience in American graduate education. The preponderance of Taiwanese students at the Massachusetts Institute of Technology (MIT) has led some to jokingly rename the school "Made in Taiwan." The trend toward educating Asia's best and brightest in American graduate schools has increased in recent years. Since 1980 the Asian student population at American universities has tripled. Currently Asians make up almost 60 percent of foreign students enrolled in US colleges and universities.[87] In 1989 there were nearly 10 times as many Chinese and Japanese students enrolled in American universities as there were in European institutions.[88] The number of Chinese (and Indian) students going into Silicon Valley's electronics industry after finishing their American Ph.D.s has given the term IC (integrated circuit) the tongue-in-cheek meaning "Indians and Chinese." Since 1990 Singapore has sent more students to the United States or Australia than to Britain, a historic turnaround for a country once colonized by Great Britain and still heavily influenced by its social and educational elites.[89] Senior Minister Lee Kuan Yew once told a journalist that if he were to live his life over again, he would choose to attend a top US university rather than a British one.[90] Today there are over

100,000 Malaysian graduates of American universities.[91] Mahathir has realized the long-term importance of human resources development, particularly of education, which has been one of the highlights of his enlightened development policies for Malaysia.

The most popular course of study of Asian students in the United States is business, with technical fields a close second. The number of students from Japan, China, Taiwan, and Korea taking the Graduate Management Admissions Test (GMAT) required for application to most American MBA programs has increased more than 70 percent between the 1987–88 and 1991–92 school years.[92] Following Japan's rapid economic growth and global industrial expansion in the 1970s and '80s, US business schools began incorporating Japanese business principles such as Total Quality Management and group-based decision making into their management courses. In the industrial capitals of autos, steel, semiconductors, and machine tools throughout the region, Japanese management practices have combined with American-style entrepreneurship to form the basis of a unique, new Asia Pacific business culture.

Japan's Deming award, named for American statistician W. Edwards Deming in honor of his work to promote manufacturing quality, exemplifies the emerging Asia Pacific business culture. Largely ignored by American businesses in the heyday of the postwar economic boom, Deming went to Japan and lectured there on quality control systems in the 1950s and '60s. Japan's industrialists took to heart Deming's lessons of total quality management and quality control circles and built a formidable industrial structure based on product competitiveness and reliability. In recognition of Deming's contribution to Japan's postwar economic miracle, the government created a prize, which is awarded to the company whose products exhibit the highest quality.[93] Thirty years later, facing stiff Japanese industrial competition, US businesses moved to adopt the theories it had earlier ignored. In 1987, the US Department of Commerce even created an American equivalent to the Deming prize, the Malcolm Baldrige award, named after a former Commerce secretary.[94]

Finally, perhaps the greatest strength of the region's civilizational cross-fertilization is the yearning of its peoples to learn from others; such curiosity and open-mindedness has been an enduring factor in the region's success. Singaporean Senior Minister Lee Kuan Yew took the lessons of Switzerland and Israel for his own country: "Switzerland, for example, [is] landlocked, but they manufacture small things like watches, high-value items, and sell to the world. . . . And Israel [was] boycotted by all [its] Arab neighbors but [is] able to grow fruits and vegetables to export to Europe, to make things to export to America."[95]

Clashes of Civilizations

Numerous challenges to Asia Pacific fusion have inevitably arisen. Most often cited are the basic differences between Eastern and Western civilizations, an incompatibility that some argue will sink the prospects for a true Asia Pacific community. "What will happen when the passive Sinic golden rule meets with the active Western golden rule?" asked former Korean Foreign Minister Han. "The East will say, 'Do not do unto others what thou dost not want others to do unto thee.' The West will respond, 'All things whatsoever you would have men do to you, do even so to them.' "[96] And he adds, "The West will say, 'You are the light of the world, you give light to everyone in the house.' The East will respond, 'Mud is used to make celadons, but it is the emptiness of the celadon that becomes useful.' " Such differing attitudes have unavoidably led to culture clashes.

Race or racial discrimination is still a factious issue in the region. The growing interdependence of the Asia Pacific has come when many Asians are rediscovering their "Asianness." This apparent contradiction has led many to suffer from identity crises of self and community.

The West has long been criticized for racial discrimination against Asia. While European powers were clearly identified as colonial masters, the perception of the United States is more complex: in freeing the Philippines from Japanese rule, the United States was heralded as a liberator, but in fighting the Vietnam War, it was reviled by some as an oppressor. An ambivalent love-hate relationship developed, as Asians became aware of a gap between the image and reality of American society. The Nobel Prize–winning Indian poet Rabindranath Tagore exemplified the tension felt by many in modern Asia. Writing in 1916, Tagore expressed his admiration of an America he had never visited because it was "the only nation engaged in solving the problems of race intimacy. Its mission is to raise civilization by permitting all races entry and widening the ideal of humanity." However, when he visited the country on a promotional tour in 1929, he was shocked by the racial attitudes he found. "Jesus," he wrote embitteredly, "could not get into America because, first of all, he would not have the necessary money, and secondly, he would be an Asiatic."[97]

Tagore was not alone among Asians disenchanted with the realities of an America that often did not live up to its ideals. There is a strain within the consciousness of many Asians of a rejection of Western ideals and beliefs, a feeling that the traditions and beliefs of East and West cannot be reconciled, and that the West will always apply a double standard that will discriminate against nonwhites. Anti-West rhetoric and emotion were particularly dramatic in the region after the 1955 Bandung Conference in Indonesia that launched the Non-Aligned Movement.

While the end of the Cold War has somewhat alleviated the North-South split, there are enduring fears in China and some Southeast Asian nations that increasing Westernization and US influence will be a threat to their native cultures, regimes, or both. As English gains more acceptance, national languages are perceived to be threatened and the old Marxist debate over the imperialist uses of English have reemerged as an issue. Malaysia and Indonesia have launched political campaigns to restrict the use of English in business and the media.[98] George Yeo predicted that Internet users around the world would one day reject the use of English as a common medium. "The widespread use of English will eventually be contested, and Internet itself will become multicultural."[99]

Nationalist Japanese politician Shintaro Ishihara, who has recently published a book with Malaysian Prime Minister Mahathir entitled *The Asia That Can Say No*, has argued for "something like the economic and cultural body of the Greater East Asian Co-prosperity Sphere,"[100] a reference to Japan's World War II Asian empire. Similarly, there has been a spate of recent popular books in the United States, such as Michael Crichton's *Rising Sun*, which have portrayed Asians, particularly Japanese, as untrustworthy villains bent on world economic domination. Politicians on both sides of the Pacific have been known in recent years to make extreme, often racist remarks to gain public support.

Yet the clash between East and West is not the only challenge to an Asia Pacific civilization. There remain substantial differences among Asian nations as well. For example, Asia has developed assorted national myths about the seas. The acrimonious debate over the name of the Sea of Japan nearly derailed a 1994 pollution control agreement between China, Russia, South Korea, and Japan when the Korean press revealed that their government delegates had accepted the term Sea of Japan, a designation Koreans reject because of the associated memories of Japanese occupation. Seoul had previously insisted on the name Tonghae (East Sea), fearing the political repercussions of condoning Japan's claim. The deadlock at the UN-sponsored conference was eventually broken with an agreement to refer to the body of water by its longitudinal and latitudinal coordinates, but the symbolic value of the debate persisted.

Such debates over nomenclature are not limited to Northeast Asia. Under Indonesia's nationalistic first president, Sukarno, Indonesia challenged the official name of the entire Indian Ocean, claiming that the "Indonesian Ocean" would be more fitting. Historian A. B. Lapian of the Indonesian Institute of Science explained that part of this problem stems from Asia's habit of naming its seas for nations, an inherently confusing and emotionally charged process. "In Europe, they do not use names of countries to describe oceans—for example, the Baltic Sea and the Aegean Sea. The United States also refers to the Pacific and Atlantic Oceans. Asia has long been unable to resolve an issue which Europe and the United States did in the distant past."[101]

The acceleration of economic growth and development offers both high returns and high risks, such as severe economic downturn that could seriously affect the stability of the region. Some economists have compared

Asia's recent economic growth with the boom in output experienced by the Soviet Union in the 1950s, arguing that the focus in the United States on the East Asian challenge is greatly exaggerated.[102]

Many parts of the region face potential development constraints or political instability because of inflation, inadequate infrastructure, and environmental degradation. In China and Indonesia the succession of Deng and Suharta respectively, could lead to serious destabilization. On an international level, there is the danger that the chronic trade imbalances that both China and Japan have with the United States could lead Washington to raise barriers to both economies, severely limiting their economic growth. The Asia Pacific's embrace of a "rule of the jungle" security environment is also chancy. The current stability of Asia's skies and sea ensured by the US Navy is currently challenged by both American budget cuts and the Asian nations' race to acquire advanced weaponry. Potentially the most destabilizing flash point in the region is in the South China Sea, where China's adventurism has been met with ambiguous American claims of neutrality.

An even more fundamental question has been directed at the viability of an Asia Pacific community. "Trade, investment, and a Pacific coastline do not necessarily make for a broader sense of community," wrote Robert Manning and Paula Stern. "Moreover, to the degree that there is a sense of identity, it tends to be Asian, not Pacific: an assertive Confucian culture; an informal, non-confrontational style; and the self-confidence of the newly industrializing economies as successful post-colonial, nonwhite societies."[103]

Yet the Confucian stereotype often applied to the region is largely irrelevant in Southeast Asia, and even in Japan, as both contain many diverse influences. The argument also ignores the emergence of a solid middle class in all of the societies in the region. By the year 2000 there will be more than 230 million people in Asia living in households with incomes greater than $10,000 per year.[104] Life expectancy in Shanghai has already surpassed that in New York.[105] This growing Asian middle class shares with its counterparts in Australia and North America a common interest in security and economic prosperity. In the future it will also demand greater political participation. The United States has already demonstrated its capacity to break not only the civilizational barrier, but also the income divide, by signing the North American Free Trade Agreement (NAFTA) with Mexico.

Finally, critics underestimate Asia's capacity to adapt. Former Philippine Finance Minister Jesus Estanislao noted that 30 years ago, combining Chinese and Malay countries together in ASEAN was a revolutionary idea.[106] There are many incentives for Asian countries to adapt again to the emerging environment of the Asia Pacific.

From Europe's vantage point, trends toward integration in the Asia Pacific may appear amorphous and undeserving of the classification of "regionalism." Asia is analogous to an Indian ink painting, in which the spaces that represent the relations among countries do not emerge in a high relief that casts clear contrasts of dark or light. Instead, a vast emptiness stretches hither and yon, through which isolated entities sometimes connect, but invariably disconnect. European regionalism, in comparison, is a precisely rendered oil painting. Europeans may concede that Asia will go global, but they question whether it will go universal. They may ask how Asia will express and realize political liberty and economic freedom of individuals, and how it will institutionalize itself as part of the world. Asia's answer will be simple and brief: it will proceed toward these goals hand in hand with the rest of the world. APEC thus will be an indispensable forum to intellectually explore the universality of Asia's experiences. Asia has also decided to follow the tried and true path of economic integration to transcend the racial and cultural legacies among nations at the regional level and has taken the first step to follow Jean Monnet's wisdom. For all the differences between Europe and Asia, the fundamental philosophy—stability and peace through economic regional integration—is strikingly similar.

Clashes of Values

Values deeply embedded in Asian and Western societies have been increasingly portrayed as conflicting, especially on human rights issues, which include the role of women in society. Critics in Asia, and even some in the United States, have argued that American philosophies such as human rights and democracy are culturally relative. This issue has strained intraregional ties, particularly when the United States has pushed publicly for internal reforms in some developing Asian nations. To many Asians, US criticisms of human rights records and authoritarian regimes appear overly self-righteous given America's domestic social ills. Often Asian leaders blame many problems in the United States—such as high levels of divorce, murder, drug abuse, and teen pregnancy—on the American premium on democratic individualism. As Kishore Mahbubani has opined, "The frontier myths, which encouraged individualism, may have finally become a liability for the United States. . . . [T]he evidence is accumulating that socially cohesive and disciplined societies are developing a competitive edge in the world today."[107]

Some long-ruling Asian leaders are concerned about the transition of Asia's developing states to pluralistic, Western-style democracies. Traditionalists worry that the loss of some long-held values is the cost of economic success. Divorce rates in Singapore, Hong Kong, and Taiwan have doubled in the past 10 years and tripled in China over the past four.[108] Potentially more dangerous to some long-standing regimes in the region is the threat posed by pluralism. Some have used cultural arguments against democratization in hopes of avoiding the inevitable.

Despite the progress on democracy that has occurred in Asia over the past 15 years, continued tensions threaten to wear down Americans unaccustomed to being rebuffed by Asian allies, long quiet because of Cold War concerns. Discovering that it cannot sway the world as it once did, the United States could potentially turn inward and spurn a global leadership role. Former Secretary of State Henry Kissinger notes that this tendency is particularly strong among the baby-boom generation of Americans, raised during the tumultuous Vietnam era.[109] That conflict has left the influential generation especially wary of engagement in Asia and prone to withdrawal when faced with a clash of values.

The diplomatic row over the caning of American teenager Michael Fay, convicted of vandalism in Singapore, became a symbol for Americans of the growing tension between the developing countries in Asia and the United States. Disputes over the East Timor issue in Indonesia and political repressions in Myanmar (Burma), and most seriously, human rights abuses, democratization, and prison labor in China have at times strained ties between the United States and its APEC partners.

These rifts, however, are not as intractable as they may appear. Despite the rhetoric emanating from Kuala Lumpur and Singapore over differing cultural interpretations of human rights and democracy, there is little evidence that Asians uniformly dismiss the concepts. South Korean President Kim Young Sam has argued that "human dignity, plural democracy, and free market economics have firmly taken root as universal values." In reference to human rights protection, former Korean Foreign Minister Han has stressed the emergence of a "globalization of values" that transcends culture.[110] This view was echoed by Japan during the 1993 World Conference on Human Rights in Vienna. Burmese dissident Aung San Suu Kyi addressed the issue of relativity this way: "If ideas and beliefs were denied validity outside the cultural bounds of their origin, Buddhism would be confined to North India, Christianity to a narrow tract in the middle East, and Islam to Arabia."[111]

As elsewhere in the world, Asia has changed as some countries in the region have demonstrated the link between codified laws, free press, and transparent government policies with sustained economic growth. Moreover, political reform and liberalization have contributed to economic efficiency. Taiwan and Korea have seen their competitiveness reinforced by the introduction of a more liberal political environment. Lee Kuan Yew, whose own government has been accused of media manipulation and censorship, gave friendly advice to Khin Nyunt, a leader of Myanmar's ruling military junta: "We are in an information age. It is not possible for him to cut off his people from some knowledge, some information of what is going on in the rest of the world."[112] Yet while

Lee has pushed for a more liberalized Myanmar, he has long criticized Philippine democracy. He has blamed excessive pluralism for the Philippines' failure to develop as rapidly as its ASEAN neighbors. Responding to Lee's charges, former Philippine Foreign Minister Raul Manglapus has argued that it was not democracy that failed the Philippines but its interlude with authoritarianism under Ferdinand Marcos, who Lee criticizes only for squandering his opportunity to exploit absolute authority. "Power tends to corrupt," Manglapus responded, quoting Lord Acton's famous saying, "and absolute power corrupts absolutely."[113]

The definition of "Asian values" has sparked intense debate among Asians. Lee Kuan Yew's argument that there is an "Asian way" based on traditional Confucian precepts has led to a lively discussion on the real character of Asian society. Longtime Korean political activist and former presidential candidate Kim Dae Jung, refuted Lee's attempt to link Confucian values and authoritarianism.[114] Kim points out that traditional Confucian concepts such as *minben zhengchi*, or "people-based politics," and the "mandate of heaven," which holds rulers accountable for their citizens' well-being, clearly rebut claims that Asian countries have no concept of political liberalism.

Despite the debate and rhetoric, many Asia Pacific countries have been at the forefront of democratization. As US Assistant Secretary of State Winston Lord assessed it, "False prophets claim a contest of values between the United States, or the West, and an Asian monolith. They assert that Asians do not share universal aspirations for individual rights. Let them tell that to the Japanese, Australians, New Zealanders, Filipinos, Thai, Koreans, Taiwanese. Let them tell that to Cambodians crossing minefields or Mongolians crossing deserts to vote."

The debate over trade and economic development models will likely continue to generate friction in the region in the coming years. Much of this struggle has been between the United States and Japan, the world's two largest economies, but the resolution of this question has far wider consequences for the region.

American revisionists claim that Japan's version of capitalism is fundamentally different from that practiced in America and Europe, and often unfair. "[Countries like] Japan behave like creatures from another economic world because they *are* from another world," argued journalist Murray Sayle. "We must either adapt to their economics or persuade them to take up ours."[115] What is worse, in their eyes, is the fact that most of the rapidly developing nations of Asia are adopting the Japanese model, a development that promises to further damage America's industrial base. Signs of such strategies are already becoming apparent, they claim. In 1987, MITI introduced its New Asian Industry Development Plan, which in the words of one scholar "gave MITI a tool to guide the market forces and thereby assert its influence" over East Asia's development.[116] Japan's official emphasis on the "flying geese" model is often pointed to as proof that Tokyo is attempting to create an army of little mercantilist Japans in the region. The fact that many Asian nations have endorsed the Japanese model has given American trade policymakers the jitters. One senior US trade official noted that in the sensitive area of car exports, "China and Korea [have been pursuing] an industrial policy to strengthen a handful of consolidated auto companies."[117] The official went on to explain that auto talks with Korea are "already [a] huge problem," despite that country's relatively small auto export capacity.

In one respect, American officials should not become too discouraged. Japan, Korea, and even China continue to follow a similar path of economic development: starting with a natural division of labor, then moving toward liberalization, and finally globalization. The economic development of the region should not be seen as either offensive or defensive. Such thinking is a remnant of the Cold War mentality of zero-sum competition and lacks historical perspective. The United States of the 19th century, like the developing East Asian nations of today, supported a government that invested heavily in infrastructure and nurtured infant industries. It is important to allow the developing countries of APEC the same opportunity to grow so that they too can enter and invigorate the global trading system as confident partners. Economic development and liberalization progress sequentially. Although the precise pattern varies to reflect the cultural and traditional backgrounds of each society, eventually both processes stimulate each other.

The centripetal forces in the Pacific outweigh the centrifugal ones. Although there are still closed markets and invisible trade barriers, throughout the Asia Pacific there is at least an intellectual agreement that the international division of labor, FDI, free trade and investment, and the transfer of technology all work for the mutual benefit of all.

A salient characteristic of those aspiring to build an Asia Pacific community is their world view of secular pragmatism. As British philosopher Bertrand Russell noted of Chinese civilization: "I know of no other civilization where there is such open-mindedness, such realism, and such a willingness to face the facts as they are, instead of trying to distort them into a particular problem."[118] This shared sense of realism, along with optimism, will be at the base of an Asia Pacific civilization. A shared interest in global free trade can provide a powerful counterbalance to the attempts to balkanize the world economic order along geographical or cultural lines. Further, strong Pacific ties will inevitably lead to true globalism.

As French historian Fernand Braudel observed of the traffic of civilizations, "He who gives, dominates."[119] The APEC belief in "open regionalism" in trade and the cross-fertilization across civilizations illustrates its potential to give, and take, the best from around the world.

Notes

1. Kishore Mahbubani, "The Pacific Way," *Foreign Affairs* 74, no. 1 (January/February 1995): 102.

2. Robert Braidwood, *Prehistoric Men* (Glenview, IL: Scott, Foresman and Company, 1975), pp. 33–34; 149–50.

3. For this theme, see an essay by Masakazu Yamazaki, "Datsu A Nyu Yo no Susume" (Discourse on Leaving Asia and Entering the West), *Ronza*, July 1995.

4. See K. N. Chaudhuri, *Asia Before Europe: Economy and Civilization of the Indian Ocean from the Rise of Islam to 1750* (Cambridge, UK: Cambridge University Press, 1990), chapter 2.

5. Walter A. McDougall, *Let the Sea Make a Noise: A History of the North Pacific from Magellan to MacArthur* (New York: Basic Books, 1993), p. 43.

6. Akira Iriye , "The United States and Japan in Asia: A Historical Perspective," in Gerald Curtis, ed., *The United States, Japan, and Asia* (New York: Norton, 1994) p. 30.

7. Quoted in Barbara Bundy, Stephen Burns, and Kimberly Weichel, eds., *The Pacific Rim: Scenarios for Regional Cooperation* (Westport, CT: Praeger, 1994), p. 60.

8. Han Sung-Joo, *Korean Diplomacy in an Era of Globalization* (Seoul: Ji Sik San Yup Sa, 1995), p. 317.

9. *Asahi Shimbun*, 29 April 1993.

10. Personal interview with Fidel Ramos, 13 January 1993.

11. Fidel V. Ramos, *Time for Takeoff* (Manila: Friends of Steady Eddie, 1994), p. 202.

12. Stanley Karnow, *In Our Image: America's Empire in the Philippines* (New York: Ballantine Books, 1990), p. 206.

13. Personal interview with Raul Rabe, 11 May 1995.

14. Personal interview with Jesus Estanislao, 10 August 1995.

15. Personal interview with Raul Manglapus, 10 August 1995.

16. Han, p. 303.

17. Enrique Cortes, *Kindai Mekishiko-Nihon Kankeishi* [Japanese translation of *Relations between Mexico and Japan in the Modern Age*] (Tokyo: Gendaikikakushitsu Publishers, 1988), chapter 2.

18. Personal interview, 8 July 1995.

19. *The Straits Times*, 13 May 1995.

20. Speech by Secretary of State Warren Christopher, University of Washington, Seattle, WA, 17 November 1993.

21. Speech by Gareth Evans before the 19th Australia-Japan Relations Symposium, 24 February 1995, Canberra, Australia.

22. *Straits Times*, 22 January 1995.

23. *Straits Times*, 22 March 1995.

24. Information Officer, Embassy of New Zealand, Washington, DC.

25. Richard Wilson, "Subregional Groupings within APEC," *NBR Analysis* 6, no. 1 (April 1995): p. 40.

26. Kenichi Ohmae, "Rise of the Region State," *Foreign Affairs*, 72, no. 2 (Spring 1993): 79.

27. Gerald Segal, "China's Changing Shape," *Foreign Affairs* 73, no. 3 (May/June 1994): 46.

28. Samuel Kim and Lowell Dittmer, eds., *China's Quest for National Identity* (Ithaca: Cornell University Press, 1993), p. 246.

29. Kim and Dittmer, p. 265.

30. Kim and Dittmer, p. 263.

31. Eishu Ochiai and Kiichi Moriwaki, *Fukuoka-shi, Kita-Kyushu-shi wa Ima* [Fukuoka city, Kita-Kyushu city, Now] (Tokyo: OS Shuppan, 1993).

32. Clifford Geertz, *Negara: The Theatre State in Nineteenth Century Bali*, (Princeton, NJ: Princeton University Press, 1980, p. 4.

33. Murray Weidenbaum, ''The Rise of Greater China: A New Economic Superpower,'' *Currents*, no. 358 (December 1993): 34.

34. *Asahi Shimbun*, 22 April 1993.

35. *Washington Post*, 30 May 1993.

36. Informal conversation with a Chinese economist, 14 August 1995.

37. *Dallas Morning News*, 8 February 1995.

38. Personal interview with Jeffrey Garten.

39. Donald Hellman, ''APEC and the Political Economy of the Asia Pacific: New Myths, Old Realities,'' *NBR Analysis* 6, no. 1 (April 1995): 36.

40. McDougall, pp. 25–26.

41. *Los Angeles Times*, 29 November 1992.

42. *Financial Times*, 8 November 1994.

43. *Reuter's World Service*, 25 October 1994.

44. *China Post*, 27 August 1993.

45. *Reuter Asia Pacific Business Report*, 4 April 1995.

46. *International Herald Tribune*, 20 June 1995.

47. *The Economist*, 4 March 1995, pp. 37–38.

48. Il SaKong, *Korea in the World Economy* (Washington: Institute for International Economics, 1993), p. 119; Vincent Cable, and Bishnodat Persaud, *Developing with Foreign Investment* (Kent, UK: The Commonwealth Secretariat, 1987), p. 44.

49. *The Straits Times*, 12 March 1995.

50. Bundy et al., p. 62.

51. Ministry of International Trade and Industry, Japan, ''White Paper on Trade: 1994.''

52. *Defining a Pacific Community* (Washington: Carnegie Endowment for International Peace, 1994), p. 18.

53. *Business Times*, 24 August 1994.

54. *Los Angeles Times*, 16 April 1989.

55. *National Public Radio*, 18 July 1995.

56. *The Straits Times*, 12 March 1995.

57. Segal, p. 48.

58. Weidenbaum, p. 34.

59. Speech by Jeffrey Garten before the Keidanren, 4 March 1994, Tokyo.

60. Personal interview with Lee Kuan Yew, 24 June 1993.

61. Weidenbaum, p. 54.

62. Randall Jones, Robert King, and Michael Kline, *The Chinese Economic Area: Economic Integration Without a Free Trade Area*, Organization for Economic Cooperation and Development (OECD) Working Paper No. 124, 1992, p. 5.

63. Jones et al., p. 20.

64. *Reuter European Community Report*, 2 March 1995.

65. *AP Worldstream*, 14 March 1995.

66. *Deutsche Presse-Agentur*, 21 March 1995.

67. *Japan Echo*, Winter 1994, p. 74.

68. *Asahi News Service*, 3 December 1993.

69. *Far Eastern Economic Review*, 18 November 1995.

70. *Asahi Shimbun*, 7 May 1993.

71. *Asahi Shimbun*, 17 May 1993.

72. *Asahi Shimbun*, 8 May 1993.

73. *Asian Business*, January 1993, p. 22.

74. Noordin Sopiee, "Megatrends in East Asia: Security and Political Implications," paper presented at the Asia Pacific Round Table, June 1995.

75. *New York Times*, 7 March 1994.

76. *Orlando Sentinel*, 2 April 1995.

77. *Washington Post*, 11 July 1995.

78. Robert Elegant, *Pacific Destiny: Inside Asia Today* (New York: Crown Books, 1990), p. 31.

79. *Washington Post*, 8 March 1991.

80. *Washington Post*, 31 March 1995.

81. *Asahi Shimbun*, 10 July, 1991.

82. Personal interview with Japanese participant in April 1995 meeting between Murayama and Do Muoi in Tokyo.

83. *Agence France Presse*, 3 May 1995.

84. *Agence France Presse*, 7 October 1993.

85. *Agence France Presse*, 3 May 1995.

86. Personal interview with Raul Manglapus, 13 January 1993.

87. *Business Times*, 20 April 1994.

88. *The Economist*, 4 February 1995.

89. *Straits Times*, 21 September 1993.

90. *Straits Times*, 18 February 1995.

91. Testimony by Ambassador-designate John Malott to the US Senate Foreign Relations Committee, 17 July 1995.

92. Graduate Management Admissions Council Five-Year Summary, provided by Washington University in St. Louis.

93. Donald Christiansen, *Engineering Excellence* (New York: IEEE Press, 1987), p. 47.

94. Reiko Kinoshita, "Marukomu Borudoriji Awodo" [Malcolm Baldrige Award], in *Puraizu* [Prize] (Tokyo: Shinchosha, 1993), pp. 160–82.

95. Personal interview with Lee Kuan Yew.

96. Han, pp. 317–18.

97. Joel Kotkin, *The Third Century: America's Resurgence in the Asian Era* (New York: Joel Kotkin, 1988), pp. 173–74.

98. Steven Schlosstein, *Asia's New Little Dragons: The Dynamic Emergence of Indonesia, Thailand, and Malaysia* (Chicago: Contemporary Books, 1991), p. 223.

99. *International Herald Tribune*, 8 August 1995.

100. *Asiaweek*, 28 April 1995.

101. *Asahi Shimbun*, 18 June 1995.

102. Paul Krugman, "The Myth of Asia's Miracle," *Foreign Affairs* 73, no. 6 (November/December 1994): 78.

103. Robert Manning and Paula Stern, "The Myth of the Pacific Community," *Foreign Affairs* 73, no. 6 (November/December 1994): 80–81.

104. Bundy et al., p. 63.

105. *Far Eastern Economic Review,* 18 February 1993.

106. Personal interview with Estanislao.

107. Kishore Mahbubani, "The United States: Go East Young Man," *Washington Quarterly* 17, no. 2 (Spring 1994).

108. David Hitchcock, *Asian Values and the United States: How Much Conflict?* (Washington: Center for Strategic and International Studies, 1994), p. 8.

109. Speech by Henry Kissinger, Frankfurt Germany, June 1995.

110. Han, pp. 513–20.

111. Quoted in "Building a Pacific Community," speech by Winston Lord before the Commonwealth Club, San Francisco, 12 January 1995.

112. Personal interview, 24 June 1993.

113. Personal interview, 15 January 1993.

114. Kim Dae Jung, "Is Culture Destiny?" *Foreign Affairs* 73, no. 6 (November/December 1994): 19.

115. Clyde Prestowitz, Ronald Morse, and Alan Tonelson, eds., *Powernomics: Economics and Strategy After the Cold War* (Washington: Economic Strategy Institute, 1991), p. 163.

116. Edward Lincoln, *Japan's New Global Role* (Washington: Brookings Institution, 1993), pp. 123–24.

117. Personal interview, 27 April 1995.

118. Quoted in Han, pp. 318–19.

119. Fernand Braudel, *The Mediterranean and the Mediterranean World in the Age of Phillip II* (New York: Harper and Row, 1973), p. 826.

2

Leaders and Diplomats

At Bogor, US President Bill Clinton joked that 2020 would find Jiang Zemin in the prime of his life, to which the Chinese president agreed, "Yes, I will be 94." Ranging in age from Mexico's 44-year-old Ernesto Zedillo to septuagenarian Tomiichi Murayama of Japan, the leaders of APEC represent the diversities and commonalities of the Asia Pacific in miniature. While President Suharto has headed Indonesia's government for more than 30 years, and Sultan Bolkiah has ruled Brunei for 26, novice Prime Minister Murayama has led his tenuous coalition government for barely one. At Blake Island, Washington, freshly elected Korean President Kim Young Sam, Bill Clinton, and Canadian Prime Minister Jean Chrétien were new forces.

Reflecting varied governmental systems, the APEC leaders ascended to power through direct elections, parliamentary decision, or military might. With shared specialities and skills they initially entered politics from myriad fields: Clinton, Chrétien, and Thailand's former Prime Minister Chuan Leekpai from law, Suharto and the Philippines' Fidel Ramos from the military, Singapore's Goh Chok Tong and Zedillo from economics, Jim Bolger from agriculture, Malaysian Prime Minister Mahathir bin Mohamad from medicine, and Chile's Eduardo Frei Ruiz-Tagle and Fidel Ramos from civil engineering.

The region's educational exchange, which has boomed in recent years, is represented by those who were educated abroad including Clinton at Oxford University, Zedillo at the University of Bradford and Yale University, Ramos at West Point and the University of Illinois, and Goh at Williams College. Mahathir has explained that he was not enticed overseas, as his education in Malaysia was already too Eurocentric, encompassing the War of the Roses and Henry VIII but omitting any Asian history.[1] Common interests can be found among their leisure time pursuits. As a boy, Bolger was an avid cricket and rugby player and Zedillo a state track champion; today, both Kim and Clinton are known for their early morning jogs. Clinton, who plays the saxophone, has a fellow connoisseur of popular music in Keating, who managed a rock band called the "Ramrods" in the 1960s.

In each of these 18 men are elements that personify the challenges that face future regional integration. Yet their interaction underlies the cooperation that has come to define the APEC process.

No Asia Pacific leader embodies these dynamics better than Clinton. The *New York Times* heralded the young president as an "Emerging Asia Hand"[2] who became familiar with the region during numerous trade and investment promotion tours—including four trips to Taiwan, three to Japan, two to Hong Kong, and one to Korea—as governor of Arkansas. Before he first ventured to Japan, he assiduously perused James Clavell's *Shogun* and Brian Kelly's *Four Little Dragons*.[3] His primary interest in the region, however, is economic, not literary. For Clinton, trade policy is foreign policy. His junkets to Taiwan included a 1985 attempt to sell 60,000 Arkansas-made parking meters for $10 million, and a 1988 trip to open an Arkansas trade office in Taipei's World Trade Center.[4] Undaunted by his state's obscurity, he once reportedly pulled out a map to show his Singaporean hosts where Arkansas was located. Another time, the US Consul General in Hong Kong, unable to convince local executives to meet Clinton, advised the governor to entice them with the prospect of imported Arkansas catfish.[5] When Clinton paid a call on Prime Minister Takeshita in 1988 to appeal for more Japanese investment in Arkansas, he even suggested that Arkansas could pay the airfare for workers to travel to Japan for retraining. Clinton's salesmanship was rewarded on several occasions, such as when a Japanese steel mill opened in his state in 1989.

Clinton's style has contrasted sharply with that of his predecessor, George Bush. Bush had broad Asian experience, including a stint as US representative to Beijing, yet he was very much a part of the East Coast/Atlanticist strategic community elite that had long guided America's Cold War foreign policy. The differences between Bush and Clinton were probably best illustrated by Bush's contemptuous comment that Clinton and Gore were "the *karaoke* kids," referring to an incident in which Clinton, as governor, enjoyed that popular, uniquely Asia Pacific brand of middle-class entertainment, including one round with the Japanese president of the Sanyo company in Osaka.[6] Britian's *Financial Times* predicted, however, "if Governor Bill Clinton's policies toward Japan are a reflection of his appetite for singing with *karaoke* machines, relations between the US and Japan should take a sharp turn for the better." (*Financial Times*, 5 November 1992).

At the same time, Clinton's commitment to protecting American workers and expanding democracy and human rights throughout the world has made his administration's relations with the Asia Pacific tense and confused. Clinton's administration soon became mired in an array of bilateral disputes over trade and human rights. The boiling point for Clinton's problems in the region came six months after the Seattle summit with the leaking of an internal memorandum from Assistant Secretary Winston Lord to Secretary of State Warren Christopher. Lord wrote that he saw US-Asian relations becoming "infected by a malaise" and warned, "[S]ome of the frictions are inevitable bumps in the road. The confluence of these individual events, however, has . . . eroded the sense of optimism and partnership forged in Seattle."[7] Despite Lord's warning, Clinton has continued to struggle with the conflicting forces within himself, his cabinet, and his country.

Indonesia's President Suharto presents many contradictions, as a temperamentally secular leader of an overwhelmingly Muslim country, a former army general who has recognized the importance of economics and trade, and a leader of the Non-Aligned Movement who has become a key ally of the United States in pursuing trade liberalization in the Asia Pacific. He has shown pragmatism and flexibility in shaping Indonesia's place as an emerging power in the region and the world. As chairman of the Non-Aligned Movement, Suharto is indisputably one of the leading figures in the developing world. He has further enhanced his credentials as a leader in the Islamic world by making a well-publicized trip to Mecca with his family in 1991.[8] Regionally, Suharto has positioned Indonesia to become not only the leading nation in ASEAN but also a strategic counterweight to the rapidly growing power of Beijing. To enhance Indonesia's strategic position, Suharto has sought to engage the United States, Vietnam, and Australia as partners. Since Bogor, Suharto has also emerged as one of the most outspoken leaders of APEC and its goal of a free and open Asia Pacific. He symbolizes the bridging of the North-South gap.

Ironically, his bold and decisive policies were made possible only because of his authoritarian power. Yet Suharto has used his power in a much more creative way than his predecessor, Sukarno, who was revered as a great independence fighter but led his country into economic ruin in the 1960s and presided over a period of 600 percent inflation. Suharto has also been more skillful in his dealings with Indonesia's partners, establishing the credo "from confrontation to cooperation."

Prior to Bogor, it was Suharto's foreign minister, Ali Alatas, who was most deeply involved with APEC. Alatas, a career diplomat who became foreign minister in 1988, was influential in the founding of ASEAN and has been an active leader within the Non-Aligned Movement.[9] His involvement in these organizations made him naturally wary of joining a group that could be dominated by Japan and the United States. Highly praised for his diplomatic acumen and impeccable record as an ASEAN promoter, Alatas represents more cautious voices. Thus, his gradual endorsement of APEC has been instrumental in smoothing the way for skeptics to accept the group. Alatas has been assisted in the APEC process by several strong and effective colleagues, including former Trade Minister (and current Ambassador to Washington) Arifin Siregar and Coordinating Minister for Trade and Industry Sastrosurarto Hartarto.

Both Suharto and Malaysia's Mahathir are leaders of rapidly developing, multi-ethnic, secularized Islamic countries that maintain a delicate power balance between an indigenous majority and an economically potent Chinese minority, yet the two have taken vastly different positions on the future of ASEAN within the Asia Pacific. Suharto has become a leading proponent of a strong APEC whereas Mahathir has focused his energies on the realization of his East Asian Economic Caucus (EAEC). Many speculate that the differences in approach are more a result of a clash of personal styles than a rational consideration of national interests. "[P]ersonality-wise they are completely contradictory to each other," notes a leading Indonesian scholar. "They never really liked each other ... because of the fact that Mahathir is showing off and everything in what Suharto considers to be a very confrontational way."[10]

Malaysia is rapidly becoming the most dynamic example of the second-generation newly industrializing economies. Its drive to becoming a developed country by the year 2020 was the idea of its colorful leader, whose car bears the plate number 2020. More than 3,000 foreign companies operate in Malaysia, whereas 2,400 have set up in much wealthier Korea.[11] Matsushita Electric, a major investor in the Malaysian economy, exports Malaysian-made air conditioners to nearly 120 countries around the world. Japan is clearly the example Mahathir uses, and he has also sought to impose the same kind of social order and cohesion that has assisted Japan in its development.

Another dynamic of Malaysia has been driven by its Chinese connections. The relationships within Malaysia between Malays and Chinese in recent years have been more harmonious as Malays have become more confident of their ability to compete in the global marketplace. That Mahathir's eldest son is married to the daughter of Liem Sioe Liong, the tycoon of the Salim Group, Indonesia's largest overseas Chinese concern, is symbolic of the changing attitudes in Malaysia.

At the same time, official relations between Malaysia and China have improved significantly. Mahathir's EAEC proposal, presented during the visit of Chinese Premier Li Peng to Kuala Lumpur, was conceived in part as an instrument of rapprochement with China. Moreover, as the fears of a communist threat and overseas Chinese economic domination have gradually waned and the need has arisen to consider ethnically Chinese constituencies in parliamentary elections, the EAEC initiative and closer relations with China in general have been in tune with domestic Malaysian political realities.

Despite the dramatic improvements in Malaysia's economy and its close economic and political relations with the West, Mahathir holds on to the legacy of the 1955 Afro-Asian conference in Bandung, Indonesia. His rhetoric of "Asia for Asians" has fallen on the sympathetic ears of millions of Asians who share his experiences and outlook. At the same time, his confrontational manner has alienated him from many of his counterparts, particularly Indonesia's Suharto. The strongest reactions have come from Washington, especially during the Bush administration. In his drive to win support for the EAEG (later the EAEC), Mahathir has often singled out the "European Americans" as the cause of Asia's problems. "[The United States] wants us to practice the kind of democracy that brings about instability, economic decline, and poverty," Mahathir warned. "With this, they can threaten and control us."[12]

At heart, however, Mahathir is not so much anti-American as anti-"big boys." As such, he will remain a player in the region because he reflects a widespread distrust and resentment of the power of advanced nations. If the world didn't have Mahathir, it would have to invent him, to borrow a phrase, for his sentiments resonate far beyond what personality alone could explain. Mahathir causes discomfort among many of his other ASEAN peers as well. However, Thai economist Narongchai Akrasanee notes that while "nobody wants to play the role of Mahathir," he is appreciated because "you don't have to be nasty, because that boy is doing everything your nasty side wants to do."

Mahathir's relationship with Australia's Paul Keating has also been strained. A minor bilateral crisis erupted between the two in 1993, when Keating, angry at Mahathir's refusal to attend the first APEC leaders' summit in Seattle, complained that the Malaysian leader was "recalcitrant." Mahathir has often publicly ridiculed Australian initiatives to strengthen ties with Asia. "You can't be Asian just by saying you are Asian," Mahathir has been quoted as saying. "Now, what Australia ought to do is let in 20 million Indians and 50 million Chinese. If they did that, then they would be an Asian country and they would qualify."[13]

Short of admitting 70 million impoverished Asians, Keating and Foreign Minister Gareth Evans have done everything possible to, in Evans's words, align Australia with "the East Asian Hemisphere."[14] While Keating's government has been a strong supporter of the APEC process, Keating's predecessor, Bob Hawke, describes Keating as "a late convert to the significance of Asia and the importance of fostering cooperation in the region."[15] Australian officials discount this charge and chalk it up to a personal feud between Hawke and Keating. In conversation, Keating stresses his deep ties to Asia and boasts of his close personal relationships with the captains of Japan's steel industry. "I've been interested in Asia all of my political life," Keating said in reply to Hawke's criticism, noting that "my first visit as prime minister was to Indonesia."[16]

Yet it is no secret that Hawke was the father of APEC. If the most critical element of politics is a sense of timing, Hawke obviously has it. When he proposed APEC in 1989, the region was primed.

And no one doubts Foreign Minister Gareth Evans's abiding interest in Australia's Asian neighbors. In 1964, as a young student, Evans spurned Europe and America in favor of travel to Japan, where he lived for eight weeks with a Japanese family. Evans often reminisces about those days and counts the experience as one factor that led him to pursue an "Asia first" policy as foreign minister.[17]

New Zealand's Prime Minister James Bolger is symbolic of the growing awareness of Asia in his country. The son of Irish immigrants, he was raised on a dairy farm, and, like many of his compatriots, became a farmer himself. As such, he has become attentive to the prodigious importance of Asia to New Zealand's vital dairy exports. Since he came to power in 1990, Bolger has led a drive to increase the education of New Zealand's citizens about the cultures and societies of their Asian neighbors. Today New Zealand has more students studying Japanese per capita than any other nation in the world outside Japan.[18] Bolger's son Matthew, 15, one of nine children, recently did a home stay in Sakai, Japan. Bolger reciprocated by taking two Japanese students into his own home.[19]

As a leader of another trade-dependent "middle country," South Korea's Kim Young Sam has played a similar role to Keating in the region. Kim, who also represents a new era in the politics of his country, has made a deep commitment to human rights, stemming from his years imprisoned by the military regimes of his predecessors. In 1983 he carried out a 23-day hunger strike against the military-backed dictatorship of Chun Doo-Hwan. "Ghandi was said to have been drinking juice [during his anticolonial fasts]," Kim recalled, "but I did not have anything but salt and water."

While Kim suffered years of persecution for his political activities, he is first and foremost a pragmatist. He broke with the opposition in 1992 to join the ruling party and become inaugurated in 1993 as the first civilian president of South Korea. Kim has also shown his practicality in foreign affairs, particularly toward Korea's longtime rival, Japan. Kim traces his ties with Japan to his childhood living on the island of Kuje Do, within eyeshot of Japan's Tsushima Island. In an interview with a Japanese journalist in Seoul, Kim was asked what influenced him most. Kim, the son of a wealthy fisherman, answered, "The sea—in a sense the sea was more than a teacher for me. . . . It fostered the spirit of freedom within me. After all, I was raised up by the sea, mentally and physically; it is my very foundation."[20]

Kim has realized that the sea connects Korea to more than just adjacent Japanese islands and the Chinese mainland and has sought to expand

Korea's orientation beyond the Yellow Sea or the Pacific Ocean to a global outlook. Under his administration, Korea has launched an ambitious process of globalization, known in Korean as *segyehwa*. Kim's Chief of Staff Han Seung-Soo described his administration's thinking: "Geographically Asia is near to us, but we think that we share universal values with countries in Europe and the United States rather than particular sorts of ones. We will go global and universal."[21] Yet Kim retains a deep sense of Confucian values, typified by the call he places each morning at 7 a.m. to his father out of filial piety.

Along with Australia and Korea, Singapore has played an important role in facilitating the APEC process. Singapore has had a tradition of free trade dating back before independence, so the APEC concept suited its regional outlook. From the start, both Prime Minister Lee Kuan Yew (now senior minister) and Deputy Premier Lee Hsien Loong enthusiastically supported APEC.

Current prime minister, Goh Chok Tong, has similarly championed the effort. Under the watchful eye of Senior Minister Lee, Goh has sought to continue Lee's tradition of regional leadership. Domestically, Goh has tried to define a role for himself outside Lee's shadow by shaping a "kinder, gentler Singapore" that emphasizes the arts, living standards, and a more open society.[22] Goh, like his counterparts in Japan, Korea, and China, has a reputation as a bland speaker but is renowned for his administrative ability and sharp intellect. He rose through the ranks of Singapore's civil service and the Neptune Orient Lines, Singapore's national shipping company, to become, at age 49, Singapore's second prime minister.

Despite Goh's efforts, his government's chronic confrontations with the Western media led to protests against a scheduled visit to his American alma mater to receive an honorary degree.[23] Goh's globalism is blended with the strong affinity for Chinese civilization he evinces through admiration of Deng Xiaoping and his attempts to learn Mandarin, which he missed during his Western education.[24]

Like his Korean counterpart, former Thai Prime Minister Chuan Leekpai has the distinction of being his country's youngest elected member of parliament. Unlike Singapore's Goh, Chuan hails from humble beginnings. Even as prime minister, Chuan continued to live in a modest wooden home in an unfashionable section of Bangkok. Chuan was the first of Thailand's 20 prime ministers to have no links with either the military or aristocracy, adding further legitimacy to his reputation as an honest and able premier.

Philippine President Fidel Ramos embodies the turbulent history of the Asia Pacific in the past half century. As a soldier, Ramos fought alongside American and Asian troops in Korea and Vietnam, as well as domestically against communist and Muslim insurgents. Ramos, as head of the national constabulary, was responsible for enforcing the martial-law order of his distant cousin, Ferdinand Marcos, a man whom ironically Ramos later overthrew in support of Corazon Aquino who called Ramos the one leader who would "fearlessly pursue the vision of this democratic society that our people fought hard to reestablish."

While Ramos has impeccable Western democratic credentials, he also has a keen interest in the democracy-building experiences of East Asia. In some Asian nations, he sees a new "communitarian capitalism," with emphasis on social harmony, which he believes is more suited to Philippine civic virtues than the traditional individualistic Anglo-Saxon model.[25] In looking toward Asia he has lived up to his pledge that ASEAN should be the Philippines' primary foreign commitment with unprecedented attempts to reach out to his ASEAN counterparts. After a trip to Kuala Lumpur, he reciprocated by asking Prime Minister Mahathir to become the first Malaysian head of state to visit the Philippines. Mahathir further encouraged the spirit of friendship when he arrived in Manila, presenting Ramos with a Malaysian-made limousine. Through economic deregulation and the reversal of protectionist policies, Ramos aims to bring the Philippines up to speed with the region's dynamism, a goal he has enshrined in his "Philippines 2000" campaign. To his detractors who would prefer that the Philippines shy away from foreign competition, he warns that "it is the cultures that live in isolation which perish."[26] In 1996, Ramos's efforts will be showcased when APEC leaders gather at Subic Bay, a site of booming Asia Pacific investment.

China's leader Jiang Zemin, like Korea's Kim, is also from a major Asian port city. As mayor of Shanghai, Jiang was known as the city's *huajiazi*, or "flower shelf," which looks pretty but does nothing.[27] In contrast, his successor Zhu Ronqi was considered a more hardworking and no-nonsense administrator. Jiang's adeptness at shifting with the political winds brought him to power immediately following the Tiananmen Square incident and earned him another nickname: "Weather Vane."[28] He is fond of quoting "men of letters" and cannot help showing off his familiarity with the great poets of the Tang dynasty when he meets with Japanese politicians. Guests from Europe and the United States have been treated to his recitations of Goethe, Shakespeare, and Lincoln. When Queen Elizabeth visited Shanghai in 1986, Jiang spoke directly with her in English and reportedly still brags about the experience.[29]

Jiang, a member of the "Shanghai mafia," is part of the third generation of Chinese Communist Party leaders, who have sought to solidify the gains made during the reign of Deng Xiaoping. Unlike their older compatriots who led Mao's peasant armies through the Long March, Jiang's generation rose through the ranks because of their technical expertise, not their revolutionary fervor. In contrast to Mao and Deng, however, Jiang does not have a sense of a grand game with the world, particularly the United States. At the informal leaders' meeting in Seattle, Jiang was the only person in the room to read off a prepared script (although he spoke without it later on).

Despite his image as a bland party functionary, Jiang's surprising propensity for singing in public, rendering communist anthems in *karaoke* style, was revealed when he tested the acoustics of the Melbourne Opera House during a tour of Australia, crooned over the intercom system of a Boeing 747, and sang and danced with Dianne Feinstein in San Francisco.[30]

Most of Jiang's problems, both domestically and internationally, stem from his position at the head of an ideologically debunked regime. The growing paradox between China's rapidly expanding market mechanisms and its stubborn embrace of the communist one-party system is increasingly apparent to the Chinese people, especially those in the booming coastal provinces. The Byzantine power struggle that has been going on in anticipation of Deng's imminent demise has also hindered Jiang's ability to provide a clear vision for the country.

Taiwan's President Lee Teng-hui has not been invited to APEC but has nonetheless cast a long shadow over Jiang. Lee's Asia Pacific credentials are much stronger, as is his personal flair and dynamism. In addition to his studies at Japan's Kyoto University, Lee holds graduate degrees from Iowa State University and Cornell University. Although he is a KMT leader, Lee represents many of the aspirations of his native Taiwanese compatriots. At a controversial 1995 address at Cornell, Lee stressed the "Taiwan experience" of economic growth and political liberalization.[31] Communist officials in Beijing considered Lee's trumpeting of the "Taiwan experience" to be political slogan targeted at achieving the much-feared "peaceful evolution" on the mainland from communism to liberal democracy.[32] While Lee has thus far not been able to attend APEC summit meetings physically he does so metaphysically through Taiwan's important role in the region and both his ideas on pet concerns such as small- and medium-sized enterprises, and agricultural development, which have been incorporated into APEC's agenda.

Two Japanese prime ministers—Morihiro Hosokawa and Tomiichi Murayama—have reflected the confusion and lack of direction that confront Japan's attempt to forge a comprehensive foreign policy. Hosokawa's participation in the first APEC summit meeting seemed to bode well for Japan's future. Urbane and charismatic, he swept into Tokyo with a new party, new agenda, and new image. One senior US official waxed laudatory: "[Hosokawa's] 'coming out party,' if you will, his debut at the leaders' meeting, was excellent. His style, his choice of clothes, the way he carried himself was a new Japan."[33] Hosokawa and Clinton together—reformist, future-oriented, and visionary—seemed to usher in a new era of US-Japan relations, one that would reassure the region of a continued partnership between its two largest economies. Yet, it was Hosokawa who resisted US demands for "numerical targets" to the last and appraised the rupture as the dawn of a "mature US-Japan relationship."

Parochial and unimaginative, Murayama is the son of a fisherman from rural Oita Prefecture in southern Japan. His premiership was the product of a strange marriage of convenience that in the eyes of the Japanese people embodied the cynical and opportunistic world of Japanese politics. "Murayama is like the round hole in the middle of a donut," one observer quipped of the prime minister's role in the coalition government. "It lacks substance, but you can't make a donut without it."

Neither of the two leaders share much in common except for a strong yearning for closer Asian ties. In this way, they are also much the same as Ryutaro Hashimoto and Masayoshi Takemura, both promising new leaders for tomorrow. From the opposition party, Ichiro Ozawa also forcefully argues for deeper Japanese ties to Asia. He has often been viewed as a "US-Japan alliance fundamentalist," yet he has exhibited a comparable attraction to Asia. But for now, chronic recession, natural and man-made disasters, and political paralysis have cast a pall on the Japanese people and underscored the pessimism felt by many Japanese voters. The power of the *kuroko*, or black mist, as influential bureaucrats are called, has also been accentuated by the chronic reshuffling of ineffectual leaders and cabinets.

Aside from ministers and heads of state, there has emerged a cadre of men and women who have guided the APEC process from behind the scenes. In the beginning, there were important Australian and Japanese figures, such as Richard Woolcott, Shigeo Muraoka, Hirokazu Okumura, and Masakazu Toyoda, who worked tirelessly to make APEC a reality. Later on, American officials such as Robert Zoellick, Robert Fauver, Sandra Kristoff and Nancy Adams, Korea's Lee See-Young, and Indonesia's Wisber Loeis worked from within their governments to cajole, co-opt, and convince their superiors and colleagues of the importance of the APEC process. EPG Chairman C. Fred Bergsten has played a similar role from outside government, keeping the process moving forward by his commitment to producing far-reaching visions and ideas through the advisory role of the Eminent Persons Group.

Without ASEAN there would be no APEC today. ASEAN stands at the core of APEC not only because of its political sensitivities, but also because of the rich experiences it provides to other members as they seek to develop and mold the APEC institution. ASEAN established a model for regional institution building that transcended the racial and political differences that have long plagued Southeast Asia. Bringing together Malays and Chinese into one cooperative regional forum was a major step toward bridging traditional suspicions. There was no superhero behind ASEAN's creation. Many officials, technocrats, and business people worked diligently and quietly to make the ASEAN idea a reality. Initially, ASEAN focused on economics as a means of avoiding more controversial political and security issues. It took off in the 1970s, largely thanks to scholars and officials such as Indonesia's Jusuf Wanandi, Thailand's Narongchai Akrasanee, Malaysia's Noordin Sopiee, and the Philippines' Jesus Estanislao, to name a few.[34]

Early pioneers of the Asia Pacific cooperation ideal included former Prime Ministers Masayoshi Ohira of Japan and Malcolm Fraser of Australia, who established the political roots of the Pacific Economic Cooperation Council (PECC) when they met in 1979, and businessman Noboru Goto, who was a founding member of the Pacific Basin Economic Council (PBEC).[35] Saburo Okita and John Crawford, the architects of PECC, particularly deserve credit for their contributions. In 1968, Okita hosted the first Pacific Trade and Development Conference (PAFTAD), which brought together academics and government officials in their private capacity to discuss regional economic issues. In a paper presented at the 1979 PAFTAD conference, Australian scholar Peter Drysdale promoted the concept of an open, consultative association of regional economies with a small, nonbureaucratic secretariat and multiple task forces that would later serve as the model for APEC.[36] Australian Ross Garnaut was another visionary scholar whose 1989 report to Prime Minister Hawke, *Australia and the Northeast Asian Ascendancy*, presented a blueprint for Australia's active support of Asia Pacific economic cooperation.[37] Drysdale recalled that in 1988 PECC approached governments to advise them that the time had come to elevate regional consultations to the official level. Without the advance work of these scholars, businessmen, and politicians in organizations such as PECC and PBEC, APEC would not have had such a solid intellectual basis for cooperation. Between 1950 and 1990, Okita traveled abroad 359 times, mostly to Asia Pacific destinations.[38]

Notes

1. Personal interview with Mahathir bin Mohamad, 20 January, 1993.

2. *New York Times*, 12 July 1993.

3. Reiko Kinoshita, *Fasuto Chiimu* [First Team], (Tokyo: Shueisha, 1993), p. 16.

4. *United Press International*, 12 October, 1985, and *Los Angeles Times*, 8 June 1995.

5. *Business Week*, 23 November, 1992.

6. Kinoshita, p. 16.

7. *Washington Post*, 5 May 1994.

8. Adam Schwartz, *A Nation in Waiting: Indonesia in the 1990s* (Boulder, CO: Westview Press, 1994), p. 175.

9. K. S. Sandhu, Siddique Sharon, Chandran Jeshurun, Ananda Rajah, Joseph L. H. Tan, and Pushpa Thambipillai, eds., *The ASEAN Reader* (Singapore: Institute of Southeast Asian Studies, 1992), p. 521.

10. Personal interview, 9 July 1995.

11. *Chosun Daily* Special, 24 August 1994.

12. *New York Times*, 14 November 1993.

13. Personal interview with C. Fred Bergsten, who attended the meeting.

14. *The Straits Times*, 24 April 1995.

15. Robert Hawke, *The Hawke Memoirs* (Melbourne: William Heinemann Australia, 1994), p. 434.

16. Personal interview with Paul Keating, 6 July 1995.

17. *Asahi Evening News*, 28 June 1995.

18. Embassy of New Zealand, "Fact Sheet," Washington, DC, March 1995.

19. Personal interview with James Bolger, 25 July 1995.

20. Keiji Kobayashi, *Kim Young Sam* (Tokyo: Hara Shobo, 1992).

21. Personal interview, 5 July 1995.

22. *New York Times*, 28 November 1990.

23. *New York Times*, 10 July 1995.

24. Personal interview, 25 June 1993.

25. Fidel V. Ramos, *Time for Takeoff* (Manila: Friends of Steady Eddie, 1994), pp. 72–73.

26. Ramos, p. 25.

27. *Washington Post*, 15 July 1989, p. A15.

28. *Washington Post*, 15 November 1993, p. A15.

29. *Washington Post*, 15 July 1989, p. A15.

30. *Washington Post*, 15 July 1989 and 15 November 1993, and *Sunday Telegraph Limited*, 30 October 1994.

31. Speech by Lee Teng-hui, Cornell University, 9 June 1995.

32. Hidenori Ijiri, *Taiwan Keiken to Reisengo no Ajia* (The Taiwan Experience and Post–Cold War Era Asia), (Tokyo: Keisou Shobo, 1993).

33. Personal interview with senior US official, 19 May 1995.

34. Personal interview with ASEAN diplomats.

35. Lawrence Woods, *Asia-Pacific Diplomacy: Nongovernmental Organizations and International Relations* (Vancouver: UBC Press, 1993).

36. Peter Drysdale, "Building the Foundations of a Pacific Economic Community," in Saburo Okita, ed., *Economic Policy and Development* (London: Croom Helm, 1985), pp. 46–57.

37. Ross Garnaut, *Australia and the Northeast Asian Ascendancy: Report to the Prime Minister and Minister for Foreign Affairs and Trade* (Canberra: Australian Government Publishing Service, 1989).

38. Koike Hirotsugu, *Ajia Taiheiyo Shinron* [A New Paradigm of Asia Pacific], (Tokyo: Nihon-keizai Shimbunsha, 1993), p. 213.

3

"Potentially Historic": Canberra/Singapore

On 31 January 1989, before a group of Korean businessmen in Seoul, Australian Prime Minister Bob Hawke, in his words, "launched my concept of Asia Pacific Economic Cooperation."[1] Hawke recalled that his speech "came to be recognized as one of seminal importance." At the time, however, it made few ripples outside government circles. Just 10 months later—a brief gestation period for such a forum—under a rainy Canberra sky, ministers from 12 nations around the Asia Pacific gathered for the first time in an official regional capacity.

Some observers speculated that the unusually inclement weather was a bad omen, just as others perceived symbolism in Australian Foreign Minister Gareth Evan's draw of a horse named "Pacific Mirage" at the Melbourne races on the last day of the summit.[2]

APEC lore has it that Hawke dreamed up the idea on the flight from Australia to Korea and had cleared it only with his host, Korean President Roh Tae Woo. Actually, Hawke was briefed on the concept prior to his trip, but Foreign Ministry officials, including Foreign and Trade Secretary Richard Woolcott, did not expect the prime minister to present the proposal in Seoul. Upon his return, Hawke ordered his diplomats, under the direction of Woolcott, to begin a full-court press on Australia's Asia Pacific neighbors to win their approval and support. Hawke specifically instructed Woolcott to "sound out the majority," to see whether there was a consensus that the United States, Canada, and the Three Chinas should be included or not included.[3]

Envoy Woolcott

While Woolcott was honored to be chosen as Australia's point man for APEC, he was concerned that Hawke's comment, coming without prior notice to any of the proposed participants except Korea, would create a stir. It indeed did. As soon as Hawke's speech was delivered, Woolcott was inundated with requests for information from the press, foreign embassies, and his own diplomats in the field. Hawke had talked about modeling APEC after the OECD but offered no details, compounding Woolcott's difficulties in formulating a coherent Australian position.[4] Woolcott and other members quickly drafted a strategy to implement the Hawke proposal, starting with a series of personal letters from the prime minister to his Asia Pacific counterparts. On 29 March, Hawke gave Woolcott his marching orders. That night, Woolcott slept fitfully, often waking to reflect "on the magnitude of the mission I was going to undertake for Australia." His schedule entailed an exhausting round of visits that would include meetings, some of which lasted for hours, with seven heads of government, 30 cabinet ministers, and over 100 officials. The next six months would find the peripatetic Woolcott in disparate locales—from the palace of the Sultan of Brunei, the world's richest man, to Tiananmen Square in the grips of student unrest, to Washington in transition from the Reagan to Bush administrations.

Woolcott chose as his first destination Australia's closest political and cultural neighbor, New Zealand. While officials in Wellington were irritated that they had not been consulted before Hawke's announcement, they welcomed the idea publicly, proudly noting that New Zealand was the first country "to be fully briefed."[5] It was encouraging to have New Zealand's support, but Woolcott knew that the real challenge would be the ASEAN nations.

Woolcott thought that "the most important country was Indonesia, because it was the largest, and ASEAN does not react to any particular proposal or policy without ascertaining Indonesia's view."[6] President Suharto and his economic and foreign affairs advisers greeted the initiative with cautious optimism, although Foreign Minister Ali Alatas expressed serious reservations about the role of China and Russia. Then–Trade Minister Arifin Siregar also noted Indonesia's support for Hawke's concept of putting ASEAN at the "core" of the process, recognizing the distaste of many of its members for wider regionalism.[7] At the time, however, Woolcott received no firm answer from Jakarta. Alatas only promised that "he would study it."

The most enthusiastic response came from Singapore's Lee Kuan Yew, whom Woolcott credits with encouraging an ASEAN consensus on the idea. Woolcott recalled that Korea was similarly supportive. "When I called on Roh Tae Woo, his opening remarks were: 'You have got no problems with South Korea about this. I've already discussed it with Mr.

Hawke, and we've agreed that this is the way ahead.' " There were some, however, who only gave a qualified endorsement of the proposal. Malaysian Prime Minister Mahathir expressed reservations about the idea of including North American countries and evinced suspicion of Woolcott's motives, questioning if he were secretly in league with Washington or Tokyo.[8] According to Woolcott, Philippine Trade and Industry Secretary José Concepcion was negative from the start, arguing for "an Asia for Asians." But other Philippine officials, including President Corazon Aquino, were more open to the idea. Then Minister of the National Economic Development Agency (NEDA) Jesus Estanislao, who had known Woolcott from the time Woolcott was ambassador to Manila, imparted some friendly advice. "I wanted to convey to him that, yes, Australia should continue to pursue the objective of APEC," he recalled, adding that "it would be helpful for ASEAN to come on board the APEC train if Australia does not appear to be too pushy for it."[9]

Woolcott's trip to Beijing was among his most memorable. At that early stage, Australia was uncertain whether to include China as a founding member. Most ASEAN nations recognized the need for Chinese participation, but stressed that Hong Kong and Taiwan needed to be included as well. Arriving just after Mikhail Gorbachev's ill-fated trip in the midst of the Tiananmen Square protests, Woolcott met with many of the top leaders, including Prime Minister Li Peng, Foreign Minister Qian Qichen, and Trade Vice Minister (now Vice Premier) Li Lanqing. Despite the domestic political crisis boiling over just outside the windows, Chinese officials expressed sincere interest in the concept. Their main concern was the issue of Hong Kong and Taiwan. China, of course, was uncomfortable with allowing their participation. Li Peng argued that "only sovereign states had ministers, and therefore by definition Hong Kong and Taiwan should be excluded."[10] Woolcott then suggested a change in terminology from a "ministerial meeting of countries" to a "ministerial-level meeting of major economies" as a potential route to avoid Chinese objections.

All of the officials and leaders Woolcott met supported Japan's participation. In Tokyo, however, Woolcott found himself in the midst of an internal struggle between the Ministry of Foreign Affairs (Gaimusho) and the Ministry of International Trade and Industry (MITI). He discerned Gaimusho's suspicion that Australia was backing an existing MITI proposal for an economic ministers' meeting. Gaimusho was unconvinced by Woolcott's assurances that foreign ministers were an integral part of Australia's concept and perhaps intervened to prevent Woolcott from meeting with Prime Minister Noboru Takeshita.[11]

In each country, Woolcott was pleasantly surprised with the warm reception he received for the APEC concept. It was particularly gratifying for Australia to finally see support for Asia Pacific regionalism after years of advocating it. Australian scholar and diplomat Ross Garnaut and fellow academic Peter Drysdale had been dedicated proponents of Asia Pacific cooperation, and Woolcott's work seemed to be the first step in fulfilling their visions. Woolcott reported his optimism back to Canberra at the end of April. Although nearly all of the seven countries he had visited were positive, Woolcott found that he needed "to assure the ASEAN countries . . . that we were not acting as a stalking horse for MITI."[12]

ASEAN's skepticism of Australia's motives may have stemmed in part from a series of similar visits these countries had received a month earlier from MITI Vice Minister for International Affairs Shigeo Muraoka, who had been dispatched to gauge the region's interest in a project conceived by MITI to establish a regional economic cooperative body in the Asia Pacific.

MITI's Mission

Muraoka visited many of the same capitals and also discovered considerable interest in economic cooperation. Unlike Woolcott, however, Muraoka found that most officials he had met, particularly in ASEAN, expressed hesitancy about American membership in the group, at least initially. Only Singaporean Trade and Industry Minister (B. G.) Lee Hsien Loong strongly urged Washington's inclusion. Muraoka, like Woolcott, met with Philippine Trade and Industry Secretary Concepcion, who was skeptical of the inclusiveness of the APEC proposal, arguing that "Asians alone can understand Asia's problems."[13] The MITI plan Muraoka was advancing, however, explicitly called for inclusion of the United States, and Muraoka patiently sought to build support for the establishment of a trans-Pacific body. When Indonesian Coordinating Minister for Economics, Finance, and Industry Prawiro Radius asked why it was important to include the United States, Muraoka responded, "It would perhaps be more effective to combat and contain US unilateral actions on trade issues if we could include the United States in the forum." Radius and his colleagues in other ASEAN nations accepted this rationale.

Initially, MITI feared that a strong Japanese push for regional cooperation would stimulate a backlash by its Asian neighbors, but during Muraoka's visits only Thailand and Malaysia expressed concern. In a conversation with Korean Deputy Prime Minister Cho Soon, Muraoka explained that Japan could not take a lead in the region because of its "lack of legitimacy due to the lingering memories of the past war." To Muraoka's surprise, Cho reportedly responded, "Japan should wipe out that kind of mental block. Do not take a wishy-washy attitude, a halfway measure."[14]

The first MITI proposal for an official Asia Pacific organization came in early 1987 when then–MITI Minister Hajime Tamura proposed a ministerial-level consultative body to discuss economic trends and cooperation among Japan, Australia, Canada, the United States, and New Zealand.

Almost immediately, Tamura's proposal encountered almost immediate opposition from the Ministry of Foreign Affairs, which feared that Japanese activism, given the legacy of World War II, might damage Japan's image in the region. While the Tamura initiative was unsuccessful, global and regional developments pushed MITI to reconsider the idea of Asia Pacific economic cooperation the following year. A strong impetus for following through with the idea came with a report from an industrial researcher at JETRO (Japan External Trade Organization). MITI official Hirokazu Okumura, based in Sydney, was one of MITI's seconded "ninjas" charged with traveling around Asia to collect information and assess local opinions. During a trip to Singapore in early 1988, Okumura learned of a US proposal to extend bilateral free trade agreements into the region.[15] Okumura pressed MITI to move ahead with an Asia Pacific forum to counter these efforts and specifically urged Japan to work with Australia.

The United States had considered the extension of a free trade area to Asia Pacific nations for some time. During the first term of the Reagan administration, both US Trade Representatives William Brock and Clayton Yeutter raised the issue during meetings with their Asia Pacific counterparts. In 1988 Secretary of State George Shultz was also intrigued by the idea of creating greater trans-Pacific links and explored a regional governmental forum on education and telecommunications. Senator Bill Bradley proposed the "PAC 8," an eight-member regional group. At about the same time, James Baker and Robert Zoellick constructed a paper, based on an analysis of the US-Canada FTA, in which they argued that regional free trade agreements could strengthen the global system. However, the Baker-Zoellick team could not pursue their initiative after they moved to the White House.

In his late January 1988 trip to Washington, Japanese Prime Minister Takeshita learned from Senate Majority Leader Robert Byrd and others of the keen interest brewing in the United States for a possible FTA with Japan and other Asia Pacific economies. Upon his return, Takeshita ordered Shinji Fukukawa, then MITI's vice minister, to study the subject, setting the stage for the Study Group for Asia Pacific Trade Development, directed by MITI's then–director general of the International Economic Affairs Department, Yoshihiro Sakamoto. Sakamoto's panel issued an interim report that recommended the creation of an Asia Pacific economic forum to avert the division of the world economy into competing regional blocs. The so-called Sakamoto Report recognized the critical state of the world economy, paying particular attention to the ramifications of the overriding need of the United States to complete the lengthy process of reducing its twin budget and trade deficits. It argued the following points:

- The region's economic and trade structure should be changed from "development through US dependency" to "development through role-sharing cooperation in the region."

- The OECD model of rigid organization is not tenable in the Asia Pacific, which requires a forum that would allow for greater diversity. Any new effort toward economic cooperation must smoothly relate to existing regional forums such as ASEAN, operate by consensus, progress gradually, and remain open to other regions.

- To promote the above ideas, Japan must expand its imports, increase its FDI in the region, and support regional human resources development.

Tactically, Sakamoto concluded that Japan should approach Australia about taking public leadership for the forum because of Australia's non-threatening nature and interest in building broader ties with both Asia and North America. Sakamoto himself had stayed in Sydney on loan to JETRO where he acquired an appreciation for the role Australia could play in the region.[16] The decision to approach Australia was opportune because of that country's simultaneous reexamination of a regional economic forum.

Ross Garnaut's report to Hawke was just one of the several proposals under consideration in Canberra at the time of the MITI initiative. Central to MITI's decision to approach Australia was a 1986 government-commissioned study by University of Melbourne professor Richard H. Snape that warned of the dangers of signing a bilateral free trade agreement with the United States.[17] Snape said Australia and the United States were not complementary economies; rather, their trade structures were very similar, strong in sectors such as agriculture and minerals. His paper also pointed out that Australia, with a large stake in indirect trade—that is, supplying raw materials for Asian exports to Europe—should pursue global liberalization rather than lock itself into a single bloc.

Masakazu Toyoda, then on the MITI trade policy planning staff and the leading author of the Sakamoto Report, said that Australia's fear of being unilaterally pressured into entering into a free trade pact made it particularly useful as a partner for Japan in developing the APEC concept.[18] Australian diplomat Geoff Brenan shared a similar analysis of the external origins of the drive for APEC: "It wasn't just the idea; it was the timing of the idea."[19] In August 1988, MITI presented the Sakamoto Report to Australian officials to broach the first official exchange of views between the two governments.

As with the Tamura proposal, MITI had difficulty persuading the Foreign Ministry to support this MITI initiative. In Jakarta, Gaimusho officials at the Japanese embassy insisted on providing an interpreter to Muraoka for his meeting with State Minister Moerdiono, who, the embassy claimed, spoke no English. After Muraoka presented the MITI proposal, Moerdiono gave a 10-minute response. However, the embassy interpreter just stated curtly that "Mr. Moerdiono would consider the idea very carefully." Moerdiono, agitated that his lengthy response had been reduced to one sentence, switched into English, expressed his interest in the proposal, and engaged Muraoka in a discussion that lasted over an hour. On his way out of Indonesia, Muraoka was pursued at the airport by an embassy official, who tried to persuade him to accept a Gaimusho summary of the conversation that stressed Indonesia's caution on MITI's concept. Muraoka dismissed the memo and proceeded to write his own version for the official diplomatic telegram.

During this period, Gaimusho was quietly instructing its diplomats in Asian capitals to lobby against the APEC idea. A trade minister of one Asian country recalled being approached by a Japanese embassy official (from the Gaimusho) who urged him not to support MITI's proposal when Muraoka called on him the next day.[20] Contradictory explanations by Japanese officials from MITI and the Gaimusho led some ASEAN ambassadors to Tokyo to directly approach MITI's headquarters in March to gauge Japan's true intentions. ASEAN was even more puzzled after Prime Minister Takeshita, in a 5 May speech in Jakarta, did not even comment on the MITI proposal.

At the time, the Gaimusho suspected that MITI's support for US inclusion was a ploy to strengthen MITI's prominence within the bureaucracy. MITI was fortunate, however, when its minister, Hiroshi Mitsuzuka, became foreign minister in the new cabinet of Sosuke Uno in June 1989. Mitsuzuka, a strong supporter of the regional initiative, was able to overcome resistance within Gaimusho during the critical months leading up to the September senior officials' meeting (SOM) in Canberra.

The first real contact between the Japanese and Australian APEC initiatives was in December 1988, when Muraoka met with Australia's Minister of Negotiations Michael Duffy in Montreal. According to Muraoka, Duffy was receptive to Japan's plans and was particularly intrigued by Japan's offer to give Australia full credit for the initiative. Muraoka recalled that he answered in the affirmative when Duffy asked, "You recommend that Australia should take a lead for the meeting? Is Japan truly satisfied with its second-fiddle role?"[21] While Australia had long been supportive of the idea, there was some concern in Canberra over Japan's eagerness. "The idea being proposed by MITI and Japan was for some in Canberra an unsettling development," Brenan said. "They were worried how it would be accepted, what would be the reaction in other capitals in the region."[22]

Tactics

While Tokyo and Canberra agreed on the basic principle of APEC, they quickly discovered differences in style and tactics. The first was over whether to include the United States. Japan had favored extending APEC to North America from the start, but Australia was somewhat reluctant. Japanese officials such as Toyoda argued that there were three main reasons for including the United States: the futility of continued sectorally focused bilateral US-Japan trade negotiations, the need for cooperation in the Asia Pacific region to counter the formation of regional blocs in Europe and North America, and the need for a new framework to cope with ASEAN's development and emergence as a new economic power center.[23]

Australia recognized the long-range need to include the United States, but it had been looking for ways to differentiate itself from the United States in its regional policy. Australia's ambivalence, however, only increased the tensions between Washington and Canberra. In a March 1989 trip to Washington, Foreign Minister Gareth Evans had a run-in with James Baker, the new secretary of state under Bush, over Australian secrecy on APEC. An Australian diplomatic cable described the exchange:[24]

> Baker said that the United States was disappointed that Australia had not talked to the United States before proceeding as far as it had. Senator Evans said that Australia had been concerned that any US participation should evolve naturally from prior consultation with a core group of Western Pacific countries rather than appearing to be preemptively imposed on them by Australia. We were telling this core group that we had no difficulties on US participation and as we had expected, the consultations were demonstrating a widespread view that the US and Canada should be involved. Senator Evans said that the exposition he had given of the initiative should be regarded as the beginning of a process of high level consultation, and it may be that the next step would be for Secretary Woolcott to come to the United States at the conclusion of his present round of discussions.

> Baker referred to discussions the United States, including himself, had had with Japan last year about regional cooperation. It had been suggested in those discussions that there should be a core group comprising the United States, Japan, the ROK and others but not Australia and Canada. Baker said he had insisted that Australia and Canada be included. He repeated his disappointment that the United States had not been consulted prior to the PM's initiative. Senator Evans pointed out (tongue in cheek) that Australia had not been consulted on that earlier occasion when our name was apparently put on the table. Baker responded (with tongue less obviously in cheek) that Australia would have been consulted before any letters were sent and wider discussion initiated. Senator Evans said, "Touché."

> All that said, Baker continued that he thought the proposal a useful idea, and if it was genuinely to be based on the Pacific Basin, it could serve a useful function. It was important that the United States should participate.

While Baker was incensed that the Australians hadn't consulted the United States sooner, he "accepted at face value their explanation that they were worried that if it included the US that ASEAN would be less likely to sign on."[25]

However, there is still some debate over Hawke's true motivations. Woolcott said that Australia's delay was also meant to discourage the United States from taking the lead. "We didn't want excessive American enthusiasm to lead to taking over the initiative," he has argued, "because we thought then that it would not get off the ground."[26] An Australian diplomat who was closely involved with the initiative explained Canberra's motivations differently. "[M]y understanding is that he [Hawke] was quite deliberate in excluding the United States. It was a chance for him to give someone the finger, as we say—get their attention by saying they can't do something."[27] He also attributed America's exclusion in the Australian proposal to the ruling Labor Party's long-held dislike of the United States.

Hawke has vehemently denied such charges. "It was the tactical question that we had at the beginning: the rather vociferous views particularly of Malaysia that there was no part in this thing for the United States," Hawke said. "The United States was quite happy for us to be taking the lead in that."[28] He also discounted the charge of the Labor Party's anti-Americanism: "By that stage I had educated the Labor Party about the facts of international life. . . . [T]he old anti-American rhetoric was not a significant element by then."[29] In his memoirs, Hawke refutes the suggestion that he even thought of excluding the United States:

> There have been some suggestions that in launching APEC I was so irritated with the United States' attitude to bilateral trade issues that I was inclined to leave the Americans out of the new regional group. This was never in my mind. There were some in [ASEAN], most particularly Malaysia, who had a well-developed antipathy towards the United States, and Malaysia certainly would have preferred to exclude the Americans. But, on any rational examination, a group seeking to maximize the chances of economic cooperation in the Asia Pacific could not seriously contemplate leaving out the major economic power, the United States.[30]

Despite Hawke's denials, there were strong reasons for Australia to exclude the United States, at least initially. By courting Asian nations first, Australia could claim another victory in its "Asianization" drive. Exclusion of North America from the Asia Pacific is hinted at in Evans's claim of Australian membership in the "East Asian Hemisphere."

Canberra calculated that the exclusion would force North America to take notice of Australia and the Asia Pacific region at large. Australia had long parroted American policies, supporting both US global initiatives such as Soviet containment and regional actions such as the Vietnam War. Despite this close political relationship, the United States had began increasingly to ignore Australian economic concerns, often inadvertently punishing Australian agricultural exporters in its attempts to retaliate against protectionist European competitors. Australia and the United States were also rapidly assuming a competitive, rather than complementary, role in international trade, particularly, as noted before, in areas such as agriculture and minerals. Although some Australian diplomats attribute Australian insistence on excluding the United States to Hawke's personal decision, MITI officials were surprised with Duffy's strong insistence on US exclusion in the group during the initial Muraoka-Duffy meeting in Montreal.[31] Mitsuzuka also recalled Evans's passionate argument against US membership during a meeting between the two.[32]

In the meantime, Tokyo sought to reassure Washington that APEC was not an effort to form an anti-American economic bloc. In April, Muraoka talked with US Undersecretary of State Richard McCormack to reassure Washington that Japan supported its inclusion. "That's all he was interested in about APEC," recalled Muraoka, "nothing else." Later Japan sent a series of high-level delegations, which included MITI Minister Mitsuzuka, to Washington to reassure the Bush administration of its commitment, despite Australia's ambiguous claims.

On 26 June, in an address to the Japan Society in New York, Secretary of State James Baker formally endorsed the APEC proposal and signaled America's willingness to participate in future ministerials.[33] When Secretary Baker made his announcement, which gave credit to both Australia and MITI, one Australian journalist commented that it was "Australia's most important foreign policy victory for a decade."[34]

The most challenging task for Japanese and Australian diplomats was enticing Southeast Asia to participate, with or without American membership. Australia and Japan had to be careful not to overwhelm the ASEAN nations, whose combined economies were the smallest of all APEC's original members save New Zealand.[35] In his 5 May speech in Jakarta, Prime Minister Takeshita stressed the starring role ASEAN would play in Asia Pacific regionalism, though he did not address APEC specifically because of internal bureaucratic infighting. Later Australia's Gareth Evans promised that ASEAN would be at the "core" of APEC, and ASEAN's voice and concerns would be central to the organization's development.

From the very start, ASEAN acted as a caucus within APEC, and at Canberra, the ministers of the six members met separately to work out their positions on the forum's agenda. These consultations among ASEAN nations prior to APEC meetings would become a tradition, even among members of the EPG. Thai EPG member Narongchai Akrasanee explained that since ASEAN ministers and officials had so much interaction, "when they go to international meetings, it is natural for them to get together."[36] It was later agreed that the chairmanship, and hence location, of annual APEC conferences would be rotated each year from an ASEAN member to a non-ASEAN member. This system was well suited at the time to APEC's "Six plus Six" membership roster of the six ASEAN nations plus Japan, Australia, Korea, Canada, New Zealand, and the United States. As six more countries have been added since that time, however, this arrangement's continued utility has been brought into question.

ASEAN finally endorsed APEC by consensus in their July Post-Ministerial Conference (PMC) in Brunei. In August, Australia issued formal invitations to the first APEC ministerial conference to be held in Canberra on 6–7 November 1989. Despite initial misgivings, several ASEAN members promptly applied to host future APEC meetings, with Singapore winning the 1990 slot. ASEAN's confidence in committing to the APEC process was bolstered by a meeting of ASEAN ministers in Kuching, Malaysia, in early 1990 at which principles for ASEAN's participation in APEC were agreed. The so-called Kuching consensus emphasized the preservation of ASEAN's identity and cohesion.

Conspicuously missing from the original 12 members at Canberra were the "Three Chinas": the People's Republic, Hong Kong, and Taiwan. In the beginning, some ASEAN nations were reluctant to include China, particularly without Hong Kong and Taiwan, as they feared that ASEAN's collective voice within APEC would be muted and their lives with Beijing would be complicated. At the time, three countries in ASEAN—Indonesia, Singapore, and Brunei—did not yet have formal diplomatic relations with Beijing, although each has established ties in the years since. There were also political considerations because of China's crackdown on student protesters in Tiananmen Square prior to the Canberra meeting.

Both Australia and Japan favored eventual inclusion of the three but differed on timing. Hawke referred to the idea of leaving China out of an Asia Pacific organization as "like getting married without having a bride."[37] Japanese officials were a bit more cautious. "The Australians were enthusiastic about getting China in the group," said MITI's Toyoda. "[However,] we were afraid that it would easily turn into a politicization of APEC if we were to discuss China's membership from the start and derail the process before it even got moving."[38]

American officials were also guarded. "There was a concern that the PRC is so big that it could swamp the process," said State Department counsellor Robert Zoellick, adding, "I wanted to get APEC off the ground, and I had some concern that too much of a focus on the Three Chinas could divert APEC from getting off the ground."[39]

While Australia was initially optimistic about China's prospects, Li Peng's refusal, in conversations with Australia's Woolcott, to allow Taiwan to participate in official meetings made immediate membership out of the question.[40] The early initiatives of Australians, Japanese, and Americans were ingenious in deciding that yearly APEC meetings would lay the groundwork for the eventual inclusion of the three Chinas by referring to members as economies, not countries, in an attempt to allow for Taiwan's inclusion without upsetting Chinese political concerns. In 1990, ASEAN acquiesced to the simultaneous inclusion of all three at the 1991 Seoul ministerial.

Japan and Australia also differed over the agenda for the APEC forum. "MITI was a bit more circumspect on what should in fact be on the agenda," Brenan said. "But once they saw the way our [proposal] was developing, they became comfortable with that, because their ideas were in there, and there were some other ideas as well that they couldn't have brought up."[41]

MITI officials remember the exchange slightly differently. "The Australians were very eager to set specific agenda items, which clearly aimed at trade liberalization," recounted Toyoda. "We also had that in our mind, but here we believed that we had to handle it very carefully. You would scare away ASEAN countries if you talked about liberalization from the start."[42] Instead, MITI focused on "enlarging the pie" by promoting economic growth rather than simply liberalizing markets. "Besides that," Toyoda went on to say, "Australia did not have any viable policy instrument for regional cooperation; that's why they almost solely focused on liberalization." Eventually both sides agreed to consider the other's positions but concentrate more fully on actualizing an actual meeting of the group.

MITI and Australia engaged in separate *nemawashi* (consensus building) efforts to initiate regional economic cooperation. Former MITI Minister Hiroshi Mitsuzuka testified that his officials, who had laboriously engineered and pushed their ideas for many months, welcomed Hawke's speech, beaming particularly brightly when they heard that Hawke had referred to "constructive talks on this issue with Japanese leadership earlier this week."[43] However, MITI officials felt that Australia alone would not be able to sway some cautious Southeast Asian policymakers, and therefore MITI could make a real difference.[44] Australian officials encouraged MITI to go ahead, partly because Woolcott had not yet been instructed by Hawke to make the rounds of the neighboring capitals. The Australians, who did not want to lose any momentum, thought that MITI could provide their concept with a strong following wind. The word "APEC," which first appeared on Hawke's formal invitation to the members that summer, had yet to be invented. Thus, Muraoka explained the MITI proposal in his meetings with top officials, while Woolcott described the Australian one. It was not until April when Muraoka and Woolcott met in Tokyo, that the two versions were finally merged.[45]

APEC's informal, off-the-cuff origins were reflected in the group's early evolution. What is most useful to consider about the period, however, was the strong role Japan played. Tokyo's activism has been obscured for two political reasons. Internally, Japan's Foreign Ministry remains skeptical of MITI's motivation in creating the body and continues to struggle with MITI over its shape and future. Externally, Japan has been concerned about the perceptions Japan's neighbors, particularly ASEAN nations, would have over its activism, given the legacy of its past region-building exercises. At the same time, Australia has been happy to take full credit, giving its political leaders a boost domestically and giving the nation a higher profile internationally. "Japan has been—while not taking a leadership role—strongly supportive of the development of the APEC process," Foreign Minister Evans said in his book on Australia's foreign relations.[46]

Canberra

The Canberra and Singapore gatherings, which comprised APEC's "warm-up" phase, were loosely organized, scarcely noticed, and accomplished little substantively. Yet, these meetings marked the first time official representatives from around the Asia Pacific sat down in a single forum. Secretary of State James Baker, a leading force driving APEC's early formation, was quoted as calling the Canberra meeting potentially historic.[47]

ASEAN delegates greeted the first APEC meeting with mixed support. Indonesian Foreign Minister Alatas noted that "Asia Pacific cooperation has already been promoted by ASEAN, thus, the currently examined cooperation should not weaken the solidarity of ASEAN."[48] Alatas also warned that institutionalization of APEC should progress only gradually, and if possible through the ASEAN Secretariat in Jakarta. On the other hand, the Philippines and Singapore welcomed APEC. At the ASEAN-only ministerial, before the first APEC ministerial in Canberra, Philippine Finance Minister Jesus Estanislao and Singaporean Trade and Industry Minister B. G. Lee pushed hard from within ASEAN to approve a continuation of the process. Lee and Estanislao argued that ASEAN's status at the center of APEC, could enhance ASEAN's influence and importance. Estanislao's "concentric circles" theory saw multilateralism as a multilayered process involving institutions at the subregional level, such as ASEAN, regional level, such as APEC, and at the global level, namely, the GATT. ASEAN had a tremendous stake in finalizing the Uruguay Round of the GATT, and an effectively mobilized APEC could help realize that goal.

ASEAN was also concerned about a diversion of foreign direct investment (FDI) away from Southeast Asia, to newly opened Eastern Europe, and began to view APEC as a means of guaranteeing continued US and Japanese economic attention.[49] "It is important that APEC secures the flow of capital from North to South, not to Eastern Europe or the Soviet Union, in order to prevent the lack of capital in the region," argued Alatas at a later APEC meeting. He noted that the European Bank for Reconstruction and Development (EBRD) had in six months committed 10 times the amount of the United Nation's total Primary Commodity Common Fund.[50]

More ominous to APEC members than internal arrangements was the threat of emerging exclusive trading blocs, especially in Europe. As Korean Foreign Minister Choi Ho-Joong said, "No one can deny that some apprehension is felt about the possibility that, in the process of this evolution [toward integration], Europe could become so preoccupied with its own problems as to turn inward despite its repeated assurances to the contrary."[51] GATT consumed the attention of the Singapore participants, who agreed to initiate action on three areas: agriculture, textiles, and the

GATT dispute settlement mechanism.[52] The members also agreed to create seven projects, including a review of trade and investment data, trade facilitation, technology transfer, human resources development, regional energy cooperation, marine resources conservation, and telecommunications.[53]

Throughout 1990, there was concern not only about a failure of the Uruguay Round but also potential divisions within APEC. In 1990 the United States was strongly focused on extending the 1989 US-Canada Free Trade Agreement (FTA) to Mexico to form the North American Free Trade Area (NAFTA). Not only did Asian nations worry that NAFTA could become a protectionist bloc in the manner of the European Union, but the Bush administration did not hide its willingness to extend NAFTA to select Asia Pacific nations, causing many to fear overwhelming unilateral American pressure to sign an FTA. Some Asian nations also were concerned about Washington's insistence on including Mexico in APEC, fearing the formation of a "NAFTA caucus" that would advance North American interests.

Fears of North American regionalism have subsequently been augmented by a similar concern over the potential for an East Asian economic bloc. In late 1990 during a meeting with Chinese Prime Minister Li Peng, Malaysian Prime Minister Mahathir bin Mohamad unveiled his proposal for an East Asian Economic Group that would include only Asian nations. Mahathir's proposal was believed to originate in his own mind without input from the bureaucracy. The Bush administration vocally opposed the EAEC concept and immediately petitioned Japan and Korea to reject the Malaysian proposal. Both of these countries greeted Mahathir's initiative with detachment, declaring only that they would consider his proposal. Mahathir's ASEAN colleagues were piqued that they had not been consulted before he launched the plan. Mahathir continued to pursue it tenaciously, although he modified the exclusive-sounding "group" to the more accommodating "caucus" (EAEC) in October 1991 by heeding the suggestion of Indonesian Arifin Siregar.

Mahathir's insistence on an Asians-only group strained his relations with US Secretary of State James Baker, who disparaged the proposal publicly. "APEC was trans-Pacific and it was inclusive, but EAEG was exclusive and draws a line down the Pacific," Baker said. "For those reasons, we were very much opposed to it."[54] Baker's position was not universally understood within the administration, however. One senior State Department official recalled that then–US Trade Representative Carla Hills gave a nod to the concept when she visited the area in 1991. "[She] had no strategic mind," he said. "We had to pull her back." As a general policy, though, the Bush administration remained firm in its condemnation of the idea and applied significant political pressure on its Asian allies to reject the proposal. At the Bangkok ministerial, Malaysian

Trade and Industry Minister Rafidah Aziz blasted the American position on the EAEC. She charged Washington with setting a double standard by pursuing subregionalism through NAFTA while attempting to block similar developments in Asia.[55]

Mahathir has grudgingly accepted the pressure to subsume the EAEC into the APEC process, which has at least temporarily lifted the tensions the proposal caused in the region. The United States has been more accepting of the group with this change in focus. As one US official put it, "We have said on occasion that a caucus within APEC, a place to share ideas and develop ideas, was fine, but if it were outside and duplicative, it would take away from the future of APEC."[56] However, US Ambassador to APEC Sandra Kristoff has warned that even as a caucus, the EAEC could propose problems.

At the same time, however, the United States has remained wary of the group's motives. A State Department position paper for Secretary of State Warren Christopher's August 1995 visit to Kuala Lumpur stated that "although [the United States] cannot object to the EAEC per se, it cannot understand how a grouping that does not admit the largest trading partner in the region could realistically be expected to deal with trade issues."[57]

While Malaysia has grudgingly agreed to focus EAEC's activities on internal consultations, it is not certain that it can play even this limited role. In fact, it is questionable whether or not there is actually consensus on APEC policy within ASEAN, let alone the entire membership of the EAEC. As an American official put it, "ASEAN does not speak as a group. They speak as six individuals."[58] Publicly, ASEAN has often shown considerable solidarity, yet on substance many point out their inability to coordinate on a range of issues.

Notes

1. Robert Hawke, *The Hawke Memoirs* (Melbourne: William Heinemann Australia, 1994), p. 430.

2. Richard Woolcott, "How APEC Came to Life," *The Australian*, 14 November 1994.

3. Personal interview with Richard Woolcott, 30 June 1995.

4. *The Australian*, 14 November 1994.

5. *The Australian*, 14 November 1994.

6. Personal interview, 30 June 1995.

7. Personal interview with Ambassador Arifin Siregar, 9 May 1995.

8. Personal interview, 30 June 1995.

9. Personal interview with Jesus Estanislao, 9 August 1995.

10. Personal interview, 30 June 1995.

11. Personal interview with Noboru Takeshita, 29 July 1995.

12. Personal interview, 30 June 1995.

13. Personal interview with Shigeo Muraoka, 12 June 1995.

14. Personal interview, 12 June 1995.

15. *Nikkei Weekly*, 15 November 1993.

16. Ministry of International Trade and Industry, Study Group on Asia Pacific Trade Development Interim Report [Sakamoto Report], June 1988, appendix A.

17. Richard Snape, *Should Australia Seek a Trade Agreement with the United States?* (Canberra, ACT: Economic Planning Advisory Council, 1986).

18. Personal interview with Masakazu Toyoda, 4 July 1995.

19. Personal interview with Geoff Brenan, 26 June 1995.

20. Personal interview.

21. Personal interview, 12 June 1995.

22. Personal interview, 26 June 1995.

23. Personal interview, 4 July 1995.

24. Extracts from the Record of Conversation with Secretary James Baker, March 1989 (O.CH 533201) obtained by the author.

25. Personal interview with James Baker, 30 June 1995.

26. Personal interview with Baker.

27. Personal interview.

28. Personal interview with Robert Hawke, 28 June 1995.

29. Personal interview with Hawke.

30. Hawke, p. 431.

31. Personal interview.

32. Personal interview with Hiroshi Mitsuzuka, 22 July 1995.

33. James Baker, speech before the Japan Society, New York, 26 June 1989.

34. *The Australian*, 14 November 1994.

35. Gareth Evans and Bruce Grant, *Australia's Foreign Relations*, rev. ed. (Melbourne: Melbourne University Press, 1993) p. 341.

36. Personal interview with Narongchai Akrasanee, 31 August 1995.

37. Personal interview with Hawke.

38. Personal interview, 4 July 1995.

39. Personal interview with Robert Zoellick, 20 July 1995.

40. Personal interview, 30 June 1995.

41. Personal interview, 26 June 1995.

42. Personal interview, 4 July 1995.

43. Personal interview with Mitsuzuka.

44. Personal interview, 12 June 1995.

45. Personal interviews with a MITI official and an Australian diplomat.

46. Evans and Grant, p. 230.

47. *US News & World Report*, 20 November 1989. Actually what he said was, "I don't know whether or not I would use the term historic yet. But I think this has the potential to qualify."

48. Personal interview with a participant.

49. *Nihon Keizai Shimbun*, 1 August 1990.

50. Personal interview with a participant.

51. "World and Regional Economic Developments, Regional Economic Outlook," speech by Choi Ho-Joong, 30 July 1990, Singapore.

52. "APEC Declaration on the Uruguay Round," 31 July 1990, Singapore.

53. APEC Ministerial Meeting, "Joint Statement," 31 July 1990, Singapore.

54. Personal interview with Baker.

55. Personal interview with a participant.

56. Personal interview, 19 May 1995.

57. Personal interview with a State Department official.

58. Personal interview, 27 April 1995.

4

APEC Vision: Seoul/Bangkok/Seattle

Seoul and the Three Chinas

It was against the backdrop of an impending breakdown of the global economic system that the APEC ministers met in Seoul in 1991. However, they were more bullish on the future of APEC. The Seoul meetings marked the first time that APEC began to catch real attention around the globe. Persistent Korean diplomacy had won the inclusion of Taiwan, China, and Hong Kong at the 1991 meeting, marking the first occasion that the three met in an official, multilateral capacity. The successful inclusion of the Three Chinas gave new optimism to APEC members, who upgraded the organization by agreeing on the goal of regional trade liberalization to further the progress of the Uruguay Round of global trade talks.

Ambassador Lee

Much of the credit for achieving this diplomatic coup lies with Korea's then–Assistant Minister of Foreign Affairs Lee See-Young, who at the time chaired APEC's senior officials' meeting (SOM). While both the Korean and American governments played a delicate diplomatic game to gain acceptance for Chinese inclusion, Lee's personal role was instrumental. In the months leading up to the Seoul ministerial, Lee made several trips to both Beijing and Taipei to negotiate membership for the two economies. Lee recalled that in the beginning, the two sides were far apart and compromise seemed elusive.[1] Although not a Chinese speaker, Lee sometimes enjoyed using Chinese calligraphy to render shared aphorisms with his Chinese friends. China's Ambassador Qin Huasun, then-director of the Department of International Organizations and Conferences in the Foreign Ministry, demanded that Taiwan agree to enter APEC officially as a province of China. Qin's Taiwanese counterpart, Wu Tzu-Dan, rejected Beijing's demands and insisted on Taiwan's entrance into the organization as "The Republic of China." Taiwan also wanted to be granted equal status to Beijing during APEC meetings, a point that Beijing strongly resisted. In the early stages, the only point that the two sides could agree upon was one that had been decided two years earlier: no APEC member would fly its flag at APEC meetings.

Although Korea had no official communications with China at the time, Lee, who had been the first Korean diplomat to visit China in 1985, had no problem in obtaining a visa. Behind the scenes, the United States was actively assisting Korea in strengthening its ties with Beijing and Moscow, and it used the Seoul negotiations as part of this process. On the other hand, Korea had ties with Taipei, which the United States had lacked since it severed diplomatic relations in 1979. Seoul was then the only APEC member that still retained diplomatic relations with Taipei. Korea could also play a more neutral role, free of the power-politics rivalry between Beijing and Washington. As one US official put it, "If it had been our ministerial or Japan's ministerial, it would have been much different. Korea was much more of a nonthreatening chair."[2] Lee stresses, however, that his negotiations with Beijing and Taipei were carried out in his capacity as chair of the APEC SOM, not as a representative of the Korean government. In any case, Lee benefited from the fact that Korea's relations with the People's Republic had warmed significantly in last few years leading up to the Seoul meeting.

Lee was not able to achieve an agreement until the August 1991 SOM in Kyongju, Korea. Just before the meeting, both Taipei and Beijing accepted a compromise plan put forth by Lee. When Lee received the news by phone of Taipei's acceptance, he was chatting in his hotel room with Bob Fauver, who congratulated him on the breakthrough. During the proceedings, Lee circulated the proposal to other APEC members, who unanimously endorsed it. The final agreement on the wording of memorandums of understanding (MOUs) between the APEC chair (Korea) and both Taipei and Beijing came in late September in New York at midnight on the morning that Chinese Foreign Minister Qian Qichen was due to leave. The Three Chinas agreed to join APEC on the following terms:[3]

> 1) The respective designations of the three parties shall be the People's Republic of China, Chinese Taipei and Hong Kong (Hong Kong will be redesignated as "Hong Kong, China" from 1 July 1997 according to the Sino-British Joint Declaration on the Question of Hong Kong signed on 19 December 1984). These designations shall be used in all APEC meetings, activities, documents, materials and other publications as well as in all APEC administrative and conference arrangements;

2) Without prejudice to the right of APEC participants to appoint their respective representatives to APEC meetings, Chinese Taipei shall be represented at Ministerial Meetings only by a minister or ministers in charge of APEC-related economic affairs, while its "foreign minister" or "vice foreign minister" shall not attend APEC meetings. Chinese Taipei's delegation may include officials of "foreign" and other ministries at or below the level of department director. Members of Chinese Taipei's delegation may use their official titles subject to the principles agreed upon in this Memorandum of Understanding;

3) Subject to the aforementioned terms, the three parties will participate in APEC meetings and activities on an equal basis with the current APEC participants.

Despite this agreement, and three letters exchanged between Korea and the three parties, China sought to introduce its own version. Shortly after signing the MOU, China submitted an "interpretative letter," the importance of which was downplayed by a senior US official. "[The letter] had no standing, and nobody accepted it," he said. "But they tried to spell out their interpretation of the agreement, which as you might imagine, was not the same balanced agreement that had been reached with Taiwan and Hong Kong."[4]

Senior Taiwanese trade negotiator and chief delegate to both the ministerial and leaders' meetings, Vincent Siew, had his own view. "The final arrangement was made that on our side we are all equal with the other side, except we have to change our name in APEC to 'Chinese Taipei,' " said Siew. "That is all. There [were] no other agreements." Siew noted that Taiwan was even reluctant to use the term "Chinese Taipei," though the name is used in other multilateral forums, and only accepted it as a last resort.

A Chinese diplomat noted that while allowing Taiwan to join APEC was a sacrifice, Beijing remained vigilant in preventing Taipei from using APEC to its political advantage. "We realized that Taiwan's participation might have some negative implications for us," he said. "We restricted the political aspects of APEC, but Taiwan tried to cross the line. Therefore we had to be stern on the issue."[5]

Since their entrance into APEC, China and Taiwan have sometimes clashed on protocol and procedural issues, but rarely on substance. Taiwan crossed the line, in China's opinion, by referring to itself as "Taiwan" instead of "Chinese Taipei" in the summary conclusion of the Working Group on Small and Medium Sized Industries.[6] Taiwan's right to host APEC meetings could be contentious in the future. Taiwanese senior official Kuo-Hsieng Shen maintained, "It is certainly conceivable that, according to APEC's cycle of rotation and fair practices, Chinese Taipei will be able to host a high-level APEC conference."[7] Yet the MOU did not specify or stipulate Taiwan's ability to host APEC conferences. China was concerned that if an APEC meeting were held in Taipei, the Taiwanese flag would be displayed in hotels. The agreement also did not address the possibility of a leaders' summit, which had not been contemplated at the time. "If there had been a concern about a potential leaders' meeting," said one American official close to the negotiations, "I don't think that the deal would have been solvable."[8]

Membership of the Three Chinas, however, has had meaning well beyond just the substance and protocol of APEC's official meetings. The inclusion of senior Taiwanese officials in Seoul led to the first official contact between Japan and Taiwan at the ministerial level since Japan severed ties with Taipei in 1971. Similar meetings were held between Taiwan's trade minister and the US trade representative.

China's entrance provided a forum for high-level Sino-US dialogue, particularly after the advent of the leaders' meetings in 1993. Hong Kong also benefited from the arrangement because it gained a voice in the development of the region's economy, which it depends upon for so much of its livelihood. At the Seoul meeting, Hong Kong noted its plans to continue its separate membership in APEC even after its reversion to the mainland.[9] The 1991 MOU stated only that "Hong Kong will be redesignated 'Hong Kong, China' from 1 July 1997," the date of its reversion to the People's Republic. Ambassador Lee noted that Hong Kong's membership after 1997 would have to be agreed upon by a consensus among APEC members at that time.

Seoul Declaration

The Seoul meeting fell at a time of increasing uncertainty around the world. Failure of the Uruguay Round in Brussels almost a year before gave rise to new worries over the round's completion. In Moscow, the Soviet Union collapsed after an abortive coup attempt by hard-line military officers. But just as the Chinese character *weiji* has the double meaning of danger and opportunity, global instability was a boost to APEC. Liberalization within the Asia Pacific was at least an acceptable fallback to a possible breakdown in global negotiations. A strong showing in Seoul also provided a welcome contrast to the turmoil in the world. The ascension of the Three Chinas into the APEC ranks displayed to many outside APEC, particularly the European Union, the seriousness of the organization.

In addition to the Three Chinas, APEC received a flood of new applicants. Papua New Guinea, the Soviet Union, Mexico, Peru, Ecuador, Chile, and Argentina all submitted requests for participation before the meeting, and India expressed its hope to join soon afterward.

On substance, Seoul limited itself to pronouncements on the Uruguay Round, calling on both members and nonmembers alike to redouble their efforts to find a compromise. The Seoul Declaration specifically pledged the forum to "a commitment to open dialogue and consensus building," noting the need to give "due considerations to the needs of developing economies."[10] As the first comprehensive articulation of APEC's mission, the Seoul Declaration was to have been adopted as the APEC Charter, but ASEAN resisted, objecting to paragraphs about establishing a secretariat and budget that were eventually omitted from the final text. Another idea that was put on hold until the following year because of ASEAN objections was the Australian proposal for an Eminent Persons Group of outside experts—modeled on the one established by ASEAN to guide the ASEAN Free Trade Area (AFTA) initiative—to provide advice and a long-term vision to the forum.[11]

Bangkok: A Secretariat and an EPG

The 1992 Bangkok meeting followed up on many of the points raised in Seoul. The EPG was formally mandated, it was agreed to expand APEC membership from 15 to 17 by including Mexico and Papua New Guinea at the 1993 Seattle meeting, and a secretariat was conceived. The Bangkok meeting attracted little public attention, however, because the United States was in the midst of the 1992 presidential election and had thus refrained from sending any ministerial-level officials to Bangkok. Japanese Foreign Minister Michio Watanabe and his Canadian counterpart were also absent. Further, President Bush's Detroit speech outlining his "strategic network" concept of bilateral free trade areas, given just a month before the Bangkok meeting, was perceived as signaling American disinterest in backing the multilateral organization.

Internal political distractions, combined with economic frustration, conspired to make the 1992 Bangkok meeting the nadir of American involvement in APEC. Both Secretary of State Baker and Undersecretary Zoellick had moved to the White House to assist President Bush's reelection campaign, so Baker's assistant, Robert Fauver, served as the acting minister for the United States. While US officials deny that they were sending a message by not sending a ministerial-level delegation, many saw USTR Carla Hills's decision to attend her daughter's wedding instead of the Bangkok ministerial as symbolic of America's growing disinterest in Asia Pacific cooperation.[12] Hills had also missed the 1990 Singapore meeting.

At Bangkok, members agreed to create a permanent Secretariat. After considerable bidding, Singapore won the right to house the Secretariat in exchange for paying all local expenses until 1995. The Secretariat was to be kept small, with staff members seconded from members and a budget formulated on the basis of relative national incomes.

With the modest annual allocation of $2 million per year, APEC did not experience the contentious debates over funding shares endemic in larger multilateral institutions such as the United Nations and the World Bank. Nonetheless, members were aware of the symbolism of funding levels. Originally, Japan volunteered to contribute up to 20 percent of the operating budget but was persuaded by the United States, limited to 18 percent because of internal rules, to match the US level. While both Taiwan and China volunteered to increase their respective shares to make up for a narrow overall shortfall, other nations privately cautioned that the total "Chinese" contribution should not exceed 18 percent.[13] In the end, however, China agreed to pay 9.5 percent, Taiwan 6.25 percent, and Hong Kong 2.75 percent—18.5 percent in all. The only other exception made was for Singapore, which voluntarily increased its share by .25 percent over the ASEAN level of 2.5 percent in anticipation of its impending reclassification as a "developed nation."

Jump-Starting the GATT: The Vancouver Meetings

In addition to the annual ministerial meetings, APEC held two special sessions of trade ministers meant to achieve progress on completing the Uruguay Round talks. The purpose of the Vancouver meetings, held in the fall of 1990 and 1992, was twofold. Firstly, the ministers sought a common endorsement of the Uruguay Round to pressure nonmembers. The second reason was internal. Members hoped to find areas that they could make progress on domestically to help break the APEC deadlock. The two meetings, particularly the 1990 gathering, were timed for maximum impact. In 1990, for instance, the APEC efforts came just a month before the Uruguay Round ministerials set for December.

The Vancouver meetings themselves focused particularly on controversial areas such as rules of origin and agricultural subsidies. Canada, an ardent supporter of the global trade regime, took the lead in the forum, pointing out the significant benefits that completing the round would have for the region. While the ministers were able to reach common positions during the talks, the meetings provoked considerable mutual recriminations within APEC.

During the meetings, Southeast Asian nations lambasted their APEC partners and the discussions for pressing the region to make concessions. After singling out US Trade Representative Hills and her Canadian counterpart, a Singaporean official said the attitudes of the North American members "have again fostered ASEAN's skepticism toward APEC itself."[14] Others singled out Japan for its reluctance to liberalize its rice markets. Thailand, for instance, expressed its dissatisfaction with Japan's reluctance to liberalize agriculture while "praising American and Canadian compromises on textiles." At the Singapore ministerial, the New Zealand delegate harshly criticized Japan's lack of progress in allowing rice imports, arguing, "It's not sufficient for everyone to ride the bus [of liberalization], someone has to be in the driver's seat."[15] In the end, the members were able to achieve a consensus supporting the Uruguay Round's completion and made some meaningful concessions in support of that goal. It is difficult to assess whether the specific commitments made at Vancouver or the overall spirit of APEC's annual meetings was more effective in furthering the completion of the Uruguay Round.

Seattle and the Era of the Summits

The 1993 APEC meeting marked a new era in the evolution of APEC. Following up on an informal suggestion by Australia's Keating, Clinton invited all 17 APEC leaders to Seattle for a first-of-its-kind informal Asia Pacific summit.[16] The historic summit of Asia Pacific leaders attracted attention from around the world. Nearly 3,000 journalists covered the conference, almost twice the number that attended the Maastricht summit, which marked Europe's biggest step toward integration.[17] As one official put it, "You have to think of this as a bit like being at a NATO meeting in 1950."[18]

While the meeting ostensibly was called to give shape to the Asia Pacific community, Europe was on everyone's minds. APEC members hoped to send a message to their European friends: stop building a "fortress Europe" or we will act. Reflecting on the first summit meeting of Asia Pacific leaders, the *Far Eastern Economic Review* concluded "The meeting . . . was the message."[19] It is clear that Europe has gotten the message: although they publicly belittle the organization, they have quietly requested observer status at APEC meetings, a request that has yet to be even acknowledged. One ASEAN diplomat reveled in the European reaction: "Yeah, they are a bit worried. But from our point of view, it is good that they are worried!"[20]

For many Asia Pacific leaders, the meeting in Seattle was also a reassurance of America's continued commitment to the region. Furthermore, some glimpsed a more outward-looking America in the policies of the new Clinton administration. Just one day before the summit, Congress had voted to approve the North American Free Trade Agreement (NAFTA). The Clinton administration took great care to reassure Asian allies that NAFTA did not signal American disengagement from global trade. Secretary of State Warren Christopher maintained, "The NAFTA vote lends further strength to APEC's support for more open trade and investment."

The leaders' summit was a huge success, surmounting many of the institutional barriers that had handicapped earlier meetings. The feeling of informality and congeniality was buttressed by the intimate settings in which the leaders met. The dress was "strictly informal," and advisers, even note takers, were banned from the room.

The summit was full of symbolism and significance for the United States and the world. It marked one of the most important post–Cold War summits, and it signified a watershed in American orientation from Europe toward Asia. It also had domestic political benefit of demonstrating Clinton's earnest and early commitment to expanded trade and jobs. The informal style of APEC was new as well: an image of relaxed relations in the Asia Pacific was projected. A meeting of the heads of state for the first time gave legitimacy to the rhetoric of an emerging Asia Pacific community. Its informal tone also signaled the new dynamics of regionalism, something vastly different from the stiff meetings of the North Atlantic Treaty Organization (NATO) or US-Soviet summit talks.

Fauver's Mission

National Economic Council official and longtime G-7 sherpa Robert Fauver played an instrumental role in organizing the Seattle meeting. Fauver, a veteran of international economic policy and diplomacy had to first win the battle on the domestic front before he entered battle on the foreign front. Within the US government, there remained considerable opposition to the idea, which had originated within White House policy circles. "State didn't see the value. Treasury, of course, didn't want it because they didn't like the APEC process anyhow," said a proponent of the summit meeting. "USTR hadn't figured out what APEC was yet."[21]

Supporters of the initiative went directly to the president, who at the time was looking for material for a speech to be delivered during his upcoming trip to Japan and Korea in July. While many foreign policy advisers criticized the summit idea as unworkable and unneeded, Clinton and his domestic political advisers jumped on the initiative. "The domestic advisers, without knowing the substance of the issue, thought it would be really positive to have 15 leaders of the free world from Asia meeting in Seattle on the West Coast," said a senior White House official. "The [David] Gergens of the world saw it as a domestic positive. The [Robert] Rubin/[Bowman] Cutter view was that it . . . showed the change from the past: new generation, new leaders, looking to Asia, not absorbed with a European focus." (The official was referring to presidential adviser David Gergen, who was then the White House "spin doctor," and economic officials Robert Rubin and Bowman Cutter of the National Economic Council, a freshly introduced apparatus of the Clinton White House.)

Clinton himself liked the idea from the start. "It was an easy sell to the president," the official said. "It took two sentences, and he was positive."[22] For Clinton, an informal summit meeting played directly to his strengths. As governor of Arkansas, Clinton was a leading member of the American Council of Governors, where he frequently used his personal charm and charisma to forge consensus among his 49 colleagues, and he felt that he could do the same in Seattle. Proponents of the summit presented their bureaucratic rivals with a fait accompli by inserting the invitation to the leaders' meeting in speeches Clinton delivered in San Francisco and at

Waseda University as part of his trip to Tokyo to attend the G-7 meeting, thereby putting an end to the debate.[23]

With the invitation on the table, there was an entirely new bureaucratic battle to be fought—this time with detractors in other nations. As in Washington, the summit's backers tried to cut as many officials out of the decision making as possible, particularly from those from foreign ministries. To accomplish this, the administration relied on communication channels between heads of government that bypassed potential opponents. In some cases, particularly Japan's, personal correspondence between Clinton and his counterparts was needed to overcome bureaucratic interference. Clinton wrote two such letters to his colleagues, one informing them of the process and the informality of the proposed meeting, and the second outlining the substance. "It was a very friendly style letter, where he also solicited their views on what they might like to do in terms of commitment," Fauver said of the first letter. "He laid out in the second letter some ideas he had for the communiqué, his vision of the future of the region, and asked them to communicate their personal views on what they might like to be recognized in the communiqué."[24]

On his first visit, Fauver swung through most of the ASEAN nations, including Indonesia. In Jakarta, Fauver encountered skepticism from influential Foreign Minister Ali Alatas. "He was concerned about [the meeting's status as] leaders-only because part of his strength has been his influence, as he is the 'dean' of foreign ministers in the region," Fauver said. Fauver was not able to travel to Kuala Lumpur because his counterparts were out of the country at the time. This was not a great setback, because Malaysia's role was marginalized anyway after Prime Minister Mahathir announced his decision not to attend the Seattle meeting. "They really lost leverage by not coming," Fauver said. "Since APEC works as a consensus body, it would have been tougher to make as much progress as we did had they been there."

Likely Fauver's greatest challenge was dealing with Beijing officials set on changing the role and participation of Taiwan. Rather than discussing the wider significance or meaning of Seattle, the Chinese were fixated on protocol. "They wanted to know who was coming from Taiwan, where were they sitting at the table," Fauver said. "When we explained that there would be no table, that they would be sitting in chairs, they couldn't figure out how you did protocol if you were sitting in chairs."[25]

As a White House official, Fauver was unable to travel to Taiwan, but he dealt with Taipei through its representative office in Washington. Fauver was able to meet Taiwan's SOM official face to face at the Hawaii meeting and was pleased by Taiwanese delegation's flexibility and interest in substantive matters. Fauver was also relieved that they did not push too strongly to send President Lee Teng-hui to the Seattle meeting, instead designating Economic Planning Minister Vincent Siew as Taiwan's ranking economic official.

Fauver's visits to other APEC countries were relatively smooth. In Seoul, then–Korean Foreign Minister Han Sung-Joo expressed support for the Seattle idea but was concerned about President Kim Young Sam's "comfort level" in speaking off-the-cuff. Korean officials worried that if he were one of the later speakers he would feel uncomfortable and perhaps forget his prepared speech. Fauver promised to allow Kim to go early, third in fact, but Fauver disputed the Koreans' claims that he lacked public speaking skills. "He ended up giving a very interesting, very good extemporaneous presentation," Fauver said.[26]

In his travels, Fauver sought to meet with officials at the highest level possible. There was a concern that excessive involvement at the bureaucratic level would unduly bog down the process in technical details and diplomatic nuances. Clinton insisted that the statement out of Seattle be genuine and truly reflect the vision and ideas of the leaders themselves. To this end, American senior officials met bilaterally with most of the invited guests to assure their participation according to American ground rules. The United States won an agreement that a draft of the communiqué would not be released until the night before the summit to avoid excessive bargaining and haggling.

The Idea

The decision to hold a leaders' meeting came quite quickly and with little preparation, in part because the groundwork had already been laid. Australian Prime Minister Paul Keating had been the first to propose the idea of an APEC summit meeting during the visit of President George Bush to Australia in 1992. Bush was reportedly interested in the idea but preferred to hold off until there was a broader consensus. Keating's idea was to transform APEC "from essentially a body talking about loose economic cooperation, to one that has real political authority and has a real agenda, and the agenda would be trade liberalization and trade facilitation."[27]

In his meeting with Bush, Keating argued that the United States needed to reorient its Asia policy in the new world order and recognize its broader interests in the region. "Up until this stage, US policy in the Pacific had been made by the United States Navy," Keating said. "It hadn't been made by the State Department or the Commerce Department."

Keating, a strong proponent of APEC as the vehicle for restructuring the Asia Pacific, followed up with letters to Bush, Japan's Kiichi Miyazawa, Korea's Kim, Singapore's Goh Chok Tong, and Indonesia's Suharto. In his letter, Keating argued that APEC's lack of annual leaders' meetings set the region apart from other regions with organizations such as NATO, the European Union, and the Non-Aligned Movement. Keating stressed that summit meetings would not only bolster APEC's normal work but also make "an important contribution to broader regional cooperation."[28] He received relatively positive replies, although Japanese Prime Minister Kiichi Miyazawa was "a little reticent at first." Japan eventually endorsed the idea. President Bush gave conditional support to the idea, but in reality he was not enthusiastic.[29] State Department Undersecretary Robert Zoellick said Bush had grown tired of international conferences and was even contemplating moving G-7 meetings to alternating years.[30] That Bush suffered "summit fatigue" actually allowed Clinton to better differentiate his message and policy from those of his predecessor. In the end, the Australian administration's efforts yielded favorable responses from all of the leaders except Mahathir.

Personalities and abilities have been magnified in the group dynamics of the informal and intimate leaders' meeting. The Seattle meeting marked the high point of the organization's six-year existence. Clinton proved to be a skillful host, and his firm grasp of the issues facing the region impressed his colleagues. "He doesn't need to read notes; he understands all the things he is doing," said Australia's Keating of the meeting. "It's not just stylized. He doesn't live off cue cards; he actually knows it."[31]

Among APEC leaders there was a strong personal dynamic, particularly among the newly elected leaders of Japan, Canada, Korea, and the United States. All of them shared the activist passions for change and reform, and optimism (at least at the time of the summit).[32] It was here where Clinton also established his personal rapport with Indonesia's Suharto. Suharto felt indebted to Clinton for meeting with him at the margins of the July 1993 G-7 summit in Tokyo in his capacity as chair of the Non-Aligned Movement. Suharto, remembering the movement's legacy established by Sukarno and Nehru, of appealing directly to Nikita Khrushchev and John F. Kennedy, wanted to set a new precedent by meeting with G-7 leaders.[33] President Clinton accepted the offer on a bilateral basis. "He was very, very thankful to Clinton," said an Indonesian intellectual close to Suharto. "So, when Clinton brought up the idea of the Blake Island summit, he said, 'Yes, I will support you, because you supported me as the chair of the Non-Aligned.' "[34]

There had been some tense moments among the G-7 when Japan, as chair, originally invited Suharto to the 1993 meeting. There was fear that allowing Suharto access to the meeting would set a precedent and concern that ongoing East Timor problems would have ramifications for the G-7's image. In place of an official dialogue, Japan facilitated a meeting between Suharto and Clinton in addition to the Suharto-Miyazawa meeting.[35] Clinton's decision to meet Suharto at the meeting, Fauver said, "was a very important recognition of the role of both President Suharto and Indonesia in the region."[36]

This rapport between Clinton and Suharto was strengthened during the informal Blake Island summit meeting. At one point after an Australian proposal to enact a voluntary investment code, Clinton turned to Suharto, expecting his opposition and said, "This is up to us to agree what we are going to do, but I'd like to make sure that President Suharto is comfortable with it." Korea's Kim, and Singapore's Goh approached Suharto about a similar meeting the following year. Suharto responded, "If all of you say so, I will accept it with great pleasure. It is a great honor for Indonesia." Suharto's acceptance paved the way for institutionalization of the leaders' meeting. Of course, because Mahathir had abstained from the meeting, making possible an atmosphere not unlike the inadvertent dynamics of the Soviet absence at the 1950 UN Security Council vote on the Korean War, consensus was reached.

However, the meeting hosted by Clinton obviously succeeded in generating a good atmosphere and feeling of camaraderie among the leaders. That result perhaps hinged more on the proactive spirit of creating something new and historic than the reactive posture toward Mahathir's challenge. As nothing succeeds like succession, the agreement to hold another summit the following year was particularly auspicious.

Vision Statement

The Blake Island, Washington, meeting in November 1993 also marked the first time American and Chinese leaders had met since the Tiananmen incident. The tone of Jiang's visit to Seattle signaled a new dynamic in Sino-American relations. The meeting came against the backdrop of a renewed pragmatism in US-China policy. The administration moved to renew China's most-favored nation (MFN) trade status, despite continued human rights problems. The bilateral meeting between Clinton and Jiang centered around commercial issues, highlighting the growing importance of trade and economics to the once politically based relationship. For instance, China is rapidly becoming one of Boeing's largest customers, as demand for domestic air travel and deregulation of the aerospace sector make it the most explosive market in the world. Jiang's visit to Boeing headquarters, in which he praised the company's "advanced technology, modern management, its highly competent staff, and strict and meticulous work requirements," underscored the evolving commercial ties between China and the United States.[37]

In addition to their bilateral meeting held before the official proceedings, Clinton and Jiang had a brief encounter during the informal leaders' meeting. According to an observer:

> Jiang Zemin and [Clinton] were the two biggest physically, just bodies. They started to mingle with brandy and coffee, and then Jiang Zemin started to walk towards the president . . . and they [began] chatting using an interpreter. And

the others kind of pulled in around them. It was clearly these two big-sized people with a whole bunch of others listening. It was very symbolic in a sense that China, the most populous, and the United States, the richest, were kind of a step out of the group. . . . They were talking, and the others were listening.[38]

While Seattle marked a turning point in recent Sino-American relations, the positive rhetoric and personal exchanges concealed many of the deeper problems that still exist between the two countries. Jiang's praise for Boeing's advocacy of China's MFN status and his quip that "for Asians, human rights don't mean the rights and privileges of the few, but the rights of the many," highlighted the lingering divergence between economic and political relations between the two countries. So did Clinton's informal meeting with Taiwan's representative Siew, a meeting that underscored the growing contact between Washington and Taipei.

Siew also met with Japanese Prime Minister Morihiro Hosokawa, the first exchange between a Japanese leader and a Taiwanese official since relations were severed in 1972.[39] The meeting came amidst growing tensions across the Taiwan Straits. Public statements set off a "volley of words" between Taiwanese and Chinese delegates. At one point during the Seattle conference, Siew referred to "two Chinas," which led Jiang to remark during the APEC meeting that "Taiwan is a province of the PRC," again provoking a strong condemnation from the Taiwanese Foreign Ministry.[40] Friction over Taiwan and human rights were only two areas of tension in bilateral US-China relations that were hardly addressed during the Clinton-Jiang meetings, though they remained just below the surface throughout.

Absent from the Seattle summit were only the leaders of Taiwan, Hong Kong (because of their political status), and Malaysia. Mahathir was still fuming over American rebuffs of his EAEC proposal, and he boycotted the leaders' summit out of protest. Malaysia also criticized the first report of the EPG, released at Seattle, which had recommended rapid action on regional trade liberalization. Malaysian Trade Minister Rafidah Aziz said, "Malaysia is wary and chary about accepting any recommendation that will radically change the original mandated form and profile of APEC beyond what it is supposed to be."[41]

Despite Malaysia's protest, APEC leaders endorsed many of the EPG's suggestions, stating in the leaders' Vision Statement: "We welcome the challenge . . . to achieve free trade in the Asia Pacific, advance global trade liberalization, and launch concrete proposals to move us toward those long-term goals."[42] They set forth a broad vision of a "community of Asia Pacific economies" boasting such attributes as a deepened spirit of openness and partnership, continued dynamic economic growth, reduced trade and investment barriers, higher incomes, improved education, and sustainable development. To this end, the leaders made specific proposals, including that APEC enhance the Uruguay Round outcome, convene a

Finance Ministers Meeting, and encourage the establishment of a Pacific Business Forum. The text of the Vision Statement also echoed the words spoken at the leaders' meeting.

During the meeting, President Clinton stressed that the Asia Pacific was an engine for increased global prosperity, not zero-sum competition with other regions. As New Zealand Prime Minister James Bolger exhorted, "It is necessary to make the countries outside of the Asia Pacific understand that the region's dynamic economies will not be a threat to them." As a way of preventing a breakdown into regional blocs, Singapore's Goh recommended the extension of "NAFTA to other APEC members" and the creation of an "ASEAN–North America Free Trade Area." Goh also noted that "in order to maintain the growth in the region, a well-balanced relationship among Japan, the United States, and China is important." Brunei's Sultan Haji Hassanal Bolkiah concurred, urging America's continued presence, as "this region profits from trade with and investment from the United States, and at the same time only East Asian dynamism can enliven the US economy." President Clinton acknowledged America's "big responsibility in promoting the region's stability and growth" and pledged continued American engagement both economically and militarily. Japanese Prime Minister Hosokawa presented a slightly different view, warning of the pitfalls of laissez-faire economics while putting forth supply-side approaches such as environmental/energy security and Small- and Medium-Sized Enterprise (SME) enhancement as measures needed to sustain economic growth in the Asia Pacific. Thailand's Prime Minister Chuan Leekpai welcomed "the approval of NAFTA-related bills in the US Congress and highly praises President Clinton's efforts for that."[43] These remarks reflected that the congeniality apparent at the Seattle meeting could even allay suspicions about the North American trade regime, which had been a source of constant fears within the Asia Pacific.

Notes

1. Personal interview with Lee See-Young, 19 July 1995.
2. Personal interview, 19 May 1995.
3. Copy of the memorandum of understanding obtained by the author.
4. Personal interview, 8 August 1995.
5. Personal interview, 27 July 1995.
6. Personal interview with a participant.
7. Personal interview with Kuo-Hsieng Shen, 9 August 1995.
8. Personal interview, 8 August 1995.
9. Personal interview with a participant.
10. Minoru Koide, "The Evolution of Economic Institutions in the Pacific Region, 1945–93: A Theory of Institutional Dynamics," Ph.D. dissertation, University of Southern California, May 1994, p. 269.

11. Personal interview, 26 May 1995.

12. Koide, p. 288.

13. Personal interview with an official in attendance, 8 June 1995.

14. Personal interview with a participant.

15. Personal interview with a participant.

16. Andrew Mack and John Ravenhill, eds., *Pacific Cooperation* (Boulder, CO: Westview Press, 1995), p. 71.

17. Rob Mikos, "The Politics of APEC," unpublished thesis, Princeton University, 1995, p. 59.

18. Jonathan Clarke, *The United States and Asia Pacific Cooperation* (New York: The Asia Society, 1994), p. 8.

19. *Far Eastern Economic Review*, 2 December 1993.

20. Personal interview, 9 May 1995.

21. Personal interview, 21 June 1995.

22. Personal interview, 21 June 1995.

23. Speech by Bill Clinton, San Francisco, California, 5 July 1993.

24. Personal interview, 24 July 1995.

25. Personal interview with Robert Fauver.

26. Personal interview, 21 June 1995.

27. Personal interview with Paul Keating, 6 July 1995.

28. Letter from Paul Keating to George Bush, 3 April 1992, obtained by the author.

29. Personal interview with Keating.

30. Personal interview, 20 July 1995.

31. Personal interview with Keating.

32. Clinton assumed office in January 1993, Kim in February 1993, Hosokawa in July 1993, and Chrétien in November 1993.

33. See Peter Willetts, *The Non-Aligned Movement: The Origins of a Third World Alliance*, (London: Frances Pinter Ltd., 1978), p. 4. After the 1961 Belgrade Non-Aligned Movement summit, the leaders dispatched Indonesia's Ahmed Sukarno and Mali's Modibo Keita to Moscow and India's Jawaharlal Nehru and Ghana's Kwame Nkrumah to Washington as special emissaries with letters appealing for further talks between the superpowers.

34. Personal interview, 9 July 1995.

35. Personal interview.

36. Personal interview, 24 July 1995.

37. *Seattle Times*, 19 November 1993.

38. Personal interview with an observer.

39. *Kyodo News Service*, 23 November 1993.

40. *South China Morning Post*, 23 November 1993.

41. Statement of Rafidah Aziz to the Fifth Ministerial Meeting, 18 November 1993, Seattle.

42. US Department of State, *Dispatch* 4, no. 28 (29 November 1993).

43. These remarks were based on personal interviews with participants and officials who knew the details of the conversation.

5

Toward 2020: Bogor/Osaka/Manila

The gains of Seattle were buttressed by the 1994 summit in Bogor, Indonesia. Again the leaders of the region (this time including Malaysian Prime Minister Mahathir) met, and they agreed upon a comprehensive trade liberalization plan. This agreement became known as the Bogor Declaration, and it marked APEC's furthest move toward free trade in the region. Bogor also saw the expansion of the group to 18 with the inclusion of Chile. The Bogor meeting was strongly focused on developmental issues, with human resources development, technology transfer, and infrastructure programs high on the agenda.

The real breakthrough was achieving consensus on the long-term goal of free trade in the Asia Pacific. As a compromise, however, the leaders agreed to adopt a two-tracked approach, reflecting the challenges many of the developing economies would face in opening up their vulnerable markets. Crossing the threshold from consultation to liberalization was not simple. The most crucial step had been taken with the advent of the leaders' meetings, in which they could do a good deal of "horse-trading" to reach a "flexible consensus" for concrete actions. Like the preceding Seattle meeting, Bogor drew world attention. Suharto's insistence that the leaders don colorful Indonesian *batik* shirts also made for photogenic group poses and a collegial environment.

Bogor

Envoy Bintoro

President Suharto chose to bypass normal diplomatic channels and use Professor Bintoro Tjokroamidjojo, his assistant for APEC affairs, to represent him in arrangements leading up to the Bogor meeting. Bintoro was a member of the influential clique of American-trained economics professors on the University of Indonesia's faculty. He had served in official capacities in the past, including as ambassador to the Netherlands and as a member of a committee dedicated to deregulating the tightly controlled Indonesian economy. Suharto choose Bintoro as his messenger because he was concerned that his vision for Bogor would not adequately be addressed if left up to the Indonesian bureaucracy, which retained some resistance to the idea of regional trade liberalization.

Suharto nominally created a steering committee for the APEC conference that included the minister for economic development, foreign minister, state secretary, and the special assistant for the Non-Aligned Movement, along with Bintoro and Suharto's top economic adviser, Widjojo Nitisastro. This group never actually met, and many of the decisions were made informally between the president and his top advisers. Suharto was so indirect in his discussions that Bintoro took advice from Suharto's chief of staff, Moerdiono to "read [Suharto's] mind ... that is how he gives instructions."[1] The core group that prepared for the Bogor summit included Bintoro, Widjojo, and Moerdiono. Widjojo, Bintoro's patron and mentor, and Moerdiono were key in formulating the substance for Bogor, according to one Indonesian scholar close to the government, while Bintoro served mainly as a sherpa to drum up regional support for the summit's agenda.

Bintoro's first trip within Asia was to Singapore, where Prime Minister Goh Chok Tong strongly endorsed the proposal and commended Indonesia for its leadership. "That kind of decision ... can only be done in Jakarta with President Suharto," Goh said. "If it could not be done there, it could not be done anywhere else, because Indonesia is in [a] position to [bridge] the North, the South, the East, and the West."[2]

Korea was a bit more circumspect. While the Koreans backed the idea of liberalization, they were concerned about their ability to make progress in the agricultural sector. Four months later, Bintoro had a surprise visit from a high-ranking official from the Japanese Ministry of Agriculture, Forestry, and Fisheries (MAFF). Flanked by both the MITI and Gaimusho officials to the APEC senior officials' meeting (SOM), he expressed similar reservations about further progress in the rice sector. Bintoro was sensitive to their concerns and assured them that Indonesia had sectoral problems as well and that Bogor would only address an overall vision for liberalization; substantive discussions were to be postponed until Osaka.

The coordination of China's and Taiwan's participation again was the tricky and thankless task of the host country. The precedent of the Blake Island formula was helpful but did not solve the problem permanently. In Beijing, Bintoro met with Trade and Industry Minister Wu Yi and other senior economic and political officials. He was particularly impressed with Wu. "She looks to me [less of a] minister of a socialist or communist country," he said. "She was very fashionable; she speaks in very professional, intellectual language." Bintoro was concerned about the caution Chinese officials expressed over the liberalization agenda Suharto had laid out for Bogor. To persuade Minister Wu, who initially seemed reluctant to accept the idea of trade and investment liberalization while China was still developing, Bintoro pointedly said, "Madame Wu . . . China is now the fastest growing country in the world. Why? Because China has been liberalized, it trades." He was gratified to receive a small smile of acknowledgment from Wu, who later dispatched her assistant to relay that she had been "receptive" to his ideas.

During his meeting with Vice President Rong Yiren, Bintoro reminded him of the commonalities of China and Indonesia: "We are both emerging markets, and our leader at Bogor reflects the aspirations of these kind of countries." Rong said China had to "represent the aspirations of the developing countries—not go too fast." In addition to expressing concern about its ability to carry out its own liberalization efforts, Chinese officials demanded vehemently that Taiwanese President Lee Teng-hui not attend.

Taiwan put strong pressure on Bintoro to win Lee's attendance at the Bogor meeting. During his first visit, Taipei officials asked that Lee participate out of respect to the close relationship between Lee and Suharto. Bintoro maintained that the leaders of Indonesia and Taiwan shared "personal, not formal" relations, and as such, Jakarta would have to stick to the formula for Taiwan's participation set in Blake Island, Washington. In early November, with one day to spare before the conference, Lee summoned Bintoro. The short notice narrowed Bintoro's travel options to one: Suharto's personal plane. Bintoro brought along his wife, daughter, son-in-law, and ex-secretary: "Of course, it was because the plane was empty, not because of shopping," he said.[3] In Taipei, President Lee expressed regret, but agreed to send Economic Minister Vincent Siew as his personal representative.

Bintoro was able to meet with the leaders or ministers of every APEC member he visited except the United States and Malaysia. American officials whom he met in April made clear that they were opposed to granting unconditional most-favored nation (MFN) status to Europe because of the potential for free riding. The United States also mentioned its desire to set a single target year for liberalization.

Mahathir's Challenge

Indonesia dealt with Malaysian officials on a different level. Malaysia had to obtain the draft of the Bogor Declaration from a third country that Indonesia had already briefed. This breach of protocol was not appreciated in Kuala Lumpur, and in November Suharto sent State Secretary Moerdiono to meet personally with Mahathir to placate him and win his approval of the Bogor agenda.[4] One regretful Indonesian diplomat commented that the delay was unintended.

A general compromise had been reached leading up to the Bogor meeting, and Indonesia had won the participation of all 18 member economies. While there was a consensus reached over the wording of the Bogor Declaration, fissures had already emerged during the informal meeting on the concept of the liberalization endeavor. The strongest challenge came from Mahathir, who argued that developing nations would never be able to catch up to the developed ones and that developing nations could not afford to open up their telecommunications and other markets. At the meeting he proposed adding an annex that would include caveats to the declaration to prevent APEC from turning into a negotiating body. Other APEC leaders greeted this initiative coolly. Singapore's Goh argued that "adding an annex to the declaration will make APEC's intention ambiguous." Philippine President Ramos concurred: "It is inappropriate to include the Malaysian opinion as a part of the declaration; it should be included at most as a note." Suharto chimed in as well: "Adding the annex as Malaysia suggested may weaken the contents of the declaration." Mahathir finally relented, agreeing to withdraw the annex. "The annex is only a note or document we presented, and we just would like our ministers to put it into consideration," he said, adding "We do not ask to have the annex attached to the declaration." Yet, several Malaysian officials were upset that Surharto kept the annex out of the declaration. The annex itself was meant to express Malaysia's reservations to the Bogor consensus. Specifically, the document noted that:

1. **Malaysia will only commit to undertaking further liberalization on a unilateral basis at a pace and capacity commensurate with our level of development.**

2. The liberalization process to achieve [the Bogor goal] **will not create an exclusive free trade area in the Asia Pacific.**

3. The liberalization process **will be GATT/WTO-consistent and on an unconditional most-favored nation (MFN) basis.**

4. The target dates of 2020 and 2010 **are indicative dates and nonbinding** on member economies.

5. The liberalization process will only cover a substantial portion of Asia Pacific trade and **should not go beyond the provisions of GATT/WTO.**

6. It is Malaysia's understanding that **decisions in APEC should be on the basis of consensus.**

7. [As] the EPG has fulfilled its mandate, **its duration should not be extended.**[5]

Despite deep divides, Suharto's flexible management of the summit allowed the leaders to reach an eventual understanding on the main points of the liberalization plan. For the final declaration, the leaders at Bogor agreed on the following points:[6]

- APEC will strive to achieve the long-term goal of free and open trade and investment in the Asia Pacific.

- APEC will complete this goal by the year 2010 for advanced economies and by 2020 for developing members.

- APEC liberalization will be open to nonmembers as well in order to discourage economic regionalism.

- To complement this process, APEC members agreed to expand and accelerate APEC's trade and investment facilitation programs.

- Members are also committed to intensifying development cooperation in the areas of human resources development, the creation of APEC study centers, cooperation in science and technology (including technology transfer), the promotion of small- and medium-sized industries, and steps to improve economic infrastructure.

Behind the Scenes

Behind the scenes at Bogor, and between Bogor and Osaka, various interests among member nations clashed. Five areas in particular have generated considerable controversy since the Indonesian summit. The first was the dual system of liberalization—by 2010 for advanced nations and 2020 for developing members. Splitting the time frame raised questions about the relative pace of the two groups and over which nation fits into which category.

The second concerned the status of APEC-related liberalization to nonmember economies. The United States has stressed that progress made through APEC should be made conditional on reciprocal action from nonmembers. Other members, particularly China, have stressed the need for unconditional MFN status. The third debate revolved around the pledge to achieve liberalization through "concerted unilateral action" (CUA). Several nations raised objections to liberalizing solely voluntarily without any coordination or review. The United States advocated dropping the term "CUA" in favor of the more nuanced "collective individual actions." There emerged a consensus, however, that much progress toward Bogor-mandated deregulation would have to be completed on an individual basis. Yet there was still a lack of agreement on how to implement comparability of each member's unilateral actions to guard against free riding.

The fourth issue that arose was over the priority and relative weights assigned to trade liberalization and economic cooperation. For the most part advanced nations favored a focus on the substantive work of reducing trade and investment barriers, while developing members hoped to gain assistance through APEC in areas such as technology transfer and human resources development. Finally, they differed on APEC's relationship with the WTO.

2020 versus 2010

The concept for a differential liberalization period originated with the EPG's report to the leaders at Bogor. The EPG originally divided the timetable into three parts, recommending liberalization by advanced countries (including Japan, Australia, and the United States) by 2010, 2015 for Korea, and 2020 for the developing states.[7] The EPG recommendation had to compete with a similar report issued by the Pacific Business Forum (PBF) that recommended complete liberalization by 2010. The PBF timetable was widely seen as too hasty, however, so the leaders chose to work from the EPG draft instead.

Actually, Suharto was more ambitious from the outset. When he talked with Australian Prime Minister Paul Keating in the spring before Bogor, he mentioned his preference for 2010, to which Keating agreed. Later, however, Suharto backed down in the face of strong resistance from China and Malaysia.[8] Suharto also had to fight with American officials, who made an attempt to delete the 2020 date to accelerate China's reform and liberalization. Washington had argued that China should receive "developed" country status in the global trade body. In addition, making further concessions to China would have been politically unpopular in the United States.

The one allowed change to the EPG draft was the result of Korean concerns over domestic rice interests. After the riots that rocked Seoul in protest of Uruguay Round rice concessions, Korea was understandably hesitant about rushing any future commitments toward liberalization. At the Bogor meeting, Suharto classified Korea, along with Hong Kong, Singapore, and Taiwan, in the newly industrializing economies (NIEs) group. But President Kim Young Sam argued that "the term 'NIEs' is insulting; thus, we would like to have the term eliminated."[9] Suharto tried to placate Kim by explaining that he used the term as a compliment, but conceded that since the United Nations used only two categories (developed and undeveloped), APEC would also do so. Kim, confident of Korea's imminent OECD membership, explained that his nation no longer was an NIE and boasted, "Korea will meet or beat 2010." It was widely believed that Seoul could meet the deadline in all areas except the highly politicized agriculture sector.

It became apparent that China, however, would be included with the developing countries at Bogor, eliciting some concerns from other APEC members. Lee Kuan Yew argued strongly that China was too big and dynamic to be included in the 2020 group.[10] Others have speculated that China might redefine itself in the future as it becomes more confident in its economic system. In the end, there was no explicit or binding decision made. Yet, in true APEC fashion, a consensus was formed among the SOM members that China belonged to the 2020 group. A clear consensus also placed Papua New Guinea and the "ASEAN Five" (without Singapore) in the same category.[11]

Fear of Free Riding

Major differences emerged between the United States and its APEC partners on the question of MFN vs. selective reciprocity. The United States, apprehensive about European free riding, insisted that any liberalization efforts undertaken through APEC be made available only through reciprocal liberalization of non-APEC member states. At the initial stage, few officials in other Asia-Pacific countries openly support the American position. Opponents of the American approach pushed for unconditional MFN status in the hopes that the additional volume of freer trade within the region would outweigh the economic losses due to free riding.

The United States believed, in the end, that other countries would come around to its perspective. "I don't see a Japanese politician standing up in the Diet and saying: 'I want to give the EC free access to my market without gaining anything from the EC,' " said one American official. "I don't see an American politician doing that; I don't see a Korean politician doing that." As the timetable of liberalization developed gradually, Australia began to shift its position toward that of the United States after the Fukuoka SOM meeting. Singapore has also warmed to the idea of extending MFN status on a NAFTA-type basis.

For its part, China was a vocal opponent of conditional MFN. "For China, the MFN issue seems to be the single issue, as if they are worried about discriminatory treatment in liberalization against China, which is not a member of the WTO, by some APEC countries, particularly the United States," said one senior Japanese official.[12]

At the Sapporo, Japan, SOM meeting in July 1995 the Chinese delegation submitted a paper that called on APEC "to take concrete measures to support non-WTO members of APEC to become members of WTO."[13] China's SOM representative, Wang Yusheng, stressed that "apart from the two timetables [2010/2020], we emphasize [nondiscrimination] is of the foremost importance."[14] The Chinese so far have apparently had broad support within APEC for nondiscrimination. At the Sapporo meeting, Hong Kong joined China in opposing the American position on selective status. The Osaka draft document stated, "The outcome of trade and investment liberalization in the Asia Pacific will apply not only among APEC economies but also between APEC economies and non-APEC economies."

Concerted Unilateral Action

To achieve a consensus among those who support conditional MFN and those who support unconditional MFN, APEC tried to introduce the controversial idea of liberalization based on "concerted unilateral action" (CUA), a term coined by Hong Kong Trade Secretary Tony Miller. "I think what we are trying to explore here in APEC is a new type of trade liberalization process—voluntary yet concerted liberalization on a peer pressure basis," said MITI's senior official for APEC, Hidehiro Konno. "There are certainly suspicious voices among some members of this very Asian way."[15]

The United States was the most hesitant to rely on CUA, fearing that APEC will be unable to achieve comparability among individual liberalization plans. Washington argued that a reliance on such measures alone is impractical in the long term and could set back the region's negotiating position vis-à-vis the European Union. Ambassador Sandra Kristoff commented, "Basically, the 'C' and the 'A' of CUA are not convincing, leaving only 'U.' The US doesn't see much value in the 'U' alone."[16]

There was some speculation that the reason the United States opposed CUA was that Washington itself would be unable to make any meaningful commitments toward realizing the Bogor Declaration. APEC Executive Director Shojiro Imanishi charged that "the US has now made a U-turn in implementing a tariff-free Asia-Pacific region by the year 2020."[17] One American businessman surmised, "The US is hamstrung," because Congress was unlikely to acquiesce to any further concessions after it approved the Uruguay Round.[18] During a senior officials' meeting in early 1995, the United States also noted that unilateral tariff liberalization might be untenable for some nations because of domestic sectoral interests and a "lack of tariff reduction" to take such steps. The latter point most likely reflected the US administration's predicament in the wake of the Democratic Party's loss of the majority in both houses of Congress in the November 1994 elections. Some observers voiced skepticism that the White House could make unilateral concessions, especially in accelerating GATT agreements, in the antagonistic domestic political environment.[19] Others perceived that the problem was rooted in the White House itself: while the Republican Congress was interested in granting the negotiating authority, the Democratic administration resisted it unless there were explicit references to labor and environment issues. In a meeting with Japanese Prime Minister Tomiichi Murayama, Australia's Paul Keating conveyed his concerns about the United States' ability to liberalize through the APEC process.[20]

The United States vigorously denied charges that it was backing away from its Bogor commitments. "The United States' commitment to open and free trade and investment by 2010/2020 remains firm and has not changed," read a joint press release by the US Embassy in Singapore and the APEC Secretariat. "The US certainly has not backed out of the APEC free trade agreement, and continues to strongly support the goal of free and open trade and investment in Asia Pacific."[21]

While the administration was not likely to secure a reduction in formal trade barriers, according to one US official, recent efforts at deregulation in telecommunications, aviation, and financial services should be enough to show America's resolve.[22] The United States also proposed replacing the term "downpayment" with "initial action" to emphasize the liberalization of qualitative nontariff barriers, not only quantitative tariff barriers.[23] Rather than focusing on specific timetables for unilateral tariff reductions and the like, the United States shifted its emphasis to the idea of a "menu" of items that could include efforts at both liberalization and facilitation.

US efforts met with skepticism from many APEC partners, however. "The US position on liberalization is not based on a long-term perspective. They do not want a unilateral approach. At the same time, they do not want structure either," said one senior Japanese diplomat after the Sapporo SOM. "In other words, they want an *orizume bento* [à la carte lunch box) rather than a full-course meal."[24] Another Japanese diplomat concurred. "I think that the US has neither the will nor the ability to liberalize further," he said. "They still have a 30 to 40 percent tariff on textiles, 25 percent on trucks, and a double digit percentage on glass. They have continued to protect these areas, and Kantor even backtracked on the textile tariff cuts that Carla Hills promised in the Uruguay Round."[25]

Malaysia and Thailand in particular rejected the emphasis on prearranged comparability, often reminding members that APEC was not created as a GATT-style compulsory organization but rather a loose consultative body based on mutual reliance. Indonesia joined Malaysia in opposing the formal negotiations on proportionality advanced by Australia, New Zealand, and the United States.

While nearly all members officially shunned the idea of formal negotiations, there was the growing realization, as APEC's agenda became increasingly ambitious, that there would have to be some sort of negotiation process. Most countries, including Thailand, recognized that without some form of agreed-upon proportionality, there was a risk of free riding by members on the slower track. A compromise was worked out in the draft of the Osaka Action Agenda within the general principles section: "The overall comparability of members' liberalization and facilitation should be considered." The inclusion of the comparability language was widely seen as the result of pressure by the USTR, which was concerned about the repercussions from the US Congress if there was no reference to comparability in the Osaka document. Despite calls for unilateral liberalization, both Asian and Western officials noted the eventual need for a process that ensures balance and fairness.

In any case, the term CUA proved to be short-lived. It actually had an earlier incarnation at the International Monetary Fund (IMF), where, according to Hong Kong's SOM delegate Tony Miller, it held the completely unrelated meaning "big boys doing what they want to do."[26] While IMF's CUA was born as an epithet, APEC's version eventually took on negative connotations and was buried in favor of "concerted liberalization." However, the basic concept remained. The new approach emphasizes a division of liberalization into two parts. The first covers areas such as standards harmonization and the simplification of standards procedures, which would be handled collectively. The second part of the process covers areas such as deregulation and tariff reduction, which would be done in a voluntary and individual way. This compromise seemed to mollify the two sides of the debate, at least during the period leading up to Osaka. The action agenda worked out at the Sapporo meeting explicitly stated this two-tracked approach.

Three Pillars

At Bogor, the APEC leaders reemphasized that there were three pillars to the APEC process: liberalization, facilitation, and development. The relative weights each member has given each of these prongs varies widely. In the debate over trade liberalization and facilitation, China, for instance, has been relatively passive, yet it began to take a spokesperson's role and formulate a position on the question of development. At the Bogor summit, President Jiang argued, "We need a practical approach for APEC, and taking a uniform approach is impractical." While he approved of the plan to achieve liberalization by 2020, he noted that it was "necessary to examine the system and sectors of liberalization by considering the diverse development stages."

China has joined Indonesia, the Philippines, and other developing members in promoting the development aspects of the 1994 declaration. "China strongly insists . . . that the developing countries should be given special treatment," one Chinese delegate said at a SOM meeting, "and that technology transfer should be included in the work of the Committee on Trade and Investment."[27] Also at Bogor, Taiwan's representative, Vincent Siew, advanced President Lee Teng-hui's vision of an APEC program for "agricultural technical cooperation." Developing countries generally welcomed Japan's Partnership for Progress (PFP) proposal, recently announced in Jakarta by Foreign Minister Yohei Kono. In SOM meetings, China endorsed Japan's PFP proposal and launched an initiative for an "APEC Fund/Pool for Economic and Technical Co-operation."[28] But some advanced members, particularly the United States and New Zealand, were skeptical of Japan's ambitions for the project, as they did not sanction using APEC as a development assistance body. The United States originally pushed strongly for expansion in this direction with then–Secretary of State James Baker's proposal for a Partnership for Education, which was meant to build on existing ties between Asian and American universities and promote the exchange of students, professors, and researchers.[29] Eventually, the project was turned over to the US Agency for International Development, which created a database of Asians educated in American institutions. Budget restraints and a shift in priority toward trade, however, lessened US interest in using APEC as a vehicle for development assistance.

In particular, some American officials saw the PFP proposal as diversionary. As an American official put it, "I am very worried about Tokyo just buying up APEC through ODA [official development assistance] funds. . . . Partners for Progress could divert us from our main task and could turn APEC into a Singapore branch office of JETRO [MITI's Japan External Trade Organization]."[30] Despite objections from within the American trade community, both AID Administrator Brian Atwood and Undersecretary of State for Global Affairs Timothy Wirth endorsed the PFP, perhaps reflecting their desire to see an overall increase in development assistance through multilateral forums rather than on a bilateral basis, given America's relative inability to provide such aid.[31]

While not yet specifying details, the Osaka Action Agenda draft noted that APEC would consider "economic and technical cooperation necessary for liberalization and facilitation." At the Sapporo SOM meeting, delegates cautioned against the formation of a separate "PFP unit," preferring to give the responsibility for implementing assistance projects to the Secretariat so as to stem the proliferation of organizations within APEC.[32]

APEC and the WTO

There was greater consensus on enhancing Uruguay Round concessions through the APEC process. Several mid-sized economies, including Australia, Singapore, and Chile, entertained the American idea of cooperative action to enforce GATT agreements.

However, the question over GATT acceleration, and the so-called WTO-plus approach (liberalization beyond the coverage of the WTO), was more sensitive. The more open economies, such as Hong Kong, Chile, Australia, and Canada, pushed for a "downpayment" on Bogor using GATT commitments.

Canada, which Sandra Kristoff dubbed "the multilateral conscience of APEC," noted that progress in this area could send a signal to other regions in the runup to the 1996 WTO ministerial conference about APEC's seriousness.[33] "What we can do in APEC can have direct relevance and importance to further liberalization efforts in the WTO," said Canada's SOM official, Len Edwards.

On this issue, Malaysia and Thailand were joined by Korea and the United States, which saw strong domestic opposition to going beyond the measures signed at Marrakesh. Korea, of course, was concerned that further concessions, particularly in agriculture, would spark another round of domestic protests. They all suffered from the "fatigue" arising from Uruguay Round concessions and had their own domestic political problems. China, which was not a member of the WTO, downplayed the importance of furthering the GATT process, focusing more on winning membership, or at least the chance to gain the benefits of the global system.

Canada proposed using APEC to push the world toward agreement on the Government Procurement Agreement (GPA), a regime that has yet to be formally ratified by any APEC member states.[34] Canada has not found widespread support for this initiative, however. Malaysia and Honk Kong had already flat-out rejected membership in the GPA, and other countries have serious reservations.

Yet these Canadian efforts have failed to impress Australian officials. Canada's enthusiasm for the WTO and its relative inaction in APEC have led to a clash between Ottawa and Canberra, with Canberra decrying Canadian passivity. In a phone call with Canadian Prime Minister Jean Chrétien last year, Australian Prime Minister Keating reportedly asked, "By the way, why are your officials on APEC such assholes? They're not in the game, they're very negative, they're not playing."[35] An Australian diplomat said of the Canadians, "They sort of drift a little bit; they talk about linkages to the WTO and things like that. It's hard to understand. Canada confuses me."

Some APEC enthusiasts felt that Canada's efforts could detract from the APEC process. Japanese government officials were split on the point. A senior Foreign Ministry official with more than 30 years' experience negotiating the GATT said, "[T]o Canada, APEC is a movement for strengthening the WTO, strengthening the multilateral liberalization. Period! The expansive interest in liberalization swelling in Asia, particularly in ASEAN, should be channeled into energy to push APEC; indeed, APEC should be used as a 'trigger' to unleash it."[36] Sympathizing with the Canadian approach, a senior MITI official who was directly in charge of Japan's APEC policy was nonetheless cool to it. "We should concentrate on the APEC liberalization action plan now lest it be distracted" by other forums such as the WTO, he argued.[37]

"Osaka-Manila"

As the Osaka summit approached, members worked hard to find a compromise that would ensure that the meeting would make a substantive contribution toward realizing the goals laid out at Bogor. Prior to Sapporo SOM meeting, Prime Minister Murayama sent a personal letter to the other APEC leaders in which he emphasized that to "enhance the credibility to the liberalization efforts of APEC, we should all bring to Osaka a package of concrete initial actions." Specifically, he pointed out the need for progress on the "acceleration of the implementation of our respective UR commitments and the broadening and deepening of UR outcomes." Murayama also requested the personal "involvement and commitment of each leader" and expressed his hope that each "will instruct [their] Senior Officials to contribute constructively to the [Sapporo SOM] meeting."

A consensus emerged that action plans should not be confined to the Osaka meeting and both Osaka and Manila should be used as forums to work out APEC's action plan. SOM delegate Sandra Kristoff coined the term "Osaka-Manila" to refer to the closely tied agendas of the 1995 and 1996 meetings.[38] By August 1995, individual action plans were slated to begin January 1997. By the Sapporo SOM meeting in July 1995, APEC members had reached a consensus on three broad areas:[39]

- **General principles.** Members agreed in principle on such items as GATT consistency, consultations, nondiscrimination, and overall balance.

- **Time frames.** Each member will submit its plan at the 1996 Manila conference and commence liberalization in January 1997.

- **Guidelines for collective and individual actions.** Members have agreed to pursue a two-track approach using both unilateral and collective actions on trade liberalization and facilitation.

During the Sapporo SOM meeting, however, several problems remained unresolved:

- **Comprehensive action.** The United States has argued that APEC liberalization should cover all areas, while Japan and Korea have maintained that certain sectors such as agriculture should be excluded. Australia and New Zealand have advocated a flexible comprehensive approach that would allow some sectors to progress at a different pace than others.

- **Consultations.** Australia and the United States have maintained that consultations are needed prior to action in order to ensure comparability in each member's liberalization plans. Thailand has argued that it is sufficient to consult after liberalization has occurred.

- **MFN status**. The United States has argued that GATT rules of consistency are adequate to cover APEC's liberalization. China and Hong Kong have objected, urging APEC to adopt an unconditional approach to granting the benefits of APEC's liberalization to nonmembers.

- **Simultaneous starting dates**. China has claimed that the agreement to divide liberalization schedules between 2010 for advanced nations and 2020 for developing economies stipulates separate starting dates for each group.

- **Concerted Unilateral Action (CUA)**. While the United States has agreed that unilateral initiatives are necessary, it opposes the term "CUA."

The EPG recommended a number of new areas such as competition policy and standards harmonization for the APEC delegates to consider at both Osaka and Manila. A central theme of the 1995 EPG report was the importance of linking the various subregional trading arrangements that account or more then 64 percent of APEC's economic output. It suggested the adoption of an "open subregionalism" within APEC that would allow nonmembers to receive the benefits of arrangements such as NAFTA and AFTA on an MFN basis.

Notes

1. Personal interview with Bintoro Tjokroamidjojo, 18 July 1995.

2. Personal interview, 18 July 1995.

3. Personal interview, 18 July 1995.

4. Conversation with a diplomat stationed in Kuala Lumpur.

5. Malaysian Reservations to Bogor Declaration obtained by the author.

6. "APEC Economic Leaders' Declaration of Common Resolve," *ASEAN Economic Bulletin*, March 1995.

7. "Achieving the APEC Vision," Second Report of the Eminent Persons Group, August 1994, pp. 41–42.

8. Personal interview.

9. Personal interview with a participant.

10. Personal interview.

11. Personal interview with Indonesian diplomat.

12. Personal interview.

13. Chinese position paper for Sapporo APEC SOM meeting, 26 June 1995.

14. Personal interview with Wang Yusheng, 8 July 1995.

15. Personal interview with Hidehiro Konno, 26 June 1995.

16. *Straits Times*, 1 April 1995.

17. *Agence France Presse*, 21 June 1995.

18. *Inside U.S. Trade*, 2 June 1995.

19. *Inside U.S. Trade*, 2 June 1995.

20. Personal interview with a participant in the meeting.

21. Joint statement by the APEC Secretariat and the US Embassy, 21 June 1995, Singapore.

22. *Inside U.S. Trade*, 23 June 1995.

23. Personal interview with a participant in the meeting.

24. Personal interview, 8 July 1995.

25. Personal interview, 2 July 1995.

26. Personal interview with Tony Miller, 21 July 1995.

27. Personal interview with a participant.

28. Personal interview with a Chinese official.

29. Personal interview with US official.

30. Personal interview, 28 April 1995.

31. Personal interview with Hiroshi Hirabayashi, who spoke with both US officials, 21 June 1995.

32. Personal interview with a participant.

33. Remarks by Sandra Kristoff, George Washington University, Gaston Sigur Center for East Asian Studies, 23 June 1995.

34. Jeffrey J. Schott, *The Uruguay Round: An Assessment* (Washington: Institute for International Economics, 1994), p. 66.

35. Personal interview.

36. Personal interview, 3 July 1995.

37. Personal interview, 26 June 1995.

38. Personal interview with C. Fred Bergsten, 31 July 1995.

39. Personal interview with participants in the July 1995 Sapporo SOM meeting.

6

Hidden Agendas

APEC was born out of fear—fear of a unilateralist or isolationist America, fear of a balkanization of the world into competing economic blocs, and fear of the potential death of the GATT-centered world trading system. It was no coincidence that the strongest initiatives for APEC's founding came from Japan and Australia. Both countries faced similar threats from the emerging forces at the end of the Cold War. Both nations also traditionally relied politically, militarily, and economically on the United States, making them especially vulnerable to an aggressive or inward-focused America. The two nations were highly trade-dependent as well and would share the benefits of the GATT system more than most of their trading partners. The fact that neither was a member of any regional bloc made the prospect of a failure of the GATT round even more dangerous.

Japan and Australia were not alone in these fears, however. Each of the founding members of APEC found themselves vulnerable in the new world order. America became increasingly reliant on East Asian export markets, as well as East Asian investment capital to finance its current account deficits. Southeast Asia found itself with a range of new competitors for markets and investment dollars, as formerly communist nations in Europe and East Asia, with their highly developed infrastructure and educated populations, made the transition to capitalism and Latin American nations such as Chile and Mexico opened up to free trade. Aside from Japan and Australia, Korea probably faced the biggest dilemma in the new environment. Facing pressure both from the rapidly industrializing economies to the south and from technologically advanced Japan, Korea was in a highly sensitive position both economically and politically. As an export-driven economy, Korea was dependent on open foreign markets and particularly defenseless against unilateralism, especially from America, which guaranteed its security against its unpredictable neighbor, North Korea. Wedged between the behemoths of China, Japan, and Russia, Korea has always played a delicate game and has seen globalization as its only viable economic and political alternative.

While the changes in the late 1980s presented serious challenges to APEC members, they also offered opportunities. The growing economic interdependence meant that cooperation in areas such as trade facilitation and macroeconomic coordination was becoming increasingly important. Substantial private-sector economic linkages also made a regional economic dialogue feasible, despite long-standing political tensions, such as those between Seoul and Beijing, and increased the likelihood of peace and stability. The economic pressures of the free market have taught many protectionist nations, such as Indonesia and China, the importance of liberalization and deregulation for their nations' continued prosperity. Smaller, trade-dependent nations quickly saw the value in the APEC theory of "open regionalism," which would give them enhanced leverage as well as encourage foreign investment and secure export markets abroad.

All of these factors led the nations of the Asia Pacific to form a community, but Asia Pacific economic cooperation was primarily born out of a changing world economic order and an uncertain power balance. Though the concepts behind it were far from original or novel, Asia Pacific economic cooperation was an idea whose time had clearly come.

After the intellectual barriers to cooperation were breached in 1989, the 12 original members began to recognize six major areas that the organization would need to address in the new economic and political landscape:

- The most immediate issue was the completion of the stalled Uruguay Round of the GATT and the maintenance and strengthening of the global trading system.

- Related to this, but less explicit, was the need to discourage the formation of regional blocs, particularly in Europe and North America, but also potentially within East Asia.

- Within the Asia Pacific, the greatest short-term challenge was continued bilateral US-Japan trade friction, which threatened to disrupt the economic and political stability of the region as a whole. Most countries wanted to defuse it.

- Over the longer term, APEC members also recognized the need to engage China, an emerging economic powerhouse, as a productive and cooperative member of the Asia Pacific.

- Most Asia Pacific nations saw APEC as a means to retain American commitment to the region, both for security and economic reasons.

- Some countries perceived political benefits from APEC participation. This has been especially true of China, which has seen APEC as a means of winning support for membership in the World Trade Organization (WTO), and Taiwan, which has seen APEC membership as another step in increasing its international prestige and acceptance. Some also wanted to discuss political issues more freely and informally,a function they found undeveloped in the region.

Impact on the Global Trade Negotiations

One of the primary goals of the participants at Punta del Este, Uruguay, when they launched the Uruguay Round of the GATT in 1986 was to discourage the rising tide of protectionism that had emerged since the Tokyo Round was completed in the 1970s.[1] This endeavor was particularly important to the exporting countries of the Asia Pacific, which were likely to bear the brunt of rising protectionist urges in Europe and North America. The stakes were so high in the region, particularly for Asian countries, that many APEC members committed to measures that caused severe domestic instability, such as rice liberalization in Japan and Korea. APEC collectively supported a successful Uruguay Round at each of its ministerial conferences and at the two special meetings in Vancouver in 1990 and 1992, which were called solely to urge member states to find areas of flexibility to facilitate the round's successful conclusion.

It is widely accepted that APEC's show of unity paid off. "[T]he additional liberalization offers that APEC developed at its Seattle summit in November 1993 made an important contribution to the subsequent success of the Uruguay Round," said Eminent Persons Group Chairman C. Fred Bergsten.[2] Almost all the leaders at the 1994 Bogor meeting subscribed to this observation. "Looking back at the Seattle meeting, we were able to make a stronger declaration toward Europe, as the Uruguay Round talks were at such a critical period," Korean President Kim Young Sam said during the 1994 Bogor summit.[3]

Australian Prime Minister Paul Keating was even more forthright on this point: "But I can say, and many other people have said this too, that if it weren't for the Blake Island meeting, we wouldn't have got the GATT signed."[4] When Fred Bergsten asked German GATT negotiator Lorenz Schomerus after the Uruguay Round why Europe abandoned its earlier demands, he answered, "The chief determinant of the successful conclusion of the Uruguay Round was the APEC summit in Seattle; they sent us a clear message. You had an alternative, and we did not."[5] Since the Seattle summit, Europe has begun to aggressively pursue direct talks with

East Asia, fearful of being locked out of the dynamic region. This kind of dialogue could add another element to the ongoing process of global economic integration. One positive result of the APEC process was that it drew European attention to the Asia Pacific, an area the continent had long neglected.

The effectiveness of APEC's efforts in pushing global liberalization forward led some officials in APEC to call for a new "Singapore Round" of the GATT to finish up business left out of the Uruguay Round. The Bogor Declaration could be a manifestation of such a concept, should countries agree on accelerating or surpassing commitments made during the Uruguay Round. There were suggestions that APEC should apply itself to areas such as competition policy, government procurement, and standards harmonization.

NAFTA and EAEC

APEC support for the GATT process has been seen by many as a counterforce to the formation of regional blocs in Europe and North America. The specific threats posed by the two blocs were somewhat different. While the European Union was basically defensive, erecting barriers to imports in order to protect European industries, the United States had considered expanding its Canada-US Free Trade Agreement to individual countries in the Asia Pacific, potentially causing trade to be diverted away from nonmember nations. MITI's 1988 Sakamoto Report specifically warned of the possible effects that both of these initiatives would have on Japan, and MITI representatives found that many of Japan's neighbors, particularly Australia and Korea, had made a similar analysis of their own situations. In Australia's case, a 1986 evaluation of the potential for a US-Australian FTA, written by Professor Richard Snape, warned of the potentially damaging effects such an agreement would have on Australia's overall trade relations and on the world trading system at large.[6]

When the US proposal first was circulated during the Reagan administration, Washington severely underestimated the negative reaction it would receive in the region. Far from embracing the proposal, most Asia Pacific nations saw the prospect of a bilateral free trade agreement with the world's largest economy as a clear threat, particularly given America's proclivity toward unilateral trade actions.

The only real exception was entrepôt Singapore, which has expressed its interest several times in entering into a NAFTA-type arrangement. "It will be good if NAFTA is expanded to incorporate countries in East Asia," Prime Minister Goh Chok Tong said. "Then NAFTA will not divide the Pacific Ocean down the middle."[7] Goh has also argued that APEC should integrate all NAFTA-type subregional arrangements and serve as an umbrella organization to harness the gains made by smaller groups. "It is desirable for APEC to link up with NAFTA and other subregional arrangements like AFTA and the Australia and New Zealand CER [Closer Economic Relations group] since their goals are the same," he said, but adds, "Do not expect any early decision."[8] Singapore's neighbors are not so confident of the benefits of tying their economies so closely with America's. Rather than as a step to bolster free trade, many view America's actions as a sinister plot to improve its own terms of trade.

Some observers have suggested that NAFTA might serve as a policy caucus within APEC, but North American officials are adamant that no premeeting consultations among the three trade partners have taken place. One senior US official argued that the NAFTA members have no need to do so: "I can tell you that there is not a NAFTA caucus within APEC. I don't think that we would want that. The overall process is so transparent that there is no need for it."[9] A senior Mexican official concurred: "We have no caucus; we have no consultative status on the discussion in APEC."[10]

The word "caucus" is a sensitive one for American officials as Mahathir's EAEC also uses the term. It would be very difficult for the United States to deny Asia its own grouping if North America had one. The United States was severely criticized by some Asian countries when it convened a special "friends of the chair" meeting in Honolulu in March 1995 to rally for the cause of liberalization. The attendees were Japan, Australia, Indonesia, Singapore, Hong Kong, and the United States—all members of APEC's "pro-liberalization" school. The fact that they had held a secret, informal meeting was later leaked to other APEC members.

Fears of a North American bloc have subsided somewhat with the strengthening of APEC. However, US officials have not yet fully ruled out the idea of offering NAFTA extensions to select countries in the Asia Pacific. This has been viewed as a "divide and rule" strategy or an "encirclement policy" in Japan. Hence, Asian countries have countered with the veiled threat of an East Asian grouping.

Not so veiled was Prime Minister Mahathir's EAEC proposal, which so effectively captured Asianist sentiment that even former Thai Prime Minister Anand Panyarachun, an avowed internationalist, defended it. "I don't see anything wrong in theory about having an East Asian Economic Caucus within APEC. . . ." he said, explaining that caucuses are prevalent in the United Nations context and that the EAEC's agenda need not even be strictly confined to APEC matters. According to Anand, the debate over EAEC's legitimacy was actually precipitated by a "conflict of personalities" between Mahathir and US Secretary of State James Baker that "was allowed to developed into a conflict of policy."[11]

ASEAN has sought to chart a new course, independent of American involvement, as four recent initiatives have illustrated. The first was the proposal for ASEAN economic ministers' (AEM) meetings between ASEAN trade and economic ministers and their counterparts in Tokyo,

Seoul, and Beijing. The controversy that this provoked in APEC was epitomized by US Ambassador to Japan Walter Mondale's criticism of the AEM as a "backdoor EAEC."[12] The second concerned the Australian-proposed ASEAN-ANZCER (Australia–New Zealand Closer Economic Relations agreement talks held in September 1995. The third was the advent in 1994 of an "Asians-only" luncheon at the ASEAN Post-Ministerial Conference (PMC). In the 1995 meeting in Brunei, Vietnam joined the gathering, which already included the six ASEAN nations plus China, Japan, and Korea.

The fourth was Singaporean Prime Minister Goh Chok Tong's proposal to hold an AEM-EU summit in 1996. Goh rejected charges that the summit was an attempt to form an exclusionary bloc, explaining that it is only intended to close the Europe-Asia side of the global economic triangle and thereby promote stability. Former US Secretary of State Baker seemed to agree, greeting it as a natural step in Europe-Asia relations. Nonetheless, some senior US officials have been decidedly wary.[13] "We certainly don't object to heads of State getting together," one official said, hastening to explain her reservations: "It's a derivative of [EAEC]. . . . It's a question of institutionalization of [EAEC]." The same official remarked that it was generally believed that the real intent of the exercise was to massage Mahathir's ego. ". . .[A]t heart this is Mahathir-spurred; this is an effort to try to placate Mahathir."

The EAEC, to some extent, offered these nations leverage against unilateral American power. "We will surely be taken lightly by the United States if we do not have bargaining power," said one American-trained Japanese trade official of the power of the EAEC concept, "because that is how Americans see the world."[14] Some speculate that the EAEC proposal led Washington to change its focus from NAFTA extensions toward a more comprehensive open regionalism through APEC. While American officials downplay the EAEC's influence, a Clinton administration official admitted that the EAEC "forced people to realize that in the long term we want to be a part of this region, that we are a Pacific nation and we need to build those ties, and if we don't there is a cost."[15]

By the mid-1990s, however, its effect was almost negligible. While the EAEC may have been useful to keep America's interest in APEC alive in earlier years, the rationale for the EAEC's continued existence became questionable after the successful completion of the Uruguay Round and the Bogor Declaration, according to Richard Wilson of the Asia Foundation. "Prior to these developments, the EAEC could have had some utility as a bargaining group, but any such role now would almost certainly prove divisive," he said.[16]

Still, there are many officials in Asia who do not subscribe to this view. The emergence of various de facto "Asians-only" forums has defused the passions swirling around the EAEC. The post–Cold War era has witnessed a struggle for new linkages. It is increasingly difficult to demarcate permanent camps within APEC, and it is still unclear how a solid caucus or group will survive in this age of mushrooming meetings (some call this trend "conference-building measures" instead of "confidence-building measures"). The APEC process must be enriched by these new forums, not diluted by them.

US-Japan Disputes

At the Bogor meeting, President Suharto commented that "trade disputes between Japan and the United States have a bad influence on all members of APEC."[17] This concern became especially acute when the Clinton administration began its strong push for "results-oriented" policies and "quantitative indicators." American use of its section 301 trade law, which allows for retaliation against countries the US Trade Representative finds to be violating free trade principles, is of particular concern in the region. In joining Japan's 1995 challenge in the WTO of threatened American sanctions over auto parts, Australian Trade Minister Bob McMullan explained that while Australia was "not taking sides in this dispute, we are not in favor of unilateral action as a means to deal with trade disputes."[18]

In a May 1995 meeting between Australian Prime Minister Paul Keating and Japan's Tomiichi Murayama in Tokyo, Keating advised Japan to push hard on APEC to lessen bilateral tensions. "[I]f Japan actively conducts itself toward the goals of the Bogor Declaration, it will cost much for the United States to resort to section 301," urged Keating. "Sitting in the special seat as APEC's chair, Japan should try to deal with the United States through trade liberalization and facilitation of APEC."[19]

Some have begun to argue for using APEC to help define these situations and reach a commonly accepted understanding. "We want the United States and Japan to multilateralize their bilateral disputes and to cushion the tension which has been a recent part of the relationship," a senior Singaporean diplomat said. "It is the reason why we support Japan's idea that within APEC maybe we can have some form of conflict resolution."[20]

A certain amount of resistance can be expected from the US side, which was reluctant to move too quickly to establish any kind of multilateralism, particularly a resolution mechanism. As one US official explained, "In the current administration, [USTR] Mickey [Kantor] and [Deputy USTR] Charlene Barshefsky have been more cautious and concerned about losing bilateral leverage."

Some American business interests opposed such a body as well. As one industry official explained, the combination of a dispute settlement mechanism and the 10- to 20-year time frame for liberalization in APEC "basically sets up the possibility of providing a shield against bilateral action."[21] In the foreseeable future, clashes between multilateralism and unilateralism will continue to haunt the United States, straining US-Japan relations and APEC as a whole. Australian Prime Minister Paul Keating remains optimistic, arguing that President Clinton's "instincts are for multilateral engagement of the US in Asia, but," he noted, "institutionally . . . probably most of his advisers still are in favor of unilateralism."[22]

The Challenge of Engaging China

As in the case of bilateral US-Japan tensions, APEC's record on engaging China has been mixed. At the Bangkok ministerial, Chinese Foreign Minister Qian Qichen noted that China's trade with and investment from the APEC region represented three-quarters and four-fifths, respectively, of its total trade and investment.[23] He stressed China's rapid economic opening and its strategy of extending its growing economic dynamism from the coastal provinces in waves of economic development.

Most members of APEC have experienced dualistic relationships with China. While investors and businessmen continue to see many opportunities in the giant emerging market, policymakers increasingly fear the impact of a rising China on regional political dynamics. In the past several years China has faced many obstacles to closer ties with the region, despite efforts on both sides to smooth the relationships. China continues to have territorial conflicts with nearly every one of its Asian neighbors, the most serious with members of the Association of Southeast Asian Nations (ASEAN) over the South China Sea.

The Taiwan issue has surfaced as one of the most explosive, as more and more Taiwanese people demand independence, or at least further autonomy, from the mainland. Worsening its international standing further has been the continued friction with Washington over human rights, missile proliferation, and America's warming relations with Taiwan. China's international reputation, particularly in the West, has still far from recovered from the 1989 Tiananmen Square incident, and its continued harassment of dissidents has kept relations between Washington and Beijing authorities chilly.

All of these international problems came at a time when China was seeking to further integrate itself into the global economy. For the past several years China has been making a bid to join the WTO but has been frustrated by American and, to a lesser extent, Asian and European objections. Most WTO members have rejected China's claims that it, by virtue of the Nationalists' signature in 1947, is a founding member of the GATT. They prefer that China receive membership under the current rules, including Article 19, which would allow members to exempt Chinese imports from most-favored nation (MFN) status in certain sectors.[24]

China's strong insistence on unconditional MFN status and its unique position as a member of APEC but not of the WTO have deepened the concerns of trading partners such as the United States, which argues against unconditional MFN in APEC liberalization. During a 1993 meeting with Australian Prime Minister Keating, former Japanese Prime Minister Kiichi Miyazawa expressed his doubts about China's ability to commit effectively to APEC given its lack of status in the GATT.[25] The United States has already laid out a number of steps China must take before it will acquiesce to Beijing's ascension to the WTO, particularly in the areas of economic reform and deregulation. The demands placed on China are much higher than those Washington has sought from other WTO applicants, and there are few Beijing can easily meet.[26] At the same time, on a bilateral basis Washington has vigorously pursued China on a number of trade and investment-related policies it claims discriminate against US companies.

With its immense size, huge economic and military potential, and uncertain political situation, China will likely be the most formidable challenge to APEC in the long term.

The American Presence

Asia Pacific nations have seen APEC as a means of preventing America's departure. Facing an uncertain security environment in the Asia Pacific, Asian leaders have been particularly keen to continue American military engagement in the region. For its part, the United States has reaffirmed its commitment to the region on numerous occasions and expressed its endorsement of multilateralism as a means of interaction in the Asia Pacific.

Yet many have argued that the United States has not developed a comprehensive policy toward the Asia Pacific in the current environment, and thus the prospects for its continued engagement remain clouded. "[T]he fundamental issue is that the United States has never had an Asia policy," argued former Australian Prime Minister Bob Hawke. "Historically, relations of the United States towards the countries of Asia were simply a residual of its Cold War policy: the containment of the Soviet Union."[27] Indeed, with the demise of the communist threat, the need and will for a continued US military presence is being increasingly questioned by some politicians and commentators in Washington, especially given America's declining relative economic position in the region.

Some have speculated that the US debate over whether to reduce its global military role has colored much of its stance toward APEC. Leaders such as Singapore's Lee Kuan Yew have suggested that the only way to ensure America's continued interest is to liberalize markets and allow increased economic interaction: "If East Asia becomes increasingly prosperous and the US does not, I can't see the US Congress voting the necessary funds to renew the Seventh Fleet and all the other things necessary to continue its role in Asia."[28] Australian Prime Minister Keating notes that the waning American security commitment to the Asia Pacific that he perceives is due in part to inadequate investment interests in the region,[29] and he expects that, with increased American investment and trade ties, the United States will base its commitment not on "some basis of altruism only, but . . . to protect its interests as well."

Given the significant costs and intangible short-term benefits of engagement, however, American politicians and commentators are increasingly calling for a reexamination of America's security role in the Asia Pacific. Some have called on the United States to abandon its commitment to Asia's security entirely. The US administration, which has had to contend with isolationist forces represented by Ross Perot and Patrick Buchanan, has started to look for something in return for their presence.

In Seattle, Clinton alluded to such a linkage in a speech: "We do not intend to bear the cost of our military presence in Asia and the burdens of regional leadership only to be shut out of the benefits of growth that stability brings. It is not right. It is not in the long-term interest of our Asian friends."[30]

The public debate over America's military commitment to the region has spilled over into administration discussions as well. During the Cold War, the institutional strength of the Defense Department prevented bilateral trade disputes from interfering with US security interests in the region. Today, this institutional barrier has largely diminished. The tension within the administration over the issue of military and economic linkage was illustrated by US Ambassador to Japan Walter Mondale's criticism of a comment by White House spokesman Mike McCurry drawing a tie between American economic and military commitments to the region.[31]

Such sentiments give the unfortunate impression that the United States is offering its military might in exchange for economic concessions from its trading partners. The result could be that long-term security is sacrificed to the pursuit of short-term trade disputes and that subsequently there could be a breakdown in the region's stability and thus its prosperity.

Calls for a direct linkage of American trade and security policies could engender a new and dangerous game. A reduced American military presence or the threat of it could jeopardize APEC and send the Asia Pacific down a path toward a damaging bloc regionalism or, worse, military hegemony. And several American officials understand this risk. "Linking security to trade as a tactic for short-term gain risks the overall relationship," Joseph Nye has argued. "The linkage between economics and security is more effective as a strategic reminder in the back of leaders' minds than in a short-term tactical sense."[32] Robert Zoellick made a similar calculation in his support of APEC and his explicit rejection of Mahathir's EAEC. "Part of what he [Mahathir] failed to recognize was that I was doing this [backing the US role in APEC] as much to keep my own country engaged as well as to have access there," he said.[33]

Both Nye's and Zoellick's comments reflect a strong, long-range view of American interests in the region. The continued stability of East Asia is critical for America's long-term prosperity. The short-term use of threats to withdraw militarily from the region may be effective in winning specific concessions on relatively minor market issues, but such actions would sour America's relationship with the region and lead many countries to reconsider their basic orientation.

Political Dimensions

APEC has taken on significant political dimensions since the leaders' meetings were initiated. There has been a growing tendency within APEC to address the underlying issues discussed in this chapter through either informal chats on social occasions or bilateral political discussions during APEC meetings. After all, a gathering of political leaders is itself an inherently political act. Indeed, Australian Prime Minister Keating emphasized the political significance, saying, "There [is] no other body where the prime minster of Japan and the president of Korea or the president of China or the president of the United States can meet together; outside the UN there is no other body."[34] Hong Kong's APEC representative, Tony Miller, pointed out that "one of the interesting things about APEC is that it is the only forum in which all three [Chinas] sit at the table simultaneously."[35] This attempt to multilateralize the relationship and develop personal ties among the leaders is exactly what Keating had in mind for his brainchild, the leaders' summits.

The formal sessions during APEC meetings, however, have remained apolitical, focusing solely on economic, development, and trade issues. This more narrow concentration has enhanced the reputation of the forum and reassured smaller member states that the forum will not be transformed into a tool of the larger nations. It has also facilitated the participation of the region's three giants—Japan, China, and the United States— which need not worry about being boxed into a smothering political pact.

At the same time, the apolitical nature of APEC meetings has allowed for bilateral consultations that would be impossible in other forums; paradoxically, an apolitical forum can enable members to engage politically. A testament to this is Taiwan's ministerial-level contact with the United States and Japan. Taiwan has seen APEC as a key part of its "diplomatic offensive" to gain more international recognition and has strategically chosen its coordinator for UN policy to simultaneously serve as its APEC SOM official. Even more significant have been bilateral meetings between

President Clinton and China's President Jiang Zemin that have been held under the cover of APEC leaders' meetings.

While valuable to both sides, the Clinton-Jiang summits have had especially strong political overtones for Beijing, which at times takes a zero-sum perspective in international relations. One Chinese official commented to his Japanese counterpart that "the most important part of the Seattle APEC summit was the bilateral meeting between the leaders of the United States and China." In China, the media suddenly found itself flushed with APEC fever.[36]

US officials sometimes felt frustrated with China's tendency to politicize that meeting. As one senior State Department official said, "Yes, we lost some negotiating strength by having invited them [to Seattle]. . . . They, I think, chose to take it as us losing capital, rather than an outstretched hand. I think that it's too bad."[37]

The automaticity embedded in the annual APEC summits has contributed to a better bilateral rapport between countries, particularly the United States and China. But scheduling bilateral meetings has been at times politically touchy. As APEC summits last only two days, there is a limit on the numbers of leaders that will be able to meet separately. At Bogor, for instance, Clinton was able to hold bilateral discussions with only four leaders: Japan's Murayama, Korea's Kim, China's Jiang, and the Indonesian host Suharto. This selection was interpreted as an insult to Malaysia's Mahathir, who had requested a meeting with Clinton during bilateral talks the two leaders held in Washington the preceding July. Clinton's rejection of talks in Jakarta with the Malaysian leader led some observers to speculate that it was a punishment to Mahathir for not attending the Seattle meeting.

While it is tempting to use APEC as a forum for formal or informal political consultations, there is a risk that such an agenda will derail the APEC process. So far, there has been a general consensus to delink political and economic issues in the Asia Pacific. Yet this consensus is delicate. Both the United States and China have used threats of economic sanctions or trade retaliation in times of political stress. Bringing these potentially dangerous disputes into the APEC process could encourage one side or another to use APEC's reliance on consensus as a means to further its political goals. There is also a potential that China could use its position within APEC to punish Taipei and its partners if political links between Taiwan and its APEC partners begin to augment the existing strictly economic ties.

In one way or another, APEC has sought to address each of the motivations discussed above. It has been particularly successful in strengthening the global trading system, both through its strong support of the Uruguay Round and its commitment to open regionalism. APEC has also served to discourage the formation of strong regional economic blocs, particularly within the Asia Pacific. It has been less effective in defusing US-Japan trade friction by dealing with it on a multilateral basis, although the current discussions of a dispute settlement mechanism hold out hope for the future. APEC's record on integrating the Chinese economy has been similarly mixed. China has moved forward with economic reforms and has strengthened its economic ties with APEC countries. But growing bilateral tensions between China and several member states have complicated the process of bringing China into the Asia Pacific community.

In the meantime, the United States has remained strongly engaged. Washington's commitment to keep a minimum of 100,000 troops in the region has been seen as a strong message that it will not turn away from the region, despite continued economic friction. However, a linkage strategy between America's security umbrella and economic concessions could pose a serious threat to the region's stability if it were tactically and directly employed.

Finally, the effects of the political dialogue within APEC remain unclear. The guarantee of annual contact among leaders was clearly a plus. However, while successive APEC summit meetings have provided a forum for Sino-US summit meetings, the quality of dialogue between Beijing and Washington has not seemed to improve noticeably. The rhetoric exchanged between Taipei and Beijing during the Seattle meeting was not a hopeful sign either. Beijing's hopes for using APEC to enhance its chances of entering the WTO remain unfulfilled.

APEC should maintain its paradoxical apolitical political dialogues in a subtle way. Perhaps the most important role for APEC is not as a forum for political debate but rather to continue to serve as an arena for intellectual interaction on regional economic issues. By bringing together the 18 leaders of the APEC forum in a discussion of areas of common interest and mutual benefit, mistrust and suspicion will gradually lessen.

Notes

1. Robert Baldwin and J. David Richardson, eds., *The Uruguay Round and Beyond: Problems and Prospects,* (Cambridge, MA: National Bureau of Economic Research, 1991), p. 1.

2. C. Fred Bergsten, "APEC and World Trade," *Foreign Affairs* 72, no. 3 (May/June 1994): 20.

3. Personal interview with a participant.

4. Personal interview with Paul Keating, 6 July 1995.

5. Story related to the author by C. Fred Bergsten.

6. Richard Snape, *Should Australia Seek a Free Trade Agreement with the United States?* Discussion Paper 86/1 (Canberra: Economic Planning Advisory Council, 1986).

7. Personal interview with Goh Chok Tong, 18 July 1995.

8. Personal interview with Goh.

9. Personal interview, 10 May 1995.

10. Personal interview, 8 July 1995.

11. Personal interview, 28 August 1995.

12. Mondale's comments were related to the author by MITI Minister Ryutaro Hashimoto.

13. Personal interview with James Baker, 30 June 1995.

14. Personal interview, 3 July 1995.

15. Personal interview, 27 April 1995.

16. Richard Wilson, "Subregional Groups Within APEC," *NBR Analysis* (April 1995), p. 40.

17. Personal interview with a participant.

18. *Inside U.S. Trade*, 2 June 1995.

19. Personal interview with a participant.

20. Personal interview, 18 May 1995.

21. *Inside U.S. Trade*, 2 June 1995.

22. Personal interview, 6 July 1995.

23. Speech by Qian Qichen, Bangkok APEC Ministerial Meeting, 11 September 1992.

24. Nicholas Lardy, *China in the World Economy*, (Washington: Institute for International Economics, 1994) pp. 44–47.

25. Personal interview with a participant.

26. Lardy, pp. 135–36.

27. Personal interview, 20 June 1995.

28. *Australian Financial Review*, 23 May 1995.

29. Personal interview, 6 July 1995.

30. Speech by President Bill Clinton to the Seattle APEC Host Committee, 19 November 1993, Seattle, Washington.

31. Personal interview with a White House official. Transcript of White House press briefing by Mike McCurry, *US Newswire*, 16 May 1995.

32. Personal interview, 22 May 1995.

33. Personal interview, 20 July 1995.

34. Personal interview, 6 July 1995.

35. Personal interview, 21 July 1995.

36. Personal interview with a Japanese diplomat.

37. Personal interview, 19 May 1995.

7

Politics of Liberalization

The issues that APEC has addressed have changed as it has developed. Today, APEC leaders recognize three broad agenda areas to be addressed: trade and investment liberalization trade facilitation, and economic cooperation.

The greatest focus has been placed on liberalization. No other issue in the organization's six-year existence has caused as much debate as APEC's attempt to realize the Bogor vision. The discussions over liberalization have focused on four themes:

- **Liberalization versus cooperation.** This issue is basically a North-South dispute over emphasis. Advanced countries have favored pushing liberalization first, seeing APEC mainly as an organization that can be used to open markets and bring down barriers. Developing nations are not as secure in their ability to compete in a fully open market and therefore have favored the use of APEC to win concessions from advanced nations on areas such as technology transfer, human resources development, and technical assistance.

- **MFN status.** APEC has become divided over the question of the circumstances under which it should grant most-favored nation (MFN) status to nonmember economies. Some have pushed for conditional MFN, forcing nonmember economies to grant reciprocal concessions in order to enjoy the benefits of APEC liberalization. Others have favored unconditional MFN, viewing APEC as a model through which the global trading system can be strengthened, regardless of the potential for nonmembers to enjoy undeserved benefits—the so-called "open region-alism" argument.

■ **The liberalization process**. There are a number of competing options for achieving the Bogor goal of free markets by the year 2020. The most serious rift comes from the choice between unilateral and collective action. The United States has stressed collective actions both because of its own wariness of the potential to achieve balance through voluntary measures and domestic political pressure to achieve concessions from trade partners in return for American liberalization. There are a number of other process issues such as sectoral limits, review processes, and timetables.

■ **The liberalization vision**. Underlying many of the differences in process are the conflicting visions of member governments on the future of the global trading system. Some members see APEC as merely a process to bolster the WTO. Others see it as either a potential EU-style trading organization, an autonomous free trade area, or an umbrella for subregional trading blocs. There has yet to be a real consensus on the long-term use of the APEC process.

Liberalization versus Cooperation

Driving the Bogor Declaration and efforts to fulfill it has been a growing philosophical convergence in the region on free trade. As economies diversify and the competition for markets and investment becomes more keen, economists and policymakers increasingly see the benefits of opening up their economy to trade and investment. The need to open markets is becoming increasingly apparent to Asian nations, and leaders have sought to convince their citizens of this need. Philippine EPG member Jesus Estanislao noted that among members of the Philippine Chamber of Commerce and Industry, long a bastion of protectionism, 70 to 75 percent of its members in a 1995 poll favored further liberalization.[1]

Indonesia, historically APEC's most protected economy, has launched an ambitious effort of market opening, starting with tariff reductions on more than 6,000 products. While Jakarta has framed its recent moves in the context of the Bogor Declaration, most observers credit the change to internal Indonesian politics. One Indonesian scholar noted that those pushing for liberalization had "another agenda to actually keep free trade, because the only way we can get rid of these monopolies of the sons and daughters and cronies is to deregulate the economy."[2]

Liberalization has only been made possible recently as Indonesians have become more self-assured in their ability to survive in the global market. This sense is partially the result of Indonesia's successful liberalization efforts in the early 1980s, after the collapse of oil prices. "We had to replace import-substitution policies with an export-oriented strategy," said former Trade Minister Arifin Siregar. "In order to boost our exports, we had to be competitive. That's why we started to deregulate the whole thing in 1983."[3] Yet, even as Indonesia becomes confident of its viability as a competitor in the open market, it still harbors some uncertainty about integrating with the "North." Thai EPG member Narongchai Akrasanee observed that even President Suharto, an avid proponent of APEC's liberalization, is of two mind: "What he talked about at the Non-Aligned Movement and what he talked about at APEC were completely different." Narongchai attributed this apparent contradiction so the "dilemma" faced by rapidly developing countries.

The issue of the pace of liberalization underlines a division that still strained APEC even after the compromise on a two-tracked approach: that between the less developed countries (LDCs), which favor a slower approach, and developed countries, which favor rapid action to bring down trade barriers.

Most developed countries see advancing free trade as the primary purpose of APEC. On the other hand, developing nations hope to get trade concessions and technology as a precursor to greater economic opening. Japan has been more sympathetic toward LDCs. An internal MITI memo noted that the United States was always pushing for a level playing field, but in the Asia Pacific, it argued, such a strategy is "like forcing Minor League players to play in Major League games."[4]

From Bogor to Osaka, the discussions on liberalization have been seen as a conflict between developed countries and less developed countries. However, the divide is not necessarily always North-South. It has often reflected the interests of particular members. Korea and to a lesser extent Japan has been very sensitive to pressures to open its rice market.

Western members also face domestic problems in liberalizing and deregulating their economies. New Zealand Prime Minister James Bolger argued at the Seattle meeting that those who opposed liberalizing trade "are not bad people but people who are fearful that their lives will be threatened in the sluggish economy."[5] President Clinton concurred, noting that "some suspect that growth in the Asia Pacific region is restraining that of the developed countries in other regions and depriving the middle-class incomes in those countries."[6] The anxieties of Europeans in particular were most likely on his mind when he said this. There is a perception, especially in the United States, that the Asian economic model is fundamentally different; this perception underlies the US position that any liberalization should be coordinated and reciprocal.

There are dangers to a one-sided push for open markets in all APEC nations. A public perception of external pressure could derail liberalization in developing countries. The 1974 Malari incident (discussed more fully in chapter 12), in which Indonesians rioted against the visit of Japanese Prime Minister Kakuei Tanaka, awoke in many Asian policymakers, including the Japanese, a feeling that moving toward liberalization too fast might invite social unrest—a sentiment that lingers some 20 years later.

For some LDCs, particularly Malaysia, Thailand, and China, market opening must not appear to be externally induced for political reasons. Antiliberalization groups sometimes try to portray the conflicts as pro-West or pro-Asian. The backers of the East Asian Economic Caucus (EAEC) in Japan and Korea, for instance, are largely those who oppose rapid liberalization. In the case of the Philippines, Secretary of the Department of Trade and Industry (DTI) José Concepcion's comment to Richard Woolcott in 1989 over the need for an "Asia for Asians" likely stemmed, in part, from DTI's traditional opposition to liberalization outside the ASEAN context.

Even in Indonesia, Suharto-sanctioned liberalization has maintained a balance with development. Coordinating Minister Hartarto explained that both liberalization and cooperation have been critical in Indonesia's case. "For Indonesia we have emphasized small and medium-sized enterprises," Hartarto noted. As Hartarto also pointed out, these businesses are owned predominantly by indigenous Indonesian *pribumi* as opposed to Indonesia's large companies, which are mainly controlled by ethnic Chinese. Liberalization had predominantly benefited the latter group at the expense of the politically important former.

Developing countries face a dilemma, however, in that while they need to protect their infant industries, they also need to attract foreign investment and technology transfer in order to become more competitive. Thus, in order to overcome the developing countries' sensitivities to liberalization, some have suggested the need to strengthen the domestic industries of less developed nations in exchange for their cooperation in lowering tariffs and informal trade barriers. Several developing countries, along with Japan, have pushed for a framework of cooperation to accompany the process of liberalization. "Liberalization and cooperation should be pursued with equal weight and emphasis, as if they were two wheels of a car," said one MITI official. "It is essential that they at least be able to envision some prospect and develop a sense of economic competitiveness they can rely upon for their survival and prosperity in the future."[7] Japan launched the Partnership for Progress (PFP) program for this reason, according to officials. An aide to Foreign Minister Yohei Kono described the PFP as an "insurance policy" for LDCs to reassure them before they run toward the liberalization goal of the Bogor Declaration that they will not be injured, because the land has already been cleared.[8]

Japan has also focused on human resources development and cultural programs. While these areas appear rather innocuous, there is some skepticism over Tokyo's motivation. As a senior US official put it, "There are two schools of thought. One school of thought is that APEC is as good a place as any to have cultural/intellectual activities. . . . The other school of thought is that this is an effort on Japan's part to divert APEC's attention away from its main job—economic liberalization."[9] US Ambassador to APEC Sandra Kristoff said that "the APEC forum should not function in a 'North-South manner' as a body to disburse official development assistance (ODA) and other funds," arguing that the job is already done by other organizations such as the World Bank and the Asian Development Bank (ADB).[10]

On a deeper level, the debate between cooperation and liberalization reflects philosophical and strategic differences within APEC. The PFP approach embodies a model of state-led development, one that conflicts with traditional concepts of laissez-faire economics espoused particularly by the United States.

Both liberalization and cooperation are necessary to sustain APEC's progress toward the Bogor goals. Members should not underestimate the reaction of the forces against liberalization and should manage their domestic political situations carefully. They must keep in mind that economic growth is not an objective unto itself. Rather, the goal is to ensure the long-term impact of economic development on enhancing the quality of life of its citizens. To accomplish this, it is critical that members work diligently, on their own and with their APEC partners, to address such issues as social and economic infrastructures, environmental protection, and the establishment of standard and balanced rules and laws.

MFN Status: Conditional or Unconditional

The question of MFN status has become one of the most salient issues in implementing the Bogor vision. APEC has to choose from three paths to opening the progress made through unilateral and coordinated liberalization to nonmembers. The first is the granting of unconditional MFN. This would open tariff reduction and rules regarding investment and procurement to all nonmembers, regardless of the actions of third parties or the relative health of affected industries in APEC countries.

The second route is through GATT-consistent MFN. The key objection raised to the GATT-based MFN approach is Article 19, the "escape clause," which allows members to apply quotas in certain sectors if imports are proved to cause "serious injury" to a domestic industry. The original agreement on these "safeguards" dictated high standards that had to be met in order to invoke Article 19, including the prohibition against selecting individual nations for restrictions. The Uruguay Round, however, added a clause that would permit GATT members to put up barriers against a certain country's products if imports from that nation "have increased in disproportionate percentage in relation to the total increase of imports of the product concerned in the representative period."[11]

The final path that is available to APEC is to grant concessions on a reciprocal basis. In other words, in order to enjoy the benefits of APEC-related liberalization, nonmembers would be required to grant the same type of commitment. This type of action is permitted under Article 24 of the GATT but would require APEC to recognize itself as a free trade area or customs union.

The United States has argued for this last route—conditional MFN status—based on its experience with European protectionism. Without reciprocity, Washington has maintained, APEC will allow the European Union to free ride to an even greater extent than it already does on the global trading system. Reciprocal concessions would help the overall global economy and add a further element of interdependence, which is becoming increasingly important for regional security. "Everybody has to be able to say that you're getting something for what you're giving," one US official said.[12]

While this line of reasoning appears persuasive, most APEC members feel that conditional MFN violates the spirit of the APEC process. A senior Hong Kong official commented that "in the American political system, on trade negotiations they have a fixation about reciprocity, which we in Hong Kong do not really understand, since it makes little economic sense, but historically they have this fixation."[13]

But the reason for America's "fixation" on reciprocity has its roots in economic and political realities. Unlike Hong Kong, or most other small- and middle-sized economies, the United States has significant bargaining power over other regions as a large export market, and it is hesitant to give up its chips—that is, reduce its trade barriers—without furthering its global goals. Europe will not reciprocate Hong Kong's, or Indonesia's for that matter, liberalization measures because the economic benefits come nowhere near to the political costs. The potential for greater access to the American market, on the other hand, presents a much more attractive prospect. In this regard, the American position can be seen to be as committed to global free trade as Hong Kong's, despite the appearance of foot-dragging.

There is also a perception, in the United States and elsewhere, that granting unconditional MFN status would preclude APEC from becoming a free trade area akin to the North American Free Trade Agreement (NAFTA). While officials publicly discount this possibility, privately some see the option as a potential response to any future breakdown in the GATT system.

Some raised the question of the effectiveness of reciprocity. Japan's SOM member Hidehiro Konno has argued that the American proposal, which he sees as based upon the Reciprocal Trade Act of 1934, is outdated and unsuitable for the current environment, in which advanced nations have reduced their tariff levels to insignificant amounts. "Industrial countries are finding it difficult to obtain concessions from [developing] countries on a reciprocal basis because they themselves have so little left to offer," Konno has written. This inability to achieve reciprocity and proportionality through multilateral negotiations, Konno noted, explains why the United States has turned toward unilateral measures to achieve concessions from its trading partners.

China's case merits special attention. Concerns about the prospect of market disruption that China and Asia in general have in many countries prompted Uruguay Round negotiators to add the new escape clause. Economist Jeffrey Schott commented that "such selective safeguards seem designed to protect against competitive exporters in Asia. In particular, it seems to presage a strategy for dealing with import surges from China."[14] China's insistence on unconditional MFN and demand for fair treatment from both non-APEC and APEC members obviously stems from this new WTO rule.

Japan and other nations see the potential for using unconditional MFN to encourage China to more fully integrate into the regional, and global, trading systems. By granting nondiscriminatory MFN to China, Beijing would have more confidence in opening up its domestic markets and deregulating its dynamic economy. China would also be encouraged to abide by international rules, such as setting up stable investment procedures and protecting intellectual property. By allowing China to compete as a normal member of the economic community, there would be a much greater willingness on Beijing's part to allow economic reforms, such as the privatization of inefficient public industries, to take place.

The dilemma over MFN boils down to a trade-off between short-term tactics and long-term interests. Singaporean Prime Minister Goh Chok Tong argued that "ideally, we should have unconditional MFN in line with the multilayered trading system," but he conceded that "in practice, the reciprocal approach is used by all regional trading arrangements to prevent 'free ridership.' " He further explained that "the concern of many non-APEC countries that they might be excluded from this growth region will be an important incentive for them to open their economies. The Seattle leaders' meeting in 1993 was a significant event that persuaded the GATT contracting parties to conclude the Uruguay Round."[15] This experience showed that APEC as a group can have a far wider impact than Asia Pacific nations individually.

Conditional MFN proponents might argue that if the mere potential for an APEC discriminatory trade arrangement can stimulate European interest in the success of global liberalization, then the actual formation of one would be even more desirable. However, given the diversity of the region, such an arrangement would not be workable. Moreover, the size and potential of the Asia Pacific economies far outweigh the need to maintain vigilance against European mercantilism. From the Uruguay

Round experience, it is clear that the European Union remains resistant to comprehensive liberalization. As their protected markets lose competitiveness over time, this tendency will only be reinforced, making GATT-style negotiations even more challenging. Practically, however, it should not give up its leverage over Europe too quickly. On a case-by-case basis, such as APEC's action on the Uruguay Round, APEC can be effective in providing implicit pressure on the Europeans to act. APEC should manage the free-rider threat that the United States so acutely perceives by using open regionalism as a catalyst for encouraging further comprehensive multilateral liberalization in the WTO. Further, it should lead the world to free trade by example, not by time-consuming and frustrating negotiations. In the end, it is in the long-term interests of all of the Asia Pacific to increase the global level of free trade, regardless of the final balance sheet or score card.

Liberalization Processes

The fundamental question regarding APEC's process of liberalization is whether APEC should become a negotiating body. The debate on CUA, which revolved around whether to take collective and/or unilateral actions toward liberalization, crystallized this question. Developing countries have insisted on a loose structure focused on CUA, while several developed-country members demand negotiated agreements to ensure comparability.

The positions of both camps basically boil down to domestic politics. Despite the declining importance of North-South issues, governments in developing countries must remain vigilant to perceptions that the big powers are imposing their policies. At the same time, several members, including advanced nations, dread the prospect of being perceived as giving away their markets to trade predators. Hence, they are under tremendous domestic pressure to be tough on foreigners. Moreover, policymakers in advanced nations such as the United States argue that they cannot win legislative approval of a liberalization package unless they guarantee that other APEC members will collectively reciprocate unilateral actions. "We need to be able to go to the Hill and to industry and say that what we're getting in APEC is equivalent to what we're giving up," said one US official.[16] American officials also are concerned that unilateral moves to reduce tariffs will carry little substantive weight, because nontariff barriers are seen as a greater culprit in the exclusion of US exports from several Asia Pacific economies.

Addressing these areas requires structured negotiations and enforcement mechanisms that are anathema to many governments in the region. It has become increasingly clear that without negotiations, advanced nations would oppose liberalization, and with negotiations, developing countries would refuse to participate.

APEC's role in the process is to facilitate consultations, not negotiations, but the group has yet to define these two terms. Wisber Loeis, who led the SOM during Indonesia's chairmanship, did not see the terms as mutually exclusive, saying, "Consultations can be argued to be one form of negotiations."[17] A further hint at maneuverability was given by one senior diplomat: "We don't like formal negotiations, but we don't mind informal ones."[18] Jusuf Wanandi has asserted, "Of course, there must be negotiations—at the end, mind you, but not the beginning."[19]

There is ample evidence to support Wanandi's point. After all, few would have guessed that the GATT ministerial meeting in Punta del Este, Uruguay, in 1986 would eventually result in more than 22,400 pages of documentation committing 123 countries to detailed tariff reductions under an umbrella World Trade Organization. In fact the impetus for moving the Uruguay Round process forward in the beginning was not prenegotiated, reciprocal tariff cuts but unilateral liberalization and deregulation undertaken primarily by developing countries as a result of internal economic realities.[20] As these efforts reinforced the confidence of developing countries in free trade, a consensus emerged on the importance of negotiating a permanent agreement to keep the world open to trade and investment. APEC is clearly heading down this path. Thus, it is important that members allow negotiations to evolve naturally and not rush to create a highly structured negotiating mechanism. Although it is often dismissed by officials in advanced nations, concerted unilateralism should not be underestimated as a force for solid trade liberalization.

The Eminent Persons Group recommended in their 1995 report that members "seek to achieve for APEC what the Punta del Este conference in 1986 and the Montreal midterm review in 1988, taken together, did for the Uruguay Round of the GATT."[21] This, they explained, involves laying out guiding principles, agendas, and timetables, as occurred during the initial Uruguay meeting. It also recommends borrowing the concept of a downpayment from the Montreal meeting to reap an "early harvest" to reinforce later actions.

Competing Visions of Liberalization

Each member of APEC country inevitably projects its vision for APEC's structure based on its own experiences and success stories. Former State Department official Robert Zoellick, for instance, has described the US vision for APEC by comparing it to America's experience in settling its far West in the 19th century. "In the case of 19th-century America, where the railroad lines went [and] where the telegraph lines went were very important in structuring the flow of commerce and influence on both sides," he said. "In the 20th century and 21st century, the questions [are] where the airline routes will go, where the telecommunications systems will go, what telecommunications systems people will use, whether people will tend to use common standards, whether they will, in the case of the US, speak English. . . . [O]ur view of APEC was to try to develop a common infrastructure on all those dimensions so as to enmesh the United States in the Pacific."[22] This could also probably be said of the "NAFTA extension" vision, yet Zoellick also realized that APEC could strengthen the global system by providing credible links to each region and discourage the balkanization of the system. "To us, APEC was also a device for emphasizing to the East Asians that we weren't just concentrating on our hemisphere," he said. "So I saw this as part of stronger ties with the then-evolving European Community, as stronger ties with Mexico and Latin America, stronger ties with East Asia, each of these being economic and political and supporting each other."

Australian Prime Minister Keating's vision is somewhat different. He argues for giving APEC a much higher profile than other regional and subregional groups. "We've seen NAFTA as being a subgroup of APEC," Keating said. "We see APEC as the overarching body . . . and you'd have these more discrete liberalized trade bodies within it, NAFTA being one."[23] Keating also sees APEC's role in strategic terms—in its ability to bring together Japan and the United States. "APEC has about it an idea that you have trans-Pacific trade and strategic linkages, which already includes the first and second largest economies in the world," he said.

Canada, and to a lesser extent Korea, have yet another approach. Realizing the benefits of global liberalization, they have sought to use APEC as a foundation for globalism and specifically to turn APEC into a WTO caucus for faster liberalization. "What the APEC trade facilitation [and] liberalization agenda offers is an opportunity to build on the WTO . . . by accelerating or deepening the cuts agreed to in the Uruguay Round," said Canadian SOM official Len Edwards. "They [APEC nations] could act as catalysts for a broader WTO action."[24]

At the Seattle meeting, Philippine President Fidel Ramos merely emphasized the need to articulate a vision, adding that "we should set up a mechanism that can find the disciplines between NAFTA and APEC." His Thai counterpart Chuan Leepkai added, "We can ask the EPG to examine APEC's relationship with AFTA and NAFTA." Singapore has looked in a different direction in linking APEC to greater global cooperation: Prime Minister Goh has often stressed his support for using APEC as an umbrella to bring together subregional groups such as NAFTA and AFTA. He has also seen interregional dialogue, such as the ASEAN plus three/EU summit, as an effective way of forging global integration. This strategy has its basis in Jesus Estanislao's theory of "concentric circles" of economic cooperation.

The competing visions of APEC's role in the global economic super-structure basically break down to five models. The first envisions the Asia Pacific, under APEC, supported by two regional blocs: NAFTA and the EAEC. The second sees the emergence of two pillars of global trade, APEC and the European Union, both competing and cooperating as autonomous units within the global system. The third model, like the one embraced by Mahathir, perceives the world as comprising three trading blocs—Europe, North America, and East Asia—in a triangular power balance. The fourth formulates a pyramid approach, with subregionals such as AFTA supporting regional groups such as APEC, which in turn provides impetus for global free trade through the WTO. Yet this model focuses on one-way pressure—that is, using regional and subregional forums to encourage global progress. APEC should support the WTO, but it must not become subject to it. APEC has its own life as a representative of the economic aspirations of the Asia Pacific community of nations. The last, and most visionary, is the one embodied by Estanislao's "concentric circles" model. This concept can be thought about in terms of waves, emanating from various organizations—regional, subregional, global, even bilateral—with each being both linked and autonomous. At the Singapore ministerial in 1990 Lee Kuan Yew said of the relationship between ASEAN and APEC that "there will be two concentric circles of cooperation, which can progress together."[25]

Estanislao's model takes into account the differing needs and circumstances of individual economies and regions yet links the progress made through each. Australia and New Zealand, for instance, through their Closer Economic Relations (CER) pact, are beginning a process whereby lawyers would need to pass only one bar exam to practice in either country. It would be unthinkable, of course, for American lawyers to practice in China through a similar agreement made through APEC. Yet such bilateral ties as CER take nothing away from regional or global liberalization.

In its 1995 report, the EPG called for the achievement of "open subregionalism," urging subregional arrangements such as AFTA and NAFTA to abide by three guiding principles: any liberalization undertaken be consistent with GATT rules, all actions taken by subregional groups should promptly be submitted to the WTO for supervision, and benefits achieved through subregional arrangements should be extended to all other APEC economies based on the EPG-suggested formula for granting APEC concessions to nonmember economies.

While this is the ideal version of the world, it is important that APEC leaders contemplate alternatives should global free trade stall. Given its immense size and dynamism, APEC provides an effective area of like-minded trading nations that could, in the place of a dormant WTO, be a strong force for promoting and liberalizing international trade. Zoellick warns that if APEC fails, countries "might want to move ahead with liberalization among the willing," which would either mean sector by sector or through free trade agreements.[26] This would clearly be a far second to the overall process under way since Bogor.

Linkages

In sum, APEC has been effective in setting its goal of free and open trade in the Asia Pacific. Yet despite the agreement on the ends, much debate remains over means. The heart of this dilemma lies with the variety of often conflicting tactics and strategies toward trade liberalization among APEC members. These views naturally reflect the particular economic and political circumstances each member faces and are therefore difficult to change.

What can be addressed, however, is the linkage between political stability and economic liberalization. Each nation in APEC—big or small, rich or poor—faces significant public and bureaucratic resistance to trade liberalization. It is up to the national governments both to educate their people on the importance of free trade and open markets and to find ways to soften the blows in those sectors that will be most seriously affected. Members must also cooperate to ensure that the economic benefits accrued through liberalization are spread to the people as a whole. It is important that APEC governments remember the common aspirations they share. In order to achieve consensus, each nation must be sensitive to the particular concerns and barriers faced by its counterparts. They must also recognize the enormous potential of linkages—between liberalization and cooperation, the costs and benefits of MFN, collective and unilateral, global and regional—that will facilitate the liberalization process.

Perhaps the most important element of the drive for free and open trade is the connection between economic and political development. These two factors are equally critical and mutually supportive. The final goal of both is the same: to improve the lives of ordinary citizens. The pursuit of both tracks, economic liberalization and political pluralism, will enhance the sense of stability and community in the Asia Pacific. Democratic politics and economic opportunities will foster common aspirations among the peoples in each Asia Pacific society. A strong middle class, enjoying access to free-flowing ideas from neighboring cultures and nations, will form the bedrock of the emerging Asia Pacific community. APEC's task is to explore the intellectual and practical linkages that will facilitate this goal.

Notes

1. Personal interview with Jesus Estanislao, 9 August 1995.
2. Personal interview.

3. Personal interview with Arifin Siregar, 9 May 1995.

4. Ministry of International Trade and Industry, "Evaluation of the U.S. Approach to APEC," internal memo, October 1993. The memo was for internal discussion; however, it referred to two positive effects of the US approach: the stimulating impact of revolutionary ideas and concepts on Asia's evolutionary mentality and the clear commitment of the United States to the Asia Pacific. On the other hand, the memo pointed out three negative effects: (1) a lack of appreciation for the policy effects as well as the economic impact—i.e., a weakening of the competitive environment of the division of labor, the very source of Asia's economic dynamism; (2) the lack of consideration for the different stages of economic development; and (3) the obsession with strengthening its bargaining position vis-à-vis the European Union.

5. Personal interview with a participant.

6. Personal interview with a participant.

7. Personal interview, 6 July 1995.

8. Personal interview, 7 July 1995.

9. Personal interview, 27 April 1995.

10. *Kyodo News Service*, 24 February 1995.

11. General Agreement on Tariffs and Trade, Article 5:2b (Geneva: GATT Secretariat, 1994).

12. *Inside U.S. Trade*, 23 June 1995.

13. Personal interview with Tony Miller, 21 July 1995.

14. Jeffrey Schott, *The Uruguay Round: An Assessment* (Washington: Institute for International Economics, 1994), pp. 96–97.

15. Personal interview with Goh Chok Tong, 18 July 1995.

16. *Inside US Trade*, 14 July 1995.

17. Personal interview with Wisber Loeis, 3 September 1995.

18. Personal interview.

19. Personal interview, 9 July 1995.

20. Schott, pp. 5–6.

21. APEC Eminent Persons Group, "Implementing the APEC Vision: Towards Free and Open Trade and Investment by 2010/2020," draft obtained by the author.

22. Personal interview with Robert Zoellick, 20 July 1995.

23. Personal interview with Paul Keating, 6 July 1995.

24. Personal interview with Len Edwards, 21 July 1995.

25. Speech by Lee Kuan Yew at the Singapore APEC ministerial meeting, 29 July 1990.

26. Personal interview, 20 July 1995.

8

The APEC Way

Summits

During a break in the historic summit on Blake Island, Australian Prime Minister Paul Keating of Australia, Korean President Kim Yung Sam, and Singaporean Premier Goh Chok Tong gathered in a corner. "Which one of us," Keating asked, "is best placed in proposing that Suharto hold the next meeting?"[1] Keating took himself out of the running, feeling that an Asian should do the asking. Eventually they agreed on Kim. During the afternoon session, Kim casually mentioned, "Why don't we hold a summit meeting again?" Goh quickly jumped in, "This summit has been a shot in the arm for APEC. I myself support holding a summit meeting again, but it is up to President Suharto."[2] All eyes turned to the Indonesian elder statesman. "If you all say so. . . . Indonesia would like to hold another summit," Suharto replied, adding, "Holding the meeting is a great honor for Indonesia."

This small episode is illustrative of the informality of APEC summits. Although Osaka marked the third consecutive leaders' meeting, the forum has no official status within APEC. Yet the practice of holding annual summits is becoming a tradition in much the same way G-7 summits evolved in the 1970s. There are no rules mandating a meeting of heads of government. In fact, each year, it is up to the leaders themselves, particularly the host, to find a consensus on scheduling leaders' talks the following year. As the incident described above demonstrates, the decisions to continue these meetings still need to be choreographed.

Still, there are some who would like to see the process ended. Japanese Foreign Minister Yohei Kono noted that several ASEAN officials conveyed their opposition to an Osaka summit, fearing that if Japan were to hold the meeting for the third year, the practice would be institutionalized.[3] These critics are likely correct. The enormous peer pressure exerted at each year's summit makes the pattern extremely difficult to break. There may be a certain appeal to leaders of small and medium-sized countries in keeping the process alive, as it gives them direct access to the leaders of the major powers. Although it may be a while before these annual gatherings are officially recognized, they are rapidly becoming a permanent fixture in the APEC landscape.

The inauguration of the leaders' summits added a new dynamic to APEC. The effect has been to speed up the process and decrease suspicion among member states. It has also forced each of the Asia Pacific leaders to focus annually on regionwide concerns, thus keeping regional issues on the top of the agenda. The summits also counteract the effects of bureaucratic inertia by providing ministers and bureaucrats with a specific mandate from their national leaders. As for bureaucrats, "They are used to routine things," said an Indonesian diplomat. "Their thinking is usually incremental, not radical, whereas the president has some other ideas. He wants to achieve something big, not just incremental."[4] An American official voiced the same sentiments: "For bureaucrats . . . 15 years is a long time in a policy context to think about what our objectives should be, and our leaders have said that is the time frame we are supposed to be talking about; it's tough."[5]

The advent of the leaders' meetings is one reason that greater emphasis has been put on flexible consensus. The freewheeling informality of these meetings has resulted in a trade-off between action and detail. The annual summits have given APEC a much more active agenda than could be achieved through ministerials or SOMs. "If the leaders actually want to do something, they can actually go and do it," said Australia's Keating. "In other words, there is no precooked agenda . . . of course, this is what bureaucrats don't like."[6] Former APEC Executive Director William Bodde noted one such example: "The ministers' reception to the EPG recommendations in Seattle was, at best, lukewarm, and it was the leaders who seized upon them and embraced the goal of free trade in the region."[7]

One lesson from APEC summit meetings, is that not all national leaders are created equal. Some, such as Australia's Paul Keating and Singapore's Goh Chok Tong, are strategic thinkers and excel in their ability to deliver on commitments back home.

Different national systems also may have an impact. Indonesian Jusuf Wanandi has suggested that the success of the Bogor and Seattle summits lies in the Indonesian and US presidential systems, which allowed these leaders to take bold steps that their parliamentary colleagues could not. "The two countries that started this idea of the leaders' meeting are very fortunate that we have the presidential system," Wanandi said.

"[T]herefore we can confine [the organization of the summits] to special personalities that can do the job on behalf of the president and not be bogged down by the process."[8]

Yet the US Congress complicates the administration's attempts to fulfill commitments to the Bogor Declaration. While a president may not have to contend with coalition rivals within his cabinet, he often must face up to the prospect of divided government.

There is no hard-and-fast evidence that an executive or parliamentary system has made a decisive difference in the ability of member states to make, or carry through on, its APEC commitments. Japan's internal power balance between the bureaucracy and politicians has been more important, for instance, than the ability of its prime ministers to ram through legislation with the aid of a parliamentary majority. Even in China, a leader supposedly free of legislative complications has to contend more with the unique political culture than with the official machinery of state.

Despite the restraints on national leaders, their direct commitment and intervention worked well in both Seattle and Bogor. Direct communication between leaders, be they President Bill Clinton's personal letters or President Suharto's personal envoy, has also been effective. Picking up on this, Japanese Prime Minister Tomiichi Murayama dispatched MITI Minister Ryutaro Hashimoto in August 1995 to both Jakarta, the 1994 APEC host, and Manila, the chair of the 1996 meeting. Just prior to the June 1995 Sapporo senior officials' meeting, Murayama also sent personal letters to all of the APEC leaders requesting that they take direct responsibility for the discussions on APEC's agenda. His personal appeal was well received by his APEC colleagues, who saw the gesture as a demonstration of the Japanese prime minister's commitment to making Osaka a success.[9] Summits have their soft spots too. The need to save face and promote a collegial atmosphere can result in misunderstandings and misinterpretations of national positions or commitments.

In Europe, leaders meet twice a year for the European Union and on average once every two years through NATO summit meetings. Before the 1993 APEC summit meeting, there were no parallel discussions in the Asia Pacific context. The experience of meeting at the head-of-state level, particularly on a regular basis, forms the foundation for a more serious dialogue.

Ministerials

Up until the Seattle summit, the primary leadership for the APEC process lay at the ministerial level. The ministerial is still the highest-level official meeting in APEC. As APEC has evolved, there has been a shift in responsibility over policy formulation in most countries from foreign ministries to trade and economics ministries. Trade liberalization will further propel this trend. As Secretary of State James Baker related to an aide during an early APEC ministerial, "You know, in a couple of years, I won't be sitting here, it will be [Treasury Secretary Nicholas] Brady sitting here."[10]

In some countries, notably Japan, this has led to some confusion over official positions on certain issues. As one US official put it, "I think Gaimusho is still in the driver's seat, but I think MITI has got its hands firmly on the map and is saying, 'No, we need to go this way. No, make a right turn here.' "[11] While ministers are finally determining their exact roles within APEC vis-à-vis their colleagues, turf battles remain a significant part of the process. From the beginning, the Japanese Foreign Ministry has been suspicious of the forum because it was the Ministry of International Trade and Industry's initiative to create it. The two ministries have pursued largely separate, and at times divergent, approaches toward APEC.

In the United States, despite Baker's prediction, the State Department is still calling the shots, although with strong input from the trade side of the administration. One US official said, "You still have the State Department in the lead. Bilateral trade negotiations and GATT negotiations come out of the USTR. Then you have the multilateral approaches somewhere in between, be it APEC, be it Summit of the Americas, be it the Caribbean Basin Initiative, and [the State Department has] to make sure that all of those approaches work together and are not inconsistent with each other."[12]

Foreign ministers have been overshadowed by the leaders since the summit was introduced. However, they have also played an important role ensuring the success of summit diplomacy. Thai EPG member Narongchai Akrasanee observed that in his nation, "Foreign Affairs officials are in favor of APEC mainly for political reasons," while "Ministry of Commerce officials . . . would prefer to work in GATT or the WTO rather than in APEC."[13] Robert Zoellick noted that APEC policymakers were aware of the deep divisions that existed within the governments in several Asian nations, particularly "between Alatas on the one hand versus other ministers in Indonesia, for example."[14] The divisions between ministers and ministries can be partly explained by jurisdictional considerations and partly by personal passions. In preparing for the Seattle meeting, Robert Fauver noted "a very interesting dynamic, that the foreign ministries are slower to see the new institutional values of [the APEC] process than the economic and trade ministries."[15] Fauver said this was true of all of the APEC members but Australia, perhaps reflecting Canberra's decision to combine the foreign and trade ministries into one. He attributed the reluctance of foreign ministries to support the process, particularly the informal leaders' meeting, to a fear of being undercut and marginalized.

There have been similar diversions between trade and industry. One Indonesian official explained the situation in his country, "As you know, we don't have a MITI ministry; we have separate ministries. Between the Ministry of Trade and the Ministry of Industry you have differences of opinion. . . . The minister of trade is usually more liberal in his thinking, whereas the minister of industry would like, of course, to protect domestic industry, which is understandable."[16]

The creation of APEC's 10 working groups has complicated the bureaucratic landscape even further. In many countries, technical ministries such as transportation and telecommunications have less international experience and more parochial interests in protecting domestic companies.

The most elusive ministerial has been in the area of finance and macroeconomic cooperation. For several years there was strong resistance, especially from Japan's Ministry of Finance (MOF) and the US Treasury Department, to putting macroeconomic issues on the APEC agenda. As one American official put it, "We had a great deal of difficulty trying to encourage finance ministries to participate. Frankly, the two biggest problems were the US and Japan. Okurasho [MOF] and Treasury dragged their feet; [they] did not want to be a full-blown part of APEC. Partly they thought there were too many foreign ministers; partly they weren't sure there was a value in the group."[17]

This situation changed after the meeting at Blake Island, where Clinton and other leaders agreed that there should be some form of macroeconomic consultations. APEC finance ministers did finally meet in 1994 in Hawaii. While there were no concrete proposals, the ministers did agree to continue annual talks. In April 1995 finance ministers gathered again in Bali, Indonesia, and they are scheduled to meet again in Kyoto, Japan, the following year. The financial crisis that hit Mexico was a strong motivating factor for continued consultations and was high on the agenda at the second meeting held in Bali in 1995.

Senior Officials' Meetings

The leaders make decisions on broad policy goals, and designated "senior officials" carry out APEC's activities. These so-called sherpas are generally foreign or trade ministry bureaucrats at the assistant secretary or vice ministerial level who on average meet four times a year at senior officials' meetings (SOMs).

In addition to their administrative work, sherpas lay out the general framework for annual ministerial and leaders' meetings. At times this arrangement has been seen as frustrating the process, since the sherpas themselves come from bureaucracies that may be less enthusiastic about APEC's progress than their national leaders are. It was for this reason that President Suharto assigned a special envoy to prepare for the Bogor summit. This practice has its origins in the months leading up to the Seattle summit, when American officials pushing for the meeting used head-of-government channels to outflank skeptical and uncooperative foreign ministry bureaucrats. William Bodde, executive director or the APEC Secretariat in 1993, complained that, even though he was on loan to APEC, White House officials kept him out of the planning process for Seattle because of his affiliation with the State Department. "I was just a pawn," he lamented of the struggle between State and the White House.[18] These types of incidents abated when Japan took the helm of APEC and used much more routine and traditional approaches. Leading up to Bogor, Indonesia convened several informal meetings of high-ranking personal representatives of leaders. In 1995 Japan established "special SOMs," informal brainstorming sessions among senior officials where they could float ideas, off the record, in search of new approaches to the Osaka agenda. In 1995 Japan scheduled two such meetings: the first in Singapore in April and the second in Hong Kong in September.

Many of the APEC SOMs personally represent the intellectual bridges they are working to establish through APEC. Most of the 1995-vintage SOM officials studied in universities abroad, primarily in Europe and the United States. Hong Kong's Tony Miller and Korea's Ban Ki Moon are alumni of the same graduate school, Harvard University's John F. Kennedy School of Government. Singapore's Khaw Boon Wan did undergraduate work at Australia's University of Newcastle, while Australia's Peter Grey is a Stanford University alumnus. Among the very few that do not have an international education are those from the United States, Japan, and China.

One concrete step APEC has taken was the creation of the Committee for Trade and Investment (CTI) and the Committee for Economics. The formation of the CTI was largely the result of a year-long effort by Assistant USTR for APEC Nancy Adams, who spent much of 1993 traversing the region to cajole other members into agreement. Both committees were created to facilitate APEC's move into substantive matters of trade liberalization. These committees, along with the SOMs and the working groups, constitute "the heartbeat of APEC," according to US Ambassador to APEC Sandra Kristoff.[19]

Working Groups

At the Singapore ministerial in 1990, APEC delegates agreed to create seven (later expanded to ten) working groups to cover a range of sectoral, educational, and environmental issues.[20] These working groups have since met annually at the ministerial and senior officials' level. An American observer termed the working groups' relations to the APEC process as akin to "planets around the sun." A Japanese official took a dimmer view, commenting that the speed at which new working groups have been created is similar to the growth of mushrooms around a tree. These groups have mushroomed to the extent that at the 1993 Williamsburg SOM, the Korean delegate proposed a rationalization of APEC meetings, particularly the working groups. He noted that each year there were 30 APEC gatherings.[21] At the 1993 Honolulu SOM, however, members finally agreed to "cluster" APEC's working groups and to make the creation of a new panel contingent upon the elimination or consolidation of at least one existing group.[22] One interesting development of APEC's sectoral working groups is that they have included business representatives along with government delegates. As an American official explained, "The working groups are unique in that a country can bring any corporate advisers along on their delegation. We urged that at the beginning, so that it would be a real-world working group with business people, not just bureaucrats."[23]

US Secretary of State Baker had originally supported the creation of APEC working groups as a means of engaging the private sector in the work of the nascent forum. Realizing that APEC would garner little political support without a strong domestic constituency, Baker pushed hard for strengthening the groups and giving business a greater stake in APEC's success. Other countries have followed the US strategy of seeking to push its own pet projects—for example, telecommunications—through the forum in order to bolster support back home. Taiwan has aggressively pursued agricultural technical cooperation, both to boost the confidence of agribusiness and related industries with accumulated know-how and because Taiwanese President Lee Teng-hui, an agricultural economist, has taken a personal interest in the subject. Canada has been a strong supporter of the work of the environmental working group, particularly in the fisheries area, a sector of paramount importance to its maritime provinces.

The Secretariat

The APEC Secretariat was given its charter during the 1992 Bangkok ministerial with this explanation: "The APEC Secretariat should be small in size, simple in structure, and flexible enough to meet APEC's needs."[24] With a budget of only US$2 million per year and a staff of 25, 12 of whom are seconded from member states, the APEC Secretariat in Singapore stands in marked contrast to its counterpart in Brussels. The differences between the two structures are not entirely coincidental. The European Union's 20,000 bureaucrats are a recurring nightmare for APEC members, fearful of losing sovereignty and effectiveness. Some governments in ASEAN have shown the strongest phobia to the creation of a permanent APEC institution. After the Secretariat installed an electronic-mail system to connect APEC officials, former Philippine Foreign Secretary Roberto Romulo complained, "It sounds like institutionalization to me."[25] An

Indonesian diplomat who recalled that "it was Minister Alatas who said in 1992 that we did not like institutionalization," assessed that today institutionalization "continues to be a bad word . . . but [nonetheless] the institutionalization is going on slowly."[26] While Malaysian Trade and Industry Minister Rafidah Aziz, ever vigilant about institutionalization, originally argued for naming the Singapore Secretariat the "Effective Secretariat" rather than the "Permanent Secretariat,"[27] the final Bangkok Declaration referred to the body simply as APEC's "Secretariat." With a minimum of institutionalization, the tiny Secretariat became quickly overburdened. A task force that was formed to look at the issue found that APEC had 75 activities in assorted fields and recommended that the secretariat be expanded to cope with its ever-increasing tasks. The decision reached at the Sapporo SOM to increase the number of loaned officials from each country by one to two, as well as to expand the local staff, was a clear sign of the permanent nature of the Secretariat.

Pacific Economic Cooperation Council (PECC) and the Eminent Persons Group (EPG)

To meet increasing demands, APEC has introduced an entrepreneurial approach. First, it has relied heavily on private organizations, particularly the Pacific Economic Cooperation Council (PECC), to provide economic and statistical analysis.

Canadian scholar Lawrence Woods has described the important role PECC has played in facilitating APEC's evolution.[28] The formula used at Seoul for including the Three Chinas, for instance, was based upon the progress made in "nonofficial" negotiations to include China and Taiwan in PECC in 1985–86.

The second instrument the organization has employed has been the Eminent Persons Group (EPG). APEC's EPG was modeled after a body set up to assist ASEAN's liberalization efforts. By most accounts, the APEC EPG has been much more effective that its earlier cousin. Thai delegate Narongchai Akrasanee, who served on both groups, noted that the recommendations of the ASEAN EPG would languish five or six years before they were implemented, but the APEC EPG's "impact was immediate." The EPG is actually heavily populated by the veterans of PECC, which first socialized APEC in the region.

APEC ministers empowered the EPG "to advance regional trade liberalization over the next decade . . . to enunciate a vision for trade in the Asia Pacific region by the year 2000."[29] As one senior American official commented, "APEC needs a group of people that will challenge it and act as the conscience for APEC—keep the APEC institution honest, as it were, and responsive to leaders' visions."[30] As EPG Chairman C. Fred Bergsten explained, "In a very important way . . . the EPG is an alternative to APEC having its own in-house institutional support." APEC made use of the Pacific Business Forum (PBF) in much the same way.

There has been some resistance to relying on the EPG or nongovernmental organizations (NGOs) for guidance. The idea of allowing external organizations to recommend policy decisions, a common practice in North America is still alien in some of the Asian nations. The current arrangement, however, is clearly preferable to the existing EU or OECD models for multilateral interaction.

Despite the diversity of its members, the group has a decided bias toward free trade. Although the general consensus in favor of liberalization enables the group to agree on broad and far-reaching agendas, it has also won it the scorn of many domestic sectors in APEC nations that see the group as a threat to their continued viability.

The reports of the EPG have at times been greeted with skepticism by national officials who see the body as either a front for American interests, a threat to sovereignty, or both. At the February 1995 SOM meeting in Fukuoka, Indonesia, Malaysia and Mexico suggested that the EPG be given only one more year to support the Bogor Declaration, then be disbanded. The United States and South Korea responded that the EPG's mandate is indefinite, and it would be improper to discuss its termination. Even in leaders' meetings, the EPG's utility has been called into question, as it was in Malaysian Prime Minister Mahathir's official reservations to the Bogor Declaration. However, Mahathir's appointment of free trader Noordin Sopiee to the EPG illustrated the Prime Minister's intellectual support for liberalization. In fact Mahathir is not the only leader to perceive that it is not bad politics to use the EPG as a "whipping boy," to deflect anger away from elected officials as they open their markets through APEC. While several governments are ambivalent about the political viability of the EPG, most would agree that its broad pronouncements have put APEC's leaders on the spot, sometimes uncomfortably so. The Philippines' then–foreign minister's following remarks tell much about the discomfort level of some ministers: "We must temper their [EPG's] boldness with our caution."[31]

Despite the occasional controversy that surrounds the EPG's work, it has contributed greatly to the progress of APEC. Its independent and visionary approach has provided an intellectual catalyst for keeping APEC's progress alive. Narongchai argued, "Without the EPG we wouldn't have those two declarations. . . . It actually helped move APEC to where it is today, whether you like it or not." APEC should reach out to other nontraditional groups as well. As an economic organization, it should, of course, redouble its efforts to gain input from the private sector. But APEC needs to look beyond business as well. The APEC-wide cooperation among local governments, politicians, academics, and NGOs could all add value to the APEC process. In order to capture the essence of the growing emerging forces of the Asia Pacific, APEC needs to shed its image as an official international organization and inject a more inclusive atmosphere that seeks to engage the interests and aspirations of people, groups, and governments at all levels. It is not a process of institutionalization but one of participation.

Membership

In its short existence, APEC has grown at a rate of about one country per year. Beginning with the six plus six equation, internal and external factors pushed the organization to expand its membership to include a broader range of nations. APEC's first expansion, which brought in China, Taiwan, and Hong Kong, was envisioned from the outset. Since then, however, the question of bringing in new economies has been politically delicate. As has been the case in the European Union, APEC faces an important choice between widening the organization by including a greater range of members and deepening the commitment among those countries that have already attained membership.

In the widening versus deepening debate, Mahathir has played a role akin to that of Great Britain's Prime Minister Margaret Thatcher within the European Union—that is, an ardent voice for widening. As the nation least supportive of the forum, Malaysia has often advocated expansion of the organization as a means of watering down the consensus-driven process. During the 1993 Honolulu SOM meeting, several members, including some ASEAN members, strongly criticized Malaysia's efforts to push through Chile's membership. One observer noted that Malaysia's obstinacy cost the meeting a half of its time. More recently, Malaysia has caused internal friction over its support of Peru's membership and calls for including India in regional dialogues.

China also seems to belong to the widening school, as China's SOM member Wang Yusheng attested that China would not object to more members. He pointed out that China supported the inclusion of Peru and Russia.[32]

On the other end of the spectrum is probably Australia, which has had a major stake in APEC's success from the very beginning. Particularly after making the Bogor commitment, APEC members have been slow to expand the organization to new members, fearing that more players would complicate efforts to achieve substantive progress.

Despite Australia's vocal commitment to deepening the APEC process, many have pointed out that Australia itself has brought in a new member, Papua New Guinea, when it served its interests, but Canberra has denied this. "It was New Zealand and Indonesia," said an Australian diplomat. "We were opposed to it."[33] Australian Prime Minister Keating was also opposed to Chile's inclusion and was angry that his foreign minister,

Gareth Evans, didn't stand up when Malaysia proposed its membership at the Seattle meeting. His frustration was particularly focused at the weakness APEC diplomats showed. "[Keating] actually wanted it to be a vote," the diplomat recalled. "He wanted people to actually look in the eye of a dangerous situation and take proper action."[34]

Former Korean Foreign Minister Han Sung-Joo noted that Chile's application came at the same time as bids from Russia, Peru, and several other countries. "Malaysia was for including Peru," he said, "and Indonesia didn't have a very good answer about why Peru had to be in while some of the other countries would not be included."[35] An Australian official also noted that the United States was also initially opposed to Chile's inclusion, sharing Keating's concern that the organization would be undermined by an infusion of new members. Treasury Secretary Lloyd Bentsen, however, intervened on Chile's behalf because of his close personal relationship with its incoming president, Eduardo Frei.[36] Chile's anticipated entrance into the NAFTA arrangement, however, will make its inclusion in APEC as natural as Mexico's, which joined just before the approval of its free trade agreement with Canada and the United States.

Japan has also been reluctant to increase the membership of the organization, fearing the precedent would increase external pressure to allow in more members. Since Chile has joined, Peruvian President Alberto Fujimori has put intense pressure on Japan to allow Peru, a PECC member, to join. "Why did the US allow Chile to be a member?" a frustrated MITI official lamented. "Since then, it has been very difficult for us to prevent a further proliferation of APEC membership."

Despite Malaysia's recent push to continue expanding the size of the organization, APEC members agreed at Seattle to enact a three-year ban on new membership. After the moratorium is lifted in 1996, however, the issue of membership will again be on the table. There is now serious talk about extending the Seattle moratorium until the year 2000, but such a decision would put a serious political strain on some APEC members. "No foreign minister wants to have an appointment after the ministerial meeting with the foreign minister of the country turned down and explain why," said one senior American official.[37]

Several neighboring nations have expressed interest in joining, including Peru, India, Ecuador, Pakistan, Argentina, North Korea, Russia, and Vietnam. As chair Japan received 10 applications for membership in 1995.[38] India has been one of the most aggressive applicants. Indian External Affairs Minister Salman Khurshid reiterated India's interest in joining APEC, noting that "geographically India cannot be separated from the Asia Pacific region."[39] Despite its lobbying efforts, there is little support in the region for India's ascension because of its geographical location, tensions with Pakistan, and uncertain economic conditions.

Vietnam is expected to eventually be given member status, however, because of its new membership in ASEAN. Geographically, culturally, and economically Vietnam is perhaps the most natural candidate on the current list of applicants. As long as economic reforms and rapprochement with Washington and Beijing continue, Vietnam could enter before the end of the decade.

Russia is the other nation that will spark the deepest debate among APEC members. In addition to admitting the Three Chinas during the Seoul conference in 1991, Korea had also considered seeking the inclusion of Russia (then the Soviet Union) and North Korea. Seoul had recently established normal ties with Moscow and won assent from North Korea to join the United Nations simultaneously, and it therefore wanted to show a good face to its northern neighbors. The military coup attempt in Moscow and the discovery of Pyongyang's nuclear program, however, killed the prospects of either country's entrance at the time. More recently, Russia has renewed its efforts to attain membership, applying particular pressure on Seoul. "In his first meeting with President Kim Young Sam, President [Boris] Yeltsin raised APEC as the first subject," said a Korean diplomat. "Yeltsin clearly used the 'North Korea card' when he pressed the issue."[40] Since the Yeltsin visit, successive Russian diplomatic delegations have pounded away at the issue. Korea has responded to Russian overtures by noting that its membership would require a consensus within APEC. Seoul has been hesitant to push the issue further because of possible objections by Tokyo.

Processes and Style

From the beginning, there has been a difference of opinion over the direction and form the APEC process should take—between an activism that moves into new areas and expands the organization's scope and a more conservative focus on cooperation and consultations. Up until the Seattle summit in 1993, the organization seemed to be headed down the path toward the latter. Meetings were generally limited to areas of broad agreement, such as Uruguay Round passage, and avoided touchy issues such as liberalization and development assistance. During this period, APEC received little attention from either the media or the business community it was supposedly created to help. Instead, it was widely written off as another "talk shop" such as the Organization of African Unity or the Organization of American States.

The Seattle summit transformed the organization in a fundamental way. "In many respects, the thing we call APEC now, the only thing it resembles about the APEC of pre-1992 is the name," said Australian Prime Minister Keating. "It is really a different body . . . the new body is an executive, head-of-government-level body."[41] At Seattle, Keating proudly remarked that "APEC is becoming as important as the IMF and the World Bank."[42]

Along with a change in substantive focus, the Seattle summit illustrated APEC's unique style within the world of multilateral organizations. As one US official put it, APEC is "involved with real interactions and flows and relationships" rather than formal structures and rules.[43] Over the years, the organization has developed its own sense of identity and style, which some have dubbed "the APEC Way." For one thing, it has retained the business orientation of its roots. "If APEC were to be nothing more than an annual dialogue among foreign ministers and trade ministers, I think that you would find that it would outlive its usefulness in a very short period of time," said US Ambassador for APEC Sandra Kristoff. "It is the business component, and the unique way in which APEC is trying to involve the business community in all of its work—from setting priorities to help [in] devising work programs—that's going to keep this organization healthy and alive for at least [until] 2010, I hope."[44] In doing so APEC has stuck with the ideas of economies rather than states, economics rather than politics. APEC has no institutional flag, nor are there national flags flown at meetings. Formal minutes are prohibited at the leaders' meetings.

Most APEC participants note the important educational value of the APEC process. Meetings between officials, ministers, and leaders build relationships and understanding between the diverse but interdependent nations of the Asia Pacific. One American official described how, in a multilateral APEC meeting, ASEAN ministers were shocked to hear Canada condemn US economic policies. The official recalled one minister's reaction: "We thought you [the United States] were the only country that really beat up on countries."[45] The official also mentioned that Secretary of State Baker "had learned a lot about Asians" during his three APEC ministerial meetings. Baker's learning process culminated in a 1991 article in *Foreign Affairs*, in which he outlined a complex and sophisticated vision of America's role in the emerging Pacific community.[46]

Informality has been the watchword throughout. "There is a bit of a culture difference," noted a US official. "APEC is an extremely collegial process. People continue to call one another by first names, even in a formal session."[47] This informality has been especially noticeable during leaders' summits. The United States started this trend when it asked leaders not to wear jackets and ties to the summit meetings. The congeniality of the process is reinforced by the absence of ministers and advisers during summit meetings; at Seattle even the interpreters were located outside the meeting rooms.[48]

Hong Kong's Miller noted that Bogor's unstructured approach to liberalization reinvigorated the APEC process. "I think in many ways the Indonesian year was quite crucial in that many players who up until then were keen on taking a structured approach to deregulation and so on began to realize that this was perhaps not either the only or the best way of doing it." He also commended Tokyo for Japan's inauguration of informal SOM brainstorming sessions, which have given an added boost to the process by allowing members to think out loud, without being held responsible for strictly representing their government's positions. Miller attributes this new type of SOM to making "Sapporo . . . in many ways the most substantive meeting so far."[49]

APEC has continued to perform the role of forum for consultations, not as a round for negotiations. "The value of APEC is not that we are going to do trade agreements in APEC," said an American trade official. "I mean, if that's all APEC were, we could do it in Geneva. We don't need it. The value of APEC is that it will help create the conditions for commercial and economic integration."[50] The members of APEC have also recognized the huge diversity in economic development. The acknowledgment of the internal variations was key to the recommendation for phased-in liberalization along two or three tiers to allow countries to meet their national goals at a more realistic pace. This approach is much different from that of the European Union, which sought to equalize member economies in a top-down fashion through an international income redistribution scheme.

Crossing the threshold toward free trade in the Asia Pacific does not just mean persuading rural voters and union members. Effecting a change in attitudes toward open regionalism will require many trade and diplomatic officials to let go of an entire culture of international trade. "[M]any of us have had years of GATT experience; most of us come from a trade perspective," said a senior US official. "The APEC process pushes the intellectual envelope and allows governments to kind of adjust, and the collegiality of the process helps one another to get to the point where something is acceptable."[51] But realizing this new form of interaction, she recognized, will mean that trade officials will have to purged themselves of the GATT mentality and remain flexible, not an easy prospect. This difference in culture is what makes APEC both so challenging and exciting. It moves the process of trade liberalization from a zero-sum to a positive-sum game—in effect, capturing the very meaning and benefits of pushing for an open trading system.

Decision Making

APEC's focus on consensus-based decision making was critical to winning support for the organization in its early stages, but unanimity is becoming increasingly difficult to maintain as the organization addresses more substantive issues. In order to receive approval of the controversial 1994 Bogor Declaration, Suharto introduced the idea of "flexible consensus," which in the Bogor case allowed Malaysia to express its objections without derailing the process. However, the word "flexible" is a tricky one. In

1993, for instance, Malaysian delegates delayed the Hawaii SOM meeting for more than half an hour when they insisted that the word "flexible" be added to modify the draft's call for APEC's "consolidation."[52]

The question of Chile's membership illustrates a weakness of APEC's flexible-consensus process. When Australia along with several other members stated that there was no consensus on admitting Chile, Malaysian Trade and Industry Minister Rafidah Aziz said that "there was no consensus against admitting Chile."[53] The case of Chile illustrates the fact that there is no clear definition of the word "consensus" among APEC members, let alone the concept of "flexible consensus."

Although it is necessary to avoid the dangers of GATT-style negotiations, there is clearly a need to ensure that APEC liberalization maintains an element of fairness and balance. The congeniality of the APEC process, particularly through the annual leaders' meetings, provides a framework through which countries can apply subtle pressure on one another without resorting to strictly legalistic and detailed trade agreements. "Back in '89 when we were trying to put this together, there was clearly a lot of misunderstanding and suspicion of other countries' motives," said Australian Ambassador to the United States Donald Russell. "There was a lot of baggage to deal with."[54]

APEC has given its members a growing awareness of their similarities and has built trust, which they can use to achieve a higher level of cooperation on substantive issues. "Over time a lot of this has shaken out," Russell said. "[Before] people felt comfortable about putting different countries in different boxes, and nothing was disturbing it; they left it that way. Initially, people seemed a bit confused, but when they start to think it through, they suddenly realize that there are links between all these countries, and it makes sense for everybody."

The peer pressure within APEC sometimes is analyzed in cultural terms and its peculiar effectiveness is highlighted. One observer attributed the success of APEC leaders' summits to the importance of shame in Asian societies.[55] William Bodde commented, on the basis of his reading of Ruth Benedict's classic work, *The Chrysanthemum and the Sword*, that Japanese leaders are particularly susceptible to this kind of pressure.[56] While it has yet to be seen whether such an "Asian way" can be effectively employed to achieve trade liberalization, particularly among democratic governments with strong legislatures, the application of subtle personal and group pressure among APEC leaders has already overcome serious obstacles, including the achievement of consensus on the Bogor Declaration.

As the range of issues that APEC seeks to address has broadened, the institutional problems have compounded. Technical agencies in many nations are not nearly as international, or flexible, as their foreign affairs or trade counterparts. It is not sufficient for APEC to rely only on the commitments of national leaders, expecting the state to act at the behest of its titular head. APEC leaders need to consciously address the internal divisions within their own governmental structure that may frustrate their ambitions.

Several APEC builders and promoters have thought about the challenges to APEC in the coming years. Jesus Estanislao emphasized the need for APEC to make an early downpayment. "I think APEC will become a pipe dream if nothing happens between now and the year 2000," he said, adding that the time has come to "give some flesh and substance to the ideal that was so gloriously proclaimed at Blake Island and reinforced at Bogor." USTR Mickey Kantor warned of "isolationist forces" in the United States, adding that "they are in Japan, and they are in China" as well.[57] Narongchai Akrasanee argued that the greatest "challenge is how to live with the US," explaining that while Japan remains more closed, it is liberalizing, whereas the United States is moving from an open and free market to greater aggressiveness against its trade partners, major and minor.[58] Bob Hawke noted more broadly that "on the two sides of the Pacific, you've got a United States which has lost its way, lost faith and confidence in so many respects in itself, where isolationist tendencies are growing, and that's counterpoised on the other side by Japan, who in a sense, I don't know whether it has lost its way, but it's trying to find its way" and adds, "that combination is potentially pretty deadly."[59]

Singapore's Tommy Koh, one of the most well-respected and talented diplomats in the region, had these friendly suggestions for his APEC neighbors: the United States should not disengage, Japan should not leave the West, China should not become a bully, and, finally, Australia should not boast so much.[60]

Beyond these assessments, several other challenges are prominent. The question of membership is one. Here, APEC needs to focus on deepening the commitment of its member economies. It has taken the first step at Bogor toward becoming an effective and potent regional organization and needs to maintain that momentum. There will be strong pressure to delay the process to incorporate new members and widen the organization to include other members of the Asia Pacific community. Indeed, the current membership leaves out many countries that by virtue of geography, history, economics, and culture are intricately interconnected with the region. The temptation to include such nations will be substantial. APEC should resist this urge, however, at least until the process begun at Bogor can be substantially begun. There remain deep divisions within the current membership over questions such as most-favored nation status and unilateral versus collective actions. Bringing in new members, which lack experience with the APEC process, will only complicate these festering questions.

Within APEC, members need to establish a consensus on the pace of progress. Far too long, mutual recriminations have been flung across the Pacific about excessive "Anglo-Saxon" activism and legalism or the obstructionist nature of the so-called "Asian way." These labels should be avoided, for such stereotypes are used mainly to hide the true issues that APEC members face in working toward greater liberalization and cooperation.

The differences between the "activists" and the "gradualists" have nothing to do with culture or race. Singapore has been more aggressive in the APEC process than Canada, for instance. What is needed is an honest discussion of the particular circumstances each economy faces in the liberalization process and a general agreement on the speed at which the organization as a whole should move forward. It is likely a consensus can be reached somewhere in the middle.

A moderate "APEC way" embodies the philosophical idea of the "golden mean." Fittingly, this concept of a "middle way" is known both to the West, by virtue of Aristotle's *Nicomachean Ethics*, and to the East, from the *Four Books* of Confucius. Perhaps for APEC, the art of the possible should be the possibility of finding the golden mean.

Notes

1. Personal interview with Paul Keating, 6 July, 1995.
2. Based on a conversation with a participant.
3. Personal interview with Yohei Kono, 31 August 1995.
4. Personal interview, 9 May 1995.
5. Personal interview, 26 April 1995.
6. Personal interview, 6 July 1995.
7. Personal interview with William Bodde, 29 August 1995.
8. Personal interview with Jusuf Wanandi, 9 July 1995.
9. Personal interview with a Japanese official.
10. Personal interview, 19 May 1995.
11. Personal interview, 27 April 1995.
12. Personal interview, 10 May 1995.
13. Personal interview with Narongchai Akrasanee, 28 August 1995.
14. Personal interview with Robert Zoellick, 20 July 1995.
15. Personal interview with Robert Fauver, 24 July 1995.
16. Personal interview, 9 May 1995.
17. Personal interview, 19 May 1995.
18. Personal interview, 31 August 1995.
19. Personal interview with Sandra Kristoff, 7 September 1995.
20. Singapore APEC ministerial meeting, "Joint Statement," 31 July 1995.
21. Personal interview with a participant.
22. William Bodde, *View from the 19th Floor* (Singapore: Institute for Southeast Asian Studies, 1994), p. 24.

23. Personal interview, 19 May 1995.

24. "Future Steps of APEC, Report of the APEC Senior Officials to the Fourth APEC Ministerial Meeting," Bangkok, 11 September 1992.

25. Personal interview with William Bodde who had the conversation with Romulo, 29 August 1995.

26. Personal interview with an Indonesian diplomat.

27. Personal interview with a participant.

28. Lawrence Woods, *Asia-Pacific Diplomacy*, (Vancouver: UBC Press, 1993), pp. 134–35.

29. "Joint Statement," APEC ministerial meeting, Bangkok, 11 September 1991.

30. Personal interview, 8 June 1995.

31. Speech by Philippine Foreign Secretary Roberto Romulo to the Seattle APEC meeting, 17 November 1993.

32. Personal interview with Wang Yusheng, 8 July 1995.

33. Personal interview, 26 June 1995.

34. Personal interview, 26 June 1995.

35. Personal interview with Han Sung-Joo, 5 July 1995.

36. Personal interview with a senior State Department official.

37. Personal interview, 8 August 1995.

38. Conversation with Japanese official.

39. *Financial Times*, 22 June 1995.

40. Personal interview, 27 June 1995.

41. Personal interview with Keating.

42. Personal interview with a participant.

43. Personal interview, 10 May 1995.

44. Remarks by Sandra Kristoff, Economic Strategy Institute/Pacific Basin Economic Council conference, Washington, DC, 30 March 1995.

45. Personal interview, 19 May 1995.

46. James Baker, "America in Asia: Emerging Architecture for a Pacific Community," *Foreign Affairs* 70, no. 5 (Winter 1991/1992): 1–18.

47. Personal interview, 26 April 1995.

48. Jonathan Clarke, "The United States and Asia Pacific Economic Cooperation," working paper of the Asia Society, 1994, p. 8.

49. Personal interview with Tony Miller, 21 July 1995.

50. Personal interview, 27 April 1995.

51. Personal interview, 26 April 1995.

52. Personal interview with a participant.

53. Personal interview, 5 July 1995.

54. Personal interview with Donald Russell, 2 June 1995.

55. Reuter Asia Pacific Business Report, 6 July 1995.

56. Personal interview, 29 August 1995.

57. Personal interview with Mickey Kantor, 20 July 1995.

58. Personal interview, 28 August 1995.

59. Personal interview with Robert Hawke, 30 June 1995.

60. Personal interview with Tommy Koh, 18 May 1995.

9

New Power Balance

The dramatic changes occurring in the political and economic environment of the Asia Pacific present both enormous challenges and momentous opportunities. Replacing the bipolar conflict of the Cold War is a new arena that encompasses both major powers such as America, Japan, and China and rising powers such as Indonesia and Korea. Yet the mere emergence of a multipolar balance in the Asia Pacific does not necessarily mark the beginning of new political and military stalemate. A new system is gradually emerging that eclipses the East-West and North-South tensions that divided the region during the Cold War. This new paradigm of regional interaction is based less on ideology and more on economic realities. At the same time, traditional political and military challenges remain.

Predicting how the balance among these major and rising powers of the Asia Pacific will evolve is not a simple task. Even the definition of power remains elusive, as each of the main powers in the region faces vastly different political, cultural, and economic constraints on their exercise of influence in the region.

In recent years, most observers have focused on China, a nation that is expected to become the dominant regional power in the next century. China perhaps presents the greatest challenge conceptually. "Territorially amorphous, economically dynamic, culturally proud, socially unstable, and politically unsettled" China, through its sheer size and momentum, will leave an unmistakable imprint on the economic and security order no matter which direction it takes.[1] Its decision to either engage the region in the dynamic Asia Pacific economic order or turn inward and focus on internal cohesion will have far-reaching consequences for the region.

Japan has emerged as the world's second largest economy, but it remains an incomplete power. Like Germany, Japan has sought to limit its leadership and participation to nonmilitary pursuits. Some of Japan's neighbors have called on Japan to become an "Asian Nordic" country that, like Sweden or Denmark, follows a UN-centered multilateral approach to international affairs. Others suggest that Japan play the role of a "global civilian power," exerting international leadership through economic and political (but not military) means. Finally, Ichiro Ozawa and others have called on Japan to shake off its five decades-old wartime legacy and become a "normal country" free from constitutional and psychological constraints to its international engagement. Within Japan, there is nothing approaching a consensus over which path to follow. External events will likely have a major impact on the direction the Japanese people choose.

The smaller emerging powers of the Asia Pacific also will need to define their place in the region. Situated between two behemoths, Korea stands poised to enter the ranks of the major powers. But as long as the political and economic questions of unification remain, it will be too absorbed in its own problems to exert a major role in the world. Some have suggested that ASEAN, too, might emerge as an axis of power in the Asia Pacific. When Vietnam is added, ASEAN will incorporate more than 400 million people within an area that has achieved record economic growth rates over the past two decades. Yet, ASEAN lacks internal cohesion economically and politically. For now, it can be seen only as a caucus at best, but in its 28-year history it has consistently surprised the region with its flexible diplomacy and creative approaches to regional problems.

In the short to medium term, the Asia Pacific will have to contend with a triangular power balance between the United States, Japan, and China. This situation is fraught with dangers, so it is imperative that relations between the three be handled with care. Political scientists have yet to settle the question over whether multi- or bipolar power structures are more stable.[2] It can be safely argued, however, that this triangular balance is more unstable than the previous bipolar one, particularly given the cultural differences and historical legacies of each of the three.

In order to both maintain this tripolar balance and accommodate Asia's rising powers, the Asia Pacific will need to search for a new security framework to replace the Cold War–era military alliance system. Yet the Asia Pacific suffers from underdeveloped regional institutions and the lack of a historic basis for regional cooperation. APEC is seen by some as a potential framework for regional security consultations, but given its nascent state and given its economic focus, this is not likely a viable alternative in the near term. Adding to this dilemma is the wide diversity in incomes, power, and size among the nations in the region.

For these reasons, the Asia Pacific will continue to look toward the United States to fill the gap. But even the American security umbrella, once taken for granted by Washington's allies in the Asia Pacific, is becoming less of a sure thing. There are growing calls in the United States for a linkage between trade and defense policies and suggestions that the United States no longer needs to guarantee the security of its main economic competitors. It is now common to hear policymakers on both sides of the Pacific talk about a "grand bargain" involving access to Asian markets in exchange for protection. It is unclear, however, how long Americans will believe that they are profiting from this arrangement. These are but a few of the enormous challenges the region faces in the new international environment.

Emerging Powers

The changing power balance in the Asia Pacific will inevitably cause friction and mistrust. The growing economic might of East Asian countries is sure to translate into stronger political and military power that may well upset the current balance. While Americans are attracted to the concept of Big Emerging Markets, New Emerging Powers conveys a slightly more ominous tone.

Heading into the next century, it seems increasingly apparent that only Germany will remain a global power within Europe. In the Asia Pacific, there are several, including China, Japan, and perhaps Indonesia and Korea. *The Economist* has estimated that by the year 2020, "only the United States, Japan, and Germany will remain in the top seven [in terms of GDP], joined by China, India, Indonesia, and South Korea." Another study has concurred with this analysis, noting that among the top 15 economies in 2020, Thailand will have displaced France; Indonesia, Germany, and Taiwan will have nudged ahead of both Britain and Italy.

Such projections have infused Asian people and policymakers with an almost euphoric sense of pride. It is this confidence that has given rise to the growing Asianization movement in the region. As one observer noted, many Asians are discovering a "sense of being 'empowered,' of being 'Asian' in the way that some elites in Europe have of being 'European,' and a sense of having 'arrived' or 'rearrived.' "[3] This optimism is increasingly embodied in the bold policies of Asia's emerging "tigers" and "dragons."

This newfound pride has manifested itself as a greater assertiveness, particularly among Southeast Asians. When Malaysian Finance Minister (and Vice Premier) Anwar Ibrahim was limited to a 15-minute visit with his Japanese counterpart, the Malaysian foreign minister urged Ibrahim to reciprocate by restricting Japanese Finance Minister Masayoshi Takemura's time when he called on Ibrahim in Kuala Lumpur. ASEAN has also bristled at China's attempts to bully the Philippines and other members over the South China Sea. Vietnam's ascension to the grouping in 1995 will further boost the organization's resolve to resist China's attempts to force territorial concessions.

Soon, several Asian economies will join Japan in the advanced nations' club. Senior US State Department officials were astonished to learn from their ambassador in Seoul, prior to a visit by President Kim Young Sam in the summer of 1995, that Korea had surpassed Russia in terms of GDP that year. To prepare for its ascension to the Organization for Economic Cooperation and Development in 1996, Seoul has undertaken an ambitious effort to "globalize" its citizens and business leaders.

Indonesia is also rapidly emerging as a major global player, seeking to become a leader both within APEC and the Islamic world. Its huge economic and military potential and strong leadership will accord it an important role in the next century. Indonesia's liberalization, accelerated by the Bogor Declaration, could be a starting point for its emergence as a global economic power. Coordinating Minister for Trade and Industry Hartarto effused that "if we [continue] liberalizing our economy, and maintaining 7 percent growth for the next 25 years, then by the year 2018, based on purchasing power parity, Indonesia [will] belong to the 'Big 5': the USA, Japan, China, India, and Indonesia."[4]

Russia may well reemerge in the medium to long term as a global player with strong interests in the Asia Pacific. Russia has traditionally played a major role in the region politically and militarily and may again turn toward the region in order to share in its dynamic growth.

Although the rise of so many diverse powers in the Asia Pacific may appear destabilizing, the new environment emerging after the Cold War offers a new framework for regional interaction. The first and most obvious change in the post–Cold War era is the end of East-West confrontation. The ideological struggle between communism and capitalism had drawn a line down the middle of the region, slicing through nation such as Korea. The end of the Cold War meant that old ties, long severed by ideological competition, could be reestablished. China, for instance, has been able to renew relations with Korea and a number of ASEAN nations. For its part, Seoul launched an aggressive diplomatic offensive to establish strong diplomatic and economic ties with both Beijing and Moscow.

The negotiated settlement of Vietnam's occupation of Cambodia removed what has been the region's most pressing security issue for the past 15 years. Now ASEAN, originally created to contain Vietnamese adventurism, has accepted Hanoi as a member. The United States also reestablished relations with Vietnam after a 20-year lapse, in part to ensure that its companies will be able to compete in the booming market against Korean, Taiwanese, and Australian investors.

Not as outwardly dramatic but perhaps even more important has been the diminishing North-South divide. First- and second-generation newly industrializing economies (NIEs) proved that the income barrier could be broken. Korea, Taiwan, and Singapore have become models for the developing world and have served as facilitators between North and South. Former Korean Trade Minister and current Chief of Staff Han Seung-Soo commented that "every nation is becoming an NIE now," and the term itself is quickly becoming out of date.[5] US Trade Representative Mickey Kantor said, "I believe that by the year 2010 almost every APEC country will be a developed country."[6] An added dimension to this trend is China, which is experiencing two tiers of economic development, with coastal provinces such as Guangdong and Fujian rapidly becoming NIEs while interior provinces such as Gansu and Shanxi remain firmly fixed in the developing world.

Indonesian President Suharto's strong push for Asia Pacific–wide liberalization, which came during his tenure as chair of the Non-Aligned Movement, was clearly symbolic of the reduction in North-South tensions. A number of aid donors in the past several years have been nations of the "South." Korea, Singapore, and Taiwan are quickly becoming major sources of development assistance, particularly toward their developing neighbors such as Vietnam.

Yet the legacy of and resentment over colonialism persists, as embodied in Malaysia's East Asian Economic Caucus (EAEC). Australian scholar Stephen FitzGerald has interpreted such movements as a sort of "decolonialization," arguing that this is why "it seems more vigorously expressed in the former Western colonies in Southeast Asia than in Northeast Asia."

In the place of East-West and North-South divisions, a common belief has arisen in the "one system" of liberal trade and investment, as Korean Han Seung-Soo put it. Certainly, the heralded "end of history" in the political sphere is premature. Yet its economic equivalent is clearly at hand. Through free trade, developing countries have at last found the formula for achieving a share of the world's wealth.

The evolution of one system in the economic sphere also bodes well politically. There are numerous cases within the Asia Pacific of links between economic liberalization and political reforms. Chile's strong economic restructuring efforts led to the creation of a solid middle class that demanded an end to the military dictatorship of August Pinochet.[7] Korea's and Taiwan's experiences have also exhibited this relationship. Stephan Haggard noted that in both cases economic development was a necessary precursor for democratization, which in turn played a crucial role in bolstering development.[8] The most significant long-term contribution of APEC could be in extending this trend to China through the opening of its markets and its integration into the regional economic system.

Despite the opportunities that this new, hospitable environment provides for accommodating the growing ranks of new powers, the emergence of a new power dynamic presents many risks and dangers. In the 19th and first half of the 20th century, the rise of Germany and Japan as global powers created friction and led to war. China's entrance into the international order as a political and economic superpower may prove to be even more challenging. The uncertainty and concern over the future of the region's power balance shared by strategists around the Asia Pacific, not least in Washington, is well founded.

Five Actors

In the post–Cold War Asia Pacific there are emerging five actors of political and economic power: America, Japan, China, ASEAN, and Europe. All five of these actors hold high stakes in the future of the region for both economic and political reasons. At the same time, each has a unique power portfolio and historical legacy that shapes and influences its perception of the region.

America and the Asia Pacific

Today, American involvement in the Asia Pacific still determines to a large extent the level of regional cooperation that is possible. However, the United States has yet to fully articulate a comprehensive regional policy in the Asia Pacific. The United States has been a strong contributor to APEC, particularly as chair in 1993, although political interest in the initiative has been unsteady. Former APEC Executive Director William Bodde noted that APEC meetings do not even "appear on the screens of White House officials" for at least two-thirds of the year. The one clear message emanating from Washington, however, has been its opposition to the EAEC initiative, despite its own efforts to create NAFTA. The United States has also remained unsure how to deal with regional initiatives outside APEC, particularly the emerging EU-Asian dialogue sponsored by ASEAN.

America's commitment to APEC seems to be a departure from its traditional pattern of relations with the Asia Pacific. The United States has played two alternating roles in the region: that of balancer or that of predominant power. From early in its history, the United States has been an active participant in the Asia Pacific security framework. As a trading nation, America was always conscious of the importance of protecting its trans-Pacific commerce against attack or control from foreign powers. Up until World War II, the United States acted as a balancer in the region, shifting its weight to ensure that no one power dominated the area. One scholar has noted that the American strategy leading up to the war was best symbolized by its support economically for the Open Door policy toward China and militarily by its sponsorship of the 1921–22 Washington Conference, which assigned relative weights to the major navies in the world.[9] In the postwar era, particularly since the Korean War, however, the United States has extended its "security umbrella" to most of the Pacific Rim nations, incorporating the region into a "hub and spoke" system centered in Washington.

The fundamental challenge to US-Asia policy is that the United States has fulfilled its historic mission to combat the Soviet aggression in the region. Despite growing calls for disengagement, America's Cold War success does not mean that the US can and should turn its policy back to the prewar model. Some policymakers, such as former Secretary of State James Baker, have sought to connect American security policy with economic realities. Baker has suggested that the United States augment its hub-and-spoke system to make a wheel, with the spokes cooperating militarily as they exchange economically.[10]

A consensus, however, has yet to emerge within the United States on its proper role in the Asia Pacific. Today, the United States faces four major difficulties in engaging itself more fully in the region. The first is the American tendency toward unilateralism in the security arena and, increasingly, in trade relations. The second issue revolves around the long tradition of moralism in US foreign policy that has at times caused friction with regimes in China and Southeast Asia. The third factor is the tendency for the United States to focus on Europe because of its deep ethnic and linguistic links across the Atlantic. The final challenge is to forge an effective Asia lobby within the United States out of the many disparate business interests and Asian-American communities.

Without a clear external threat, many Americans have become wary of making sacrifices to multilateral entities such as the United Nations or the World Trade Organization. Americans have maintained a clear distrust of multilateral security institutions, exemplified by Congress's rejection of membership in the League of Nations after World War I. Public disenchantment with the United Nations has already led to laws being passed that prohibit American troops from serving under foreign command. Increasingly, Americans are unwilling to bear the burden of world leadership if it means keeping the peace in Bosnia or giving foreign aid to Africa without receiving tangible benefits for the United States.

America's attitudes toward the Asia Pacific are even more complex. The United States clearly has a strong economic incentive for engagement in the Asia Pacific, yet it is precisely in the trade arena that most Americans are disillusioned. The United States has faced chronic trade deficits with almost every one of its East Asian APEC partners, and there is a growing public perception, fueled by political pundits and journalists, that East Asia's economic rise is to blame for America's relative decline.

The most contentious issue of the past decade between the United States and its Asia Pacific partners has been its increasing use of unilateral measures to resolve trade disputes. The American congressional response to the Asian economic challenge has been to pass bill after bill meant to force American presidents to "get tough" on America's Asian trading partners. Recent American efforts at managed trade have been in direct contradiction to its rhetoric in support of free trade and have eroded its credibility among its trading partners. Trade laws such as section 301 and antidumping regulations have also angered America's allies, not only because they rely on the unilateral economic might of the United States but also because of their automaticity and their occasional extraterritoriality. Australian Prime Minister Keating has likened American trade retaliation against its Asia Pacific trade partners to using a "heavy-headed sledgehammer to crack [a] nut."[11] The American public, however, has generally supported such measures, viewing them as a means of forcing others to play by fair (read American) rules.

Moralism has been a salient feature of American foreign policy for much of its history, and Americans have also increasingly supported a linkage between trade policy and moral issues. In recent years, however, this tendency has greatly complicated its relations with Asia. This has been particularly true of the Clinton administration, which has become embroiled in a number of incidents such as China's imprisonment of American human rights activist Harry Wu and the Michael Fay caning case in Singapore. As US Congressman Jim Kolbe (R-AZ), in a speech entitled, "Are We Losing Asia?" commented, "One can hardly avoid noticing a tremendous disconnect between the grand ambitions of the Clinton Asia policy and the muddled reality it has helped to create. From Singapore to China to Japan and Korea, it is ironic, unfortunate, and tragically unnecessary from the standpoint of the US national interest that today our relations are eroding with almost every single major Asian nation. So much for Asia first."[12] Although the Clinton administration officially delinked China's lack of human rights protections and its MFN trade status, the implicit threat of linking human rights to trade concessions has alarmed policymakers in the region. Singaporean statesman Lee Kuan Yew warned that if the administration continued to try to force China to accept human rights protection, "the United States will find itself all alone in the Pacific."[13]

Some cynical Asian commentators have accused the United States of using moralism as a cover for advancing its own economic and political agenda. This characterization is woefully oversimplified. American foreign policy has long been driven by the moralistic zeal of its people. Indeed, it was able to rally support to fight both World War II and the Cold War on the basis of abstract Wilsonian ideals rather than cold rational logic. Today, the need for Americans to see the world as good versus bad has been illustrated by US National Security Adviser Anthony Lake's doctrine of "enlargement." This policy aims to spread democracy and human rights to a handful of nations, including China, that the administration has dubbed "rogue states" and "backlash countries." Yet this same sense of moralism has the potential of turning American inward. Henry Kissinger has pointed out that throughout its history, "America has oscillated between a missionary and an isolationist tendency, between thinking that it was too good for this world and believing that it had a mandate to reeducate the entire world."[14]

Perhaps what is of even greater concern is the potential for American moralism to spark a new cold war with China. "It is a fascinating question as to why the United States has hoped and upon occasion demanded that the world's oldest civilization reject its past and embrace the values of the world's youngest civilization, said Sinologist Michel Oksenberg."[15] China, more than any other nation in the region, has seen American demands on human rights and democracy as a thinly veiled attempt at hegemonism. Complicating this clash has been the warming ties between the United States and rapidly democratizing Taiwan, which many Americans see as a more reliable, and palatable, partner in the region.

America's ties across the Pacific are also heavily influenced by its links across the Atlantic. From the very beginning, the United States has had a complex relationship with Europe. Although the United States has traditionally sought to avoid becoming entangled in European conflicts, it was drawn into two major European wars in this century.

In recent years America has again tried to downplay its Atlantic ties. US Secretary of State Warren Christopher commented that Washington needed to rethink its "Eurocentric" orientation adding that "Western Europe is no longer the dominant power in the world."[16] Indeed, the end of the Cold War has shaken the alliance and threatened to remove the very underpinnings of the multilateral NATO alliance structure. Asia should not view cooling US-European ties as a positive development, however, for two reasons. First, American withdrawal from Europe would signal a real trend toward isolationism in the United States that would likely be extended to Asia as well. The second threat stems from the possibility of America turning away from its European commitments because of fatigue over European economic regionalism. European protectionism could provoke the United States to build its own economic bloc in North America, causing significant collateral damage to Asia Pacific economies.

At the same time, the dynamics of American isolationism may turn from being European-generated to Asian-generated. As Richard Rovere and Authur Schlesinger Jr. noted in their 1951 classic, *The General and the President: And the Future of American Foreign Policy*, "Among oceans, the Pacific has always been the favorite of American isolationists. This is true for the simple reason that the Pacific is not the Atlantic. Isolationism is opposed to the introduction of 'European ideas' in American politics; it has never had to oppose the introduction of 'Asian ideas' because scarcely anyone has tried to introduce them." Yet greater Asian assertiveness in expounding its ideas may well generate calls to return to America's roots. Some are beginning to say that America's destiny lies across the Atlantic, not the Pacific. William Hyland, for example, has argued that America should emphasize its traditional cultural ties with Europe over its "superficial alliances" with Japan and Korea.[17]

One factor that has been lacking in the United States has been a strong mutual dialogue and exchange of ideas with the Asia Pacific. Millions of Americans have an interest in the Asia Pacific through business, scholarly, or ethnic ties. These voices must reverberate in the domestic American political debate in order to deepen US links to the Asia Pacific. Business has contributed heavily to the debate over US-Asian ties. In the debate over China's MFN status, US business groups lobbied hard on Beijing's behalf. American businesses have also been successful in persuading the United States to normalize relations with Hanoi.

Although Asian-Americans remain a relatively small group, their numbers and influence are increasing rapidly. Asian-Americans account for about 8 million citizens, up from only 255,000 in 1940. In California, 1 in 10 residents is of Asian ancestry, and if current trends continue, Asian-Americans will surpass African-Americans by the year 2020.[18] Despite their growing population, Asian-Americans remain underrepresented in America's interest-group politics. The main reason for this political weakness has been a lack of internal cohesion among Asian-American groups. During the Seattle summit, for instance, there was an outpouring of excitement among the city's Asian-American population, but this enthusiasm was limited and divided. US Congressman James McDermott (D-WA) noted that just before the summit "the Filipinos were excited that their president was coming, and the Japanese and Chinese, but no interest in the other guy's person."[19] Given their minority status, it is necessary for Asian-Americans to cooperate in order to focus the nation's attention on Asia.

In the new geopolitical environment, the United States will need to rethink its Asia strategy. First, it should build a multilateral "fan" security apparatus to reduce both the financial and political burdens of regional engagement. The United States should modify its unilateralist approach to be more in tune with multilateral and regional arrangements being explored in the Asia Pacific. Second it needs to temper its moralism with realism. America has the right to object to the human rights practices of its partners, but it must keep in mind the potential damage to its political and economic prestige that results from incessant criticism and pressure.

America also needs to engage in a comprehensive dialogue with the Asia Pacific in order to bridge the cultural and structural issues that plague its relations with the region. These discussions, however, should remain a two-way street and should focus on developing ideas and concepts rather than attempting to impose one system on the other side. Those in the United States with a stake in the region, particularly businesspeople and Asian-Americans, need to focus political debate on the issue of US–Asia Pacific relations.

Despite the difficulties for American relations with the Asia Pacific, its participation in the region is crucial for continued stability and prosperity. In security terms, American naval hegemony has provided open lanes for air and sea traffic. The US military presence in the region has also discouraged Japanese and Chinese adventurism and prevented a regional arms race. The United States also remains a major economic force in the region. A more intangible benefit of America's engagement has been its ability to lead. Neither Japan nor China has the capacity or legitimacy within the region to exert a leading political role in the region.

Americans should be reminded of the strong incentives for it to stay engaged in the Asia Pacific. More than half of the world's economic growth is concentrated in East Asia. The region remains a major, or the major, market for many of America's most competitive products such as aircraft and avionics, electronics, and telecommunications. Quite simply, the region is too important for America to ignore.

Japan's Reexamination of Its Place in the Asia Pacific

Japan is also beginning to find an effective outlet for leadership in the region through the imaginative use of foreign aid and economic expertise. Although still dependent on the United States for military protection, Japan has emerged as the world's second largest economic power and its premier financial center. Hailing the "flying geese" model of development, Tokyo has encouraged overseas investment in infrastructure and production facilities in sectors no longer competitive in high-cost Japan. Through both official development assistance (ODA) and foreign direct investment (FDI), Japan has found channels in which to recycle its global current account surplus.

At the same time, Japan has incrementally assumed an independent role in the region since the late 1980s. In resuming economic aid to China shortly after the Tiananmen incident, Japan broke from its traditional pattern of following America's line. For the first time since World War II, Japan dispatched troops for peacekeeping operations abroad as a major contributor to the UN peacekeeping effort in Cambodia and has since sent contingents to several other areas of the world.

MITI's initiation of APEC in the late 1980s was another manifestation of Tokyo's new activism in regional economic and political affairs (see chapter 12 for further discussion of Japan's role in the region). In the coming years, Japan will have a more delicate relationship with the United

States as it tries to define its role and mission in East Asia. Potential rivalry between China and the United States, Japan, or both could add new challenges for Japanese foreign policy.

China's Emerging Role in the Asia Pacific

China's keener interest in the Asia Pacific was shaped gradually during the 1980s, as its neighbors one by one joined the ranks of the newly industrializing economies and appeared to be on their way to developed-country status. Through that decade, the Beijing government worked toward easing the country from socialism to a market economy. Through its use of deregulations and special economic zones (SEZs), China has mounted one of the most outstanding economic growth drives the world has ever seen. The World Bank has predicted that China's share of world output between 1980 and 2010 will be 50 percent higher than that recorded by Japan in its dynamic growth period from 1950–80.[20] China is likely to emerge as a complete power, not unlike the United States in that it combines economic strength with political and military muscle. China has become increasingly integrated with the economies of the Asia Pacific. Huang Xiang, the director of China's Center for International Studies, a state-sponsored think tank, noted in 1984 that China belonged to the emerging "one united market in the world, where capitalism and imperialism prevail."[21] Huang Xiang specifically emphasized the importance of the Asia Pacific region to China and pointed out: "The Asia Pacific region could have a genuine impact on the world, both politically and economically, if China would develop and come to represent the developing countries of the region.[22] However, he argued that regional cooperation should be limited to economic and cultural dimensions to the exclusion of political and security issues.[23] China has worried about the US influence in the politico-military field in the region.

Its new awareness and realization of an economic future that depends on its relationship with its Asia Pacific neighbors can perhaps be seen as a radical change of China's perspective on the region and its place in it. As Japanese Sinologist Ryosei Kokubun argued, "In a way, it can be interpreted that China has started to relativize its position in Asia, a clear departure from its traditional Sino-centric vision of the world."[24]

However, China's relationship with APEC has been complicated. A senior Chinese diplomat has argued that China seeks APEC-style open regionalism because "China is for free trade." He further claimed that China seeks to use open regionalism because "we want the US to live up to free trade; we do not want the US to unilaterally impose its own trade law on others."[25] Chinese policymakers are becoming interested in strengthening cooperation with Japan development cooperation in APEC. China is one of the largest aid recipients, and Japan is the world's largest aid donor. This relationship has allowed the two to work together within APEC to advance cooperation programs, as China's support of Japan's Partners for Progress initiative illustrates. One reform-minded Chinese economist, an adviser to Vice Premier Zhu Ronqi, said that China and Japan should also explore ways to conduct a closer policy dialogue in macroeconomic policies. "It is still premature," he commented, "but after the *renminbi* becomes a convertible currency, it will be meaningful for both to discuss the implications of their respective macroeconomic policies on the *renminbi*-yen exchange rate, which will have a major impact on the Asia Pacific economy as a whole."[26]

At the same time, Chinese leaders remain unconvinced as to whether APEC and similar multilateral organizations are economically beneficial or are just part of an effort to prevent Beijing from taking its rightful place in the region. One Chinese diplomat commented that "China had long viewed the United Nations as a tool for the US and the West to dominate the world." He added that "China has never shown strong multilateral diplomacy and has not excelled at multilateral conceptualization."[27] China has also remained suspicious of attempts to forge regional cooperation in the Asia Pacific, interpreting them as either American or Japanese ploys to expand their influence. China has long cast a wary eye on the Pacific Economic Cooperation Council (PECC), which it has seen as an endeavor by Tokyo to translate its economic power into regional political power.[28] China also dismissed James Baker's "fan" concept, which he had outlined in a *Foreign Affairs* article, as a maneuver meant to impose a new, American-led, order in the Asia Pacific. At the time, the Chinese cynically predicted that the United States would be unable to support this new system given its weakening economic and financial power.[29] As noted Sinologist David Shambaugh said, "Beijing is particularly critical of what it perceives to be a new effort by the US to dominate post–Cold War Asia."[30] Shambaugh argues that China sees a comprehensive strategy forming in Washington to use multilateral political and economic frameworks and bilateral pressure on trade and human rights to prevent China from achieving its proper role. Kokubun has noted that China remains deeply suspicious of the power of both Japan and the United States, which it sees as the two potential powers that could interfere with its drive to become the preeminent country in the region.[31]

Skepticism exists among China's partners as well, especially with Beijing's aforementioned lack of transparency, particularly in the military arena. Other Southeast Asian policymakers likely share the cautions expressed by former Philippine Foreign Secretary Raul Manglapus: "[There is reason to distrust China] because of its potential as a military power and its traditional historic thinking that it is the Middle Kingdom in this part of the world."[32] There are divergent views of China's "threat."

Some Asians maintain that China has traditionally played a nonaggressive role in the region. Malaysian Prime Minister Mahathir has discounted the Chinese threat: "I don't think that China, at this moment, poses a threat.... No, China is going to concentrate on giving its people a good life."[33] Others have noted that while traditional China was not expansionist, a "Westernized" China with Western concepts of strategy could be dangerous indeed. As the late Indian Prime Minister Jawahadal Nehru put it, "History has proven that a unified and strong China was always expansionist."[34]

China has made repeated claims that it does not seek regional military hegemony, that it will instead focus on economic renewal, deferring military development until well into the future. According to one Chinese officer, "If we compete with economic needs, we will be in competition with the economy, and that is not in China's interest.... When China modernizes we will have more resources ... but, if we don't have economic growth now, we will not modernize later."[35] President Jiang Zemin, mindful of the emerging threat perception of China abroad, emphasized in his Seattle summit debut that "a peaceful and prosperous China will contribute to the world and therefore will not be a threat."[36]

Despite such claims, China has launched a recent military buildup. Official Chinese figures show a double-digit increase in the military budget over the past six years. Foreign estimates have put this figure at three to five times this rate due to China's accounting system and multiple sources of funding. There have been reports, in fact, that even Chinese military leaders do not know the real figure of Chinese military spending. More worrisome to China's neighbors has been its modernization program.[37] While overall troop levels have been cut substantially, China has embarked on an aggressive procurement effort to bring its military hardware up to modern standards.

Moves by the United States to improve ties with Taiwan have met with scorn in Beijing. The visit by Taiwanese President Lee Tung-hui to receive an honorary degree from Cornell University led the Chinese to accuse the United States of "brazenly creating 'two Chinas' or 'one China, one Taiwan,'" violating the so-called "three communiqués" that govern US relations with the two countries.[38] China suspects the United States of playing a "Taiwan card." There has been friction between Beijing and Tokyo as well, although Japan has taken a far more conciliatory approach than the United States. A recent Chinese nuclear test, however, sparked strong condemnation from Tokyo, which suspended a portion of its economic aid program to the People's Republic. When Japan plays its "Hiroshima card" in this manner, China is likely to counter with remembrances of its own victimization at the hands of Japan during the war—its "wartime guilt card." Thus, recriminations continue in a vicious circle.

China expert Michel Oksenberg questions Japan's and America's ability to bring China into a constructive relationship. "China's strategic culture, the Chinese predisposition to use force, their traditional and contemporary military doctrines, and their theories of deterrence—remain ill understood in either the United States or Japan," he wrote.[39]

There is hope, however, that China will see the attractiveness of engaging the Asia Pacific and will thus become a responsible economic actor. For the first time in its 46 years of existence, the People's Republic does not face a direct challenge to its security. As a recent report on China's strategic role in the region noted, "There is a window of opportunity of perhaps two decades in which (as China's power grows) we can seek to make future peace, stability, and economic growth more likely."[40]

Many of the new crop of Chinese leaders, such as Jiang Zemin and Zhu Ronqi, have achieved their status on the virtue of their economic policy skills rather than their ideological orthodoxy. As China becomes increasingly interdependent in capital, technology, labor and natural resources with the Asia Pacific, its ability to turn away from regional integration is less and less tenable. Political liberalization is inevitable, and in the meantime no amount of repression can reverse the economic opening of China's coastal provinces. APEC liberalization helps China achieve sustainable growth. But the ability to harness this tremendous potential depends on Beijing's ability to show flexible leadership within the region.

ASEAN: A Fourth Leg?

While the Association of Southeast Nations, or ASEAN, has been dubbed "the most successful regional body outside the European Community,"[41] its military and economic power is a far cry from that of its neighbors to the north. Certainly ASEAN still cannot be called a "pole" or a "power center" in the traditional sense. However, its strategic location and present economic growth, combined with its diplomatic prowess, have made it a force to be reckoned with in the region. It is likely to grow stronger, as Vietnam's inclusion will swell ASEAN's market to 420 million consumers and Laos, Cambodia, and Myanmar are expected to expand the market further by the end of the century. Lauding the scope of ASEAN's activities, Thai Foreign Minister Kasem Kasemsri notes, "ASEAN is fast becoming a global player."[42] Since its hesitant first days in APEC, ASEAN has become increasingly confident in its role as "core" of APEC. Through a number of forums such as APEC, the ASEAN Post-Ministerial Conference, and the ASEAN-EU plus three summit, ASEAN has found strength in unity. From the first APEC meeting in Canberra, ASEAN ministers perceived the value of gathering separately to pursue a common policy on regionwide issues. In 1993 Thai Prime Minister Chuan, as chair of the ASEAN standing committee, proposed that ASEAN hold a summit prior to the APEC meeting in Seattle. While that initiative was blocked by President Suharto, Thailand and the Philippines have pushed strongly for a separate ASEAN summit in Osaka.[43] The ASEAN members of the Senior Officials' Meetings and the Eminent Persons Group also often meet prior to official sessions to compare notes.

ASEAN nations have become increasingly interested in engagement in the wider Asia Pacific as a result of its economic success over the last two decades. Long worried about domestic political stability, these countries have found that the best strategy for soothing internal discord has been to rely on "national resilience" by providing a strong domestic economic base. At the same time, ASEAN's economic dynamism has been heavily reliant on both foreign investment and export markets to absorb domestic products, making integration with their wealthier neighbors crucial for their continued economic viability.

ASEAN was founded in 1967, primarily as a political group to counter Vietnamese communist aggression. Besides its success at maintaining a unified position against Vietamese expansion, ASEAN's greatest achievement has been economic growth and expanded trade, although it was not originally dedicated to economic integration. Since its inauguration, all of the ASEAN economies, with the exception of the Philippines, have enjoyed growth rates greater than 5 percent per year. In some cases these rates have approached or exceeded 10 percent.[44]

In 1992 ASEAN launched the ASEAN Free Trade Area (AFTA), which targeted tariff levels on selected manufacturing and service sectors. ASEAN has remained more reliant on external trade than on intra-ASEAN commerce. With a couple of exceptions, ASEAN nations share almost identical economic profiles and export the same types of products. Since it first began to explore AFTA in 1987, the growth in intraregional trade has been negligible, despite a 17 percent increase from 1985 to 1990 in trade with the rest of the world.[45] Specifically, many ASEAN nations have become dependent on both Japan, for investment, and the United States, for export markets. These trade and investment patterns increase ASEAN's interest in greater Asia Pacific economic cooperation.

ASEAN has faced challenges cooperating in the economic sphere. As Indonesian scholar Hadi Soesastro has remarked, "ASEAN is both too small and too big. On the one hand, ASEAN is too small to be effective in its external economic diplomacy in view of the changes that are taking place in the world economy. . . . On the other hand, ASEAN is considered too big in the sense that despite restructuring of each of the ASEAN economies they are still diverse and at different levels of development and thus, integration among all its members tends to be shallow."[46]

Following the fall of communism, ASEAN nations began to worry that American and Japanese investors would divert their money from Southeast Asia to the newly opened markets in Eastern Europe. As a result, Southeast Asian nations overcame fears that APEC would subsume ASEAN, realizing the greater importance of maintaining American and

Japanese economic engagement. According to Soesastro, "APEC can be seen as an insurance policy. . . . [T]he incorporation of the US and Japan in APEC could be managed to ASEAN's advantage."

More recently, similar concerns have affected ASEAN's relations with China, a country that offers greater long-run investment opportunities than ASEAN does. Japanese Emperor Akihito's 1992 visit to Beijing, coupled with what has been dubbed a "Japanese economic rush" into China, despite the Japanese recession, has led ASEAN nations to worry that foreign aid and investment will go to China rather than Southeast Asia.[47] One of the reasons that ASEAN countries have made a pitch to introduce important deregulation policies recently is their realization of the decline in investment from Japan by as much as 25 percent in the early 1990s, which coincided with a significant rise in FDI into China.[48] At the same time, however, ASEAN nations do not want Japanese investment to lead to domination by Tokyo.

The United States could counterbalance Japan's superior bargaining and dominant position. ASEAN countries have walked a fine line, however, in their relationship with Washington. Several countries fear the power of unilateral American pressure to open markets and to institute democratization and human rights protection. As one Southeast Asian observer pointed out, "[There is] a persistent inability on the part of the ASEAN states to define a coherent response beyond a common recognition that the US should have a security presence in the region."[49] While Singapore, Indonesia, Philippines, and even Malaysia have offered military facilities such as logistics and repair stations, ASEAN nations have stopped short of allowing a large permanent military-base presence in the region.[50]

ASEAN's active engagement in the Asia Pacific's security system is a departure from its past attempts to distance itself from the region's great powers. During the Cold War, several Southeast nations sought to remove external powers from the region. In 1971 ASEAN promulgated a Zone of Peace, Freedom, and Neutrality (ZOPFAN) in Southeast Asia to express its desire to stay outside big-power rivalry.[51] More recent statements from ASEAN, however, have signaled a desire to see increased military and economic engagement from outside.

There are two reasons for ASEAN's change of heart. The first is the declining American military presence in the region. Following the collapse of the Soviet Union and the closing of US bases in the Philippines, ASEAN nations have become increasingly aware of the "power vacuum" that was emerging in their part of the world. Fearing that either China, Japan, or India would move into the gap, ASEAN nations have sought to reverse America's withdrawal by offering naval access agreements and in the case of Singapore, limited base facilities.[52] As Indonesian military chief General Try Sutrisno (now vice president) has argued, a declining American military presence in the region could encourage states such as Japan and China to "emerge and vie for influence in the region."[53] This gives further reason for ASEAN to endorse the APEC process.

The ASEAN Regional Forum (ARF) has yet to resolve any major security issue, including the festering dispute between China and nearly every ASEAN member over the islands of the South China Sea. So far, however, China has been wary of ARF, fearing it is a ploy to limit China's ascension to a "fuller" role in the region. "[China] see[s] the US as the driving force behind the ASEAN Regional Forum and as attempting to dictate the Forum's agenda," David Shambaugh wrote.[54]

The increasing perceived threat of China already has moved once hostile nations closer toward cooperation. One Indonesian scholar noted that President Suharto's close relationship with Australia's Paul Keating, including their cooperative leadership roles in APEC, is part of an Indonesian strategy to consolidate its relationship with its southern flank to prepare for threats from the north—that is, China. Australia has welcomed its new relationship with Jakarta and shares its concern over Chinese encroachment. The Philippines' Raul Manglapus commented that the Australians "had realistically come to the conclusion that they should get together with Indonesia, not only for economic purposes, but for purposes of security."[55] Australia's emerging partnership with Indonesia is a striking departure from the past. During President Sukarno's tenure, "Australia (population 11 million) was terrified of the hostile Indonesians (population 160 million) sitting one hundred miles across the Torres Straight," noted one observer.[56]

In sum, ASEAN faces challenges in dealing with each of the power centers in the Asia Pacific. With China, they are strategic and territorial. Its problems with the United States often stem from issues such as democracy and human rights. Japan also presents a problem for Southeast Asian nations, which both crave and fear the immense capital that Tokyo showers on the region.

Perhaps the real challenge for ASEAN is the growing difficulty of coordinating its own policies toward APEC or the wider Asia Pacific. Singapore, for instance, has been a leading proponent for American economic and security involvement as well as for APEC. Indonesia has been similarly supportive of APEC but is still suspicious of American political interests in the region. Malaysia falls on the other end of the spectrum, openly calling on Japan or China to counterbalance America. Malaysia and Thailand have presented alternatives for ASEAN, hoping to increase its integration with Northeast Asia and engage Europe in a dialogue to offset the influence of the United States.

From a practical standpoint, it is clear that APEC provides a useful tool for achieving ASEAN's economic, political, and strategic goals. Economically, APEC locks the region into an area that includes its greatest export markets and investment sources. APEC's embrace of open regionalism is also consistent with ASEAN's goals of preventing the regional bloc formation of Europe and North America. In political and strategic terms, APEC can bolster the ARF process by increasing the dialogue of the region's major powers—Japan, China, and the United States. Thai economist Narongchai noted that his nation's diplomats "are so keen on APEC because they think that this is a forum where you have the three powers there."[57]

ASEAN can and will play a significant role in keeping the balance of power in the Southeast Asian region. On the Spratly Islands issue, for instance, nonclaimant countries such as Indonesia, Singapore, and Malaysia have tried to facilitate a negotiated solution. Singapore in particular has been able to present itself as a nonthreatening honest broker. Although China has agreed to refer the matter to the United Nations, it has yet to ratify the Law of the Sea Treaty, which governs such disputes. So far, China has insisted on dealing with the issue on a bilateral basis. This case, however, demonstrated ASEAN's strong cooperative efforts, which have made it more difficult for China to ignore ASEAN's collective will. "One chopstick is easy to break," commented one ASEAN official on his organization's response to China's moves. "Several together are much more difficult to deal with."[58]

Europe: Partner or Pariah?

Europe was relatively slow to appreciate APEC's importance and initially Europe dismissed it. One MITI official related a minor (and much joked-about) episode before the first APEC meeting in Canberra in which a French official argued that France warranted membership in APEC because of its sovereignty over New Caledonia (the MITI official had to consult a map to verify his claim). The MITI official apparently did not take France's interest seriously at the time. The 1991 decision to include the Three Chinas sparked Europe's interest in the organization. The 1993 Seattle APEC summit meetings deepened Europe's growing concern over the potential power and influence of an Asia Pacific free trade area and was a major factor in Europe's compromise in the Uruguay Round negotiations (as was discussed in earlier chapters.)

While individual European nations have pursued aggressive and balanced policies toward the Asia Pacific, the European Union as an institution has been hindered by internal squabbles. In 1993, for instance, Belgian Foreign Minister Willy Claes, who was about to assume the EC Council of Ministers presidency, suggested that APEC and the European Union maintain informal contacts, or perhaps even mutual observer status. These comments won Claes an immediate rebuke from many of his European colleagues and forced the abandonment of the idea.[59] Despite its problems in articulating a common Asia Pacific policy, Europe has already established deep economic ties with the region. In 1992, total trade between Europe and Asia surpassed that across the Atlantic and East Asia has become Europe's largest external customer for its food, clothing, chemicals, and textiles.

Germany has spearheaded the European efforts to gain leverage in the dynamic Asian markets. The German government has set out 10 key strategies to raise Germany's profile and access to Asia, including support for the participation of China and Taiwan in the World Trade Organization, cooperation in the United Nations and other multilateral forums, coordination of efforts in Asia with Germany's EU counterparts, and the promotion of increased dialogue between Germany and both Japan and APEC. The government has initiated these measures out of a concern that its businesses were preoccupied with Europe and slow to understand the impact of emerging Asian markets. Foreign Minister Klaus Kinkel argued that "[i]f the German business community was as active in the growth markets of Southeast Asia and China as the Japanese are in Europe, we would have less unemployment."[60] As part of these efforts, Chancellor Helmut Kohl led 40 top German executives on a state visit to China in 1993.[61] Germany's vigorous and successful Asia policy has limited itself to engaging the region on strictly commercial terms. One observer has remarked that among European economies, Germany has the most similarity with those in Asia. "If anything, Germany shares more characteristics with Japan, particularly where the capital market is concerned; there exists a more corporatist style of economic management," he argued.[62] Indonesian scholar Jusuf Wanandi remarks that Germany is more welcome in the region because it does not have the colonial legacy of its continental neighbors. "They also have no hangups about the human rights thing and all that," Wanandi observed.[63] Bonn's 10-point strategy paper noted the importance of human rights but added that "mutual knowledge and recognition of, as well as respect for, societal, cultural, and religious differences are, however, indispensable."[64] Germany's efforts have won it numerous business deals in the region. Between 1987 and 1993, Germany more than doubled its exports to East Asia, an increase of over $13 billion.[65]

Yet Europe is not a single entity. There are deep divides within the community over economic and foreign policies, and in regards to Asia, some European countries, such as Germany, have been much more effective than others. France, Germany's main competitor for European leadership, has been the one country that has suffered from its mix of politics and economics. Anti-Asian rhetoric, such as former French Premier Edith Cresson's charge that Japan was scheming to conquer the world, has given Paris a rather dim image in the Asia Pacific.[66] This sentiment was compounded by a later prime minister, Edouard Balladur, who called for an economic alliance between North America and Europe to oppose low-wage Asian competitors. In a bilateral meeting between Clinton and French President François Mitterrand during the 1993 Tokyo G-7 summit, Clinton referred to Balladur by name when he expressed his strong objections to the proposal.[67] France's recent nuclear tests in the South Pacific have even led to calls for a boycott of French products in Australia, Japan, and elsewhere.

In 1994, a study initiated by the Commission for European Communities recommended a comprehensive European strategy toward East Asia. The report noted that in many ways, Europe already had strong ties with the region, including foreign aid (between 1976 and 1991 Europe disbursed three times the amount of assistance given by the United States), bilateral and multilateral dialogue, including periodic direct EU-ASEAN ministerial talks, and investment.[68] At the same time, the panel recommended that EU members redouble efforts to attract foreign investment, participate in political and security dialogues, and shift the emphasis of trade policies from defensive to proactive. One step being considered is the strengthening of cooperation between the European Union and ASEAN. In 1996 the two organizations are planning their first-ever leaders' summit, which is to be held in Thailand. Singaporean Prime Minister Goh Chok Tong has described the growing Asian-European dialogue as a move to tie up the "two ends of a ribbon. At one end are the prospects in the Asian economies, and at the other end are the prospective investors in Western Europe and elsewhere."[69]

Europe's entrance into the Asia Pacific power game could alter the already complex triangular balance between the United States, Japan, and China. In economic terms, the Europeans see Asia's potential to absorb its high-end exports such as aircraft and view its developing markets, particularly China's, as an attractive destination for direct investment. Politically, Europe does not face the same challenges as the United States, which is intimately involved in the region's affairs. A German strategy paper noted that Bonn has "no direct security interests in the Asia-Pacific region."[70] This further cements the US perception that Europe essentially is a free rider in the region. In fact, Europe has seen an opportunity to exploit Asian-US political tensions to its own advantage.[71] Europe's renewed interest in breaking into Asia has been compared by one observer to the competition between France, Germany, Britain, and the United States in the late 19th century to establish an economic presence in the "open door" era in China.[72]

The development of an ASEAN-EU dialogue has sent ripples across the Pacific Ocean. Some American officials have become concerned that the summit meeting is a ploy to "gang-up" on the United States. Australian Prime Minister Paul Keating, who brushed off claims that the meetings would have any significance, takes a similarly negative view. "This has come out of Europe's almost paranoid interest in APEC," he argued.

"They see APEC as developing itself into an exclusive trade body."[73] His colleague from New Zealand, James Bolger, was more positive. "We believe ourselves that the meetings can do nothing but good to break down the lingering concerns of the Europeans that somehow or other the Asia Pacific region is doing something untoward that they're not familiar with and might be to their disadvantage," he commented.[74]

Yet, there are some Asian and European officials who do harbor some ulterior motives. According to one MITI official, a French official said, "Perhaps, it will be the first opportunity to design the post–Cold War world without an American role or participation."[75] Both French President Jacques Chirac (then-mayor of Paris) and British Prime Minister John Major expressed their support for the EAEC when they visited Kuala Lumpur in 1993. Their move was seen as an attempt by European countries to play an "EAEC card" in order to prevent the United States from enjoying all the benefits of the rising East Asian economic tide.

There is some room for maneuverability. Both regions have been the victim of American trade retaliation and have strong motivations for countering Washington's power. This shared perception has led each region to explore the idea of forming a countervailing force vis-à-vis the United States. Europe has tended to exploit internal disputes among APEC members, particularly between the United States and Japan. When Japan appealed America's decision to impose tariffs on Japanese automobiles, for instance, Europe asked to be a party to the appeal, despite its own tarnished track record on auto import restrictions. Yet like the EAEC proposal, the potential for direct Asian-European ties has sent a strong message to the United States on the need to cultivate its relationships with its Asia Pacific partners. The United States has traditionally viewed Asian-European talks suspiciously and in some cases with hostility, just as some Americans saw the Anglo-Japanese alliance earlier in the century as gradually developing into an anti-US pact.[76] America's concern in part stems from its legacy of anticolonialist, anti-hegemonic engagement in the Pacific characterized by its 19th century Open Door policy with China. Perhaps old habits die hard.

Despite the probable ulterior motives in Paris or Kuala Lumpur, most Asian officials see increased Asian-European ties as a natural process of global economic interdependence, not as an affront to the United States. Indonesian Ambassador to Japan Wisber Loeis noted, "Europe is as important as Japan and the United States because Japan is our largest customer and supplier, the United States is number two, and Europe number three, so we need all three." Singapore's Premier Goh argued: "The global economic order in the 21st century will be supported by three principal regions, namely North America, Europe, an East Asia. The proposal for a meeting of leaders from Asia and Europe is meant to close the Asia-Europe side of the triangle and add to global economic stability."[77] EU

Executive Commission President Jacques Santer argued that EU-Asian talks should be seen as part of the emerging "grand triangle" among Europe, Asia, and North America.[78]

The United States in turn can play its Europe card. The United States and Europe have strong and pervasive ties. Trans-Atlantic security relations, as embodied in NATO, are still much stronger than US alliances with Asia. Many foreign policymaking elites in the United States have emerged from the Atlanticist mold as well, cementing strong personal ties across the Atlantic that are only beginning to form across the Pacific Rim.

Recently, the United States and the European Union agreed to explore the possibility of a Trans-Atlantic Free Trade Area (TAFTA), that would link Europe with the NAFTA area. As a practical measure, such an agreement is likely unworkable since the European Union and United States compete in and protect many of the same sectors. Yet rhetorically, it is a reminder that the United States retains strong links across the Atlantic that it could use if locked out of Asia. So far, however, Europe appears to remain the primary target, not partner, of American regionalization efforts.

Triangular Game

Interestingly, the three leading powers of the Asia Pacific—America, Japan, and China—have each found it difficult to exert leadership within APEC. Of the three, the United States has perhaps the strongest experience in multilateral institutions, but top American leaders have tended to see APEC as useful only for "event diplomacy." Japan, while active in the early planning stages, has played even less of a leadership role in the process. Of the three, China has adopted the lowest profile, and it has yet to clearly articulate its interest in the forum.

One observer has noted of these preeminent power centers: "These are three nations of breathtaking cultural arrogance, and each of them is powerful in different ways. The mix is potentially explosive."[79] Triangular power balances are nothing new to the Asia Pacific. Starting in the late 19th century with rivalry between Japan, Russia, and the United States and continued with the Cold War version of Russia, China, and the United States, the notoriously unstable triangle has been more the rule than the exception. Today Russia has largely dropped out of the picture, although it could one day be a wild card in the equation. Replacing it is Japan, which, while still bound by its bilateral security treaty with the United States, will be growing increasingly confident in its ability to play an independent role. How one predicts the relationship's development depends on perspective. An idealist would argue that the future balance will be cooperative, with the three powers bound in a web of mutually beneficial, productive trade relations. This is the future envisioned by the Clinton administration in its attempts to elevate APEC into the primary forum for regional interaction.

Realist theories of international relations would suggest a different outcome along the Pacific Rim. Realists scoff at the suggestion that APEC will provide a mechanism through which Japan, China, and the United States could share leadership in a constructive manner. According to political scientist Richard Higgot, "Despite aspirations, there is little likelihood at this stage (. . . the rhetoric of the Seattle Summit notwithstanding) that APEC has sufficient institutional strength to provide '. . . a convenient regional framework within which Japan can move towards a position of shared policy leadership with the United States.' "[80] Higgot criticizes the reliance on the beneficial role of the market in institution building in the region: "Market-led theories of integration and cooperation are underwritten by too robust a notion of rationality and have little or no theory of politics to sustain them."[81] While optimists may see these realists as overly cynical and may point to the current growth of economic interdependence in the region as proof of a "posthegemonic" world, at least in China strategic thinkers take theories of power dynamics very seriously and remain skeptical of any initiatives that claim to be power balance–neutral.

There are also internal factors that concern many of the smaller nations in the Asia Pacific. One of the greatest worries is that nationalism, dormant during the ideologically centered Cold War, will reemerge in Japan, China, or both. As one scholar has noted, East Asia has no tradition of multilateral power arrangements: "The historical pattern has been one of domination by the strongest regional power, principally by China and, in the first part of the twentieth century, Japan. There is scant regional experience of international relations among states of like capacities practicing European-style balance of power politics."[82]

Asian-style hegemony has traditionally been couched in terms of regionalism and ethnic solidarity rather than open power relationships. During World War II, Japan's militaristic nationalists subjugated much of the region in the name of Asianism. In the minds of many Asians, Japan's reluctance to publicly examine its wartime record, as Germany has, is an ominous sign for its future intentions. Recent comments by politicians such as former Foreign Minister Michio Watanabe, who claimed that Japan's prewar conquest of Korea was a "peaceful merger," have raised ire around the region.[83]

Similar concerns surround the region's relations with China, especially given its rapid economic growth and military potential. Asians remember a Sino-centric system of tutelage in which all nations in the region were under the "benevolent" domination of the "Middle Kingdom" before the coming of European imperialists. While Beijing's control was not as absolute as many Chinese would like to believe, the image of a paternal, hegemonic China is popular among modern nationalists.[84] The reassertion of China's international position has become more pronounced in recent years as the ailing Beijing government seeks to legitimize itself through the use of nationalistic rhetoric.

The concern over America's role is somewhat opposite to that of China and Japan. While few countries favor outright dominance from Washington, the United States is seen as a useful balancer to Chinese and Japanese ambitions. Singaporean Senior Minister Lee Kuan Yew has warned that if the United States withdrew from Asia, "[t]here could then be only two outcomes concerning the two major regional powers, Japan and China. They either merge or there would be a takeover of one by the other—a colossus so big, that the United States and Europe will not be able to balance its weight."[85]

After the Sino-US relationship deteriorated due to Lee Tung-hui's visit to the United States, some Chinese strategists have started to talk about *lian ri fan mei* (alliance with Japan to counterbalance the United States) in informal discussions.[86] A Sino-Japanese alliance would be devastating to smaller Asian countries. After Japanese Emperor Akihito's visit to Beijing, Philippine President Fidel Ramos used the analogy of two elephants: When elephants fight each other, some grass gets trampled under foot. But when elephants mate (which they do on their sides), even more grass gets crushed.[87]

Lee Kuan Yew has argued that a continued American presence in the region, along with a partnership with Japan, is vital for the region's stability. Lee speculates that "if Japan gets too close to China, the balance will be very difficult to maintain because then it becomes again uncomfortable for the rest of Asia."[88] Lee hopes that the power balance will evolve along the lines of an "isosceles triangle, where America and Japan will be closer than China and Japan."

This argument stands in striking contrast to the analysis by Malaysia's Mahathir, who first coined the elephant analogy to apply to the US-Japan relationship. Mahathir argues that Asia has nothing to fear from a potential Sino-Japanese alliance: "[T]hey will balance themselves because Japan has a natural fear of China and China has a natural fear of Japan."[89]

For their part, American strategists almost uniformly endorse a continued partnership with Japan in the event of a trilateral power rivalry. Both countries have several characteristics that would support a continued alliance, including a shared belief in democracy, free trade, and, more generally, the status quo. At the same time, short-term bilateral tension has led some in both countries to flirt with the idea of using a "China card." Some Japanese argue that a Sino-Japanese alliance is more natural than its current US ties because of the long historical, cultural, and racial links between the two countries. For its part, the United States can hark back to the anti-Japanese Sino-US alliance of the 1930s.

But as Sinologist Michel Oksenberg has warned, "Neither Tokyo nor Washington should look upon China as a counterweight to the other. Such strands of thought exist in both capitals. . . . Our readings of history caution against such views. Efforts to use China for tactical advantage give

Beijing excessive influence. The strategy yields Beijing the opportunity to play Washington and Tokyo against each other. Such a strategy assumes a greater capacity to manage tensions within a triangle than the three capitals possess."[90]

Henry Kissinger has warned that the United States should minimize its antagonism of China. "Tensions between China and the United States tempt Japan into acting as mediator, which in practice implies a degree of dissociation from the United States," he wrote. "Moreover, Japanese mediation could easily generate temptations to achieve hegemony in Northeast Asia."[91]

The United States and Japan can and should cooperate in order to integrate China as a responsible nation in the world system. Historian Walter McDougall has pointed out the benefits of a continued alliance, arguing that "Japan and America, pooling their complementary strengths, can assist Korean unification, the development of China and Siberia and provide the foundation for a multilateral regime, with minimal danger to themselves or threat to others."[92] Despite the opportunities that lie in a continued partnership, they have yet to be explored.

The fate of the region's security lies in large part in the hands of these three major powers. The membership of all three in the APEC forum necessarily makes it an important body through which to influence the strategic atmosphere in the region. According to one senior US official, "What will hold APEC together is that the US, China, and Japan are all balanced off one another. Frankly, there is much of Asia that is not comfortable with the giants of Japan and China, and one of them being more prominent than the other, and sees the US as a counterforce; in the same sense they would not like the US dominating. This goes in all ways, and they view Japan and China as good counterweights to the United States. In some sense, I think the beauty of APEC is in the fact that these three enormous players are offset, and it provides a comfort level for everyone else in the region . . . even for us."[93] Yet it will not be enough for the region's three main players to simply achieve a balance that simply canceled each other out in APEC. Each will need to explore means of exerting entrepreneurial leadership in conjunction with smaller APEC through members and each other. They should see APEC as a chance to learn to share leadership through on-the-job training.

The Politics of Regionalism

The United States has simultaneously facilitated and hindered efforts to forge regionalism in the Asia Pacific. Focused on the political and military necessities of the Cold War, American strategists often viewed multilateral cooperation as little more than an instrument to check communism in East Asia. Former US National Security Adviser W. W. Rostow, for instance, maintained many years ago that Asia Pacific regionalism would be key in preventing either China or the Soviet Union from dominating Southeast Asian and Indochina—an eventuality that, in his words, would threaten the "vital interests of India, Japan, the United States, Indonesia, and Australia."[94]

In the 1950s and 1960s the United States launched the Southeast Asian Treaty Organization (SEATO) in response to the perceived threat from Chinese and Vietnamese communists. SEATO included both independent Asian nations such as Thailand, and European nations, notably Great Britain, that retained colonies in the region. Despite its high-minded goals, the organization quietly disappeared from the scene in the mid-1970s having fulfilled no notable role. Rostow argued that the North-South conflict was the major contributing factor to the failure of America's attempt to create regional security organizations in the Asia Pacific. Raul Manglapus, who served as secretary general of the founding conference of SEATO noted, however, that the forum "suffered from the disadvantage of having been drawn up entirely in Washington."[95]

Efforts to achieve economic cooperation are still often seen in *Realpolitik* terms. The US proposal to extend NAFTA to individual Asia Pacific economies led many to accuse Washington of pursuing a divide-and-rule strategy. APEC has also been viewed skeptically by some Asian leaders. Thai Prime Minister Anand Panyarachun originally thought Australian Prime Minister Bob Hawke's APEC initiative was only a front while the "United States decided to take a backseat, pretending that they were not so interested."[96] When Malaysia's Mahathir learned of the proposal from Australian envoy Richard Woolcott, he was immediately suspicious of the designs of both Japan and the United States.

Yet American involvement was key to the normalization of relations among many Asia Pacific nations, a prerequisite for regional institution building.[97] Following World War II, American security guarantees and military engagement enabled Japan to reestablish ties with Australia, New Zealand, Korea, and Southeast Asian nations, which shared in the comfort of the American security blanket. The US-Japan security alliance remains important in supporting Japan's relations with its neighbors, particularly China and Korea.

Despite the reestablishment of economic and diplomatic links after World War II, for much of the past 50 years there has been significant resistance from Asian countries themselves to regionalism. Korean and Japanese proposals for regional economic cooperation in the 1960s all failed to gain support from other Asian nations. In 1980 Prime Minister Masayoshi Ohira's pan-Pacific cooperation proposal was gracefully rejected, and a few years later Korean President Chun Doo-Hwan's proposed Pacific summit was totally ignored. Only ASEAN was able to organize itself into a coherent group, although it took more than a decade to really establish itself. For many years, the word "multilateralism" was a bad word among Asian policymakers, who worried that it was a catch phrase for American disengagement. The term "regionalism" revisits a different, but equally ominous, connotation of Japanese domination. This situation was much different from that in Europe, where America played a role in NATO more akin to "first among equals" than paternal leader and Germany was accepted as a new partner, not a lingering threat.

Another crucial factor that explained the lack of regionalism was the absence of an economic incentive. "Regional economic cooperation . . . made little sense, from either the American or the Asian point of view: cut off from traditional markets on the Asian mainland by the Cold War, allied export strategies were reoriented toward the US market, where access was best guaranteed by bilateral bargaining and membership in global organizations such as the General Agreement on Tariffs and Trade (GATT), not by multilateral regional initiatives," said American scholar Miles Kahler. This strategy had far-reaching consequences for the region. Rather than strengthening regional economic interdependence during the postwar period, Asian countries focused on building strong ties across the Pacific.

Today this situation has changed dramatically. The diversification of trade and investment ties have supplanted the bilateral flow formerly common in the Asia Pacific. APEC has a higher rate of intraregional trade than the European Union, providing further incentive for economic cooperation.

A wide gap still remains in terms of regional frameworks between security and economics. Because of earlier economic circumstances, the security framework in the Asia Pacific evolved much differently from that constructed in Europe. Rather than an overarching, NATO-style military pact, Washington maintained a web of bilateral treaties with its key allies in Asia. This "hub-and-spoke" system gave it both greater leverage and a larger burden in its engagement in the region.

Central to America's Asian security strategy was Japan. Both Japan's historical legacy and America's desire to ensure that bilateral relations remained close discouraged the creation of a regional security arrangement. The Cold War also worked against the cause of regionalism. Soviet leaders from Brezhnev to Gorbachev often called for multilateral security dialogue in the Asia Pacific, but Washington firmly rejected such an initiative, viewing it as a ploy to increase Soviet influence in the region. Americans also rebuffed suggestions from Australia and Canada creating in the Asia Pacific an arrangement like the Conference on Security and Cooperation in Europe (CSCE, now the OSCE).

With the Cold War's end, the United States is no longer averse to multilateralism in either the security or economic realms. Former US Secretary of State James Baker's "fan" concept was perhaps one of the earliest conceptual attempts to modify the traditional "hub-and-spoke" strategy. Baker envisioned a framework, which, while centered on an American deterrent and balancing, would encourage Asian nations to cooperate directly to bolster their mutual security. The US decision to downplay the hub-and-spoke model is due in large measure to the increasing cost of being the "hub" and signals its search for a more equitable, "burden-sharing" relationship.

Economically, the United States would like Asians to diversify their export markets so that it is no longer the only "hub" for Asia's exports and can thus begin to correct its bilateral trade imbalances with the region. Encouraging intraregional trade would reduce another of the burdens that the United States shouldered during the Cold War. At the same time, it is in the interest of America's Asian trading partners to diversify. An end to the hub-and-spoke arrangement may be to Asian countries' advantage in another sense: there appears to be a link between America's "hub-and-spoke" security system and its propensity to use bilateral trade leverage. Between 1977 and 1994, the United States initiated nearly twice as many section 301 cases under its trade law against APEC partners as it has against the European Union. Even more telling, perhaps, is that it has publicly threatened to invoke 301 on 23 cases in the Asia Pacific compared with only 9 in Europe in this same period.[98]

The relationship between the United States and Asia is moving toward a more equitable one. The United States remains the linchpin of the Asia Pacific security system. This system, however, has loosened significantly with the mantling of the Cold War–era camps. Today, power has diffused, and for the first time in decades, Asia Pacific nations are exploring alternative models of security, such as the ASEAN Regional Forum. In another break with the past, Japan is being increasingly engaged in the security dialogue of the region.

Some nations in the Asia Pacific are also reexamining the role of the United States in the region's economic system. "East Asia is accepted as a powerhouse," said Australian Ambassador to Washington Don Russell. "But it is a powerhouse that needs the US less and less, as trade and investment expand rapidly within Asia." In fact, one Malaysian commentator, Chandra Muzafar, accused the United States of trying to use APEC to "hitch a ride" with the more dynamic Asian economies.[99] This may be true, but it is also the reason for the engagement of China, Japan, and Europe in the region. For the United States and Asia as well, this is an important way to help fill the gap between security and economics and should be seen as a part of the "grand bargain" maintaining the US presence in the region—presence that has facilitated the region's rapid growth in trade and commerce over the past five decades.

The New Asia Pacific Order

APEC embodies a vision beyond the traditional realm of concerns about power balance and military competition. APEC enthusiasts dream that

APEC someday will integrate the political interests of the region, much as the market has integrated their economic interests. They hope that APEC will seek to go beyond the question of hegemonism and realize a region that shares a collective goal of peace and economic prosperity.

It is too early to tell how the future power balance will shake out. Will it be a Mahathir-style Asian coalition lining up against North America and Australia, or perhaps a triangular game between Japan, America, and China? Most leaders and observers hope that the expanding economic and intellectual linkages around the Pacific will lead to the establishment of a true "post-hegemonic" order in the Asia Pacific. This is perhaps the unwritten political vision APEC represents.

There are good reasons to be optimistic. A racial bloc would be strongly opposed by almost all countries in APEC, particularly Singapore, Korea, Japan, the Philippines, and Australia, which feel strong bonds with both East and West. The reliance on international trade and the common interest of North America and East Asia in preventing the formation of exclusive blocs also give ample reasons for discarding the idea of an Asian bloc.

The triangular game of balance-of-power politics portends more risky scenarios. It is true that the region has had a tradition of triangular power structures, and the interests of all three nations are clearly diverging on many issues. There is also the question of geostrategic comparative advantage. Japan and the United States are both strong maritime powers. Both country's bitter memories and lessons of Asian continental engagement ensure that they will not challenge continental China on its home turf. China, with its army of 3 million, however, presents a new question. It has not had a serious blue-water fleet in 400 years, yet its rapid economic growth may enable it to build a fleet to rival its Pacific neighbors if it so chooses. Were it to move aggressively into Southeast Asia, Taiwan, or the Persian Gulf, both Washington and Tokyo would have to respond decisively or it would pose a serious question as to whether they see the threat in the same way.

In order to prevent Chinese adventurism, it is imperative that freedom of navigation be maintained along Asia's sea lanes. The Taiwan Straits, the South China Sea, and the Straits of Malacca are all vital to their own country's, and the region's, economic well-being. Freedom of navigation lies at the foundation of APEC, since the free trade on which APEC's prosperity depends presupposes it. After all, the Asia Pacific civilization is a maritime civilization. If China were to acquire naval superiority in the Western Pacific, the region's prospects could be severely dampened.

Historically, China has followed a pattern in its relations with external powers: When it has perceived a threat from the north, it has been benevolent to the south. When the threat emerged from the south, it has sought warm relations with the north. With the collapse of the Soviet Union, China no longer faces any competition from its northern borders. This dynamic makes it crucial for China's neighbors to formulate a strong stand that, while offering China the benefits of trade and economic integration, draws a firm line against aggression and intimidation.

Rather than waiting for such a challenge, it is important that both Japan and the United States move boldly toward creating an effective regional system. It is clearly in the interest of both countries to maintain military stability in the Asia Pacific. Equally important to both is to prevent China from becoming, as one observer put it, "a dissatisfied revisionist power, bent on upsetting the regional status quo and redressing the humiliations and losses of territory it has suffered over the last several centuries."[100] It is imperative that Japan and the United States convince China that positive economic engagement is in its best long-term interests. Should it believe that more could be gained from aggression, there is no doubt that it could use its leverage to destabilize the region and drive a wedge between the United States and Japan, an eventuality that could have chilling ramifications for the entire Asia Pacific. Simultaneously, the interests of Japan and the United States are increasingly overlap those of ASEAN. All three value free trade, the rule of law, freedom of navigation, the peaceful resolution of disputes, and a multilateral framework in which to settle regional issues.

It is difficult to analyze how APEC has affected the emerging power dynamics in the region, but it is possible to speculate on how the regional body will address these issues. Perhaps APEC's greatest feat in a strategic sense has been its incorporation of all four actors—the United States, Japan, China, and ASEAN—under one roof. Its focus on economic cooperation and trade facilitation has served to channel the energies of these powers into greater economic interdependence, at least in the short and medium terms. In this regard, APEC may affect the power dynamic in the region in a constructive way. At the same time, there is the possibility of the reverse case—that is, political issues and problems could push their way onto the APEC agenda.

Perhaps the greatest challenge for APEC will be to avoid upsetting the power balance between Japan, China, and the United States. In addition to the "cultural arrogance" of these three major powers, each of them faces serious political problems that hampers further commitments to APEC's evolution. The American challenge is its aversion to multilateralism. Its philosophy is committed to changing the world and "if you cannot change it, contain it." Japan's problem traditionally lay in internationalism. Its adage is "adapt to the world; if you cannot, close yourself." What China fears most is interdependence. Its attitude is to "adopt the world; if you cannot, reject it." All three outlooks on international interaction will likely plague at least one, and possibly all three powers. If any were to revert to isolation, however, APEC's endeavors would likely have to be seriously curtailed.

In addition to a traditional reluctance to commit and engage, the United States, Japan, and China each face serious internal problems. America, which has experienced a relative economic decline, is reconsidering its role in the world after 50 years of exhausting and costly engagement. Japan is in the midst of a major transformation in its domestic political and economic systems and finds itself with a weak leadership that lacks a vision for Japan's role in the new international environment. For its part, China is attempting to further its spectacular economic gains, achieved through a more open economy, while holding onto an outdated ideology of autocratic communism.

There is little APEC can do to affect the emerging relations between these three nations directly. However, its annual forums and working groups provide a regular mechanism through which the three can work on a positive-sum basis toward agreement on less-controversial economic issues. In the long run, their experience working cooperatively should help build confidence and reduce suspicion over each other's foreign policy goals and initiatives. APEC in fact provides great opportunities for the three major powers to learn how to exert more entrepreneurial leadership. So far, none of the three has taken such a leadership role within the process, and each remains unsure of how APEC will contribute to their own regional and global objectives. Their skeptical postures toward APEC serves as a reminder of the delicate position the organization plays in the region's power-politics dynamic.

Notes

1. Yoichi Funabashi, Michel Oksenberg, and Heinrich Weiss, *An Emerging China in a World of Interdependence* (New York: The Trilateral Commission, 1994), p. 3.

2. Robert Gilpin, *War and Change in World Politics* (Cambridge, UK: Cambridge University Press, 1981), pp. 88–89.

3. Speech by Stephen FitzGerald to the 1994 Asia Leaders' Forum, Bali, Indonesia, 14 September.

4. Personal interview with Hartarto, 16 August 1995.

5. Personal interview with Han Seung-Soo, 7 July 1995.

6. Personal interview with Mickey Kantor, 20 July 1995.

7. John Williamson, *The Political Economy of Policy Reform* (Washington: Institute for International Economics, 1994), pp. 225–231.

8. Stephan Haggard, *Pathways from the Periphery* (Ithaca, NY: Cornell University Press, 1992), pp. 254–70.

9. Akira Iriye, *The Cold War in Asia: A Historial Introduction* (Englewood Cliffs, NJ: Prentice-Hall 1974), p. 17.

10. Gerald Curtis, ed., *The United States, Japan, and Asia,* (New York: Norton, 1994), p. 238.

11. *New York Times,* 2 May, 1994.

12. "Are We Losing Asia?" speech by Jim Kolbe before the National Strategy Forum, Chicago, 20 May 1994.

13. *New York Times*, 2 May, 1994.

14. Speech by Henry Kissinger, "Global Outlook for the 21st Century," Frankfurt, Germany, 5 July, 1995.

15. Curtis, p.105

16. *New York Times*, 25 November, 1993.

17. William Hyland, "The Case for Pragmatism," *Foreign Affairs*, 47 Winter 1991/1992.

18. *Straits Times*, 12 March, 1995.

19. Personal interview with James McDermott, 7 June 1995.

20. World Bank, *China's Emergence: Prospects, Opportunities, and Challenges* (Washington: The World Bank, 1994), p. 5.

21. Kazuko Mori, "Chugoku to ASEAN—Saigi kara Kyoryoku e" (China and ASEAN, from Suspicion to Cooperation), in Tatsumi Okabe, *ASEAN no 20 Nen—Sono Jizoku to Hatten* (ASEAN's 20 Years—Its Resiliency and Development) (Tokyo: Nihon Kokusai Kenkyu-jo, JIIA, 1987), p. 149.

22. Ryosei Kokubun, "Chugoku ni totte no Ajia Taiheiyo Kyoryoku (Asia Pacific Cooperation for China) in Tatsumi Okabe, *Posuto Reisen no Ajia Taiheiyo* (Post-Cold War Asia Pacific) (Tokyo, JIIA, 1995) p. 109.

23. Kokubun, "Asia Pacific Cooperation," p. 109.

24. Kokubun, "Asia Pacific Cooperation," p. 109.

25. Personal interview, 27 July 1995.

26. Personal interview with a Chinese economist, 14 August 1995.

27. Personal interview, 14 August 1995.

28. Personal interview with a PECC member, 9 July 1995.

29. Kokubun, "Asia Pacific Cooperation," pp. 118–119.

30. David Shambaugh, "Growing Strong: China's Challenge to Asian Security," *Survival*, Summer 1994, p. 51.

31. Kokubun, "Asia Pacific Cooperation," pp 118–119.

32. Personal interview with Raul Manglapus, 10 August 1995.

33. Personal interview with Mahathir bin Mohamad, 20 January 1993.

34. Paul Kreisberg, et al., *Threat Perceptions in Asia and the Role of the Major Powers: A Workshop Report* (Honolulu: East-West Center, 1993), p. 14.

35. "Sino-American Military Relations: Mutual Responsibilities in the Post–Cold War Era," a report by the National Committee on United States–China Relations, Inc., 1994, p. 10.

36. Personal interview with a participant.

37. "Sino-American Military Relations," p. 6.

38. *Far Eastern Economic Review*, 1 June 1995.

39. Curtis, p. 108.

40. "Sino-American Military Relations", p. 6.

41. Speech by Robert Scalapino, Manila, 13 January 1993.

42. InterPress Service, 2 August 1995; Reuters, 28 July 1995.

43. Personal interview, 31 August 1995.

44. Gautam Jaggi, *Association of Southeast Asian Nations (ASEAN): Chronology and Statistics*, Working Paper No. 95-4 (Washington: Institute for International Economics, 1995), p. 19.

45. Janadas Devan, *Southeast Asia: Challenges of the 21st Century* (Singapore: Institute for Southeast Asian Studies, 1994), p. 31.

46. Hadi Soesastro, "ASEAN Economic Cooperation in a Changed International Economy" (photocopy).

47. Kin Wah Chin, "ASEAN and the Major Powers (US, Japan, China)," Asia Pacific Forum, International conference on ASEAN, Manila, unpublished paper, 13 January 1993.

48. Personal interview with Hidehiro Konno, 26 June 1995.

49. Chin, 13 January 1993.

50. *Straits Times*, 3 November 1994.

51. Michael Leifer, *Dictionary of the Modern Politics of South East Asia* (London: Routledge, 1995), p. 260.

52. Mark Hong, *East Asian Regional Security: A Singapore Perspective* (New York: Columbia University, East Asia Institute, 1994), p. 6.

53. *International Herald Tribune*, 20 October 1992.

54. Shambaugh, "Growing Strong."

55. Personal interview with Raul Manglapus, 10 August 1995.

56. John Roche, "Indochina Revisited: The Demise of Liberal Internationalism," *National Review*, 3 May 1985.

57. Personal interview with Narongchai Akrasanee, 28 August, 1995.

58. *Financial Times*, 31 July 1995.

59. William Bodde, *View from the 19th Floor,* (Singapore: Institute for Southeast Asian Studies, 1994), p. 8.

60. "The Federal Government's Concept on Asia," Bonn, 1994.

61. *Christian Science Monitor*, 18 November, 1993.

62. Brian Bridges, *EC-Japanese Relations: In Search of a Partnership,* (London: Royal Institute of International Affairs, 1992), p. 16.

63. Personal interview with Jusuf Wanandi, 9 July, 1995.

64. "The Federal Governments Concept on Asia," Bonn, 1994, p. 51.

65. *Direction of Trade Statistics Yearbook,* (Washington: International Monetary Fund, 1994), pp. 206–07.

66. *Asahi Shimbun*, 13 January, 1990.

67. *Asahi Shimbun*, 10 July, 1993.

68. "Towards a New Asia Strategy," Commission of the European Communities, Brussels, 1994.

69. *Business Times*, 22 April, 1994.

70. "The Federal Governments Concept on Asia," Bonn, 1994.

71. *Business Week*, 31 July, 1995.

72. *Christian Science Monitor*, 18 November, 1993.

73. Personal interview with Paul Keating, 9 July, 1995.

74. Personal interview with James Bolger, 31 July, 1995.

75. Conversation related to the author by a Japanese trade official.

76. Ian Nish, *The Anglo-Japanese Alliance,* (London: University of London Press, 1972), pp. 363–64.

77. Personal interview with Goh Chok Tong, 18 July, 1995.

78. *Washington Post*, 23 June, 1995.

79. *Newsweek*, 22 November 1993.

80. In Andrew Mack and John Ravenhill, eds., *Pacific Cooperation: Building Economic and Security Regimes in the Asia Pacific Region* (Boulder, CO: Westview Press, 1995), pp. 74–75.

81. Mack and Ravenhill, p. 78.

82. Mack and Ravenhill, p. 112.

83. *Washington Post*, 6 June 1995.

84. Lowell Dittmer and Samuel Kim, eds., *China's Quest for National Identity* (Ithaca, NY: Cornell University Press, 1993), p. 217.

85. Hong, "East Asian Security."

86. Personal interview with a Chinese scholar familiar with the arguments, 20 July 1995.

87. *Asahi Shimbun*, 15 May 1992.

88. Personal interview with Lee Kuan Yew, 24 June 1993.

89. Personal interview with Mahathir.

90. Curtis, p. 109.

91. *Washington Post*, 15 June 1993.

92. *New York Times*, 29 August 1993.

93. Personal interview, 26 April 1995.

94. W. W. Rostow, *The United States and the Regional Organization of Asia and the Pacific, 1965-1985* (Austin, TX: University of Texas Press, 1986).

95. Personal interview with Manglapus.

96. Personal interview with Anand Panyarachun, 31 August 1995.

97. Peter Drysdale, *International Economic Pluralism: Economic Policy in Asia and the Pacific* (New York: Columbia University Press; Sydney: Allen and Unwin, 1988), p. 247.

98. Thomas O. Bayard and Kimberly Ann Elliot, *Reciprocity and Retaliation in U.S. Trade Policy* (Washington: Institute for International Economics, 1994).

99. Mack and Ravenhill, p. 91.

100. Mack and Ravenhill, p. 115.

10

Japan's Interests

Fifty Years

The last time Japan held an Asia Pacific regionwide summit meeting was in 1943, when Japan invited the rulers of China, Manchuria, the Philippines, and Burma, along with leaders from Thailand and "Free India," to a Greater East Asia Conference. That year was a turning point in World War II: Japan withdrew from Guadalcanal Island early in the year, Navy Commander in Chief Isoroku Yamamoto was killed during his inspection of the front lines in April, and the garrisons on Attu Island were defeated in May. The general public in Japan, as well as in Asia, began to sense that Japan was more on the defensive. The refusal of Thailand Prime Minister Pibun Songgram to attend the conference was a signal that the once pro-Japanese Thai government had begun to waver.

In formulating the sequence of the delegates' speeches, Prime Minister Hideki Tojo bypassed Japan's two most common alphabetical systems for the most obscure one, the *Iroha* method, which is the only one to order "Japan" first. Thus, the conference opened with Tojo's explanation of the war and Japan's "Greater East Asia" plan. He condemned the conquests of the British Empire and the expansionism of the United States as attempts to subordinate Asia. It was in response to those aggressors, he explained, that Japan "inevitably but resolutely came to fight against the challenges against Asia." Furthermore, Japan's ambitions were "fundamentally different from the Old Order of the US and UK, which engaged in fraud and plunder to further their own prosperity." Japan instead aspired to create family-type links with Asian nations; of course, in this family Japan would be the "father" who possessed absolute power.[1] While Tojo's speech promoted the idea of "Asia for Asians," Asia's technological defeat was already in plain view at the conference, where visiting Asian leaders were chauffeured around in the best cars Japan could offer: American-made Buicks.

Asian leaders greeted Tojo's "One Asia" concept apprehensively. President José Laurel of the Philippines and Prime Minister Chandra Bose of India refused to submit their speeches prior to delivery, not wishing to subject themselves to Japanese scrutiny. In retrospect, that conference was a desperate and ultimately unsuccessful bid to form an anti-West bloc in Asia.

Fifty years after Japan's defeat, Asia was free, and representatives of APEC economies were to be invited to Osaka, Japan, as equal participants. The region was not focused on war, but on economics, and was growing and thriving in peace. Japan's chairmanship of APEC was fortuitous, as the chance would not come again for many more years.

Osaka was a particularly appropriate city to host the APEC conference, as it perhaps has become more interdependent with Asia than any other city in Japan. Today, more non-Japanese Asian peoples live in Osaka than in Tokyo. Osaka is at the core of what is called the Kansai region, a six-prefecture domain including Kyoto and Kobe, which exceeds the economic power of Canada. Historically, this Japanese port has ushered in Asian culture and art. During the early years of the Tokugawa Shogunate, about 350 trading ships traveled between Osaka and East Asian ports in China, Taiwan, Vietnam, Thailand, and the Philippines.

For most of the postwar era, Japan saw Asia through the Cold War prism that polarized the region. Asia was not an organic, comprehensive, or cultural entity, but a sharply divided ideological battleground; the region was rent by wars in Korea and Vietnam and other smaller conflicts. Accordingly, Japan's relationship with Asia was fragmented: it was decades before diplomatic relations with South Korea or China were established, recognition of North Korea has yet to be achieved, and a territorial dispute with Russia is still unresolved. It was not only the Cold War milieu that precluded a regional strategy; Japan shunned a regional approach in view of its wartime legacy.

However, Japan has recently begun to rediscover its geography and history. With the end of the Cold War, Asia's importance to Japan has reached a new zenith. Asia surpassed the United States as Japan's largest trading partner in 1988, and it surpassed the United States in 1991 as Japan's largest export destination.[2] Although Japan's trade with the United States declined from 38 to 32 percent between 1985 and 1994, trade with Asia jumped from 23 to 40 percent.[3] Other contributing factors are the flow of Japanese foreign direct investment (FDI) into the region, and the ascendancy of a new generation that is less encumbered by the past and is increasingly sharing some aspects of a common culture. Japan's dispatch of UN peacekeeping personnel to Cambodia in 1991 was widely heralded as a signal of more active Japanese involvement in the region.

Asia had been taking note of Japan much sooner than Japan did Asia. Japanese soldiers that arrived in their countries in the 1930s and '40s were replaced in the 1950s and '60s by Japanese merchants dressed in company uniforms that identified the new breed of Japanese in Asia. Tokyo rose from the devastation of the war as the proud host of the 1964 Tokyo Olympics. Korea successfully emulated this "rite of passage" to economic development when it hosted the Seoul Olympics in 1988, and China fervently desired to have the magic repeated with its own bid to host the games.

Asian countries expect to pattern their efforts to become advanced economies on Japan's development path. On a trip to Japan in 1961, Malaysian Prime Minister Mahathir bin Mohamad took note of the fact that Japan had already erased most of the results of the war. This remarkable "ability to bounce back," according to Mahathir, was the reason that he decided Malaysia "should look at Japan."[4] He said some have asked him, "Why do you want to copy somebody who copied from somebody else?" to which Mahathir responds, "The original source has lost its momentum."

In the 1970s, Sapporo's *chikagai* (underground shopping malls) appealed to Rafidah Aziz, Malaysia's flamboyant minister of trade and industry, who fondly recalled taking her small children on vacation to enjoy the abundance of snow and tempura that Sapporo offers. The lifestyle of Japan's middle class resonates with Asia's emerging "middle class." Aziz emphasized the efforts that her government has made to promote an equitable distribution of income, which has allowed Malaysia to develop a sizable middle class.[5] Raul Manglapus, former foreign minister of the Philippines, recalled that when he was in exile in the 1970s and early '80s, Japan was one of the few countries in which he could make a speech without being held responsible by the police. The fact that Japanese people "maintained their traditional discipline without giving up political rights" was Japan's success story from Manglapus's perspective.[6] Manglapus was tortured by the Japanese *kempeitai* during the war. His son is a graduate of Japan's Sophia University.

The 1980s and '90s saw Japan's trade with Asia enhanced by increased investment flows to the region. While Asian nations were accustomed to seeing Japanese men in their country, the 1990s have brought an influx of Japanese tourists, including women. Japanese culture has permeated the region.

Although the rise of Japan and the increasing peace and prosperity of Asia have been the success stories of the postwar era, Japan still lacks confidence. Indeed, recent traumas have dealt a crushing blow to national self-esteem. Japanese leadership has been debilitated by chronic political instability since 1993. The deflationary implosion that has affected the economy since 1990 prompted a deep recession, exacerbated by financial crises. Most recently, the Great Hanshin earthquake and terrorism of fanatical cults have gravely shaken the population. These negative events taken together have cast a pall on the national psyche, generating pessimism. In fact, journalists have labeled 1995 an *annus mirabilis* in Japan.

Perhaps sensing the erosion of confidence within Japan and the danger that would portend, Senior Minister Lee Kuan Yew of Singapore offered words of encouragement, telling a leading Japanese banker: "Japan should have confidence in itself. . . . I have recently switched from a Mercedes to a Lexus. Lexus is really good. . . . Everybody says that German Braun is the best electric shaver, but I think Matsushita's is superb. You can use it while you take a bath."[7]

Japan in 1995 was different from Japan in 1979, when government officials prepared all night to ensure that Japan's first-ever chairmanship of the Group of Seven (G-7) summit would be a success, putting forth a series of policies to reduce tariffs and cut the trade surplus. LDP politicians, Kasumigaseki bureaucrats, and the public alike were proud and honored to host the meeting, as it clearly endorsed Japan's arrival as an economic power and "member of the club."

On the eve of the APEC summit in 1995, however, Japan seemed to lack similar determination. The nation already had attained the status of economic superpower to which it had aspired in 1979. Whereas 1979 found Japan in pursuit of the one-dimensional goal of economic growth, 1995 found Japan with unclear aspirations of political and regional power, and at a loss as to what the next goal should be and how it should be achieved. At the Fukuoka senior officials' meeting (SOM) in February 1995, Japanese senior officials intimated that Indonesia was backing away from Bogor, to which Indonesia very pointedly told Tokyo: "Don't hide behind us!" In view of such statements, a puzzled senior diplomat from Singapore asked: "Instead of viewing the chair as an opportunity, Japan seems to regard it as a burden. Why?"[8]

This lack of direction and will seemed to stultify Japan's chairmanship of APEC, and concerned friends sensed the danger. At a Japan-Australia Summit Conference in May 1995, Australian Prime Minister Paul Keating warned Prime Minister Tomiichi Murayama that progress in APEC was still tenuous. He explained that unlike the solidly established G-7, where the loss of "one wheel clasp" in a given year does not cause the wheel to fall off, such a loss in APEC would indeed collapse the entire vehicle.[9] Following consultations with Indonesian President Suharto in June 1995, Singaporean Prime Minister Goh Chok Tong expressed worries about

Japanese leadership, telling a press conference that signals from APEC senior officials indicated that "the Japanese hosts may not be going full steam ahead to come out with a concrete plan" for Osaka.[10] Others had already questioned Japan's ability to lead. Singaporean official Kishore Mahbubani surmised, "If Japan's contribution to APEC suffers in such comparison [to Seattle and Bogor], Japan's claim to international leadership would also have been dented."[11]

Throughout six years of APEC experience, Japan remained a mystery to the other Asia Pacific countries, as very few new initiatives or inspirations emanated from Tokyo. Japan's prime ministers left Blake Island, Washington, and Bogor without significantly imprinting their voices or spirits on the proceedings.

Contrary to the general perception that Japan was skeptical of the endeavor, the Ministry of International Trade and Industry (MITI) had been quite active in conceiving the APEC concept behind the scenes. However, Japan did not lead the way to initiate APEC, and in later years was seen as reluctant to support the summit. The view of Japan as a member of the "go slow" club persisted, as illustrated by Kishore Mahbubani's assessment: "Japan, China, and Malaysia want to hold back" on free trade.[12]

On liberalization, Japan did not take a lead. While Japanese leaders did not try to sabotage APEC's efforts, they did prove to be in Australian Prime Minister Robert Hawke's words, "followers rather than leaders."[13] At Bogor, Murayama discreetly asked President Suharto for special consideration for the agricultural sector in liberalization. Japan's greatest stumbling block has been its inability to articulate its vision or message in a comprehensive big picture. A US official remarked that Japan's APEC proposals tended to have "no geopolitical relevance."[14]

However, as preparations for the Osaka summit proceeded, particularly after the Sapporo SOM in July 1995, the perception of Japan's leadership gradually changed. Japan's chairmanship was "determined, meticulously thorough, and quite courageous," said Tony Miller, Hong Kong's SOM representative. During his trip to Washington, Australian Trade Minister Robert McMullan observed: "Japan's attitude has shifted markedly in the lead-up to Osaka with clear indications of its preparedness to take a leadership role in achieving regional trade liberalization." He further reminded his American audience: "It is also important that the US is not left behind in steps toward greater cooperation in the region."[15] Even US officials who had been skeptical of Japan's ability to lead were heartened by the Sapporo outcome. In the words of US Trade Representative Mickey Kantor, "Out of Sapporo comes a tremendous hope, given Japanese leadership, which was very, very evident there, that we can make concrete goals, timetables, [and] establish areas of concern."[16]

A new confidence was seen in Japanese officials themselves, one of whom effused that Japan was perfectly suited to the chairmanship role in 1995. He explained that although Japanese bureaucrats could not have drafted the far-reaching vision set out in Indonesia, they were well-equipped to logically formulate the details needed to actualize the Bogor Declaration.[17]

Yet, the jury is still out. Japan's political instability prevents it from taking a strong initiative and playing a more significant role in liberalizing its markets, particularly agriculture. Its agricultural constituencies, long protected and politically powerful, have also been resistant to the rationalization and restructuring of the rice sector that would make it more competitive. As this vicious circle has progressed, the Japanese government has remained unable to formulate a new agricultural policy in the 10 years since the Punta del Este meeting, which kicked off the Uruguay Round, even though it has known well enough the inevitability of liberalization. The case of rice is symbolic, for it revealed Japan's inability to reform or rejuvenate itself; such complacency in stalemate situations may be increasingly common in the coming years. APEC, in this sense, tests Japan's political will and ability to reinvigorate its economy and market. For Japan, Osaka presents a watershed for its future. It will test whether Japan will be in renewal or in decline in the emerging Asia Pacific renaissance.

Japan and APEC

1989–92: Canberra, Singapore, Seoul, Bangkok

During APEC's formative years from 1989 to 1992, Japan, as well as the United States, conspicuously refrained from asserting influence over the APEC process. A noted scholar has surmised that both countries were skeptical of the endeavor.[18] However, a deeper historical examination shows that Japan's MITI in fact played an important, behind-the-scenes role in urging Australia to form the group.

As was shown in earlier chapters, MITI endeavored to remain low-key at APEC's incipience because some Southeast Asian nations were apprehensive that Japan might dominate them in an APEC devoid of the United States. Memories of Japan's earlier attempt at a "Greater East Asian Co-Prosperity Sphere" had not yet dissipated and indeed still remain. Japan perhaps tried to quell some of these fears by insisting on North American membership.

Moreover, Japan reassured its Southeast Asian neighbors by ardently promoting ASEAN's development, starting with the first conference in Canberra, where Japan announced a plan to promote human resources development to help develop technologies and form a labor network in the region. At the same time, it stressed that APEC would not form an economic bloc.

Near the time of the 1991 Seoul meeting, Japan advanced five principles for economic development, and the following year, Japan proposed standardized economic statistics, intellectual property rights, and specifications for industrial products in the region, and expressed an interest in developing competent business managers and promoting personnel exchanges.

It is notable that the above-mentioned Japanese proposals from 1989 to 1992 did not focus on liberalization as a primary objective. In fact a series of MITI reports actually reveal a two-pronged strategy of liberalization and development for APEC. For example, before APEC had even been proposed, the 1988 MITI Sakamoto Report laid out a range of possible futures for the economies of the region, among which a vision of cooperation, aimed at stabilizing the world's economy, stood out as the best-case scenario. A major objective was keeping the Asia Pacific open to the rest of the world. To help achieve that rosy picture, Japan would spearhead development initiatives—human resources training, expanded economic cooperation, and promotion of technological exchanges, as well as expanded imports and the facilitation of FDI.[19]

MITI's vision paper for the region for the year 2000 was the first practical, long-term plan for APEC; it emphasized the "flying geese" developmental pattern. The 1993 follow-up to that paper not only thoroughly analyzed developmental issues such as infrastructure and energy efficiency, but also clearly stated: "The most important issue in the economic development of this region is the promotion of trade and investment liberalization."[20] MITI, from the start, did not view liberalization and cooperation as conflicting goals. Instead, it maintained the need for balance between the two.

1993–94: Seattle and Bogor

Since APEC was elevated to the summit level in 1993, Japan has not taken a leadership role. Before the 1992 Bangkok summit, Vice Minister Koji Kakizawa, in his meeting with Australia's Foreign and Trade Minister Gareth Evans, preconditioned Japan's support for Australia's leaders' meeting proposal on the acquiescence of the ASEAN nations.[21] A US senior official observed of her Japanese counterparts: "They resisted Blake Island; they resisted Bogor."[22] The perception already had gelled.

While Miyazawa had offered tentative support to an APEC leaders' meeting when Prime Minister Paul Keating mentioned it in 1992, Japan did not finally approve it until July 1993. Japan publicly explained that the attendance of the Three Chinas was the reason for caution. Japan feared that a leaders' meeting in APEC would inevitably cause the Taiwan issue to surface, thereby complicating and perhaps derailing the whole process. Yet it also came from the reactive rather than proactive style of diplomacy practiced by the Gaimusho, Japan's Ministry of Foreign Affairs. "There was a danger of ASEAN collectively boycotting the leaders' meeting proposal at the time. The US had not formally prepared until the US-Japan summit talks at the Tokyo G-7 summit in July. Therefore, we had to be cautious," said Koiichiro Matsuura, a seasoned Japanese diplomat and G-7 sherpa.[23]

The pressing domestic debate over rice liberalization was another concern. MITI also was worried that the United States, in its haste to institutionalize APEC, did not fully consider the different stages of development of the member economies. In addition, MITI bureaucrats were apprehensive of APEC promoting regionalism at the expense of globalism. They thought the United States might want to counter EU regionalism with an Asia Pacific equivalent and they were accordingly concerned that the United States viewed APEC as merely a card to be used against Europe. On the positive side, MITI welcomed the stimulus that the US proposal provided to the evolutionary process and was encouraged by the signal of US commitment to Asia.[24]

Japan was even slower in agreeing to the goals of Bogor, withholding formal support for the proposed 2020 deadline until late October.[25] Japan's ASEAN emphasis was evident during the Bogor preparations, when Japan proposed that APEC discuss cooperation to aid the development of infrastructure in developing countries and decide on a common energy policy to avoid supply-demand imbalances.

1995: Osaka

Japan's Foreign Minister Yohei Kono put forth the Partners for Progress (PFP) initiative in 1994 at the Jakarta ministerial meeting to address cooperation between industrialized and developing economies in the areas of financial, human, natural, and administrative resources. Although PFP was welcomed in the November 1994 Jakarta Ministerial Joint Declaration, confusion about what the proposal actually meant generated a good deal of skepticism, and a June 1995 wire report speculated that the scant attention given to the proposal in an internal APEC document was a signal that Japan had shelved the plan entirely.[26] Some APEC members have been concerned that PFP detracts from APEC's bold trade liberalization goals. Such members have been prone to conclude that Japan is more concerned with sustaining Southeast Asian economic growth than in liberalizing trade. Others have been doubtful of the initiative's practicality. For example, the United States and Malaysia have pointed to the possible redundancy of APEC and non-APEC economic assistance.

Unfortunately, PFP invited instant suspicion before Japan fully explained it. A draft outline of the PFP proposal showed that the Ministry of Foreign Affairs sketched out five PFP projects, mainly dealing with human resources development, that might aid the promotion of trade and investment in the region. However, the wording was vague on the logistics of the projects, stating that APEC members would "utilize the facilities established and other results achieved" from bilateral aid to "implement regional cooperation in the APEC region more efficiently and effectively."[27] This lack of specificity has allowed Japan's intentions to be misconstrued.

Seeking to better understand the PFP proposal, representatives of Indonesia and the Philippines at the SOM in Fukuoka in February 1995 asked Japan for clarification, and a New Zealand representative expressed the view that APEC should not directly supply assistance.[28] Comprehension of this proposal was not much improved by the April SOM in Singapore, where a developing-country official interpreted the PFP proposal as an indication that Japan planned to supplement its ODA budget with a separate category of APEC assistance, whereas the representative of a developed nation pointedly asked, "Is Japan trying to buy out the region?"[29]

At the Sapporo SOM, the PFP received support from a number of SOM members, not the least of whom was a delegate from China. Chinese enthusiasm was clearly demonstrated by his remarks that PFP could be an important "sub-milestone" for APEC's progress toward realization of the Bogor vision.[30] However, this was both good news and bad news for Japan, as most developed countries increased their vigilance on the prospect of APEC turning into another aid agency.

It is Japan's position that rather than detract from APEC's liberalization and facilitation goals, PFP will complement and promote them. Foreign Minister Kono explained that the primary objective of PFP was to smooth the way for liberalization among differently paced participants.[31] APEC nations that are "graduating" from Japan's ODA—that is, Singapore and Korea—have expressed a keen interest in becoming "new donors" through PFP.[32] To jump-start the program, Japan has started to sound out developing expertise and an institution-building mechanism to deal with intellectual property rights. Clearly, such a project would not only enhance liberalization but also appeal directly to the United States, which has so aggressively pursued the issue with China.

Japan's Agenda

Japan's interests in APEC are multifold: to promote globalism in and from the region, to contain US unilateralism and prevent Europe and the Western Hemisphere from becoming protectionist, to strengthen ties with

ASEAN, to engage China in the region, to ensure the US security presence, and to elevate Japan's status from a regional political power to a global political power by strengthening its ties with the Asia Pacific.

Japan and its Asian neighbors have been the beneficiaries of the global trading system over the past 50 years, and that system has propelled Asia's success. A look back to the 1920s and '30s provides a reminder of the havoc wreaked when the disintegration of liberal international economic order led to bloc economies and pushed Japan into exclusive regionalism. MITI's Sakamoto Report concluded that by opening up markets toward regions other than the Asia Pacific, a new regional forum would enable the whole world to increase exports to Asia, reducing any perceptions that Asia could pose a "threat" as a trading bloc.[33]

Japan's trade structure is now truly global; in 1993, 37 percent of Japan's trade was with Asia, 33 percent with the Western Hemisphere, and 18 percent with Europe.[34]

In light of this interest, Japan would like to use APEC as a counterforce to prevent its worst nightmares of the 1920s and 30s from being repeated. To further bolster the global trading system, Japan may hope to use APEC as a warning signal to the European Union and the North American Free Trade Agreement (NAFTA) parties not to turn protectionist. The concern raised in the first APEC Eminent Persons Group report in 1993 is still very much alive: namely, that NAFTA may signal that "the United States—the traditional leader of the global trading system—may be 'going regional' or at least hedging its bets."[35]

The absence of a multilateral framework in the region tends to provoke US unilateral action, and intensified US-Japan economic friction could exacerbate protectionist sentiment, as some in the United States would fear the maturation of some East Asian economies into successive "second or third Japans." Japanese officials already have seen the rapid momentum of these two drives manifested in the auto parts talks during 1993–1995 and in the strong inward-looking forces in the US Congress. In the words of one Japanese diplomat who has kept in touch with US APEC policymakers, Japan sees the United States as "extremely reluctant to endorse the general principles of liberalization, whether it is nondiscrimination or consistency with the GATT/WTO agreement."[36]

From the start, engaging the United States in Asia to avoid choosing between the two has been a hidden agenda of Japan. MITI's insistence on the inclusion of the United States in APEC in early 1989 illustrated this intention. Some MITI officials—particularly those who argued for regional integration—were interested, further, in receiving something in return for liberalization. For example, Japan would agree to a free trade agreement or area in return for a US-Japan dispute settlement mechanism, which later could develop into an APEC-wide mechanism. With the Bogor Declaration, APEC nations agreed to examine a proposal for a dispute settlement mechanism to supplement that of the World Trade Organization (WTO). As evidenced in the Sakamoto Report, MITI has long been interested in developing such a mechanism, perhaps to curtail the US use of its section 301 trade law.[37]

The Japanese government has avidly pursued a dispute mediation mechanism not only in APEC, but also in GATT and the WTO. Although Japan voiced worries in 1988 that the GATT dispute settlement mechanism could be abused by countries that demanded arbitration panels before exhausting bilateral negotiations, Japan's confidence in the GATT dispute panel has since been bolstered.[38] The GATT ruling in favor of Japan in 1990 that the European Community's so-called "screwdriver" law on the assembly of industrial goods was in violation of international trade rules was heralded by the press as a signal of Japan's new willingness to take complaints to the GATT.[39] Japan's ambassador to the GATT told his colleagues in Geneva just before the launch of the WTO that he expected the WTO to implement an effective dispute settlement mechanism.[40] By May 1995, Japan was ready to test the mechanism, and it lodged a complaint with the WTO against US unilateral auto sanctions.

Japan's concern about US unilateralism is shared by other APEC countries. South Korean Vice Minister for Foreign Affairs Lee See-Young explained that the resentment of South Koreans toward section 301 is akin to that of Japanese nationals toward the US Immigration Act of 1924, which effectively excluded Japanese and all Asians except Filipinos.[41] Some countries hope to use APEC to defuse tense and chronic US-Japan trade disputes. Paul Keating recommended to Murayama in their 1995 meeting that Japan take bold steps toward the creation of an action plan at the Osaka summit by emphasizing its potential to smooth the US-Japan relationship. According to Keating, Japan's enthusiastic support for realizing the Bogor targets would greatly affect the US stance, helping to tie the Americans into a more constructive multilateral approach. Indeed, the United States would have more difficulty pursuing 301 actions, would be undermined in its criticism of Japan's closed markets, and would be confronted with its own reluctance to liberalize key sectors. However, Japan's official line is that the defusing of bilateral tensions is not an objective of APEC policy and that APEC should be promoted on its own merits, but any positive side effects on the US-Japan trade relationship are welcome.[42]

APEC, with its ASEAN "core," is an instrument that Japan is using to strengthen its ties with ASEAN. Like the United States, Japan's so-called "Asia policy" once could be more accurately described as a construct of bilateral relationships. However, ASEAN, as an established and successful regional institution, provides a conduit to bring Japan's policy to the multilateral level.

Japan's APEC policy has been shaped to a large extent by its consideration of what Gaimusho refers to as ASEAN's "sensitivity." At the time of the 1990 Singapore meeting, Eastern Europe had begun to adopt a market economic system, and the ASEAN nations feared a shift of international flows of capital and technology from East Asia to Eastern Europe. In response, MITI Minister Kabun Muto assured ASEAN countries that their development would continue to be a priority for Japan. At the 1992 Bangkok meeting, Japanese Vice Foreign Minister Koji Kakizawa, mindful of Indonesian Foreign Minister Ali Alatas' position that APEC still did not need a Secretariat, asked that the SOM consider Minister Alatas' remarks when they examined the Secretariat issue.[43]

Japan's emphasis on the development leg of the Bogor Declaration's triadic goal of liberalization, facilitation, and development to a great extent stems from its desire to strengthen its ties with ASEAN. Japan's EPG representative, Professor Ippei Yamazawa, views the three as equally weighted, whereas the United States, for instance, assigns primacy to liberalization.[44] Professor Yamazawa's view is endorsed by Japan's SOM representative, Hidehiro Konno, who said that whereas Japan regarded liberalization and cooperation as "two wheels of a car" before, it now views liberalization, facilitation, and cooperation as "three pillars" with equal emphasis.[45]

Through ASEAN's initiative, the major players in the region including Japan have sat down together as "dialogue partners" and since 1994 have been participants in the first multilateral security arrangement in the Asia Pacific, the ASEAN Regional Forum (ARF). ASEAN, in fact, has leverage over Northeast Asia in the APEC context—another dimension that Japan values. Ichiro Ozawa, for instance, argued that ASEAN's support for Japan's contribution to the Cambodian peacekeeping effort "considerably deflated Chinese and Korean criticism that Japan's personnel contributions are signs of a renewed militarism. As a result, both China and Korea have begun to exhibit an 'understanding' of Japanese personnel contributions that include the SDF."[46] Other Japanese officials are not as frank but share the same calculations and sentiments. Indeed, ASEAN has provided Japan an entryway into the region. Accordingly, Japan is inclined to look at its improving ties to ASEAN as its one shining success in Asia. In the words of Japan scholar Gerald Curtis: "The strengthening of Japanese-ASEAN relations is one of the outstanding achievements of postwar Japanese diplomacy."[47]

From Japan's perspective, APEC has the added benefit of creating a place for China in the international community. Japan, which has a great stake in stabilizing China, looks to APEC to defuse heated US-China issues in a more structured way. The apocalyptic picture of millions of refugees descending upon Japan from the Chinese land mass is the Japanese media's favorite nightmare scenario of a disintegrated China. Japan has good reasons to fear the nationalism that would be unleashed if China's economic reform and open door policy failed. Another concern is China's advances into the South China Sea, which have ramifications for Japan's oil lane access.

Furthermore, Japan is increasingly nervous about the strain between China and Taiwan, which poses difficulties for Japan and the United States. As China specialist Michel Oksenberg has written, "Both countries would be deeply torn, but ideological proclivities of the United States would tug in Taiwan's direction, while Japan's economic priorities would propel it in the mainland's direction."[48] This factor explains Japan's initial reluctance to include the Three Chinas in APEC in early 1989 and to elevate APEC to the leaders' level in early 1993. For example, in Canberra, Japanese Foreign Minister Taro Nakayama took a cautious position on the Three Chinas issue, arguing that it was necessary to watch China's domestic situation more carefully. He thought that Taiwan's inclusion might complicate the Japan-China relationship but that Japan should support Hong Kong's inclusion if the others so agreed.

Yet, as one of the largest investors in China, Japan has a great interest in engaging China in the region so that it adheres to international law. APEC could be a starting point for China's engagement.

Japan also hopes that APEC could help promote a convergence of views on development and human rights so as to prevent a rift in the US-Japan relationship. A reconciliation of US and Japanese positions was signaled when the Clinton administration embraced the strategy of "comprehensive engagement" with China, including the delinkage of human rights from most-favored nation (MFN) trade status. Moreover, on issues such as intellectual property rights, Japan has taken a similar stance to that of the United States. However, underlying tensions were evident in Prime Minister Hosokawa's comments to Clinton in Seattle when the Japanese leader cautioned that it would not be wise for the West to impose its own standards of democracy on less developed countries. He then lobbied for US support of future Chinese bids to host the Olympics. These comments, and particularly Hosokawa's remarks on human rights in Beijing four months later, led to Winston Lord's evaluation of Hosokawa as "undercutting" the US position in his famous "malaise memo."[49]

Japan would like APEC to develop into the net that ensures US presence in Asia, augmenting the anchor of the US–Japan security treaty. Koichi Kato, chairman of the LDP's Policy Research Council and a strong contender for premiership, outlined the need for the US military presence in Asia, especially in light of China's uncertain future. He answered those who have asked why NAFTA is deemed acceptable when the EAEC is not by explaining that the security presence of Japan and/or China is not a prerequisite for NAFTA nations' economic security and welfare, whereas Asia needs the US presence.

Finally, Japan, which is already a regional and global economic power, would like to attain the status of a global political power. Some argue that the end of the Cold War has lessened Japan's power and prestige as a G-7 member and has thus required the nation to strengthen its regional ties to ensure another venue for participation. Ichiro Ozawa has written that "the twin pillars of Japanese diplomacy have been its membership in the Asia Pacific community and in the community of the advanced democratic nations of the West. "The end of the Cold War, however, has stripped the latter approach of its significance, while the remarkable rise of the Asian economies suggest that Japan's ties to the Asia Pacific region can only strengthen."

Others argue that Japan can boost its international standing by its close ties with the Asia Pacific region—the most powerful "constitutency in the world"—which would give it leverage vis-à-vis the European Union and the United States. Another Japanese aspiration is a permanent seat on the UN Security Council, which would give it the status of a global political power. To achieve this, it will need the backing of an "Asia Pacific caucus," or perhaps an "APEC caucus." Yet forging such a support group would be challenging. Indonesia, for instance, harbors its own ambitions, while China and Korea remain wary of increasing Japan's political stature.

Japan is actually best suited to lead within the new dynamics of multilateralism and regionalism that APEC symbolizes. As Japan simply does not have a strong military, its interests lie in a peaceful framework in which countries influence each other subtly. APEC nicely fits into Japan's Asian strategy to help overcome the region's distrust of Japan.

ASEAN, as the foundation of APEC, has been more forthcoming with Japan. Already APEC has recognized the advent of Japan as a regional power, as it puts Japan on the same par as the United States on the APEC plane. Both countries are equal contributors, at 18 percent each, to the APEC Secretariat. A US senior official confided that although Japan initially wanted to contribute more than 20 percent, the United States said it would not offer more than 18 percent and hoped that Japan would refrain from offering more.[50] While the $2 million operating budget is minuscule, the fact that both the United States and Japan are equal contributors is symbolic.

Moreover, Japan may find APEC to be a useful arena in which to explore the modus operandi of an eventual shared leadership role with the United States in the region. Peter Drysdale, one of the pioneering thinkers of Asia Pacific regionalism, has observed that APEC offers ". . . a convenient regional framework within which Japan can move towards a position of shared policy leadership with the United States."[51] A US administration official who deals with APEC has observed that over the last few years, working closely with Japan on APEC "helped us realize that there is more to our relationship than just the framework of some of the bilateral tension."[52] Yet there is no deliberate effort to forge a position of shared leadership on APEC policy. Japan fears that other APEC members, particularly ASEAN countries, could perceive a US-Japan condominium.

Japan has tried to forge a close relationship with Australia and New Zealand in pushing its agenda. Murayama expressed his willingness to cooperate with Australia by saying "Let's take a lead in APEC with Japan and Australia hand in hand." As Australian Ambassador to the US Donald Russell astutely observed, Australia, Japan, and Korea all do not want to choose between Asia and the United States.[53] All have bilateral alliances with the United States, are geographically situated between the Asian and American land masses, and have their respective problems with Southeast Asian countries. Japan has the legacy of World War II, Korea still suffers from a lack of interaction with its southern neighbors, and Australia, which only changed its racially discriminatory immigration policy in 1973, has its own history to overcome.

Japan's special attention to the needs of Australia and New Zealand can be seen as an effort to form a forum for their mutual concern. Lack of mutual trust between Japan and Korea perhaps has prevented the two from taking a coordinated step to express their views and interests. By moving on two tracks—through the positive and proactive Australian channel as well as the cautious and reactive ASEAN channel—Japan hopes to strengthen its bargaining chips vis-à-vis the United States.

Options

Before APEC's inception, Japan could have chosen one of two routes: regionalism in the Asia Pacific or a US-Japan Free Trade Area (FTA). In fact, in 1988, MITI examined the feasibility of both approaches and concluded that the first option was preferable. The FTA scheme was discarded partly because the United States was not interested—an October 1988 ITC report indicated that the United States perceived Japan's markets to be "invisibly" protected and thus invulnerable to an FTA—and partly because Japan was seen as "too equal" in the words of then US Trade Representative Clayton Yeutter, who referred to the fact that Japan's size precluded it from entering a hierarchical arrangement such as NAFTA. Japan chose the right option. Perhaps there was no other viable alternative to regionalism for Japan to counteract and prevent the potential balkanization of the world trading system and exclusive blocs precipitated by the seclusion of Western Europe and the United States in their respective regions. Asia Pacific regionalism was the best insurance policy against the emergence of regional blocs. Yet Japan could have developed various forms of regionalism in Asia. It was the correct decision of Japan, particularly MITI, to strongly insist that the US should be made an integral part of the new regional arrangement. It was a strategic move to prevent the

US from disengaging from Asia and entrenching itself in the Western Hemisphere.

Japan's activism in the Asia Pacific, which has increased in the past decade, has been gradually accepted, as Japan's commitment to APEC has demonstrated. APEC and the ASEAN Regional Forum (ARF) in tandem have helped Japan facilitate its relations with Asia. More importantly, APEC has provided a means for Japan to gradually find a regional and multilateral framework for its Asia policy. Equally importantly, APEC has finally given Japan's Asia policy the chance to emerge as an Asia Pacific Asia policy. Although these opportunities have yet to be fully developed, they provide Japan with an unprecedented occasion to reorient its basic role in the Asia Pacific.

With regard to APEC's critical liberalization and cooperation agendas, Japan has not been able to pursue a dynamic policy and to have an impact on APEC's evolution because of its inability to put these issues into the larger picture and express its positions in an articulate manner. In the liberalization debate, Japan has not been able to play a leadership role. The impenetrability of Japan's markets has hampered the government from delineating a clear cut strategy. Instead, Japan attempted to use its bureaucratic discretionary instruments such as the PFP to smooth the way for developing nations. Japan's ineffective APEC diplomacy was a result of its lack of a political leadership that could prioritize its interests in the forum and the region.

Notes

1. See Yusuke Fukada, *Reimei no Seiki* (Century of the Dawn), Bungei Shunju, 1991, pp. 35–36.

2. *Direction of Trade Statistics Yearbook* (Washington: International Monetary Fund, 1994).

3. *The Business Times,* 19 April 1995, p. 15.

4. Personal interview with Mahathir, 20 January 1993.

5. Personal interview with Rafidah Aziz, 19 January 1993.

6. Personal interview with Raul Manglapus, 15 January 1993.

7. Conversation with Lee Kuan Yew related to author by Yo Kurosawa, president of the Industrial Bank of Japan.

8. Personal interview, 29 January 1995.

9. Personal interview with an official who attended the meeting, 8 June 1995.

10. *The Straits Times* (2 June 1995): 1.

11. Kishore Mahbubani, "The Pacific Impulse," *Survival* (Spring 1995): 119.

12. Kishore Mahbubani,"The Pacific Way," *Foreign Affairs* (January/February 1995): 110.

13. Personal interview with Robert Hawke, 28 June 1995.

14. Personal interview, 18 April 1995.

15. Speech by Australian Trade Minister Robert McMullan to the Asia Society in New York, 20 July 1995.

16. Personal interview with Mickey Kantor, 20 July 1995.

17. Personal interview.

18. Miles Kahler, "Institution Building in the Pacific," in *Pacific Cooperation*, Andrew Mack and John Ravenhill, eds., (Boulder, CO: Westview Press, 1995).

19. "Interim Report by the Study Group for Asia Pacific Trade Development," chaired by Yoshihiro Sakamoto, 13 June 1988.

20. MITI follow-up report to "Vision for the Economy of the Asia Pacific Region in the Year 2000 and the Tasks Ahead," November 1993.

21. *Asahi Shimbun*, 25 July 1992.

22. Personal interview, 27 April 1995.

23. Interview with Koiichiro Matsuura, 24 July 1995.

24. MITI internal memorandum, October 1993.

25. *Kyodo News Service*, 6 November 1994.

26. *Kyodo News Service: Japan Economic Newswire*, 20 June 1995.

27. A draft *Partners for Progress* (PFP) report (Ministry of Foreign Affairs, Japan, 6 July 1995) obtained by the author.

28. Personal interview with participants in the meeting.

29. Personal interview, 27 April 1995.

30. Personal interview, 10 July 1995.

31. Personal interview with Yohei Kono, 31 August 1995.

32. Personal interview with a participant in the APEC Senior Officials Meeting in Fukuoka in, February 1995.

33. "Interim Report by the Study Group for Asia Pacific Trade Development."

34. Derived from the *1994 Direction of Trade Statistics Yearbook*, International Monetary Fund, Washington, pp. 257–59.

35. *A Vision for APEC: Towards an Asia Pacific Economic Community*, Report of the Eminent Persons Group to APEC Ministers, October 1993, p. 17.

36. Personal interview with Japanese diplomat, 8 July 1995.

37. Personal interview with Hidehiro Konno, 26 June 1995.

38. *International Trade Reporter* 5, no. 25 (22 June 1988): 924.

39. *1992—The External Impact of European Unification*, vol. 1 no. 24 (23 March 1990): 5. *International Trade Reporter* 7, no. 11 (14 March 1990).

40. *Japan Economic Newswire, Kyodo News Service*, 9 December 1994.

41. Yoichi Funabashi, *Nihon no Taigai Koso* [A Design for a New Course of Japan's Foreign Policy], (Tokyo: Iwanami Shoten, 1993), p. 96.

42. Personal interview with a Japanese government official.

43. Personal interview with a Japanese official.

44. Ippei Yamazawa, "What the Osaka Agenda Should Look Like," *NBR Analysis: APEC at the Crossroads* (Seattle: National Bureau of Asian Research, 1995) vol. 6, no. 1.

45. Personal interview, 31 July 1995.

46. Ichiro Ozawa, *Blueprint for a New Japan* (Tokyo: Kodonsha, 1994).

47. Gerald Curtis, ed., "Meeting the Challenge of Japan in Asia," *The United States, Japan and Asia: Challenges for US Policy* (New York: Norton and Company, 1994), p. 222.

48. Michel Oksenberg, "China and the Japanese-American Alliance," in Curtis, p. 121.

49. *Washington Post* (5 May 1994): A38.

50. Personal interview, 8 June 1995.

51. Peter Drysdale, *Open Regionalism: A Key to East Asia's Economic Future?*, Pacific Economic Papers 197, 1991, as cited in Andrew Mack, and John Ravenhill, eds., *Pacific Cooperation: Building Economic and Security Regimes in the Asia Pacific Region,* (Boulder, CO: Westview Press, 1995).

52. Personal interview, 26 April 1995.

53. Personal interview with Donald Russell, 2 June 1995.

11

Japan's Dilemmas

Japan and the EAEC

Japan has been inclined to view its Asia policy as an integral facet of its policy toward the United States. This approach was molded during the Cold War. During those decades, US diplomacy enabled Japan to resume diplomatic ties with its neighbors. For example, the United States facilitated Japan–South Korea normalization in 1965, and US normalization of relations with China allowed for the resumption of Japan-China relations. Overall, ideological and geostrategic constraints prevented Japan from establishing its own relations with Asia.

But Japan's US-centered approach to Asia has been more difficult to pursue now that the Cold War has receded. Following APEC's birth in 1989, Japan's APEC policy was instantly challenged by divergent forces within Japan's body politic. Far from the hoped-for "shared leadership" between Japan and the United States in APEC, their relationship was often strained. Malaysian Prime Minister Mahathir's proposal in 1990 for an East Asian Economic Group (EAEG), which he later amended to an East Asian Economic Caucus (EAEC), pointed up these divisions and underscored a key dilemma for Japan. As one Japanese diplomat sighed, the proposal "came too early and caught Japan off guard."

When Mahathir devised a Look East policy in the early 1980s, it was to encourage Malaysia to emulate its East Asian neighbors, especially Japan. An avowed "Japan fan," Mahathir cultivated business links between Malaysia and Japan, especially in the electrical and automotive sectors. Thus, in December 1990, when Mahathir proposed an East Asian

Economic Group (EAEG) as a trade bloc to counteract bloc formation in Europe and North America, he naturally envisaged a leadership role for Japan.

The following year, a Malaysian monarch, addressing a dinner for Japan's visiting imperial couple, made an unusual plea for Japan's leading role in the group. Mahathir reworked his proposal in October 1991 to be more palatable to Japan and Malaysia's ASEAN partners by transforming his bloc-forming "group" into a pressure-asserting "caucus." He also made a strong pitch to Prime Minister Kiichi Miyazawa in January 1993 that Japan's representation of Asian interests at the G-7 summit in Tokyo in July would be enhanced if there was a meeting of the East Asian countries to develop a consensual stand (as reported in *Far East Economic Review*, 28 January 1993).

Japan's hesitancy to join the EAEC aggrieved Malaysian leaders, who responded with vitriol. In 1992 the Malaysian MITI minister told her Japanese counterpart that it was strange that Japan must always comply with the United States. In an August 1994 meeting, Mahathir chastened Prime Minister Tomiichi Murayama, stating that "Japan should stop apologizing for World War II and start being a world leader." Later that year, Mahathir suggested that the EAEC would be created without Japan's participation and that he was uncertain whether he would participate in the APEC Osaka conference.[1]

The strain between the two countries was most clearly revealed just prior to the Bogor leaders' meeting when Foreign Minister Yohei Kono dispatched Ambassador Nobuo Matsunaga to Kuala Lumpur to obtain Mahathir's commitment to attend the Osaka leaders' meeting. Matsunaga had to depend on a private channel to arrange the meeting, as diplomatic efforts had failed. In the end, Mahathir was not forthcoming, promising only to "make up my mind after looking into the Bogor meeting results." When he canceled his official visit to Japan scheduled for September 1995, he explained his reticence on the question of his Osaka attendance: "Once you have decided, you are no longer interesting."[2]

While Mahathir had high hopes for Japan's participation, his exclusion of North America and Oceania concerned Japanese leaders, rendering them unable to offer support for the proposal. During meetings with their Malaysian counterparts in April 1991, Prime Minister Toshiki Kaifu and Foreign Minister Taro Nakayama were cautious. In September 1992, even though Japan was increasingly alarmed by the North American Free Trade Agreement (NAFTA), MITI Minister Kozo Watanabe was still wary of embracing the EAEC, explaining that it might further drive NAFTA into regionalism.[3] Miyazawa made the same argument to Mahathir, adding that East Asia should remain open to thwart protectionism in the European Community as well.[4]

The United States pressured Japan not to accept the EAEC. Former Secretary of State James Baker was opposed to the EAEC from the outset; "his reaction was instantaneous," in the words of one US senior administration official.[5] Baker publicly warned that Mahathir's group could "draw a line down the Pacific."[6] He also sent a memo to Japan requesting Japanese opposition to the EAEC. Korea, worried at the initial stage about a Japan-centered grouping, was believed to sympathize with Baker.[7] Baker's main concern was that the US-Japan alliance could be harmed by the divisiveness of the EAEC. However, Japan was already torn by the proposal and could neither reject nor accept it.

This was to change somewhat. At a bilateral meeting between Japanese and South Korean foreign ministers in Seattle in 1993, Foreign Minister Tsutomu Hata had responded to a press question about the status of the EAEC by saying that the most desirable option would be for the EAEC to be a caucus within APEC.

Now that the APEC leaders' meeting has been institutionalized, Japan's guarded, noncommittal stance has been gradually replaced by an acceptance of the EAEC as a caucus within APEC. Former Prime Minister Yasuhiro Nakasone, who was opposed to EAEC when it was first proposed, arguing for its safe incorporation under a huge umbrella.[8] "Make it true to the name 'a caucus in APEC,' " was Nakasone's advice to Mahathir. Thus, Japan appears to have moved from opposition to precondition. Although the Japanese government still maintains that it is "looking into the matter"—a phrase one MITI official explains is a euphemism for "no"[9]—it increasingly predicates its own membership on that of Australia and New Zealand. MITI Vice Minister for International Affairs Yoshihiro Sakamoto said that Japan's consistent policy has been to advocate inclusion of Australia and New Zealand in the EAEC, in some part to avoid their incorporation into NAFTA.[10] This policy was strongly reiterated in May 1995 by Foreign Minister Kono.[11] This is also the position that Japan has taken on Prime Minister Goh Chok Tong's call for another grouping designed to exclude the United States: an EU-ASEAN plus 3 summit, and Malaysia's proposal for a "6 plus 3" ASEAN Economic Ministerial (AEM) meeting, in which Japan, Korea, and China would sit down with ASEAN.[12]

While Prime Minister Murayama agrees that Australia and New Zealand should be included in the EAEC, he reportedly does not support the anti-EAEC argument for special consideration of the US-Japan relationship and has been frustrated by the perception of Japan as "parroting the Washington line" and "dancing a choreographed role" to please the Americans. "What is wrong with the EAEC?" he asked when MITI briefers emphasized their cautious position.[13] One such briefer, who described Murayama as "obviously pro-EAEC," said that because Japan has for too long automatically viewed the United States and Asia dichotomously, he stressed to Murayama that Indonesia, deep down, was also cautious on the EAEC.

Where Does Japan Belong?

Japan has been traumatized by the protracted debate that the EAEC and related proposals have inspired. Former Thai Prime Minister Anand

Panyarachun is critical of Japan's "not being able to have any independent point of view," and said, "they keep on changing their stances. First, they say if all of ASEAN agrees to the idea, they would have no objections to joining and then later they again shifted their stance. They said that they would have to wait until Australia and New Zealand are included or something like that. So we don't know what the Japanese stand is or if they are going to keep upping the ante all the time."[14] The EAEC encapsulates many of Japan's strategic and historical considerations—East versus West and North versus South—and it nags at the core dilemma: where does Japan belong? There is something within Japan's national psyche that is drawn to the notion of an all-Asian group. Some fear that if Japan rejects the EAEC proposal today, it may suffer tomorrow if or when the United States disengages from the region and China dominates it.

Prime Minister Mahathir evokes latent Asianist sentiment in the hearts of many Asians, including those in Japan. In April 1995, the Japanese politician Shintaro Ishihara told *Asiaweek* magazine about an "invisible yet evidently common Asianness" that flows in the blood of Asians. The 1992 book that he coauthored with Mahathir, *The Asia That Can Say No*, argues that to be faithful to its Asian roots, Japan must join the EAEC.[15] At the same time, there is worry among Japanese who experience a certain déjà vu when looking at Mahathir. One Japanese diplomat wondered if prewar Japanese Pan-Asianists shared the same feelings.[16]

To Japan's Pro-American (or Western) politicians, the EAEC looked like *dokumanju*, red bean sweets with poison inside. Former Prime Minister Noboru Takeshita and Kiichi Miyazawa have taken a cautious stance because of its ramifications for Japan's relationship with the United States. It was *Shinshinto* strongman Ichiro Ozawa, however, who argued against the EAEC in the most explicit terms: "We must be wary of ideas, such as the East Asian Economic Caucus (EAEC), that encourage a drift toward bloc economies," adding that "the EAEC and other bloc ideas will only obstruct development."[17]

Nonetheless, Mahathir's EAEC proposal has crystallized Japan's embryonic Asianist yearnings: the "pro-Asia" bureaucrats who have obtained important posts in the Ministry of Finance and the Ministry of Foreign Affairs are often more inclined to support the EAEC, some politicians have promoted an EAEC federation and Finance Minister Masayoshi Takemura gave clear support to Mahathir in January 1995, promising that Japan would try to persuade the United States to accept the creation of the EAEC. Younger MITI officials are more receptive to the EAEC, although the ministry's top ranks remain cautious.

Japanese officials who are fatigued by constant trade battles with the United States are perhaps more welcoming of Mahathir's idea than others. The contentious US-Japan "framework" talks, for example, allowed MITI Minister Ryutaro Hashimoto's political fortunes to rise in proportion to his toughness against US Trade Representative Mickey Kantor. Although Hashimoto has adopted MITI's caution on the EAEC, he warned Henry Kissinger that Japan might turn to the EAEC if NAFTA became a closed trading bloc.[18] Voices in support of EAEC are increasingly heard from various corners: from business leaders in the associations Keidanren and Keizaidoyukai, to revisionist bureaucrats in Kasumigaseki, to Prime Minister Murayama.

Implications for Regional Politics

The EAEC has complex political implications. From an economic standpoint, Japan's trade with East Asia has surpassed that with the United States. In keeping with the saying that "politics will follow economics," some see the EAEC as an instrument to reorient Japan politically toward East Asia, to account for the region's increased economic importance. They do not regard the EAEC as an alternative to APEC but a complement to further promote the global system.

Membership in the EAEC is enticing to some Japanese leaders because it would provide Japan with leverage against the United States. The EAEC could be used to balance any US inclinations to go protectionist with NAFTA or to expand NAFTA into East Asia. Such leverage would not be limited to the US-Japan bilateral relationship; it could be employed in the APEC context too. In Jakarta, MITI Minister Hashimoto hinted at this strategy when he warned his counterpart Mickey Kantor: "If you stick to a numerical target approach, you will be criticized by all the other APEC countries."[19] Cho Soon Sung, chairman of the Trade, Industry, and Energy Committee in Korea's National Assembly and a parliamentarian who strongly opposes rice liberalization, suspects that EAEC is indeed "a ploy by Japan, which has wanted to use the EAEC to brake the liberalization of APEC pushed by the US." Cho admires what he perceives as Japan's strategic acumen, saying that it would also be good for Korea to be able to resist "new colonization" by the United States through liberalization.[20]

In addition, the EAEC proposal inexorably draws Japan into the politics of ASEAN. Within ASEAN, Malaysia and Indonesia have a close relationship, yet each has its own interests in promoting EAEC and APEC, respectively. There in fact may be some degree of personal rivalry between President Suharto and Prime Minister Mahathir. When Mahathir led the charge for an EAEC, he did not first consult with his ASEAN friends, Suharto included. Under the leadership of President Suharto, Indonesia bounded to the forefront of APEC. Each of these leaders stands to gain by garnering Japanese support. Which way Japan tilts would affect significantly the internal balance of ASEAN.

Since its inception, ASEAN has played a unifying role between Sinic and Malay societies in Southeast Asia. Mahathir, however, would prefer the racial bridging to stop with Asians, and thus would value Japan, the preeminent Asian power, as a member of the EAEC. Suharto, on the other hand, has sought to form links farther afield, hence his strong support for APEC. Japan's endorsement of APEC would be another validation of his efforts.

There is another dimension of EAEC: the politics of identity. For Mahathir, the East Asian identity crystallized in the EAEC is a politically necessary vehicle to overcome and transcend sharply distinct ethnic identities among the Malaysian populace.

A final political dimension of the EAEC proposal is that it points to the struggle between China and Japan for ASEAN. ASEAN is a key component of the Asia policy of both nations. China has supported the EAEC in a much more unqualified manner than has Japan. Its embrace of the EAEC, as former Korean Foreign Minister Han Sung-Joo notes, may be an attempt to show ASEAN a friendlier face.[21] In Japan, there is great uneasiness over China's interest in a "Greater China" that would encompass ASEAN. Japan has accordingly placed ASEAN at the heart of its Asia policy. One of the dangers of Japan's new Asianist thrusts lies in the tension between Japan and China to acquire power and influence over the Southeast Asian subregional area. It will inevitably stimulate China's interest in extending the influence of a "Greater China" sphere in the region.[22]

EAEC runs the risk of intensifying the China-Japan rivalry without having a built-in mechanism to balance the two major powers. A Chinese diplomat has said that Japan will lose credibility among Asian nations if it does not support the EAEC, explaining that while "Japan still sticks to the West even though the Cold War was over five years ago," this posture "will not be a plus to Japan's future."[23] Yet a Japanese senior diplomat, after hearing the comment, wondered aloud whether China was not unhappy to see the issue cause discord within Japan and tension in the US-Japan relationship.[24]

In summary, the drama surrounding the EAEC proposal underscores many serious quandaries surrounding Japan's relationship with the Asia Pacific that will remain for a long time to come. It first points to the fact that an Asia policy that is subsumed by US policy is no longer tenable for Japan in the post–Cold War era. Neither Japan's East-West dilemmas nor its North-South legacies will soon disappear. Membership in the EAEC is appealing to those with a defensive mind-set, who would argue that the EAEC will protect Japan from being ostracized from the region in the future. At the same time, the prospect of an all-Asian grouping forces Japan to consider its interests across the Pacific and around the world.

As a result of the debate and deliberation forced by the EAEC proposal, a compromise position emerged in 1995 wherein Japan would support the EAEC as a caucus with APEC if it would also contain Australia and New Zealand. The sharp edges of the EAEC have been somewhat softened by Goh Chok Tong's EU-ASEAN plus three proposal, which is welcomed as a new global linkage.

Suspicious reactions to the EAEC proposal from various players revealed how underdeveloped the Asia Pacific is in terms of communication and mutual understanding among governments about each other's motivations. Moreover, myriad political ramifications spring from the EAEC's relationship to ASEAN. Within ASEAN, the tension between Mahathir and Suharto suggests that the EAEC is navigating risky political waters. Japan's inability to deal with the EAEC proposal most cogently highlighted Japan's need for a comprehensive Asia Pacific policy.

Internal Politics

The political scene in Japan with regard to APEC is dotted with familiar landmarks: bureaucratic turf battles between ministries, Japan's "Achilles' heel" of rice liberalization, the problems presented by Japan's decision-making style, and the qualities of Japanese leadership.

Bureaucratic Rivalry

At Canberra and Singapore, APEC nations asked not only about the "Three Chinas," but about the "Two Japans": MITI and Gaimusho, Japan's Ministry of Foreign Affairs. The two ministries had a serious fight over APEC at its inception. Gaimusho, which had scant involvement in APEC's economic ministerial process until it was upgraded to the leaders' level in 1993, was jealous that MITI helped Australia to orchestrate APEC from the very beginning. Moreover, Hawke's initial words on APEC in Seoul caught Gaimusho off guard, since Australian representatives had promised at an Australia-Japan ministerial committee a few days before to consult Japan before making any further moves.

Gaimusho's reluctance to facilitate MITI's APEC objectives was illustrated when it declined to send anyone with MITI's head of international trade policy, Shigeo Muraoka, on his "promotion tour" for APEC in March 1989.[25] Gaimusho's plan was to ask ASEAN to reject MITI's proposal, as it had its own competing scheme for an expanded ASEAN foreign ministers' conference that would include ASEAN, Japan, the United States, Canada, Australia, New Zealand, and the European Community, but changed its stance after Prime Minister Noboru Takeshita visited ASEAN countries in May 1989. Gaimusho, which argued for a more comprehensive dialogue among regional countries, complained that MITI's proposal would limit discussion to trade and investment. Furthermore, the MITI version would curb bureaucratic involvement in Asia Pacific cooperation to MITI and Gaimusho, whereas Gaimusho thought that more ministries should be involved.

In the lead-up to the first APEC ministerial, the one matter on which the two ministries agreed during the preparatory stage was that since the Tiananmen Square incident precluded China's participation, none of the Three Chinas could be included. At the first ministerial meeting in Canberra, the MITI/Gaimusho split was revealed even at the official dinner. Both Japan's foreign minister and MITI minister clamored for a seat at the head table, where the chief delegates from each country were to be seated. In the end, the Japanese delegation received a lesson on the costs of hubris: neither Japanese minister was put at the head table; rather, both were assigned seats of secondary importance.[26]

The ministries were so divided that representatives of each routinely held separate meetings with the SOM chairperson until the 1991 conference in Seoul, when Minister Lee See-Young invited the MITI and Gaimusho representatives to meet with him jointly.[27]

A MITI/Gaimusho divide was also evident in the struggle to come up with a selection for Japan's member of the Eminent Persons Group. Professor Ippei Yamazawa of Tokyo's Hitotsubashi University was eventually chosen. As an expert who had been asked to do research for both agencies, he was a compromise of the two agencies' preferences. Each had demanded that its favorite scholar be nominated, and neither would back down until Prime Minister Miyazawa pressed them to do so after he was chastised for Japan's delay by Prime Minister Paul Keating in Canberra in May 1993.[28]

Gaimusho's interest in APEC may have originally been compromised by concern that APEC might eclipse the Pacific Economic Cooperation Council (PECC), a private sector/public sector organization with which Gaimusho has long been involved. Moreover, since ASEAN has been at the core of Japan's foreign policy toward Asia, Gaimusho is characteristically sensitive to ASEAN's wariness of Pacific-wide institutions.

Hiroshi Mitsuzuka, who was appointed minister of foreign affairs in 1989 after serving as MITI minister, recalled intense bureaucratic infighting on this issue. Just after his appointment to the Foreign Ministry, he called in all of his top officials and told them point-blank: "You are principally in charge of foreign policy. However, as a commercial, nonmilitary power, Japan needs to vigorously pursue trade policy. Thus, I genuinely hope that Gaimusho and MITI will coordinate trade policies, especially APEC policy, very well." Mitsuzuka cited as the reason for Gaimusho's resistance its concern about an adverse effect on Japan's ASEAN relationships. Foreign Ministry officials remembered well

ASEAN's cool response to former Prime Minister Masayoshi Ohira's call to form a Pan-Pacific forum a decade ago. He added, "Besides that, Gaimusho could not put up with MITI intruding into their jealously guarded turf—Asian diplomacy. It was their pride." His appointment as foreign minister marked a turning point in Gaimusho's support of the proposals by MITI and Australia. "Gaimusho, however, turned its attention to Cambodia peace settlement issues as their major arena for new Asian diplomacy, and have started to feel more confident of themselves," said Mitsuzuka.[29]

A US administration official observed: "There is plenty to do in APEC that is not trade. . . . But I think they [the Ministry of Foreign Affairs] haven't quite figured out what their role is."[30] On several occasions when it has tried to contribute to APEC, Gaimusho has been spurned. For example, at the first APEC ministerial meeting, Gaimusho's proposal for a cultural exchange program was not taken as an agenda item at Canberra, while MITI's proposals were accepted.[31] At Seattle, Gaimusho again proposed a cultural exchange program with which Prime Minister Morihiro Hosokawa was not enthusiastic; he opted for MITI's energy and environment development and small and medium-size enterprise projects instead.[32]

Gaimusho, which is automatically involved at summit-level conferences, expected the advent of the leaders' meetings to guarantee the ministry a larger role in formulating APEC policy. The precedent it looked to was the G-7 summit, which had boosted Gaimusho's standing vis-à-vis MITI and other government agencies. Gaimusho is certainly home to a renewed interest in Asia. Its Asian Affairs Bureau increasingly attracts able young bureaucrats, rivaling the North American Affairs Bureau. As the ministry in charge of official development assistance, it has always targeted Asia more ODA than any other region. Kazuo Ogura, deputy minister of foreign affairs, has passionately argued that the image of Asia has been reversed recently, into a region characterized by "positive values, nonartificial and solid substance."[33] The ranks of Ogura's Asianist followers seem to be swelling in Kasumigaseki. However, Gaimusho has yet to establish its solid status in APEC. The organizational inertia of the Foreign Affairs bureaucracy is strong. Even though it reviewed its organizational charts in 1993 to put more emphasis on policy planning by establishing a Foreign Policy Bureau, it did not respond to the new dynamics of regionalism in the Asia Pacific, especially in APEC.

In the prewar days, a South Seas Affairs Bureau was created to deal with Southeast Asia and Oceania. Following the war, Oceania was moved back into a bureau with Europe.[34] Today, Australia and New Zealand remain in the European and Oceanian Affairs Bureau, which is an anachronistic "relic of the old Commonwealth days," in the words of a Japanese official.[35] In contrast, Korea's Foreign Ministry has been more geographically correct. The same bureau that deals with its Asian neighbors handles Australia and New Zealand; it was renamed from the Asia Bureau to the Asia Pacific Bureau in 1994.

Gaimusho's debut as a major player in APEC during the Seattle meeting in 1993 was marred by the poor performance of its lead bureau for APEC, the Asian Affairs Bureau. In the words of one Gaimusho official: "Translations were poor; logistics were bad; there was no script, no scenario."[36] In the wake of that disaster, APEC responsibility was transferred to the Bureau of Economic Affairs. A longtime APEC sherpa raised the question of why, given the importance of APEC to Japan's foreign policy, Gaimusho has not assigned APEC policy to a vice minister, just as it has traditionally charged a vice minister for international economy with G-7 policy.[37]

During the preparations for the 1995 Osaka meeting, MITI and Gaimusho managed to work together much better, and bureaucratic politics almost disappeared. An American official noted the division of labor that seems to characterize the two: MITI's Hidehiro Konno takes care of the substance while Gaimusho's Hiromoto Seki manages the process. Hong Kong SOM representative Tony Miller likened the cooperation between Gaimusho and MITI to a team in a three-legged race, implying that the two agencies had begun moving in lockstep.[38]

Yet latent distrust occasionally resurfaces, as it did over the Partners for Progress issue. MITI suspiciously regarded the PFP proposal as a Gaimusho plot to gain power in APEC, especially since MITI was not consulted before Konno broached the idea. By mid-1995, MITI and the United States were labeled by one Japanese official as the two foremost opponents of PFP.[39]

The question of increased bureaucratic involvement remains to be answered. While the Ministry of Finance (MOF) continues to have a quiet voice in APEC policy, Finance Minister Takemura's strong stance on the yen-dollar issue at the APEC finance ministers meeting in Bali in April 1995 indicated that the situation may be changing.[40] However, banking and finance are very much cartelized in Japan, and, as a US official noted, MOF bureaucrats, like their counterparts at the US Treasury, still hesitated to join in the APEC process.[41]

Rather, MOF seems more interested in strengthening ties with its counterparts in ASEAN countries. For example, MOF took the initiative to host the first Japan-ASEAN finance ministers' meeting at the 1994 International Monetary Fund conference in Madrid. At this inaugural meeting, the ministers discussed exchange rate and yen loan issues and agreed to meet twice a year at the margins of the IMF and Asian Development Bank meetings.[42] The fluctuating yen-dollar exchange rate and the dizzying escalation of the yen are further concerns. Many East Asian central bankers, mindful of the necessity to repay yen loans, are keenly interested in the currency's stabilization.

The MOF may also try to curb APEC competition-policy initiatives, both because of its proposed heavy regulation of the financial and insurance markets and its control over appointments to Japan's Fair Trade Commission (FTC).

As for the other ministries, a senior US official noticed at a senior officials' meeting (SOM) that despite the trade component in telecommunications and transportation, the relevant Japanese ministries did not really think that APEC applied to them and resisted direction from MITI and Gaimusho.[43] The same official, struck by Japan's foot dragging before the June 1995 APEC transportation ministers' meeting in Washington, DC, said: "We have 14 or 15 ministers who have already accepted, and Japan is saying maybe we should postpone."[44]

The fierce turf battle between MITI and the Ministry of Posts and Telecommunications (MPT) is revealed at APEC telecommunications discussions, where the representatives of both will always angle to secure Japan two seats at any table, even though other delegations are all represented by one person. Because they cannot rely on one another, they maintain separate information networks and independently support different Japanese projects. As telecom ministerials become institutionalized, MPT seems intent on trying to use APEC as a realm in which to reign over MITI, according to US administration sources. MITI, which is under pressure from textile companies and other industries to provide them with protection, certainly does not always take a free trader's perspective. Yet, MITI and Gaimusho are the only two agencies in Japan's bureaucracy that recognize their stake in pushing for liberalization. Other agencies that are not so inclined are extremely vigilant of the specter of liberalization wherever their issues are concerned.

Japan's Achilles' Heel

The single most crucial obstacle to Japan's taking an initiative or playing a more forthcoming role in trade liberalization is rice. Prime Minister Kiichi Miyazawa repeatedly referred to this domestic political hindrance as Japan's "Achilles' heel." In May 1993 a Japanese official noted that Miyazawa twice made this point in reference to the Uruguay Round: during his summit meetings first with Prime Minister Keating of Australia and second with Prime Minister Jim Bolger of New Zealand. Although Japan finally agreed to the GATT provisions for rice liberalization, it did so with a minimal pledge to import 4 percent of domestic consumption in 1995 and gradually increase the amount to 8 percent by the year 2000.

Japanese politicians and agriculture constituencies were especially attentive to any concessions the government might make on rice in the months preceding the APEC leaders' summit in Seattle. A MITI official explained that Japan had to maintain a low profile in APEC, so as not to arouse any unnecessary suspicions among these constituencies.[45] In 1990, when APEC was considering a declaration to push the Uruguay Round, the trade ministers of Korea and Japan were worried about the tariffication of trade barriers as they faced severe impediments in the agricultural sector.[46]

Before the Jakarta meeting, the Ministry of Agriculture, Forestry, and Fisheries (MAFF) repeatedly cautioned Gaimusho that agriculture products should be awarded the special status of "nontradeable goods," apparently in order to prevent them from being liberalized. A puzzled Gaimusho official inquired why MAFF was then insisting on a special status, when it did not do so in the Punta del Este meeting of the Uruguay Round in 1986. MAFF's answer was, "That's why we should not make a similar mistake again," referring to the rice liberalization decisions forced on them in the Uruguay Round agreements. MAFF seems to be maintaining a "wait and see" posture, at least for the five years until 2000, when the World Trade Organization (WTO) will resume a review process of the Uruguay Round agreements, including rice liberalization. The ministry has made clear it is reluctant to give up its bargaining chip so readily.[47]

Prime Minister Murayama, Foreign Minister Kono, and MITI Minister Hashimoto twice met in the prime minister's office to discuss APEC policy before the Jakarta conference. They were all concerned that a commitment by Japan in the APEC context to liberalize agriculture would adversely affect the ratification of the Uruguay Round. Murayama, under heavy pressure from the MAFF, finally said that while he understood its position, he himself would have to judge what would be appropriate to say in Jakarta, given the atmospherics of the meeting. He indeed raised the agriculture issue in the leaders' meeting. In addition, he privately appealed to Suharto in Jakarta for special consideration of "nontradeable aspects of agriculture" in liberalization.[48] Yet, as Suharto's special envoy Bintoro Tjokroamidjojo rightly perceived after receiving a surprise MAFF visitor (see Chapter 5), most of these requests and pleas are a matter of political ritual that allows Japan's political leaders to demonstrate to their constituencies that they "have fought until the last man."

Japan thus faced an acute dilemma. As chair at the Osaka meeting, it needed to demonstrate unilateral liberalization actions to set a good example and live up to the general principle of comprehensiveness (that is, no exceptions in areas of liberalization). However, Japan's SOM members requested a waiver for its agricultural sector from the comprehensiveness list at the Sapporo SOM meeting.

Decision-Making Style

Japan's APEC policy is also constrained by the unique combination of Japan's decision-making mechanisms and processes. Decisions on foreign affairs in Japan are routinely retarded by "bottom-up" consensus building known as *nemawashi*, the dominance of the "domesticists" over the internationalists, and the manner in which domestic political institutions must achieve mutual parity in burden sharing.[49] Furthermore, the different sectors of Japan's bureaucracy seem to exercise veto power against each other, especially when they lack strong direction from the political leadership.

They have tended to prevent any bold actions or initiatives. It is for these reasons that *gaiatsu* or "foreign pressure" became an integral factor in Japan's decision making, allowing the internationalists' voices to be heard and providing the necessary catalyst to overcome the inertia caused by bureaucratic gridlock. The harnessing of international impetus to effect domestic political change was honed during the lengthy de facto one-party rule of the LDP. *Gaiatsu* also was brilliantly manipulated by Prime Minister Yasuhiro Nakasone in the G-7 context. More recently, MITI appeared to employ Australian *gaiatsu* to override the resistance to APEC exhibited by the Foreign Ministry.

With the fall of the ruling party in 1993, *gaiatsu* began to work less reliably. This was illustrated by the unprecedented breakdown in the US-Japan "framework" talks in 1994, which led to drawn-out negotiations on auto parts. The reason for this is threefold. First, there is now a difference in the interaction between *gaiatsu* and *naiatsu* (pressures from within) in Japan. The dynamics of Japan's current coalition government differ from that of the old LDP regime, in which competing LDP factions provided a testing ground for US *gaiatsu*. Each faction tried to demonstrate that it was most adept at managing the US-Japan relationship. In addition, US *gaiatsu* had the most success when it affected Japanese industries with an interest and stake in opening up markets to imports. Coalitions would form between the Japanese industry that would benefit from greater openness and the US industry that would gain export opportunities.

Second, the rice liberalization agreed upon in the Uruguay Round has changed the face of Japanese politics. Although rice is still Japan's Achilles' heel, politicians are no longer as cowed by the prospect of the agricultural cooperative's retaliation. Their newfound confidence is also seen in their stance toward the United States. In the past, US threats to open Japan's agriculture markets, particularly the rice sector, were likely to sway politicians to compromise on trade. By eliminating Japan's sanctuary market for rice, the Uruguay Round deprived the United States of a bargaining chip.

Third, the allure of nationalism has grown in the transition period following the Cold War. Thus a "tough on the US" portfolio has a certain appeal to the electorate and has been successfully wielded by politicians such as MITI Minister Hashimoto.[50]

Given the new dynamics of a more interdependent world order, bilateral *gaiatsu* may yield the United States less than a regional or multilateral type of *gaiatsu*, such as that exerted in GATT/WTO and APEC. In the GATT round, for instance, the minimal increase in rice market access was only made possible by Uruguay Round multilateral negotiations, not by the filing of a petition by the US Rice Millers Association with the Office of the US Trade Representative to initiate a section 301 action against Japan's closed rice market. Already, *gaiatsu* has begun to shift from bilateral to multilateral forums.

"Leadership from Behind"

Japanese leaders appear loath to take international initiatives. Prime Minister Mahathir was particularly frustrated by Japan's lack of bold action on his EAEC proposal. Rather, Japanese leaders have preferred a more subtle, behind-the-scenes approach. An Australian scholar has termed this style as Japan's "leadership from behind."[51] Part of the reason for Japan's inhibition on foreign policy is the memory of its invasion and colonization of neighboring countries. Japanese leaders are further constrained by their special consideration of US concerns. Both politicians and the public alike are inclined to view strong and charismatic Japanese leaders with suspicion. Former Prime Minister Yasuhiro Nakasone is a case in point. Although voices around the globe hailed him as one of Japan's most talented and effective leaders, he failed to gain the same level of admiration in Japan. In fact, he was known to sigh that he was a "prophet who is not welcomed at home."

In Seattle, Japanese Foreign Minister Hata was serendipitously invited by a young local couple to attend their wedding banquet, which was held in the room adjacent to the one where a dinner was hosted by Japan's Consul General. In response to their request for a small speech, Hata recited his favorite poem:

> Better to look foolish
> if it increases harmony between you.
> Better not to have everything ideal. . . .
>
> If you have a telling remark to make,
> enfold it in reticence.
> Bear in mind that truth can hurt the other.[52]

Although these words are from an epithalamium, Hata regards it as his philosophy of leadership as well. He believes in the value of consensus and recognizes that it is a time-consuming process. "APEC building is no exception," he said.[53] In Japan, such thinking is perceived not only as the Japanese way, but as the Asian way. Yet, viewed from the other side of the spectrum, it also reflects the problem of Japan's leadership. And this consensual decision making, which is both a cause and an effect of Japan's political immobility, has hindered Japan from making timely decisions on foreign policy as Japan has become a major world player. It works against Japan's leaders in the international context, allowing them to be too easily co-opted.

Japan's weak political leadership, however, is not a hereditary malady. Japan has had effective leaders in this era, such as Prime Ministers Shigeru Yoshida, Eisaku Sato, and Yasuhiro Nakasone. These leaders, however, were aided by the fact that Washington had already mapped the big picture. This arrangement allowed Japan to enter the GATT in 1955, the UN in 1956, the OECD in 1964, and the G-7 in 1975. Also, Japan was able to normalize relations with China in 1972 and promulgate the Japan-China Peace and Friendship Treaty in 1979 as part of the anti-Soviet strategy. Those leaders were adept at fine-tuning and balancing US strategic imperatives with Japanese domestic requirements. Their one-dimensional economic rehabilitation strategy ultimately succeeded, but now Japan is paying the price of their success. Although Japan has fulfilled its economic goal, it now finds itself in a new era without a blueprint for tomorrow's Japan. The nation is beyond the point of "catching up" with the West, and Japanese leaders do not see the next goal so clearly.

The power vacuum created when the LDP was removed from power in 1993 has cast a dark shadow over the inept political leadership. Political instability has hampered any Japanese leader from taking bold action. A senior diplomat confided that he was exceedingly frustrated with the lack of commitment and ineffective leadership from the *Kantei*, or the Prime Minister's office, in APEC liberalization policy formation. "Whenever you go to *Kantei* for a decision, you are told to go to the three different parties [of the coalition government] to get consensus before you come to see the prime minister," he complained. "But if you go to the three coalition parties for their input, you will surely end up having the lowest common denominator."[54]

The strength of Japan's government has traditionally been the "routine power" exercised by bureaucrats. But this type of leadership is not suited to the radically changing global environment. Japan has often been called a country in which politicians reign while bureaucrats rule. With a set of clear, long-term national goals such as economic reconstruction, growth, and anticommunist defense policy, bureaucratic and administrative prowess functioned effectively. However, it has proved to not work well in a crisis, such as the oil shock in 1973 or the 1990 Persian Gulf Crisis. Japan faces a serious challenge to its leadership style, for the international environment is radically changing. Mapping Japan's future course for Asia policy and the US-Japan relationship is one of the most crucial tasks Japan faces. It requires strong political leadership.

Another factor that will continue to affect Japan's political leadership is generational change. Tensions arising from the generation gap tend to cloud Japan's view of Asia and the United States. The old guard, such as former Prime Ministers Noboru Takeshita and Kiichi Miyazawa, has always viewed the US-Japan bilateral relationship as the cornerstone of Japan's foreign policy and was willing to make Asia policy subordinate to US policy. However, younger politicians such as Finance Minister Takemura and MITI Minister Hashimoto have explored a new direction. They are trying to rebalance the emphases on the United States and Asia in Japan's policy.

In sum, Japan's domestic politics has at times impeded its progress in APEC. Like bureaucracies the world over, Japan's is riven by "turf battles" among ministries. Fierce competition between MITI and Gaimusho limited Japan's role in APEC, especially during the early years. Although this rift is beginning to disappear, new ones are emerging as other ministries, perhaps harboring the "watchdog" instinct to guard their own turf, begin to take a more vigorous interest in APEC.

A reluctance to liberalize rice has been foremost in Japan's domestic political considerations. Given the sensitivity of the issue, Japanese leaders have fastidiously tried to avoid being perceived as crusaders for or even contributors to liberalization in APEC.

As for Japanese decision making, the end of the Cold War has brought a change in the reliance on US *gaiatsu* to overcome sectoral interests. This brand of outside pressure, which became embedded in Japanese political culture during the uninterrupted reign of the LDP, cannot survive in the new political atmosphere.

A new type of mutual *gaiatsu* is emerging that is better suited to multilateral forums such as APEC. APEC can and should provide this kind of catalyst or political "cover" for all its political leaders when they liberalize their respective markets and economies. It can help them avoid the protectionist and nationalist reactions at home that would ensue from bilateral negotiations. Finally, Japan's leadership has yet to clearly reveal its intent in APEC. Japanese leaders are hampered by a number of factors, including Japan's wartime legacy, a Japanese tendency toward consensus building, confusion over Japan's role in the world, and political instability. The resolution of these problems will necessarily take time. However, as Japan grapples with these issues, it can begin in APEC to experiment with new varieties of leadership.

Notes

1. *Nihon Keizai Shimbun*, 30 November 1994.

2. Personal interview with Japanese diplomat, 8 July 1995.

3. *Asahi Shimbun*, 9 September 1992.

4. *Far Eastern Economic Review*, 23 January 1993.

5. Personal interview with US official, 19 May 1995.

6. Personal interview with James Baker, 30 June 1995.

7. Ph.D. dissertation of Minoru Koide, University of Southern California, 1993.

8. Personal interview with former Prime Minister Yasuhiro Nakasone, 18 November 1994.

9. Personal interview with MITI Economic Cooperation Bureau Director Hidehiro Konno, 25 June 1995.

10. Personal interview with Yoshihiro Sakamoto, 8 June 1995.

11. *Asahi Shimbun*, 30 May 1995.

12. Personal interview with Yohei Kono, 31 August 1995. Kono stressed this point in the ASEAN PMC meeting in the summer of 1995 but was told that ASEAN could not reach a consensus on it before the first summit.

13. Personal interview with MITI Minister Ryutaro Hashimoto, 3 July 1995.

14. Personal interview with Anand Panyarachun, 28 August 1995.

15. *Asiaweek*, 28 April 1995.

16. Yoichi Funabashi, *Nihon no Taigai Koso* [A Design for a New Course of Japan's Foreign Policy] (Tokyo: Iwanami Shoten, 1993).

17. Ichiro Ozawa, *Blueprint for a New Japan* (Tokyo: Kodansha, 1994) p. 13.

18. Ryutaro Hashimoto, *Vision of Japan* (Tokyo: Bestsellers, 1994), pp. 70–71.

19. Personal interview with Hashimoto.

20. Personal interview with Cho Soon Sung, 26 July 1995.

21. Personal interview with Han Sung-Joo, 5 July 1995.

22. Funabashi, pp. 105–06.

23. Author's conversation with Chinese diplomat.

24. Personal interview, 11 April 1995.

25. Personal interview with Hiroshi Mitsuzuka, 22 July 1995.

26. Personal interview with a trade minister who attended the meeting.

27. Personal interview, 2 July 1995.

28. Personal interview, 2 July 1995.

29. Personal interview with Mitsuzuka.

30. Personal interview, 26 April 1995.

31. *Nikkei Shimbun*, 24 October 1989.

32. Personal interview, 3 July 1995.

33. Kazuo Ogura, "Ajia no Fukken no Tame ni" (For the 'Restoration of Asia'), *Chuo Koron*, Summer 1993. English translation in the *Straits Times*, 16 July 1993.

34. Susumu Yamakage, "Ajia Taiheiyou to Nihon" (Asia Pacific and Japan), in Akio Watanabe, ed., *Sengo Nihon no Taigai Seisaku* (Japan's Postwar Foreign Policy) (Yuhikaku, 1985).

35. Personal interview, 4 July 1995.

36. Personal interview with Japanese senior administration official, 3 July 1995.

37. Personal interview, 24 July 1995.

38. Personal interview, 21 July 1995.

39. Personal interview with senior Japanese administration official, 4 July 1995.

40. *New York Times*, 10 April 1995.

41. Personal interview, 27 April 1995.

42. Personal interview with Masayoshi Takemura, 17 June 1995.

43. Personal interview, 26 April 1995.

44. Personal interview with a senior US administration official.

45. Personal interview, 26 June 1995.

46. Koide, p. 257.

47. Personal interview with a Japanese official.

48. Personal interview with MITI Minister Ryutaro Hashimoto, 3 July 1995.

49. Yoichi Funabashi, *Managing the Dollar: From the Plaza to the Louvre* (Washington: Institute for International Economics, 1987).

50. See also Leonard Schoppa and Herman Schwartz, "On a Collision Course with Japan," *Chicago Tribune*, 2 June 1995, p. 19.

51. Alan Rix, "Leadership from Behind," in R. Higgot, R. Leaver, and J. Ravenhill, eds., *Pacific Cooperation in the 1990s* (Australia Fulbright Commission, 1993), p. 65.

52. Hiroshi Yoshino, *Epithalamium* (translated by Kii Nakano).

53. Personal interview with Tsuotomu Hata, 4 July 1995.

54. Personal interview with a diplomat.

12

Japan and the Asia Pacific

New Affinity for Asia

An "Asianist" wave has engulfed Japan. Today, many Japanese perceive Asia not only as a region of dynamic economies, but also as a chic hot spot. Asia's boom has also proved to be Japan's boon. For instance, when Japan was in a deep recession in 1995, with only seven out of ten female college graduates finding jobs in what has become known as the "super glacial period," the recruiting efforts of Yaohan, a worldwide Japanese retail chain headquartered in Hong Kong, were enticing. Yaohan's ads proclaimed that the company was seeking "100 talented, ambitious and English-speaking Japanese women under the age of 25" to join the ranks of its Asian business troops.[1]

Asia does not just present an opportunity for young Japanese, it delivers a message. Trends in Japanese media suggest an increasing fascination with the region. News articles about Asia in Japan's leading newspaper, *Asahi Shimbun*, increased from 1,000 stories in 1985 to more than 6,000 in 1994.[2] As for the general public, a survey by Japan's weekly magazine *AERA* showed that a predominantly young readership would prefer Asia over the United States if Japan had to choose between the two in the pursuit of its foreign policy.[3] The wording of this question highlights the "either/or" nature of public discourse on the subject. Thoroughly Western-trained business leaders are no exception. For example, Yotaro Kobayashi, chairman of Fuji Xerox, forcefully advocates the "re-Asianization of Japan" by strengthening ties with Asian neighbors and distancing itself from the United States. Newspaper publisher Toshiaki Ogasawara recently announced his "conversion" to a new conception of "East Asian identity."[4]

Japan is perhaps experiencing its third Asianist wave. The first took place during the Meiji Restoration in the late 19th century and the early 20th century when an Asia-first policy was championed by intellectuals such as Junzan Sugita, author of *Koa-saku* (Plans for Asian Prosperity), a book which detailed several ways to avoid Asia's colonization by Europe. Sugita was a member of the Jiyu-Minken Undo (Freedom and People's Rights movement) whose members not only sympathized with Japan's less fortunate colonized and semicolonized Asian brethren, but also perhaps feared eventual colonization of Japan. To stem the tide of colonization, leading intellectuals promoted the idea of Japan forming a coalition with Asian neighbors such as Korea, China, Vietnam, and India. Such partnerships would be based on the shared "Asianness" of Japan and the other nations, especially China, which merited the phrase *dobun doshu* (same character, same ethnicity).

These benevolent intentions were eventually supplanted by a hegemonic vision of Japan as the lead organizer of Asia. To the hegemonists, there were two courses that Japan could choose: ignore Asia or conquer it. Great educator Yukichi Fukuzawa argued for the first. He put forth a "dissociate from Asia" policy that warned against forging partnerships with Asia's corrupt rulers, whom he termed "Japan's bad friends." Many *Ajiashugisha* (Asianists) found the second way as the only option to survive against Western powers, particularly Russia. First Japan conquered Korea, and then Manchuria. Even idealistic activists such as Sugita came to advocate Japanese invasion of Asia to counterbalance the West. After Sugita visited Qing China, he changed his views, because he had been devastated by the backwardness and ignorance of the Chinese leaders. He gave up on the coalition strategy to counter the West, fearing that such an alliance with a decadent China would only drag Japan into an abyss. Therefore, he began to argue that Japan should enter the West, for if Japan waited for China to reform, both would be swallowed by the West.[5]

The 1930s brought the second Asian wave, in the guise of Japan's plans for a Greater East Asia Co-Prosperity Sphere. After the Great Depression, the world economy was composed of competing economic blocs. In 1933, Japan became the world's largest exporter of cotton cloth. Japan's massive intrusion into British India's textile market prompted Great Britain to form an Imperial Preference system, which later became the Commonwealth. Japan's response was to turn to Asia. The wave that began in the 1930s culminated in Japan's hosting of the Greater East Asia conference in Tokyo in 1943. These first two waves were born of Japan's aversion to the West rather than compassion toward Asia. The imperialistic sentiment that these waves inspired eventually led to Japan's invasion of East and Southeast Asia.

Noted Korean economist and current Mayor of Seoul Cho Soon has warned that the "re-Asianization" of Japan today without true spiritual and psychological links to fellow Asians could lead to another Greater East Asian Co-Prosperity Sphere.[6] However, there are signs that the cresting of this third wave is different. This time, Japan is becoming peacefully enmeshed in Asia through greater travel, business interaction, and person-to-person links. Japan has come to consider its Asian neighbors to be "normal" foreign countries, in the same way that Japan has long viewed America and Europe, and this allows for more equal intra-Asian relations. At the same time, the collapse of the bipolar world order has sparked profound soul-searching within Japan; the resurgence of Asianist yearnings coincides with the desire to define a new national identity.

Reevaluation of Western Ties

Japan's new Asianism is inherently driven by psychic yearnings for it to disassociate itself from the United States. For years, Japan played the "little brother" to its American "big brother." The end of the Cold War has prompted a reevaluation. Wasuke Miyake, a former diplomat, has suggested that Japan shift its diplomatic emphasis from the United States to Asia. He argued: "Until now, Japan has often listened to American voices and persuaded Asians. From now, Japan needs to listen to more Asian voices and persuade Americans."[7] Within Japan, American revisionist theories, as well as the popular perception of American trade negotiators as abrasive auto parts promoters, stoke anti-American sentiment. The 1989 bestseller, *The Japan That Can Say No*, by Shintaro Ishihara and Akio Morita, was a precursor of more widespread *kenbei,* or dislike, of the United States. One of the characteristics of Japan's swing back to Asia has been the Japanese perception of being rejected by the West. Japanese thinker and China scholar Yoshimi Takeuchi once observed Japan's Asianism in prewar years as a "mood or a state of mind which does not contain any set value system in and of itself, but only reflects a reaction to other [Western] ideas."[8]

More nuanced ways to distance Japan from the United States have emerged, however. More and more, voices calling for *nyua nyuo* (enter Asia, enter the West) have been heard. Recognition of Japan's stake in the global economy and the critical underpinning of the US-Japan security relationship have put a limit on the excessive Asianist thrusts in the mainstream. Heightened concern about US disengagement also give Asia-firsters second thoughts. Yet, Asianist drives will continue to take on tones of dissociating from the United States.

Japan's rediscovery of Asia parallels the heightened interest of European countries in their own region. Just as Europeans have come to acknowledge their commonalities, increased interaction with Asia and the sharing of popular culture has revealed to the Japanese people the mutual interests they share with other Asians.

Asian regionalism has also come to be seen as a counterforce against the European Union's single market. Deep concern over European integration was strong in the late 1980s and early 1990s. European integration simultaneously sanitized and immunized the bad connotation Japan assigned to regionalism in the past: bad politics and bad economics. The advent of the North American Free Trade Agreement (NAFTA), which showed that even the United States could be "adulterated" by regionalism, was another factor. The US embrace of regionalism shook the intellectual foundation of the multilateralist school of Japan's GATT followers, who had solidly built up its influence in policymaking circles.

Japan as Role Model

The endeavors of many Asian countries to emulate Japan's economic success have now come to fruition. Indicative of this achievement are the success of Malaysia's Look East policy and the World Bank's affirmation of the "East Asian miracle," that materialized as a result of prudent allocation of physical and human resources.[9] Japan promoted the World Bank project and tried to put forth an East Asian developmental model for use by the less developed countries.

Moreover, the trend seems to be spreading. According to influential Australian economists, "The East Asian success is now influential outside the region, most importantly in South Asia."[10] The recognition of the "Japanese model" in Asia has given Japan new confidence in itself and an enduring interest in the region. Former Foreign Ministry Spokesman Masamichi Hanabusa has suggested that "Japan should, and can, make intellectual contributions to the global aid community in years ahead by undertaking studies on East Asian success in development."[11]

The end of the Cold War has unleashed new sentiments and motivations in Japan to rediscover Asia. Now that ideological boundaries have largely deteriorated, Japan's trade and investment is free to flow in new directions. Emancipated from Cold War restraints, Japan has been able to explore new approaches to Cambodia, Vietnam, North Korea, and Mongolia. Once the territorial issue with Russia is resolved, Japanese ties to Siberian and Maritime Russia will also be reinvigorated.

At the same time, the fading of the Cold War mentality has led some to believe that Japan can now, for the first time, afford to distance itself from the United States. While nations were once strategically and ideologically engaged globally on the Cold War's global chessboard, a sense of regional preferences is emerging, as evidenced by the trend toward selective engagement. With groups such as the European Union and NAFTA already established, there are some who argue for an Asian one. Finally, with the end of the Cold War has also come the realization that the US model is not the only one. This has sparked an interest in Japan in defining the Japanese model and its relevance to the world.

The Evolution of Japan's Asia Policy

Haunted by the failure of the Greater East Asian Co-Prosperity Sphere and World War II, Japan has for years shunned the concept of regionalism and the strategy of approaching Asia as a whole. From a political perspective, there was the danger that a coherent Asia policy could be mistaken for a resurgence of prewar "Asianism" and evoke painful memories of political domination by an ambitious hegemon. From an economic perspective, regionalism has been seen as portending a malevolent exclusivism that could disrupt the system of free trade.[12] Indeed, Kensuke Yanagiya, a former Gaimusho official who formulated Asian policy for a long time after the war said that authorities in his ministry "actually made a point of not articulating what could be called an Asia policy."[13] Moreover, regionalism simply has not been fostered institutionally in Asia in the manner of the North Atlantic Treaty Organization or the European Community in Europe. Such organizations helped to alleviate some of Germany's tensions with its Western European neighbors. While there is a certain degree of equality among European nations that nurtures these frameworks, Japan's emergence as the first non-Western industrialized nation and its subsequent pursuit of hegemony left a legacy of schisms and inequality in Asia.

1951, the year in which the San Francisco Peace Treaty was signed and the occupation of Japan came to an end, marked the beginning of a new postwar era in Japan's relations with Asia. At the time, Asia Pacific countries harbored deep suspicions of the newly independent Japan. Australia and New Zealand, for instance, demanded a military alliance with the United States, the ANZUS pact, in return for their signature of the treaty. Japan's first interactions with the region were through war reparations, which eventually totaled $1.5 billion paid to 11 countries.[14]

Japan's postwar course of renewing its relations with Asia was distinctly shaped by Cold War dynamics. Japan's Asia policy was subsumed by its US Asia policy, which pursued three main objectives: to transfer Japan's exports from China to Southeast Asia, to maintain a stable supply of materials to Japan from Southeast Asia, and to promote an organic integration of US, Japanese, and Southeast Asian markets. After the war, the United States wanted to dissociate Japan from Asia and integrate it into the international order. At the same time, these objectives, which were mapped out by Washington, fit the interests of a Japan that aspired to become accepted by the international community.

As the Cold War wore on, a huge gap emerged between Japan's rapidly deepening relationship with the United States on the one hand and Japan's difficulty in forging better relationships with its East Asian neighbors on the other. Although Japan and Australia signed a trade pact in 1957, it was not until 1974 that Japan concluded a trade agreement with the Philippines.

Yet, within the boundaries of US interests, Japan took initiatives in organizing regionwide cooperation. In 1966, Foreign Minister Etsusaburo Shiina greeted counterparts from Malaysia, Singapore, the Philippines, South Vietnam, Laos, and Cambodia in Tokyo. They had come to attend the first South East Asia Development Ministerial Conference, which was the first official international meeting Japan hosted in the postwar era.[15] Indonesia joined the following year. This endeavor was seen by some as an *ukezara*, or "receiving saucer," for Japan's economic assistance. Shiina, mindful of US strategy, perhaps designed his proposal to complement President Lyndon Johnson's plan for a $1 billion development package for Southeast Asia.

While Shiina's conference was a clear anti-North Vietnam maneuver, there were also anti-China overtones. These were even more pronounced in the anticommunist ASPAC grouping founded in 1966 by Korean leader Park Chung-Hee. That group comprised Australia, New Zealand, the Philippines, Thailand, South Vietnam, Malaysia, Taiwan, Korea, and Japan.

The year of those inaugural conferences also marked the birth of the Asian Development Bank (ADB). Although some Asians argued that the ADB should be an Asian-only enterprise, Japan characteristically insisted on US participation. It was during the mid-1960s that Japan began to encounter Asians' deep mistrust of and resistance to Japanese leadership. A common concern was that Japan's official development assistance (ODA) might lead to political influence. Illustrative of the Asian nations' apprehension was the decision of ADB members to locate their headquarters in Manila rather than Tokyo, for which Japan had actively campaigned.

The 1970s brought a realignment of Japan's Cold War strategy and marked a new phase in relations with Asia. Having adhered to the tenets of US strategic concerns, Japan was stunned by the Nixon *shokku* of the 1970s, which was delivered in three parts: the US administration's unilateral advances toward China, its action to end the convertibility of the dollar to gold, and its embargo of soybean exports. The tremors from Nixon's attempt to realign the power politics of the region through his new China policy were particularly strong in Japan. As Tokyo University Professor Susumu Yamakage succinctly described it: "The pretext of Japan's Asia Pacific diplomacy, in a single swoop, collapsed."[16]

The 1973 oil crisis further awakened the Japanese to their own natural resource needs and security interests. These events stimulated Japan to explore the possibility of *dokuji gaiko* (more autonomous diplomacy).

As Japan embarked on a new campaign to ingratiate itself with resource-rich countries, it was soon beset by another shock: the violent riots that Prime Minister Kakuei Tanaka met with when he visited Thailand and Indonesia in 1974. His disastrous trip pointed to the inadequacies of Japan's "resource diplomacy" and more broadly to the problems that one-dimensional economic diplomacy posed. The anti-Tanaka protests were not only staged against "Japanese economic imperialism" but also directed at the elite business class with Japanese connections and the overseas Chinese business community, particularly in Indonesia's case. Indeed, Indonesia's Foreign Minister Adam Malik told the press that Indonesian resentment against ethnic Chinese was a factor in the violence.[17] The riots more broadly indicated a backlash against the opening up of the Indonesian economy, which had been largely state-owned since 1958, and have been described as a turning point in Indonesia's economic policies. Soon after Tanaka's visit, Indonesia's investment laws were changed to prevent 100 percent foreign ownership.[18]

Japan has always been prone to be made a target or a scapegoat, as Japanese investment has been most visible in the region. ASEAN nations again showed their displeasure when they refused to invite Prime Minister Takeo Miki to their first summit meeting in Bali in 1976. At that point, Japan began to take vigorous new initiatives toward ASEAN, which culminated in the first ASEAN-Japan Forum in 1977.[19] Prime Minister Takeo Fukuda further strove to correct the errors of the past in his famous "heart-to-heart" speech in Manila in 1977, in which he made strong overtures toward ASEAN.

In the late 1970s, Japan began to fear the disengagement of the United States from Asia. The fall of Saigon and President Jimmy Carter's pledge to withdraw from Korea sparked this concern. Vietnam's invasion of Cambodia and the Soviet Union's invasion of Afghanistan again evoked images of falling "dominoes," and Japan's Asia policy rapidly reestablished the primacy of Cold War concerns. Fukuda's successor, Masayoshi Ohira, who took over in 1978, promoted a "pan-Pacific design" that widened the scope of Japan's regional diplomacy and reflected an acknowledgment of Cold War realities.

"Market Asia" emerged in the 1980s as the de facto unifying theme of Japan's policy in the region. Since the 1985 Plaza Agreement, Japan's foreign direct investment (FDI) has achieved new prominence over Japan's ODA. The infusion of Japanese money combined with other factors, such as China's implementation of new open-door policies, to promote the globalization of Asia's economies. Japan's investment was followed by the investment of the NIEs in ASEAN, which led to the emergence of "new NIEs." Asia exploded into a chain reaction of success stories. Democratization accelerated as economic development fostered democratic forces throughout Asia. The so-called Miyazawa Doctrine, put forth by

Prime Minister Kiichi Miyazawa in Bangkok in 1992, did not lay out a new direction for Japanese foreign policy but simply endorsed the market forces that had already begun to transform Asia.

The 1990s and the end of the Cold War have brought Japan's Asia policy to a new stage. Increasingly, politics and a greater spirit of independence have been infused in Japan's approach to the region. The passage of the peacekeeping operations bill and the dispatch of Self-Defense Forces personnel to Cambodia was the starting point for a new political and security dimension to Japan's Asia policy.[20] In September 1992, Japan sent over 600 SDF personnel and civilian police to Cambodia as part of an overall 1,800 troop deployment. In addition, with the advent of APEC in 1989 and APEC leaders' meetings in 1993, Japan has begun to prioritize a more regional and multilateral Asia Pacific policy. Along with APEC, MITI has begun to emphasize AEM&M, an acronym for the ASEAN Economic Ministers and MITI, a ministerial group that first met in Manila in October 1992.

Although Japan has followed the US line on policy issues concerning Myanmar and Vietnam, Japan has taken steps toward a more independent policy on China. Prime Minister Morihiro Hosokawa's comments on China and human rights are a case in point. Japan's new voice was resoundingly heard at the 1990 Houston G-7 summit. Former Vice Minister for Foreign Affairs Hisashi Owada emphasized that Japan played an instrumental role in persuading the others that China should not be isolated.[21]

The formulation of a thoughtful China policy is something that Japan owes itself and the region, since the emergence of China on the world scene promises a new era of interdependence in Asia. Full diplomatic relations were finally restored between China and all the ASEAN states in the early 1990s. Japan's commitment to engaging China in the international community may be the best contribution that Japan could make. Japan's balancing act between the United States and China has constrained Japan's movement. Furthermore, that China is one of the last bastions of communism prevents Japan from engaging more fully with Beijing.

East versus West, North versus South

Situated at a crossroads between East, West, North, and South, Japan is often perceived as linking those compass points. Actually, Japan's unique position may actually be at the root of myriad dilemmas that reverberate in Japan's relations with the Asia Pacific. Throughout history, Japan has tried to reconcile the dimensions of its identity, which are pulled in different directions. Japanese people remain ambivalent about Asia. An *Asahi Shimbun* poll from August 1994 asked whether Japan's relationship with Asia or with Europe and the United States should get first priority. Of those polled, 28 percent favored Asia, 6 percent favored Europe and the United States, and 60 percent said importance should be attached to both. When asked whether Asia would take the place of Europe and the United States in the 21st century, only 27 percent said yes; 59 said no. One scholar has connected the public's preference for attention to both Asia and the United States/Europe revealed in these polls to an emerging interest in the Asia Pacific. He found that since the late 1980s, Japanese prime ministers began to mention "Asia Pacific" more often than "Asia" alone in their speeches.[22]

However, like a pendulum, Japan has often seemed to swing between East and West, as if it must only link with either one or the other at a given time. Japan's internal debate over whether to join the East Asian Economic Caucus (EAEC), Malaysian Prime Minister Mahathir's all-Asian club, is often framed as a decision to choose one alliance over another. While Japan is proud of its membership in the nearly all-Western Group of Seven (G-7), Mahathir's Asianist philosophy—epitomized in statements such as ". . . if you resent the Europeans, you naturally appreciate the Asians"—also has a certain resonance.[23] The angst provoked by the EAEC proposal is but the most proximate example of Japan's East versus West dilemma.

In prewar days, the East-West division was almost institutionalized in the political class, which contained the Western faction, *Eibieha*, and the competing Asian faction, *Ajiaha*. On the night of the fateful day in 1933 that the Japanese delegation walked out on the League of Nations in protest for its censure of Japan's 1931 invasion of Manchuria, the Japanese officials in Geneva sang "Come back to Asia. . . . Oh, back to Asia." Indonesian statesman Mohamad Hatta, who together with Sukarno led Indonesia's independence movement in the late 1940s, was intrigued by the surge of the "come back to Asia" sentiment when he visited Japan around the time of Japan's departure from the League of Nations. He perceived it as a kind of national therapy, in which Japan sought to immerse itself in the East as an antidote to rejection by the West.[24]

Following World War II, the pendulum swung back to the West. Japan allied itself closely with the United States under the leadership of Prime Minister Shigeru Yoshida, who strove to bring Japan into the West through economic reconstruction and commercial diplomacy. This philosophy, retroactively referred to as the Yoshida Doctrine, shaped a Japan whose own Asia policy was heavily influenced by the United States. For example, in 1955 the Hatoyama cabinet first asked the permission of the United States before deciding to dispatch a delegation to attend Indonesia's Bandung Conference of Asian and African leaders.

In Cold War days, there was a definite divide between the Pacific and Asia. The Pacific was defined more in security and military terms, as a "zone" or a "theater." Asia, on the other hand, was seen in cultural or racial terms. Developed countries of the North inhabited the Pacific, whereas less developed countries of the South made up Asia. To some eyes, Japan's induction into the G-7 club in 1975 perhaps can be seen as the culmination of Japan's disassociation from Asia.

Actually, membership in the G-7 has revealed Japan's uncertainty about its place in the world. Indeed, it seemed more important for Prime Minister Yasuhiro Nakasone that Japan be accepted as a member of the West (*Nishigawa no Ichiin*) rather than be treated as another economic power; he vied primarily for membership in the "Western club," not necessarily the "economic club." At the same time, it became a tradition for Japan, as a member of the North, to solicit the views and requests from Asian capitals before G-7 meetings. In 1975, when Prime Minister Takeo Miki went to the first G-7 summit at Rambouillet, France, he could not help from saying that Japan would attend as a representative of Asia, which would hence try to infuse perspectives from the South.[25]

However, Japan was not welcomed as a full-fledged member of the Western club, as Prime Minister Masayoshi Ohira painfully discovered. As a Japanese leader who diligently labored to strengthen trans-Pacific ties, Ohira was an especially proud host of the first Tokyo G-7 summit in 1979 and considered it a great accomplishment that Japan had become, in his words, a "member of the West." Thus, when the leaders of United States, United Kingdom, France, and Germany met for an exclusive "G-4" inner-core breakfast meeting before the summit, Ohira was profoundly devastated. That instance brought back memories of Japan's experience in the League of Nations; although Japan was a charter member of the Council of Ten, it was humiliated by being squeezed out of the Council of Four. Japan was told that the members of the Council of Four were all chiefs of state or prime ministers. Colonel Edward M. House informed Viscount Nobuaki Makino, the former foreign minister who would one day become the father in law of Prime Minister Shigeru Yoshida, that the Big Four were discussing matters of European concern.[26]

At the same time, improvement of relations with its Asian neighbors has been an alluring prospect in Japan's eyes, as it would enable it to play an "Asia card" when dealing with the United States. The diplomatic machinations of Prime Minister Nobosuke Kishi in the late 1950s serve as an example. Kishi, who visited six Southeast Asian nations before his meeting with US President Dwight Eisenhower and Secretary of State John Foster Dulles, explained his goal: "to build Japan's place in Asia and impress upon Eisenhower that Japan is at the center of Asia, and strengthen my position when I negotiate with Eisenhower for changing the US-Japan relationship into a more equal one."[27]

Japan's new moves toward Australia in the past decade or so also reflect to some extent its eagerness to overcome its East-West dilemma. Japan's need for raw materials and export markets for manufactured goods has certainly attracted it to Australia. The 1973 oil crisis awakened MITI to its vital interest in strengthening ties with resource-rich countries such as Australia.

The driving force of economics dates back more than a century. In the late 19th century, diplomat Manjiro Inagaki argued for an alliance between Japan and Australia. He pointed out the strategic importance of a Japan-Australia alliance before the conclusion of the Anglo-Japanese alliance: "It has often puzzled me why Japan does not hold closer relations with Australia, especially as Australia is becoming one of her most important neighbors in commerce. I can certainly predict that if this suggestion comes to pass that together they will in the future hold the key of the Pacific trade."[28]

There is more at work than just economics. Japan has perhaps sought a "soul mate" in its South Pacific friend. The fact that Australia is an English-speaking country, a member of the OECD, and basically a Caucasian nation may make it attractive to Japan, especially when it has problems with the United States. Furthermore, Japan has been extremely uncomfortable with the racist Asian-only concept, which reminds Japan of its serious mistakes in the prewar days.

The East-West dilemma was clearly perceived by Prime Minister Kiichi Miyazawa, who attempted to address the problem. His view, as analyzed by Asia scholar James Morley, was a conception of Japan that was neither Eastern nor Western, but "Pacifican."[29]

Japan's approach toward Asia has been further complicated by the North-South tensions that have permeated the Japan-Asia relationships. The slogan *hokujin nanbutsu* (Northern man, Southern material), which gained currency in the 1890s and became especially strong after 1910, put forth the notion that Asia was but a source of raw goods to fuel Japan's growth. Leading up to the Pacific War, the policy of *nanshin* (southward advance) informed Japan's approach to the region: it was an area in which to project Japanese power.

In the 1950s and '60s, Japan's reparations were perceived as a means to develop both export markets for Japanese finished products and import sources for raw materials. During these years, "economic cooperation" and "resource diplomacy" were the concepts used to explain Japan's relationship with the region.

Japan has suffered strained relations with its neighbors in Northeast Asia. Thus, a special diplomatic emphasis has been put on Southeast Asia, especially ASEAN. In 1980, a study group created by Prime Minister Ohira embraced foreign aid as a major pillar of Japan's comprehensive national security and stressed: "Japan's world historical mission is to play a leading role in creating an order between the North and the South."[30] Miyazawa's 1992 Bangkok speech echoed the Fukuda Doctrine's emphasis of the importance of ASEAN in Japan's foreign policy. In terms of promoting Japan-ASEAN cooperation, the Japanese business association Keidanren has advised an increase in person-to-person ties, a larger role for Japan as an absorber of products from ASEAN, the promotion of technology transfer, and the training of engineers.[31]

Japan's image of its place in Asia has great pertinence to the discussion of the North-South dimension. The well-known analogy of Japan as the leader of a flock of Asian geese in part reflects Japan's hierarchical views of social organization. There is a tendency for Japan to project its own highly ordered social structure onto the world scene.[32]

Particularly in Asia, foreign relations have tended to be unequal, dating back to the centuries when Japan was under China's tribute system, although Japan did not accept that designation. In modern history, Japan's pursuit to dominate a Greater East Asia Co-Prosperity Sphere revealed this hierarchical mind-set, which has been well-suited to bilateral relationships and alliances and has allowed Japan a high comfort level in its Anglo-Japanese and US-Japan alliances. However, this mode of thinking does not so easily adapt to multilateral or regional relationships where all nations are presumed to be on equal footing.

Japan's view of Asia, and its own role in it, is challenged by new economic realities. The old flying-geese analogy has been updated by a Chinese scholar, who compares the Asian economy to a train with Japan leading the front car and China pushing as a caboose.[33] Yet another conception portrays the Asian economies as elevators at different levels, where Japan has ascended to the top, the "four tigers" are at the next highest level, and the industrializing economies such as Malaysia are rapidly following. At any rate, the traditional leader-follower dynamic between Japan and Asia is becoming more complex.

Over the past two decades, Asia has undergone tremendous transformation, as the development of the NIEs progressed through the 1970s, democratization took root in the 1980s, and APEC, with the ground-breaking Bogor Declaration, paved the way for liberalization in the 1990s. During this progression, the tensions and ideological passions that used to inflame North-South relations have become subdued. The LDCs are now more self-confident. The infrastructure that Japan's ODA helped install has propelled further growth. As a result, Japan is increasingly more comfortable with its own role in the region.

Although the North-South dilemma is lessened, weighty problems remain, foremost among them the conceptually challenging question of China's role in the region. Malaysia's EAEC proposal also threatens to create some North-South challenges. Within APEC, a North-South divide occasionally reappears, especially during discussions of liberalization and development. Both goals have been endorsed by all; indeed, Indonesia has forged a bold path toward liberalization, while Japan devotes much attention to development. Nonetheless, development is still most ardently pressed by the South, and liberalization by the North. Japan's stance can perhaps be understood best from a wider historical perspective. The riots of Tanaka's 1974 visit to Southeast Asia were inspired by anti-Japan, anti-Western, and anti–market opening sentiments, and they cast a long shadow over Japan's policymakers.

Policy Concerns

There are several policy issues pertaining to the Asia Pacific that are destined to influence the future course of Japan's involvement in the region, as well as its role in the world. The manner in which Japan manages its markets and trade surplus, uses its ODA, articulates a coherent policy on the security front, defines a human rights policy, and strengthens its civil society will be especially critical. Finally, Japan must come to terms with its past.

Trade Imbalances

Of the obstacles that Japan confronts in translating its new Asianist thrusts into policies that will fit into a globally minded agenda, market issues have particular relevance. Japan sustains large trade surpluses with its Asia Pacific trading partners such as Korea, Malaysia, Singapore, and Taiwan, but its biggest one—$51 billion in 1993—is with the United States.[34] These surpluses persist despite the fact that both Japan's foreign direct investment in Asia and its imports from the region have increased. The chronic surpluses are in part the result of barriers to imports that still exist in Japan.

As East Asian economies continue to grow and mature, they will increasingly seek access to the markets of the world's second largest economy. Already, graduates of Japan's foreign aid program have requested greater market access. Observers have noted that at almost every intergovernmental talk between Japan and Korea, "Seoul has constantly argued that the Japanese government should promote imports from Korea."[35]

In the face of East Asia's economic growth, Japan's barriers are ultimately debilitating. Indeed, Japan does have the potential to absorb more of the region's imports. By opening its markets, Japan could reduce imbalances and thus give Japan's trading partners a chance to accumulate yen. It has been argued that a more open market will spur Japanese investors to invest abroad, as they are more likely to see returns if their debtors are able to earn yen by exporting to Japan.[36]

Japan's trade imbalances also have implications for its relationship with the United States, where the phenomenal size of Japan's trade surplus is often cited as if it were a direct measure of the impenetrableness of the Japanese market. The US government has been increasingly concerned about the corrosive effects of the trade disputes on the US-Japan relationship.

To alleviate tensions with both East Asia and the United States, Japan should remove its remaining barriers and deregulate its economy to attract inward foreign investment. In doing so, Japan would reinvigorate its own economy as well as promote the growth of its trading partners in the Asia Pacific. The Keidanren has calculated that deregulation would boost national income by $1.8 trillion and create 740,000 new jobs from 1995 to 2001. Furthermore, the Economic Planning Agency has estimated that although 3.5 million manufacturing jobs would be lost, 4.25 million service jobs would be gained, making Japan's economy look more like other industrial countries.[37]

The Role of the Yen

Japan's FDI and ODA have rapidly increased in Asia. From 1986 to 1989 alone, Japan's FDI to ASEAN increased seven times to $4.8 billion, considerably affecting the region's GDP. In this period, Japan's total investments in East Asia were $19.8 billion compared to $21.1 billion in the European Community and $33.6 billion in the United States, which both have much higher GDPs. The influence of this investment was evidenced by the fact that Japanese factories employed 600,000 more workers in East Asia than in the United States and European Community combined.[38] Japan has already surpassed the United States as the greatest source of FDI to the region. The result of this increased Japanese FDI is that Asian economies have become more resilient to deflationary pressure from other industrial countries. According to Malaysian MITI Minister Rafidah Aziz, increased Japanese FDI has warmed East Asian nations' feelings toward Japan, and they have increasingly tried to attract even more Japanese FDI.[39] An American scholar has argued that Japanese foreign investment has directly contributed to the formation of a true "region" in Pacific Asia: "East Asia is becoming a product-based region, one in which Japanese-style institutions show signs of extensive diffusion."[40] Malaysian as well as Thai businesses have established trading companies on the Japanese model.[41]

The influx of FDI has been stimulated in part by Japan's ODA programs, which increased rapidly through the 1980s after Japan overtook the United

States as the largest donor of bilateral foreign aid to the region in 1978.[42] Now, however, Japan's ODA is reaching the point of diminishing returns. As countries such as Singapore and Malaysia "graduate" from donor status, they receive more loans and fewer grants. Paying back such loans is a daunting prospect, given the surge in the yen's value. Japanese Foreign Ministry officials have been known to lament that their ODA is no longer as highly desired.[43] Increasingly, graduating countries want Japan to open its market rather than giving them ODA. In an increasingly interdependent Asia, we now may see the change suggested by politicians such as Koichi Kato, who urges that Japan must go one step further to appease its Asian neighbors, who demand market deregulation and technology transfers from Japan.[44]

As a result of FDI and ODA, the yen is increasingly ubiquitous in Asia. Multinational companies in Asia have shifted to holding more yen, and about 40 percent of all Japanese exports are denominated in yen, up from 34 percent in 1988.[45] Moreover, the yen now denominates an increasing share of Asian debt: China's debt is 21 percent in yen, Indonesia's 40.7 percent, the Philippines' 38.3 percent, and Thailand's 52.1 percent. With an eye on the plummeting US dollar, Asian nations have increased yen holdings in their foreign exchange reserve portfolios. For example, the Bank of Indonesia announced in April 1995 that 36 percent of its foreign currency reserves were denominated in yen.[46]

However, while Japanese capital is welcome throughout Asia, the yen is not. The US dollar is still the dominant currency in transactions, despite its weak state. Japan still is not able to use its market power due to bureaucratic regulation and artificial impediments. Although Singapore and Malaysia argue for fewer dollars and more yen in their central bank reserves, Japan is reluctant to give yen for reserve currencies. It is crucial that Japan make yen available to stimulate the region's growth and encourage inward investment. This does *not* mean that Japan should pursue a yen-bloc strategy.

Economist Jeffrey Frankel has argued against the supposition that a yen bloc has already formed in Asia, explaining that although trade between Japan and other Asian countries increased substantially in the late 1980s, the intraregional trade bias did not increase. He concluded that the yen's role in the region is not yet as great as Japan's importance in regional trade.[47] Economist Takatoshi Ito identified two main reasons for the yen's low stature: Japan's domestic financial markets are overregulated, and Asian countries are concerned about the political implications of holding yen.[48] The United States and Japan must work together to stabilize the yen and dollar to preclude formation of a yen bloc.

US-Japan Security Link

In the 1990s, the US-Japan security arrangement appears increasingly anachronistic to some, and its very rationale is open to question. There is an emerging consensus that the utility of the Yoshida Doctrine—under which Japan spoke softly but carried a big checkbook—died with the end of the Cold War and was buried when Kiichi Miyazawa left his post as prime minister. Two prospects stand out: "globalization" of the alliance— that is, extending the US security umbrella to encompass all of Asia, or "localization" of Japan's military, in which the United States would serve as the "cap on the bottle." Globalization, which could be perceived as Japan underwriting the global US military presence, may be an unattractive option in Japan. But neither is the Japanese public likely to embrace the "cap on the bottle" strategy, which amounts to a US "containment" of Japan that could easily lead to an "encirclement" of Japan by the United States in concert with Japan's Asian neighbors. Either course poses political problems for Japan. Many argue that the "regionalization" of the US-Japan alliance, allows more room for maneuvering.

Although the US-Japan alliance was primarily designed to protect Japan, many in Asia argue that the US-Japan umbrella should extend Asia-wide—the "regionalization" course. While the hub-and-spoke arrangement of US bilateral arrangements in the region still exists, the Japanese government seems to be quite interested in pursuing other types of regionwide, multilateral approaches. In a meeting with ASEAN's dialogue partners at the ASEAN Post Ministerial Conference (PMC) in Kuala Lumpur in 1991, Foreign Minister Taro Nakayama proposed that the PMC be additionally used as a forum to discuss security, stating that it would institute a "process of political discussions designed to improve the sense of security among [Asian countries]."[49] In 1994, the ASEAN Regional Forum (ARF) for security dialogue actually came into being.

Regional security frameworks were also endorsed by a distinguished panel of military and civilian experts known as the Higuchi Commission, which was formed by Prime Minister Morihiro Hosokawa to evaluate Japan's security needs in the new world order. The commission's report, released in August 1994, recommended that Japan strengthen the following three pillars: multilateralism, autonomous capability, and the US-Japan alliance.[50] It stressed that Japan should actively deal with international disputes and fully participate in UN peacekeeping operations, including contribution of forces. Particular emphasis was given to the need to reaffirm the crucial importance of the US-Japan security regime now as a new base for an "alliance for peace" for the security of the entire Asia Pacific.

The modality for successfully enmeshing these recommendations in a coherent security policy has yet to be formulated. Pressing regional concerns indicate that the US-Japan security treaty is not yet irrelevant, and a recent report by American scholars cites a wide-ranging survey of Japanese leaders who agree on this point.[51] Although Japan will not be able to take a leading role in the security arena any time soon, its supportive role should further enhance broader Asia Pacific regional security. However, the balance between support of multilateralism and support of the US-Japan alliance needs to be carefully watched, for there is the risk of supplanting the US-Japan alliance rather than supplementing it. Through its new engagement in Asia, Japan should encourage the United States to help build a new Asia Pacific community fortified by strong security commitments.

Civil Society

The divisive issue of human rights in Asia points directly to the role of civil society, and to Japan's role in building it. Through its ODA program, Japan has the opportunity to invest not only in the hard infrastructure of the region, such as roads, bridges, and telecommunications networks, but also in the "soft" intellectual infrastructure. Indeed, the region's future hinges on critical issues such as human rights, democratization, education, women's and children's rights and welfare, population concerns, and environmental protection.

Japan is coping with these issues by using ODA as a policy tool. Japan's ODA Charter, drafted in 1992, espouses four principles. These political tenets perhaps were designed to answer criticisms that Japan's ODA is motivated solely by economic self-interest. The charter states that Japan must consider the following characteristics of a given country when disbursing aid to it: trends in military expenditures and weapons deployment, progress on democratization and human rights, the fostering of market-oriented economies, and attention to environmental problems. While these standards are laudable, they have yet to be effectively applied, so Japan's influence on progress in donor countries on these issues has not grown. For example, Japan is the largest aid provider to China, India, and Pakistan—three countries that cause varying degrees of concern among nuclear nonproliferation experts. Yet, it has not responded strongly in accordance with its charter principles. Accordingly, China does not listen to Japan's requests not to test nuclear weapons, and India and Pakistan are not forthcoming on whether they possess nuclear devices.[52]

Japan has been equally ineffective in enforcing the principle of human rights enshrined in its ODA Charter. It is true that there are different paths toward democratization. Indeed, the unique experiences of the United States, Japan, Taiwan, Korea, and the Philippines have shown that there is no single model. However, universal values of human dignity do exist. Thus, to summarily ascribe all conflicts over human rights to culture clashes is not honest. Japan must take a firm, supportive position on the UN Human Rights Declaration and by doing so help diminish the polarization of the issue along cultural lines. Japan does not need to wield ODA as a mechanical threat or punishment. Rather, Japan should endeavor to enforce the principles of its charter through subtle pressure—that is, the foreign policy "stick" of a gardener, not a mechanic.

Subtle foreign pressure is not the only force that will lead to recognition of universal human rights in Asia. The most persuasive voices for change may come from within Asia's own civil societies. It is therefore crucial for individuals in Japan and Asia to work to build and strengthen this dimension. In mandarinate society, bureaucracy (*kan*) traditionally reigns supreme over civil society (*min*). Thus, constraints on intellectual dialogue and freer policy discussions are common in the mandarinate cultures of Northeast Asia, as is bureaucratic control of money, personnel, and ideas. Japan has been hindered by the lack of meaningful policy alternatives from outside its powerful bureaucracy. As other East Asian countries move toward greater democracy, they too stand to benefit from stronger civil societies.

The Problem of Historical Legacy

Japan's relations with the Asia Pacific are still infected by the lingering issue of Japan's wartime guilt and culpability. The problem continues to fester, effectively constraining Japan's foreign policy. Matters such as the redress for wartime "comfort women," for example, have only now been brought to the surface. In the words of Prime Minister Goh Chok Tong: "The history of the Second World War is still very fresh in people's minds. The older-generation leaders in other parts of Asia are still alive, and they can recall that part of Japan's history."[53] This point was illustrated when Prime Minister Tomiichi Murayama visited China in May 1995. The Communist Party newspaper, the *People's Daily*, greeted him with an article on Japanese brutality during the Sino-Japanese war.[54]

Several obstacles have prevented Japan from putting the war to rest, as Germany has more successfully done. First, few politicians have been willing to risk challenging the status of the emperor with a comprehensive condemnation of the war. Second, the mentality of Japan as a victim has endured since the nuclear bombs were dropped on Hiroshima and Nagasaki. Third, Japan's old-guard nationalists thrived in the tense Cold War atmosphere sparked by Korea, Vietnam, and smaller regional conflicts. At the same time, Japan has not had the benefit of institutions such as North Atlantic Treaty Organization or the European Community to foster a sense of shared regional values. Fourth, whereas Germany's neighbors vigorously demanded apologies in the immediate aftermath of the war, many of Japan's victims were silenced under authoritarian regimes.

The death of Emperor Hirohito, the end of the Cold War, and the fall of the conservative LDP's de facto one-party rule led to Prime Minister

Hosokawa's new approach. Along with his reformist colleagues, Hosokawa began formulating a new policy toward the region, which he launched soon after he took office with his candid apology for Japan's actions in World War II. Given the fact that wartime guilt is still an explosive and unresolved issue, apologies by recent Japanese prime ministers may indeed help to improve the atmosphere.

During his May 1995 visit to China, Prime Minister Murayama apologized not only in words, but also in actions: he became the first Japanese leader to visit the Marco Polo bridge, which stands close to the spot where the Sino-Japanese War began in 1937. He also apologized repeatedly during his August 1994 trip to Southeast Asia and offered his "profound and sincere remorse and apologies" to wartime "comfort women," who had been forced into prostitution, with the Japanese military playing a role in recruiting them for Japanese soldiers.

Although apologies are necessary, it is also necessary to move beyond them. Moreover, the picture of remorse painted by the apologies of Prime Ministers Murayama, Hosokawa, and others has been indelibly marred by the comments of cabinet ministers in both the Hata and Murayama administrations who have tried to rationalize Japan's invasions. For example, comments by Prime Minister Hata's justice minister, Shigeto Nagano, that the Nanking massacre was a fabrication and by Murayama's Environment Agency director, General Shin Sakurai, that Japan had not pursued a war of aggression have forced their resignations.

It perhaps will be an agonizing but inevitable process for Japan to finally come to terms with the past. Yet a post–Cold War environment unfettered by ideological barriers offers Japan the opportunity to initiate confidence building with its former colonies and its neighbors.[55] Positive developments such as APEC are moving Asia toward a new sense of community, which bodes well for the resolution of the problems of history.

Notes

1. *Asahi Shimbun*, 28 July 1995.

2. Data from the *Asahi Shimbun* database on NiftyServe, as cited by Akihiko Tanaka, "Japan's Security Policy in Asia," unpublished paper, March 1995.

3. *AERA*, 22 December 1992.

4. Toshiaki Ogasawara, "An East Asian Identity," *Japan Times Weekly*, International Edition, 15–21 February 1993, p. 7, as cited in James Morley, "Japan and the Asia Pacific: Defining a New Role," The Asia Society, Asian Update Series, May 1993.

5. Bunzo Hashikawa and Sannosuke Matsumoto, eds., *Kindai Nihon Seiji Shisoshi* [The History of the Political Philosophy of Modern Japan], (Tokyo: Yuhikaku, 1971), pp. 259–64.

6. *Nihon Keizai Shimbun*, 27 October 1991.

7. *Asahi Shimbun*, 10 December 1994.

8. Yoichi Funabashi *Nihon no Taigai Koso* (A Design for a New Course of Japan's Foreign Policy) (Tokyo: Iwanami Shoten, 1993) p. 107.

9. *The East Asian Miracle*, a World Bank Policy Research Report, (New York: Oxford University Press, 1993).

10. Asia-Pacific Economics Group, *Asia Pacific Profiles 1995* (Canberra: The Australian National University, 1995).

11. Masamichi Hanabusa, "A Japanese Perspective on Aid and Development," in Shafiqul Islam, ed. *Yen for Development* (New York: Council on Foreign Relations Press, 1991), p. 95.

12. Yoichi Funabashi, "Japan and the New World Order," *Foreign Affairs* (Winter 1991/ 1992): 63.

13. Personal interview.

14. Susume Yamakage, "Ajia Taiheiyou to Nihon" (Asia Pacific and Japan), in Akio Watanabe, ed., *Sengo Nihon no Taigai Seisaku* (Japan's Postwar Foreign Policy), (Tokyo: Yuhikaku, 1985), pp. 136–142.

15. Yamakage, p. 145.

16. Yamakage, p. 156.

17. Richard Halloran, *New York Times*, 17 January 1974, p. 3.

18. See also Adam Schwarz, *A Nation in Waiting: Indonesia in the 1990s* (Boulder, CO: Westview Press, 1994), pp. 34–35.

19. Wilfrido V. Villacorta, "Japan's Asian Identity: Concerns for ASEAN-Japan Relations," *ASEAN Economic Bulletin* (July 1994): 82.

20. Sueo Sekiguchi and Makito Noda, *Japan in East Asia*, Ushiba Memorial Foundation Study on Prospects of Economic Interactions among Countries in East Asia, September 1992.

21. Hisashi Owada, *Sankaku kara Souzou He* (From Engagement to Creation) (Tokyo: Toshishuppan, 1994), p. 272, pp. 330–331.

22. Tanaka, p. 5.

23. Personal interview with Mahathir bin Mohamad, 20 January 1993.

23a. *Bungei Shunju Ni Miru Showa Shi*, (History of Showa in Bungei Shunju Magazine) Vol. 1 (Tokyo: Bungei Shunju, 1988) p. 185.

24. Kenichi Goto, *Kindai Nihon to Indoneshia* (Modern Japan and Indonesia), (Tokyo: Hokuju Shuppan, 1989), p. 49.

25. Yoichi Funabashi, *Samittokurashi* (Summitocracy) (Tokyo: Asahi Shimbun, 1991), p. 418.

26. Charles Mee, *The End of Order, Versailles 1919* (New York: E. P. Dutton, 1980), p. 188.

27. Yoshihisa Hara, *Kishi Nobusuke* (Tokyo: Iwanami Shoten, 1995), p. 190.

28. Manjiro Inagaki, *Japan and the Pacific* (London: T. Fisher Unwin, 1890), p. 57.

29. Morley, p. 3.

30. Shafiqul Islam, "Beyond Burden-Sharing: Economics and Politics of Japanese Foreign Aid," in *Yen for Development* (New York: Council on Foreign Relations Press, 1991), p. 215.

31. "How Cooperation with ASEAN Should Be Promoted: Interim Report of the Keidanren Committee on Cooperation with Asia," in Kazue Sugiyama and Stephen Leong, eds., *Japan and East Asia* (Kuala Lumpur: Institute of Strategic and International Studies, 1994), pp. 43–53.

32. Robert Scalapino, "Perspectives on Modern Japanese Foreign Policy," in *Foreign Policy of Modern Japan* (Berkeley: University of California Press, 1977).

33. Author's conversation with Prof. Shi Min, Chinese Academy of Social Sciences.

34. *Direction of Trade Statistics Yearbook* (Washington: International Monetary Fund, 1994).

35. Sekiguchi and Noda, p. 18.

36. Speech by Richard Koo at the Economic Strategy Institute/Pacific Basin Economic Council Conference, Washington, DC, 30 March 1995.

37. *Asia Pacific Profiles 1995*, p. 50.

38. Noordin Sopiee, "Megatrends in East Asia: Security and Political Implications," paper presented at the Asia Pacific Round Table, June 1995.

39. Sugiyama and Leong, pp. 9–10.

40. Richard F. Doner, "Japanese Foreign Investment and the Creation of a Pacific Asian Region," in Jeffrey Frankel and Miles Kahler, eds., *Regionalism and Rivalry* (Chicago: University of Chicago Press, 1993), p. 159.

41. Katzenstein and Rouse, 1993.

42. Bruce M. Koppel and Robert M. Orr, Jr., "Power and Policy in Japan's Foreign Aid," in Koppel and Orr, eds., *Japan's Foreign Aid: Power and Policy in a New Era* (Boulder, CO: Westview Press, 1993), p. 344.

43. *Washington Post*, 18 April 1995.

44. Koichi Kato, "Japan's Asia Policy and the US-Japan Relationship," background paper for Shimoda '94 conference, 1994.

45. *Chicago Tribune*, 17 April 1995.

46. *Jiji Press*, 18 April 1995.

47. Jeffrey Frankel, "Is Japan Creating a Yen Bloc?" in Ross Garnaut and Peter Drysdale, eds., *Asia Pacific Regionalism* (Pymble, New South Wales: Harper Educational with the Australian National University, 1994), pp. 227–49.

48. Takatoshi Ito, "The Yen and the International Monetary System," in C. Fred Bergsten and Marcus Noland, eds., *Pacific Dynamism and the International Economic System* (Washington: Institute for International Economics, 1993), pp. 299–322.

49. *Asahi Shimbun*, 22 July 1991 (evening edition).

50. "The Modality of the Security and Defense Capability of Japan: The Outlook for the 21st Century," Report to the prime minister of Japan by the Advisory Group on Defense Issues, 12 August 1994.

51. Michael Green and Richard Samuels, "Recalculating Authority: Japan's Choices in The New World Order," *NBR Analysis*, December 1994.

52. *Nikkei Weekly*, 20 March 1995, p. 1.

53. Personal interview with Goh Chok Tong, 25 June 1993.

54. *New York Times*, 7 May 1995.

55. Yuji Suzuki, "Japan's New Leadership in East Asia," prepared for an international conference on "The New Asian-Pacific Era and Korea" by the Korean Association of International Studies, August 1992.

13

Japan's Role: Beyond Bridging

Kaikoku: "Open Country"

As it has elsewhere in the world, economic liberalization in Japan has historically combined political and social reforms. The Meiji Restoration in the 19th century and early 20th centuries and the post–World War II era are the most proximate examples. Economic liberalization was pursued in tandem with such measures as outlawing discrimination against *bura-kumin*, the pariahs of Japanese society, during the Meiji years. The Meiji government, suffering some backlash, opened Japan's door to the outside world. This period in Japan's history has come to be called *kaikoku*, which literally means "open country" and contrasts to the *sakoku* or "closed country" rule of the Tokugawa shogunate. Following World War II, a new constitution established a democracy in which women had the right to vote. In both cases, Japanese leaders were challenged and confronted by nationalist and Asianist reactions and counterforces. Liberalization was often perceived as being forcefully imposed by European, Anglo-Saxon, or American powers.

APEC liberalization is an entirely new case. The pressure to liberalize in APEC comes not only from the West but also from the East—in fact, from around the Asia Pacific. While APEC's domain is regional, it has an even broader reach. The dynamics of liberalization not only connect and enrich the region but also provide impetus for global free trade through the World Trade Organization (WTO). As a Carnegie report pointed out, APEC's open regionalism—which is a positive force for global free trade and investment—helps to solve the globalism versus regionalism quandary that Japan, among others, faces.[1]

Japan has always experienced tension between traditionalists and modernists during periods of change; "adjust and adapt" was the slogan of the devoted supporters of the modernization school. Japan scholar Edwin Reischauer has noted additional dilemmas, including the psychological pulls of Japan's East-West and North-South tensions.[2]

Moreover, the distinctions made in Japanese society between the understanding of *honne* (one's own personal motivations) and *tatemae* (principles for the general good) and between *ura* (private) and *omote* (public) behavior are often misunderstood by others. The *ura/omote* distinction fosters a tendency for Japan to take a "two-faced" approach, telling one thing to the United States and another to Asia, usually to avoid an unpleasant atmosphere with each. At an informal meeting of Japanese officials, one of them confided that in APEC it is more difficult for Japanese officials to employ such "double talk." "That's why the Japanese delegation is so quiet in that multilateral forum!" quipped another, inviting laughter from the others.[3] The third *Kaikoku*—APEC liberalization—will inevitably reform this dichotomous mind set.

Civilian Power

The economic focus of APEC is a great boon for Japan, which has been evolving into a unique type of power: one that takes pride in economic prowess without military might. As Japan tries to convey its own message and to come to terms with its past, APEC can support Japan's emergence as a first true "global civilian power."[4] As definitions of power change with the end of the Cold War, Japan can and should seize the opportunity to define this new role. Japan's postwar democratic institutions and peace strategy have been underpinned by its constitution, which reflects the same visionary ideals as Franklin Roosevelt's "four freedoms," the Atlantic Charter, and the United Nations Charter. Rather than abandon this foundation to build a military-based one in the image of old-style global powers, Japan should adhere to its unique power portfolio and seek ways to use its economic strength to gain global political power. Japan must accordingly actively engage in promoting world peace while exercising military restraint. In the old world order, these two goals were assumed to be in conflict. By successfully pursuing both of them to become a new type of global civilian power, Japan can contribute to building the "civilianization" of the international community, thereby fostering an environment that favors Japan's own national interests.

The international environment in the Asia Pacific does not necessarily help Japan pursue this goal: the region is still governed by the "rule of the jungle" and lacks regional institutions such as NATO or the EU; the gaps of income, culture and tradition appear to be unbridgeable; and civil societies have yet to mature in most countries. Japan is already confronted with the risks of North Korea's potential nuclear weapons capability, and China's conceivable interest in projecting naval power into the South China Sea.

Although the Asia Pacific has been an inhospitable place for a civilian power, there are signs that it is changing. Encouragment can be gained from the Korean peninsula, where South Korea appears resilient enough to absorb the shocks of unification, were it to occur. In China, reform and open door policies have stimulated growth in the coastal areas and nurtured a middle class, so that China has more stake than ever before in economic interdependence. ASEAN's growing influence is another stabilizing factor. Multilateral frameworks such as APEC and ARF are contributing to a new sense of community. Furthermore, the United States is aware of its new economic interest and stake in the region. Finally, through pursuing the path of a global civilian power, Japan itself can contribute to regional stability, which in turn will provide a salutary climate for such a power.

Globalism

Particularly salient in APEC is the opportunity to link global and regional thrusts. Although Japan has emerged as the preeminent economic power of the region, the nation has been prevented from formulating a regional strategy. As the obstacles to creating such a strategy diminish, Japan has recently initiated a new activism in its Asia policy. Although a new Asia policy is critical, Japan should not aim to be solely an Asian power. The international economic system and Japan's trade figures, in particular, show that such a strategy is untenable. Asia is too small for Japan. Indeed, Asia is too small for Asia. In mapping a regional strategy, Japan must look to a globalized Asia Pacific, which is precisely the region encompassed by APEC. As a former US diplomat has assessed, the world situation today demands not just regional answers but global responses.[5]

Within the new regional thrusts lurks the danger of too much zeal for going regional. It is to Japan's great advantage that APEC links Asia with the Pacific, keeping the United States engaged in the region and preventing the North American Free Trade Agreement (NAFTA) from becoming a US corollary to the British Commonwealth. APEC thus sets the stage for Japan to pursue a new brand of "Pacific globalism."[6] The group brings together the three main Pacific powers of Japan, the United States, and China, as well as the regions of Northeast and Southeast Asia. The Asia Pacific, embodied in APEC, holds the key to the compatibility of regionalism and globalism, because, as a Korean economist concludes: "As long as East Asia perseveres as a regional force for globalism, regionalism may serve as a complement to globalism."[7]

Transnational Linkages

Japan will undergo a restructuring to adapt to the new Asia Pacific dynamics. This change will affect the power balance between the center and the periphery of Japan's political structure by diffusing the excessively concentrated central government power into the local governments. At the dawn of the Meiji era, Japan underwent a dramatic restructuring, when a coalition of "outer" domains, such as Satsuma in southern Kyushu and Choshu in western Honshu, took control of the imperial court.[8] The new rulers endeavored to replace the Tokugawa feudal system with a centralized government that would facilitate Japan's modernization. Today, a different sort of revolution is needed. While the traditional system was organized from the center to govern the periphery, a new structure should evolve to put the periphery at the center. This movement is already evident in the new activism of local governments and communities in Japan. Prefectures and cities on the Japanese island of Kyushu have been particularly active in initiating links with neighbors in Asia. Fukuoka even decided to name itself the "Gateway to Asia." The "one village, one specialty" campaign, launched by Oita Governor Morihiko Hiramatsu in 1979 to encourage each village concentrate on one product, has become a renowned development model in the region. Local-level diplomacy is Hiramatsu's forte; to explain his ideas he has traveled to the Philippines and Korea and has received local leaders from Malaysia, Indonesia, China, Taiwan, and Russia.

Such cross-border, local-level cooperation has flourished in Asia, driven by economic complementarity, geographic proximity, political and economic policy frameworks, infrastructure, and market access.[9] Philippines President Fidel Ramos explains that it is an "easily organized way of protecting . . . against trade blocs in the developing countries."[10] The phenomenon has been described as a harbinger of a new world order, in which nation-states are coexisting and competing with region-states and political units coexist and compete with economic units. APEC, with its "member economies" rather than "member states," seems to aptly fit this scenario. Yet, the APEC experience shows that politics has certainly not lost all relevance. It has been the prolonged peace and reduced political tensions in Asia that have allowed the economies to flourish.

Community

The sense of community that APEC inspires points to another opportunity for Japan to contribute. Japan has great potential, as well as numerous resources, for local and regionwide community building. The private sector, especially nongovernmental organizations (NGOs), are already transforming mandarinate culture. Despite countless government restrictions, NGOs are increasingly thriving in Asia. Gradually, governments of developing nations throughout the region are recognizing the potential utility of this sector in furthering national development goals. The rapid proliferation of NGOs in many countries has prompted a new growth in "umbrella organizations" to provide a networking framework for NGOs, thereby reducing duplication of effort and providing new opportunities for cooperation.[11]

Communist rulers still hold no respect for NGOs, as was demonstrated by the Chinese government's treatment of NGOs in Huairo at the United Nations' Fourth World Conference on Women in September 1995. Nonetheless, NGOs have the increasing support of the private sector. Private wealth created from the expansion of non-state-owned enterprises in China has fueled a boom in Chinese NGOs. The number of philanthropic foundations almost quadrupled in Taiwan during the period from 1980 to 1990.[12] Japanese corporations that have embraced the spirit of "corporate giving" now allow employees to take leaves of absence to volunteer for philanthropic causes. Moreover, the face of Asian NGOs is changing, as they evolve from branch offices of US organizations into homegrown enterprises.[13]

Japan's Priorities

Japan's APEC strategy is straightforward: to help build an Asia Pacific community and to help strengthen the global economic system. Japan can and will have its interests recognized and realized through the commitment to these twin goals by Japan and the other APEC members.

On the crucial question of liberalization and cooperation, Japan should make liberalization its primary priority, followed by cooperation. Both objectives are equally important in APEC community building. However, Japan should use and harness its market power, not its bureaucratic power, to promote the economic welfare of the region. More importantly, Japan should help to find a way for both to effectively complement and interact. As for the question of most-favored nation status, Japan should raise the lofty goal of unconditional MFN. Further, it should set an example by liberalizing its own markets and economy. With due respect to subregional cooperation, Japan should concentrate on APEC building as its major target. Japan should try to avoid inordinate Asianist zeal and excessive tactical calculations, which the EAEC type of "Asians-only" caucus perhaps has inspired. With such a narrow focus, it is too easy to lose sight of the big picture. That type of myopia can be averted if subregional groupings are submerged and fused into the regional and global context. In failing to take a more vigorous initiative in strengthening ties with Asia and Europe, Japan revealed a dearth of diplomatic imagination. The EAEC has proved to be another such "blind spot" in Japan's foreign policy. Japan should review and reform the entirety of its policy apparatus and decision-making mechanisms so as to promote its APEC policy more forcefully. Such measures will foster stronger Japanese leadership, which has been one of the missing links in APEC thus far.

Japan, as it moves toward a cohesive APEC policy, should endeavor to put it in the larger political and strategic context. In the bigger picture, US engagement in the region and the US-Japan security arrangement feature prominently. Japan's new policies will have implications for the overall US-Japan relationship, whose future in turn will affect the entire Asia Pacific.

Japan's new Asia Pacific strategy should be combined with its global strategy to strengthen the international system. Japan should promote policy dialogue and mutual cooperation with Europe to prevent both Asia and Europe from becoming protectionist and exclusively regional, and to rekindle the spirit of trilateral cooperation with the United States in a new environment. Japan's consultation with Germany is particularly important to cement the weakest link in the triad structure, as both have special weight and responsibilities in their respective regional economies.

To circumvent lectures by its Western partners and give credence to the argument that approaches to respect and realize human rights vary from developed to less developed countries, Japan can and should play a significant role, along with other Asian countries, in articulating and pursuing a cogent alternative to safeguard human dignity.

Finally, Japan must come to terms with its past. The intellectual exercises of reflecting on and learning from history must be institutionalized in Japanese society. This is not the responsibility of government alone; the private citizens of Japan, as well as those from around the Asia Pacific, have a role to play. In Europe, a precedent was set by Frédéric Delouche, who edited a secondary school textbook of European history, *The Illustrated History of Europe,* that was written jointly by historians from 12 European countries. It would be worthwhile for historians in the APEC region, in a private capacity, to contemplate a similar endeavor: to consolidate the histories of all 18 APEC countries and publish the final text in all the languages of APEC by the year 2020.

Beyond Bridging

Japan must overcome two unique features of its perception of its place in the Asia Pacific: the belief that Japan is destined to be differentiated from Asia by virtue of an inherent Japanese "exceptionalism" and the antiquated notion that Japan's purpose is to bridge the East and West. By subscribing to such views, Japan obscures its vital interests in the Asia Pacific.

The concept of Japanese exceptionalism in part derives from geography, history, and culture. The Japanese archipelago, which has endured neither invasion nor colonization, is home to an almost homogenous population. The 250-year reign of the Tokugawa family, which enforced a rule of *sakoku,* or "closed country," fostered Japanese insularity.

Japan's concept of its exceptionalism has at times been manifested as a myth of uniqueness. In fact, Tadao Umesao, one of Japan's most noted anthropologists, proclaimed that "it is a fiction that Japan is a part of Asia," as "Asia will not be able to achieve a highly developed industrial society like Japan's."[14] Umesao enumerated several measurements of the difference between Japan and Asia: higher education enrollment, literacy rate, number of sick, average longevity, number of telephones per capita, and number of cars per capita.[15] In all of these categories, the gap between Japan and Asia has narrowed over the past two decades. Exceptionalism can also be seen in the 1957 retrospective written by Prime Minister Shigeru Yoshida, one of the architects of Japan's postwar foreign policy. He asserts: "Together with Africa, Asia outside Japan is marked by low standards of living and is an uncivilized, backward region."[16]

Also contributing to the sense of exceptionalism has been Japan's position in Asia since the late 19th century. Of all the Asian nations, Japan alone competed as a member of the North and of the West. The first non-Western nation to fully modernize, Japan was the only Asian "member of club," a pattern extended to Japan's membership in the Group of Seven (G-7).

Japan's uniqueness is disappearing as other Asian countries rapidly modernize, the North-South gap closes, and distinctions of East or West become less relevant. Recently, the Japanese have been taken aback by what has been termed the "bypassing" phenomenon: American firms such as Goldman Sachs spurning Japan to deal with other Asian businesses. Shock at this phenomenon can only be explained by a lack of awareness of the fundamental changes taking place in the Asia Pacific. Japan cannot expect to maintain privileged relations with the United States when Asian countries are rapidly becoming major players.

Japan should welcome this transformation of the Asia Pacific. For the first time in modern history, Japan can begin to establish a new rapport with its neighbors and overcome its isolating sense of uniqueness.

Voices both from within and outside Japan have long advised Japan to act as a "bridge" between the Asian and Western nations in various circumstances, including APEC. At a news conference at Bogor, Foreign Minister Yohei Kono hinted at the role Japan was trying to play between ASEAN and the United States, saying that Japan would offer "guidance to people new in associating with Asia."[17] Some Asians, such as Thailand's Vice Premier Supachai Panitchpakdi, have forcefully advocated such a bridging role for Japan.[19] Japan's inclinations to play this role may indeed spring from goodwill. There is much merit to the idea that Japan is uniquely qualified to understand both Asia and North America, and there are many cases in which Japan can serve the international community well by acting as an intermediary to facilitate communication and understanding.

However, the true meaning of and motivation behind Japan's claims to serve as a bridge are a bit unclear. A US official complained: "The whole notion of APEC was that there wasn't to be any division between the East side of the Pacific and the West side that needed to be bridged. . . . They [Japan] are not being leaders in the chair, they are being searchers, they are searching the tea leaves for the middle ground."[19] A MITI official confessed her own concern that Japan is increasingly perceived as lacking the ability to articulate its own agenda, serving only as a "bat" to drive home the ideas of others.[20]

The idea that Japan's destined niche is to serve as an East-West bridge took new hold of the national psyche after the Tiananmen incident of 1989, when the US-China relationship abruptly deteriorated. There is a strong inclination, particularly among Japanese politicians, to find psychological satisfaction and political reward in promoting this bridging role. When it comes to the perceived room for US-China or US-Asia relations, this posture also, to a great extent, reflects Japan's deep-rooted "either/or" world view. It clouds Japan's vision of its role and mission in the new world order and stifles its potential to reach out regionally and globally. The bridging role itself is not a viable objective, and to solely aspire to that role is mere posturing. Rather than hastily cobbling together a policy to address the short-term concerns of its neighbors, or dividing its interest somewhere between the sum of the two sides, Japan must first delineate its own long-term interests. Foremost among those interests is building APEC.

The inadequacy of the bridging role was tragically demonstrated by Nitobe Inazo, the author of *Bushido* and Japan's premiere internationalist who served as Under Secretary General to the League of Nations in prewar days. Nitobe, who studied in the United States, married a Philadelphia native, and became a Quaker, fervently aspired to serve as a bridge between Japan and the West. A self-proclaimed bridge across the Pacific, he is memorialized today on both sides of the ocean; his face appears on the 5,000 yen note in Japan, and a garden in British Columbia bears his name. However, Nitobe ultimately failed to achieve his goals. He simply was unable to explain Japan's invasion of Manchuria, which he himself viewed ambivalently, to his Western colleagues. His biographer explained: "When he started, he rode the ascending wave of Japanese internationalism so well. . . . [But] during the last four years of his life, it became increasingly difficult to bridge the chasm within Japan between the internationalists like Nitobe and the expansionists of the Japanese army.[21] He sadly could not succeed as a bridge, as foundational questions could not be answered by posturing.

Nitobe's story has another significant moral. In his book on Japan published in 1931, he expressed regret about the dissolution of the Anglo-Japanese alliance in 1922.[22] Only a decade earlier, Nitobe, a disciple of Woodrow Wilson, had argued for abandoning the alliance in favor of Wilson's League of Nations. Indeed, he was not alone among Japanese internationalists asserting that the alliance was outdated. As a secret military pact, it ran counter to the thinking of the day. Having pinned all their hopes on the League of Nations, Japan's internationalists were left in a precarious position when the League collapsed.

Although today's US-Japan security arrangement markedly differs from the archaic Anglo-Japanese one, there is still a lesson to be learned from the experience of that ill-fated alliance. It highlighted the inadvisability of enthusiastically supplanting a known regime with an untested alternative. It is wiser to employ the new system to complement the old. In the present-day scenario, Japan should strive to harness the resources of the US-Japan alliance to further develop and strengthen APEC.

APEC is already on course for growth into the next century. The very fact that the first two words of its appellation are being gradually standardized as "Asia Pacific," rather than "Asia-Pacific," is symbolic. Just as the words "Asia" and "Pacific" do not need to be linked with a hyphen, the actual regions do not need to be linked by a bridge, for they are already becoming fused together.

Notes

1. *Defining a Pacific Community* (Washington: Carnegie Endowment for International Peace, 1994).

2. Edwin O. Reischauer, *The Japanese*, (Cambridge, MA: Harvard University Press, 1977), pp. 377 and 414.

3. Conversation with Japanese government officials in Tokyo, March 1995.

4. See Yoichi Funabashi, "Japan's International Agenda for the 1990s," in Yoichi Funabashi, ed., *Japan's International Agenda* (New York: New York University Press, 1994).

5. Morton Abramowitz, president of the Carnegie Endowment for International Peace, 25 June 1995.

6. See Yoichi Funabashi, "Japan and the New World Order," *Foreign Affairs* (Winter 1991/1992).

7. Soogil Young, "Globalism and Regionalism: Complements or Competitors," in C. Fred Bergsten and Marcus Noland, eds., *Pacific Dynamism and the International Economic System* (Washington: Institute for International Economics, 1993), p. 126.

8. Robert A. Scalapino, "Perspectives on Modern Japanese Foreign Policy," *Foreign Policy of Modern Japan* (Berkeley: University of California Press, 1977).

9. Chia Sio Yue and Lee Tsao Yuan, "Subregional Economic Zones: A New Motive Force in Asia Pacific Development," in Bergsten and Noland, eds., *Pacific Dynamism and the International Economic System*, pp. 111 18.

10. *International Herald Tribune*, 30 November 1994.

11. Tadashi Yamamoto, ed., *Emerging Civil Society in the Asia Pacific Community*, (Singapore: Institute of Southeast Asian Studies with the Asia Pacific Philanthropy Consortium, 1995), pp. 8–11.

12. Yamamoto, p. 10.

13. Yuko Iida Frost, "Strategic Management of American NGOs in the Asia Pacific Region: Save the Children Federation's Model," master's thesis for Yale School of Management, May 1995.

14. Tadao Umesao, "Ajia Taiken No 50 Nen," (50 Years of Asian Experience), *Umesao Tadao Chosaku Shu*, vol. 6 (Chuo Koron, 1989), p. 15.

15. Umesao, p. 15.

16. As cited by Yoshibumi Wakamiya, "Asianism in Japan's Postwar Politics," background paper for the Shimoda Conference, 1994.

17. *Daily Yomiuri*, 17 November 1994.

18. *Asahi Shimbun*, 21 February 1995.

19. Personal interview, 27 April 1995.

20. Personal interview, 3 July 1995.

21. John F. Howes and George Oshiro, "Who Was Nitobe?" in John F. Howes, ed., *Nitobe Inazo: Japan's Bridge Across the Pacific* (Boulder, CO: Westview Press, 1995), p. 21.

22. Thomas W. Burkman, "The Geneva Spirit," in Howes, ed., *Nitobe Inazo*, p. 202.

Appendices

Appendix A: A chronology of APEC

Year	Events in APEC	Events in the world and the Asia Pacific
1987		
January	Japanese MITI Minister Hajime Tamura calls for the creation of a "Pacific Rim Trade and Industrial" ministerial body.	
December		Third ASEAN summit concludes in Manila.
		General Roh Tae Woo defeats two opposition candidates to become president of Korea.
1988		
January	Following a visit to the United States, Japanese Prime Minister Noboru Takeshita instructs MITI to explore the prospects for economic cooperation in the Asia Pacific. MITI launches a study under the direction of International Affairs Division Chief Yoshihiro Sakamoto.	
June	MITI Interim Report on Asia Pacific economic cooperation (Sakamoto Report) completed.	
August	Japan and Australia hold unofficial trade meeting in Tokyo to discuss the findings of the Sakamoto Report.	General Chatchai Choonhavan becomes prime minister of Thailand after parliamentary elections.
September		Summer Olympics held in Seoul, Korea.
October		US International Trade Commission (ITC) releases a report recommending against a free trade agreement with Japan.
November		Vice President George Bush defeats his Democratic opponent for the US presidency.
December	Senior MITI official Shigeo Muraoka meets with Australian Trade Minister Michael Duffy to discuss strategies for implementing regional economic cooperation.	

Year	Events in APEC	Events in the world and the Asia Pacific
1989		
January	Australian Prime Minister Bob Hawke announces his plan to create APEC during a speech in Seoul. Later he writes letters to each of his counterparts in the region explaining the proposal.	Bush succeeds Ronald Reagan as president of the United States.
March	MITI dispatches Shigeo Muraoka to gauge support in the region for the APEC concept (March: ASEAN, Hong Kong, Korea; April: US).	
	Australian Trade and Foreign Affairs Secretary Richard Woolcott begins a round of visits to prospective APEC members (March: New Zealand; April: ASEAN, Korea, Japan; May: Hong Kong, China, US, Canada).	
	Australian Foreign Minister Gareth Evans meets with US Secretary of State James Baker to discuss the APEC initiative.	
	Woolcott meets with Japanese officials from MITI and the foreign ministry to discuss APEC.	
April-May	Prime Minister Takeshita visits ASEAN nations but does not publicly advocate the APEC concept.	
June	MITI Minister Hiroshi Mitsuzuka becomes foreign minister, breaking internal bureaucratic opposition to the APEC initiative.	Chinese soldiers open fire on pro-democracy demonstrators in Beijing's Tiananmen Square, provoking widespread international condemnation.
	In a New York speech, Secretary of State James Baker announces US support for the creation of APEC.	In the midst of a major political scandal, Prime Minister Takeshita announces his resignation and is replaced by Foreign Minister Sosuke Uno.
July	ASEAN ministers meeting in Brunei endorse APEC by consensus.	Japan's ruling Liberal Democratic Party (LDP) is dealt a stunning defeat in an Upper House election. Uno resigns, and in August former Education Minister Toshiki Kaifu assumes the premiership.
September	First senior officials' meeting (SOM) held in Sydney.	

Year	Events in APEC	Events in the world and the Asia Pacific
1989		
November	**APEC inaugurated at ministerial conference in Canberra. Twelve economies represented.**	The Berlin Wall is dismantled amidst a wider movement in Eastern Europe to break the stranglehold of communist regimes.
		Geoffrey Palmer replaces David Lange as prime minister of New Zealand.
1990		
February	ASEAN foreign ministers meet in Kuching, Malaysia, to agree on terms of APEC membership.	Lower House elections in Japan give an unexpected boost to the LDP government of Prime Minister Kaifu.
March	SOM held in Singapore.	
May	SOM held in Singapore.	Prime Minister Kaifu, in a trip through South and Southeast Asia announces the Kaifu Doctrine, which includes making official development assistance (ODA) contingent upon the political and military policies of target countries.
June		Boris Yeltsin is elected President of the Russian Republic. He embarks on a major privatization effort to stimulate the flagging Russian economy.
July	**Second APEC ministerial is held in Singapore.**	
August		Iraq seizes Kuwait, provoking the United States to assemble a multinational force to protect Saudi Arabia. Many APEC members contribute personnel or money to the operation.
September	Special APEC trade ministerial convened in Vancouver to discuss the ongoing deadlock in the Uruguay Round of GATT negotiations.	New Zealand Prime Minister Palmer resigns and is replaced by fellow Labor Party member Michael Moore. Parliamentary elections in October oust the Labor Party from power and bring in a National Party government led by James Bolger.

Year	Events in APEC	Events in the world and the Asia Pacific
1990		
October	SOM held in Seoul.	Germany officially reunifies.
		Parliamentary elections held in Malaysia.
		Goh Chok Tong succeeds long-ruling Singaporean leader Lee Kuan Yew as prime minister of Singapore. Lee retains the title of senior minister.
November		US holds midterm congressional elections.
December		Malaysian Prime Minister Mahathir bin Mohamed unveils his proposal for an East Asian Economic Group (EAEG).
		GATT Uruguay Round talks in Brussels reach an impasse.
1991		
January	Korean diplomat Lee See-Yong, chairman of the APEC SOM, embarks on a mission to incorporate the Three Chinas (Hong Kong, Taiwan, and the People's Republic) into APEC. After several months of shuttle diplomacy, Lee brokers an agreement during eleventh-hour negotiations in New York.	
February		US–led coalition launches a 100-hour offensive against Iraqi troops in Kuwait and southern Iraq. Iraq agrees to accept all UN resolutions, including reparations, related to its invasion of Kuwait.
		Military junta ousts Prime Minister Chatchai in Thailand. In March, junta appoints respected diplomat Anand Panyarachun as head of the military-backed government.
March	SOM held in Cheju-do, Korea.	

Year	Events in APEC	Events in the world and the Asia Pacific
1991		
August	APEC members endorse the secret memorandum of understanding (MOU) during SOM meeting in Kyongju, Korea, that sets out the terms for membership of the Three Chinas.	Attempted military coup d'état fails in Moscow.
September		Philippine Senate rejects an agreement worked out between Manila and Washington to extend the lease on the Subic Bay Naval Base. Clarke Air Force Base in Angeles was destroyed earlier in the year by the eruption of Mount Pinatubo.
October		Peace accord signed in Paris between the Cambodian government and three opposition factions. Prince Norodom Sihanouk named head of a national reconciliation government in November. United Nations agrees to dispatch troops and monitors to oversee the disarmament of Cambodian factions and the transition to democracy. Japan is among several Asia Pacific nations that contribute forces to the UN effort. UN personnel are later targeted by guerrillas loyal to the Khmer Rouge faction, which dropped out of the four-party agreement. UN withdrawals in September 1993 after peace plan completed.
		East Asian Economic Group (EAEG) officially renamed East Asian Economic Caucus (EAEC).
November	**Third APEC ministerial held in Seoul. China, Taiwan, and Hong Kong officially join. Fifteen economies represented.**	LDP faction leader Kiichi Miyazawa replaces Prime Minister Toshiki Kaifu after a party vote.
		Indonesian troops clash with separatist demonstrators in Dili, East Timor. Jakarta is harshly criticized abroad. Relations with Canberra are particularly strained.

Year	Events in APEC	Events in the world and the Asia Pacific
1991		
December		Soviet Union is dissolved and replaced by a looser and smaller Commonwealth of Independent States (CIS). Soviet President Mikhail Gorbachev retires from politics.
		Paul Keating ousts Robert Hawke during a party caucus to become prime minister of Australia.
1992		
January		Chinese President Yang Shankun endorses EAEC during talks with Malaysian Premier Mahathir.
		Fourth ASEAN summit meeting held in Singapore. Agreement is reached on implementing AFTA. Leaders also agree to begin a security dialogue with members of the ASEAN Post-Ministerial Conference (PMC) including China, Japan, Russia, and the United States.
March	SOM held in Bangkok, Thailand.	General Suchinda Kraprayoon appointed Thai prime minister after elections. Demonstrations erupt among citizens angry that Suchinda, who was not elected to parliament, was chosen as premier. In May, Suchinda resigns his post.
April	Australian Prime Minister Paul Keating recommends APEC be elevated to the leaders' level. Keating sends letters supporting an APEC summit to US President Bush, Japanese Prime Minister Miyazawa, Indonesian President Suharto, and Singaporean Prime Minister Goh.	
May		Fidel Ramos wins the Philippine presidential elections.
June	SOM held in Bangkok, Thailand.	Parliamentary elections held in Papua New Guinea.
		Former Thai Premier Anand is reappointed to head the Thai government until elections are held in September.

Year	Events in APEC	Events in the world and the Asia Pacific
1992		
August		South Korea recognizes Beijing and severs all official ties with Taiwan.
September	**Fourth APEC ministerial convenes in Bangkok.** US fails to send ministerial-level delegates. Foreign ministers from Japan, Canada, and Malaysia also do not attend. Secretariat and Eminent Persons Group (EPG) established. Special trade ministerial held in Vancouver to help stimulate the completion of the Uruguay Round talks.	Indonesian President Suharto hosts the summit meeting of the Non-Aligned Movement in Jakarta. Elections held in Singapore; ruling party loses seats but maintains strong majority. Chuan Leepkai chosen as Thai prime minister after general election. President Bush calls for a "strategic network" of FTAs that would extend NAFTA to individual economies in the Asia Pacific during a speech in Detroit.
November		Arkansas Governor Bill Clinton defeats George Bush in US presidential election.
December	SOM held in Washington, DC.	Former dissident Kim Young Sam elected president of Korea.
1993		
January		Unified European market comes into effect. Japanese Prime Minister Miyazawa visits ASEAN and announces the "Miyazawa Doctrine," calling for increased cooperation between Japan and Southeast Asia over security and political matters as well as economic concerns.
March		Jiang Zemin assumes the presidency of China.
April	SOM meeting held in Williamsburg, Virginia, to discuss trade facilitation measures to be included in the Seattle Declaration.	
June	APEC SOM in Seattle held to explore the possible adoption of an APEC investment code.	

Year	Events in APEC	Events in the world and the Asia Pacific
1993		
July	President Clinton announces his plans to hold an informal APEC leaders summit at the Seattle APEC conference on his way to Tokyo to attend a G-7 meeting.	At the annual ASEAN economic ministerial in Singapore, members agree to endorse the EAEC as a caucus within APEC rather than a separate organization. ASEAN Regional Forum officially established.
		Indonesian President Suharto meets with US President Clinton and Prime Minister Miyazawa in bilateral talks held during the Tokyo G-7 summit.
		Following the defection of several key members of the LDP, elections oust the government of Prime Minister Miyazawa. Morihiro Hosokawa, head of a small reformist party, is chosen to head an unstable seven-party coalition government.
September	APEC SOM meeting convened in Honolulu to discuss the upcoming Seattle conference.	
October	First EPG report released.	Landslide elections in Canada unseat the government of Kim Campbell. Jean Chretien's Liberal Party forms new cabinet.
		The North American Free Trade Agreement (NAFTA) is approved by the US Congress and enters into force in 1994.
November	**APEC informal leaders' meeting held on Blake Island outside Seattle. Fifth APEC ministerial meeting.** Leaders agree to form an "Asia Pacific community" and hold a second summit meeting the following year. Mexico and Papua New Guinea added to the forum, bringing total membership to 17.	
December		GATT Uruguay Round completed.

Year	Events in APEC	Events in the world and the Asia Pacific
1994		
February	SOM held in Jakarta, Indonesia.	
March	Bintoro Tjokroamidjojo, special representative of President Suharto, meets with minister and officials of APEC member-states in preparation for the Bogor summit meeting. Chinese officials demand that Taiwan not be allowed to attend. In November Bintoro is summoned to Taipei for talks with President Lee Teng-hui, who agrees not to participate in the Bogor talks.	
	First APEC finance ministers meeting held in Oahu, Hawaii.	
April		Final act of the Uruguay Round signed in Marrakesh, Morocco, pledging the GATT's 123 members to significantly reduce tariff levels.
		Japanese Prime Minister Hosokawa resigns amidst charges of financial impropriety. Foreign Minister Tsutomu Hata forms a minority government after Social Democratic Party leaves coalition.
May	SOM held in Bali, Indonesia.	
August		Ernesto Zedillo wins the Mexican presidential elections after the assassination of the leading government party candidate.
September	SOM held in Jogjakarta, Indonesia.	
November	Suharto dispatches Minister of State Moerdiono to Kuala Lumpur to confer with Prime Minister Mahathir about the planned Bogor agenda.	The Republican Party captures both houses of Congress in mid-term US elections.
	APEC leaders' meeting held in Bogor, Indonesia. Sixth APEC ministerial. Leaders pledge to create free trade in the Asia Pacific by the year 2020 based on a formula suggested by the EPG. Chile is accepted as the last member before a three-year moratorium is placed on APEC's expansion, bringing membership to 18.	

Year	Events in APEC	Events in the world and the Asia Pacific
1994		
December		The Mexican peso collapses on international exchange markets, creating a major financial crisis in Mexico and other developing-country markets.
1995		
February	SOM meeting held in Fukuoka, Japan, to discuss means of implementing the Bogor vision.	
April	Special SOM convened in Singapore to brainstorm issues related to the Bogor Declaration.	Ruling party wins by a landslide in Malaysian parliamentary elections.
	Second APEC finance ministerial held in Bali, Indonesia. Delegates focus on the impact of the Mexican financial crisis.	
May	Indonesia announces the first "downpayment" on the Bogor Declaration in the form of a unilateral reduction in tariffs on over 6,000 products.	
June	Japanese Prime Minister Murayama urges his counterparts in a letter to make progress at the Osaka summit a personal priority.	Taiwanese President Lee Teng-hui pays a visit to the United States to speak at a university commencement.
		Australia calls for the creation of an Indian Ocean counterpart to APEC during a first-ever gathering of 23 Indian Ocean nations.
July	SOM officials agree at Sapporo meeting to adopt a two-tracked approach to liberalization, clearing the way for a consensus on the November Osaka summit.	
August		Vietnam officially joins ASEAN, becoming its seventh member.
September	Special SOM held in Hong Kong to finalize action agenda.	
October	SOM held in Tokyo to prepare for leaders' summit.	
November	**APEC leaders' meeting and seventh ministerial conference scheduled for Osaka, Japan.**	

Year	Events in APEC	Events in the world and the Asia Pacific
1996		
March	Third APEC finance ministerial to be held in Kyoto, Japan.	First EU-ASEAN plus 3 (China, Japan, and Korea) summit talks slated for Bangkok.
November	**Eighth APEC ministerial conference slated to be held in Manila, Philippines.**	
1997	**Canada to host the ninth APEC ministerial conference.**	Hong Kong to be returned to China in July. Status within APEC will be determined by consensus.
1998	**Malaysia scheduled to chair the tenth APEC ministerial conference.**	

Appendix B: Intra-APEC trade, 1983 and 1993[a]

	Australia		Brunei		Canada		Chile		China		Hong Kong		Indonesia		Japan		Korea	
	1983	1993	1983	1993	1983	1993	1983	1993	1983	1993	1983	1993	1983	1993	1983	1993	1983	1993
Australia			22	63	661	1,185	0	114	794	3,015	902	3,089	610	2,173	10,927	19,985	1,301	4,505
Brunei	22	59			0	8	0	0	4	11	14	28	0	44	2,469	1,543	229	[2]
Canada	676	1,538	1	8			121	264	1,795	2,567	773	2,886	214	714	8,053	14,476	1,072	3,069
Chile	9	100	0	0	167	331			183	486	31	415	18	167	644	2,643	140	911
China	623	3,527	14	12	1,494	3,688	104	395			8,342	95,671	231	2,185	10,007	38,004	0	9,080
Hong Kong	812	2,401	8	31	844	1,576	17	76	7,507	32,568			247	900	5,962	24,825	1,038	7,366
Indonesia	592	2,100	0	49	206	707	0	97	199	2,139	728	1,765			14,003	18,532	639	4,683
Japan	9,961	18,552	2,419	1,427	7,246	14,670	509	2,382	10,012	18,085	6,482	29,974	13,471	17,420			9,622	31,580
Korea	1,066	4,313	258	[2]	1,098	3,136	80	751	0	8,220	1,070	8,496	715	4,323	9,413	30,934		
Malaysia	644	1,831	49	210	193	897	0	71	401	1,788	401	2,953	118	1,103	5,897	17,366	1,003	3,377
Mexico	36	176	0	0	1,185	3,530	18	341	44	280	30	603	31	198	2,469	5,058	252	1,135
New Zealand	1,805	4,541	3	6	227	285	0	32	171	396	145	517	287	222	1,895	3,042	134	695
Papua New Guinea	534	1,605	0	0	8	5	0	6	43	118	26	61	0	39	464	856	53	[186]
Philippines	231	569	69	57	135	471	0	55	188	494	541	1,854	424	342	3,049	7,266	358	1,253
Sinapore	1,065	3,444	376	894	241	921	0	83	681	4,892	2,256	9,867	6,593	5,165	5,917	20,291	938	4,649
Taipei	1,215	3,578	93	71	1028	2,988	58	593	0	14,395	2,354	15,790	730	2,752	7,707	31,881	428	3,703
Thailand	287	1,414	175	245	169	925	0	80	330	1,351	566	2,703	258	703	3,527	18,843	314	2,300
United States	6,380	12,543	414	555	98,054	202,207	1,787	4,133	4,466	27,609	9,707	41,430	6,801	8,485	68,134	162,841	14,540	36,066

a. Brackets denote 1992 figures.

Source: International Monetary Fund, *Direction of Trade Statistics,* 1994, 1989.

	Malaysia		Mexico		New Zealand		Papua New Guinea		Philippines		Singapore		Taipei		Thailand		United States	
	1983	1993	1983	1993	1983	1993	1983	1993	1983	1993	1983	1993	1983	1993	1983	1993	1983	1993
Australia	741	1,922	13	169	1,730	4,148	460	1,515	276	597	1,173	3,152	1,215	3,578	280	1,463	6,376	11,815
Brunei	47	191	0	3	1	11	0	0	66	62	544	851	93	71	130	215	78	510
Canada	3,991	689	673	3,264	226	334	5	5	132	343	267	818	1,028	2,988	201	918	90,790	213,794
Chile	5	118	21	335	7	28	0	6	2	55	15	153	58	593	4	101	1782	4,307
China	427	2,303	64	168	145	502	50	108	102	430	1,040	4,309	0	14,395	373	1,335	4,650	42,497
Hong Kong	441	2,863	22	595	135	344	24	58	423	1,520	2,082	9,114	2,345	15,790	434	2,495	9,388	19,873
Indonesia	156	1,261	18	193	291	203	2	38	207	368	6,593	5,165	730	2,752	154	715	7,123	8,657
Japan	6,144	18,646	1,832	4,960	1,760	3,095	432	795	2,326	5,938	7,083	24,189	7,707	31,881	3,776	18,205	65,453	158,368
Korea	900	3,005	155	1,140	143	656	42	[171]	310	1,016	885	4,809	428	31,881	335	2,409	13,582	32,556
Malaysia	13	258	7	237	106	334	6	66	321	526	7,931	24,539	720	3,703	839	2,715	3,889	16,988
Mexico					26	176	0	0	113	41	20	172	0	3,958	14	148	26,101	82,381
New Zealand	126	442	17	175			56	77	76	135	288	407	159	688	57	159	1448	2,573
Papua New Guinea	2	72	0	0	58	79			12	82	152	178	11	552	1	37	111	157
Philippines	322	720	92	39	74	138	9	75			549	1,877	299	37	83	379	3,967	8,705
Singapore	5,027	17,183	11	168	297	283	146	176	429	1,410			782	1,367	1,154	7,428	6,728	24,726
Taipei	720	3,958	0	668	159	552	11	37	299	1,367	782	6,257			358	3,074	16,777	42,550
Thailand	976	2,829	1	142	44	184	2	49	69	341	1,450	7,731	358	6,257			2,098	12,751
United States	3,991	17,305	17,992	78,687	1,559	2,955	115	147	3,624	7,878	8,215	29,029	16,777	42,550	2,234	13,383		

Appendix C: APEC organizational chart

Informal Economic Leaders' Meeting (LM)

Ministerial Meeting (MM)

Budget and Administration Committee (BAC)	Senior Officials' Meeting (SOM)	Eminent Persons Group (EPG)

Committee on Trade and Investment (CTI)

- Evaluation of regional free trade areas within the APEC region such as NAFTA and AFTA.
- Four current projects—tariff data base, simplification of customs procedures, market access, investment regulations handbook.
- Promotion of greater liberalization of trade and investment through discussion of mutual recognition of investment principles, standards and certification, etc. Publication of a follow-up to the EPG report.
- CTI evolved from the Informal Group on Regional Trade Liberalization (RTL).

Economic Committee

- Discussion of economic trends and issues.
- Implementation of the recommendations outlined in Japan's "Vision for the Economy of the Asia-Pacific Region in the Year 2000 and Tasks Ahead" and the follow-up report.
- Collection of economic data and short-term economic forecasts.
- Macro- and microeconomic policy dialogue.
- Japan's 3Es Study—examination of the ways of harmonizing economic growth, energy security, and environmental protection.

(10 Working Groups—WG)

	Shepherd	Project
Trade and Investment Data Review	Indonesia, Japan Singapore, United States	• Economic data review aiming to establish near-comparable data. • Possible creation of an APEC database.
Trade Promotion	Indonesia, Korea Malaysia, Thailand	• Exchange of trade information. • Seminars, fairs, and training courses.
Investment and Industrial Science and Technology	China, Indonesia Japan, Philippines	• Assessment of an investment and technology information network. • Assistance in the construction of a technopark—manuals, seminars, etc.
Human Resources Development	Australia, Canada, Indonesia, Japan, Korea, Malaysia, Thailand	• Creation of a network between the various human resources institutions throughout the region (business management, economic development, industrial science and technology, etc.).
Energy	Australia	• Examination of ways of improving energy supply and demand. • Assessment of environmental issues, energy conservation, and technology transfer, etc.
Marine Resources Conservation	Canada, Indonesia, New Zealand	• Examination of such issues as marine pollution and the ocean dumping of wastes.
Fisheries	Indonesia, Japan, New Zealand, Thailand	• Cooperation in the management of fisheries resources.
Telecommunications	United States	• Survey of the telecommunications environment. • Creation of a basic network for electronic data interchange.
Transportation	United States	• Survey of the basic transportation infrastructure throughout the region and recommendations for future improvements.
Tourism	United States	• Study of ways to reduce barriers to promote tourism.

Index

Air travel, 23
Alatas, Ali, Indonesian Foreign Minister
  on APEC Secretariat, 198
  on ASEAN versus APEC, 67
  attitude to Seattle summit, 81
  on capital flows, 67
  on institutionalization, 140
  profile, 45–46
  turf battles, 136
Anand, Panyarachun, Thai Prime Minister, 109, 177, 207–8
Anti-communism, 6, 7, 111, 176. *See also* Cold War
ANZUS pact, 227
Argentina, 76
ASEAN (Association of Southeast Nations)
  ASEAN Economic Ministerial (AEM) "6 plus 3" meetings, 109–10, 207
  ASEAN Regional Forum (ARF), 168, 198, 238
  assurances about APEC, 2
  as caucus within APEC, 64
  China and, 167–68, 230
  common interests with Japan and US, 181
  competition from Eastern Europe, 67, 166
  free trade area (AFTA), 8, 77, 166
  Gaimusho and, 211–13
  human rights, 167
  Japan and, 166, 192–93, 197–98, 229
  Japan-ASEAN finance ministers' meeting, 214
  Korea and, 18
  Malay society, 210
  as model, 52–53, 77

new course of, 109–10
origins, 166
Philippines, 18
politics of, 209
Post-Ministerial Conference (PMC), 18, 110, 238
as regional power, 165–69
security issues, 167–68
Sinic society, 210
Three Chinas and, 65
US and, 167–68
ASEAN Five, 95
ASEAN Free Trade Area (AFTA), 8, 77, 166
ASEAN Regional Forum (ARF), 168, 198, 238
ASEAN-ANZCER. See Australia-New Zealand Closer Economic Relations
ASEAN-EU plus three summit, 165, 171, 207, 211
Asia
  Asian way, 147, 149
  as the "East," 19
  Japanese attempts to lead, 187–88
"Asia for Asians," 57, 58, 122, 188
Asia Business News (ABN), 27
Asian Development Bank (ADB), 123, 228
Asia Pacific Economic Cooperation forum (APEC)
  choice of meeting sites, 64
  congeniality, 79, 145, 147
  consensus, 82, 92, 116, 145, 146–47
  economic dimensions, 2–3, 4, 5–6
  effectiveness, 128
  engaging China, 112–13

Comparative advantage, 26
Concentric circles theory, 67, 128, 129
Concepcion, José, Philippine Secretary of Trade
 and Industry, 57, 58, 122
Concerted unilateral action (CUA), 96–98
 Bogor Declaration, 93
 concept of, 3
 domestic politics and, 126
 opposed by US, 93, 102
Conference on Security and Cooperation in
 Europe (CSCE), 178
Conflict resolution, 111
Confucian culture, 17, 34, 37
Containment, 113. See also Cold War
CUA. See concerted unilateral action
Cultural arrogance, 181
Culture, 15, 31–38

Decision-making processes, 146–49
Defense Department (US), 114
Deming, W. Edwards, 31
Democratization, 239
Deregulation of Japan, 235–36
Development assistance, 98–99, 119, 194–95,
 196, 236–37, 239–40
Discrimination, racial, 32
Disneyland, Tokyo, 28
Division of labor, international, 26
Divorce rates, 35
Drysdale, Peter, 53, 58, 200
Dulles, John Foster, Secretary of State (US), 232

E-mail system,
 APEC, 138
 ASEAN, 18
East Asian Economic Group/Caucus (EAEG/
 C), 68–69
 as bargaining tool, 109–10
 evolution, 205–07
 Japan and, 122, 206–11, 231
 North-South challenges, 234
 political implications for the Asia Pacific,
 209–11
 South Korea and, 122
 support for, 207–09
 suspicious reaction to, 211
East versus West, 31–38, 230–32
Eastern Europe
 breakdown of authority, 20
 competition from, 9, 67, 166
 FDI and, 67
EC. See European Community.
Eco-tourism, 28
Economies, analogies of Asian, 234
Ecuador, 76
Educational exchange, 99
Educational levels, 24, 30
Eisenhower, Dwight, US President, 232
Eminent Persons Group (EPG)
 1993 report, 196

1995 recommendations, 129
ASEAN members of, 166
at Seattle summit, 134
and term "community", 1
functioning of, 140–41
Japanese turf battles over, 212
liberalization timetable and, 94
Malaysia protests, 92
mandated, 77
open subregionalism, 102, 129
English language, 29–30, 32–33
EPG. See Eminent Persons Group
Estanislao, Jesus, Philippine Finance Minister,
 34, 57, 67, 120, 128, 129, 148
Ethnic conflicts, 10
Ethnic diversity, 4
EU-ASEAN plus 3 summit, 165, 171, 207, 211
European arrival in Asia, 16
European Bank for Reconstruction and
 Development (EBRD), 67
European Community, 1
 Council of Ministers, 169
European Union (EU)
 Asian concern over single market, 226
 bureaucracy of, 139
 compared to APEC, 3, 22
 divisions within, 170
 economic potential for Asia, 169–72
 equalization scheme, 146
 Japanese investment, 236
 leverage of APEC, 62, 107–108, 196, 201
 liberalization, 126
 membership issues, 142
 protectionism, 124
 reaction to APEC, 79, 169
 as regional bloc, 108
 regular meetings of, 135
Evans, Gareth, Australian Foreign and Trade
 Minister, 19, 55, 62, 64, 66, 142–43

Fair Trade Commission (FTC) of Japan, 215
Fauver, Robert, 74, 77, 80–82, 83, 136
"Flexible consensus" concept, 146–47
Flying geese developmental pattern, 38, 193
Foreign debt of Asian nations, 237
Foreign direct investment (FDI), 24
 Japan, 24, 161, 188, 193, 228, 236–37
 South Korea, 24
Foreign ministers, role of, 135–36
Foreign Ministry of Japan, 136. See also
 Gaimusho
Fraser, Malcolm, Australian Prime Minister, 53
Free riding issue, 95–96
 Bogor Declaration, 93
 Europe, 91
 open regionalism, 126
 reciprocity and, 125, 127
Freedom of navigation, 180
Fukuda Doctrine, 234
Fukuda, Takeo, Japanese Prime Minister, 229

Other Publications from the
Institute for International Economics

POLICY ANALYSES IN INTERNATIONAL ECONOMICS Series

BOOKS

Completing the Uruguay Round: A Results-Oriented Approach
to the GATT Trade Negotiations
Jeffrey J. Schott, editor/*September 1990*
                        ISBN paper 0-88132-130-3   256 pp.

Economic Sanctions Reconsidered (in two volumes)
    Economic Sanctions Reconsidered: Supplemental Case Histories
    Gary Clyde Hufbauer, Jeffrey J. Schott, and Kimberly Ann Elliott/*1985, 2d ed.*
        December 1990
                        ISBN cloth 0-88132-115-X   928 pp.
                        ISBN paper 0-88132-105-2   928 pp.

    Economic Sanctions Reconsidered: History and Current Policy
    Gary Clyde Hufbauer, Jeffrey J. Schott, and Kimberly Ann Elliott/*December 1990*
                        ISBN cloth 0-88132-136-2   288 pp.
                        ISBN paper 0-88132-140-0   288 pp.

Pacific Basin Developing Countries: Prospects for the Future
Marcus Noland/*January 1991*
(out of print)   ISBN cloth 0-88132-141-9   250 pp.
                        ISBN paper 0-88132-081-1   250 pp.

Currency Convertibility in Eastern Europe
John Williamson, editor/*October 1991*
                        ISBN cloth 0-88132-144-3   396 pp.
                        ISBN paper 0-88132-128-1   396 pp.

International Adjustment and Financing: The Lessons of 1985-1991
C. Fred Bergsten, editor/*January 1992*
                        ISBN paper 0-88132-112-5   336 pp.

North American Free Trade: Issues and Recommendations
Gary Clyde Hufbauer and Jeffrey J. Schott/*April 1992*
                        ISBN cloth 0-88132-145-1   392 pp.
                        ISBN paper 0-88132-120-6   392 pp.

Narrowing the U.S. Current Account Deficit
Allen J. Lenz/*June 1992*
(out of print)   ISBN cloth 0-88132-148-6   640 pp.
                        ISBN paper 0-88132-103-6   640 pp.

The Economics of Global Warming
William R. Cline/*June 1992*
                        ISBN cloth 0-88132-150-8   416 pp.
                        ISBN paper 0-88132-132-X   416 pp.

U.S. Taxation of International Income: Blueprint for Reform
Gary Clyde Hufbauer, assisted by Joanna M. van Rooij/*October 1992*
                        ISBN cloth 0-88132-178-8   304 pp.
                        ISBN paper 0-88132-134-6   304 pp.

Who's Bashing Whom? Trade Conflict in High-Technology Industries
Laura D'Andrea Tyson/*November 1992*
                        ISBN cloth 0-88132-151-6   352 pp.
                        ISBN paper 0-88132-106-0   352 pp.

Korea in the World Economy
Il SaKong/*January 1993*
                        ISBN cloth 0-88132-184-2   328 pp.
                        ISBN paper 0-88132-106-0   328 pp.

Managing the World Economy: Fifty Years After Bretton Woods
Peter B. Kenen, editor/*September 1994*
ISBN paper 0-88132-212-1   448 pp.

Reciprocity and Retaliation in U.S. Trade Policy
Thomas O. Bayard and Kimberly Ann Elliott/*September 1994*
ISBN paper 0-88132-084-6   528 pp.

The Uruguay Round: An Assessment
Jeffrey J. Schott, assisted by Johanna W. Buurman/*November 1994*
ISBN paper 0-88132-206-7   240 pp.

Measuring the Costs of Protection in Japan
Yoko Sazanami, Shujiro Urata, and Hiroki Kawai/*January 1995*
ISBN paper 0-88132-211-3   96 pp.

Foreign Direct Investment in the United States, Third Edition
Edward M. Graham and Paul R. Krugman/*January 1995*
ISBN paper 0-88132-204-0   232 pp.

The Political Economy of Korea-United States Cooperation
C. Fred Bergsten and Il SaKong, editors/*February 1995*
ISBN paper 0-88132-213-X   128 pp.

International Debt Reexamined
William R. Cline/*February 1995*
ISBN paper 0-88132-083-8   560 pp.

American Trade Politics, Third Edition
I. M. Destler/*April 1995*
ISBN paper 0-88132-215-6   360 pp.

Managing Official Export Credits: The Quest for a Global Regime
John E. Ray/*July 1995*
ISBN paper 0-88132-207-5   344 pp.

Asia Pacific Fusion: Japan's Role in APEC
Yoichi Funabashi/*October 1995*
ISBN paper 0-88132-224-5   312 pp.

SPECIAL REPORTS

1 Promoting World Recovery: A Statement on Global Economic Strategy
   by Twenty-six Economists from Fourteen Countries/*December 1982*
   (out of print)   ISBN paper 0-88132-013-7   45 pp.
2 Prospects for Adjustment in Argentina, Brazil, and Mexico:
   Responding to the Debt Crisis
   John Williamson, editor/*June 1983*
   (out of print)   ISBN paper 0-88132-016-1   71 pp.
3 Inflation and Indexation: Argentina, Brazil, and Israel
   John Williamson, editor/*March 1985*
                         ISBN paper 0-88132-037-4   191 pp.
4 Global Economic Imbalances
   C. Fred Bergsten, editor/*March 1986*
                         ISBN cloth 0-88132-038-2   126 pp.
                         ISBN paper 0-88132-042-0   126 pp.
5 African Debt and Financing
   Carol Lancaster and John Williamson, editors/*May 1986*
   (out of print)   ISBN paper 0-88132-044-7   229 pp
6 Resolving the Global Economic Crisis: After Wall Street
   Thirty-three Economists from Thirteen Countries/*December 1987*
                         ISBN paper 0-88132-070-6   30 pp.

WORKS IN PROGRESS

The list below describes research in progress at the Institute. It is intended to inform our customers about our current research agenda. We do not accept back orders for books in this section because of the uncertainty about publication dates.

Global Firms and National Governments
Edward M. Graham

Mismanaging the World Economy: The Demise of the G7
C. Fred Bergsten and C. Randall Henning

Trade, Jobs, and Income Distribution
William R. Cline

Trade and Labor Standards
Kimberly Ann Elliott and Richard Freeman

Regionalism and Globalism in the World Economic System
Jeffrey A. Frankel

Overseeing Global Capital Markets
Morris Goldstein and Peter Garber

Global Competition Policy
Edward M. Graham and J. David Richardson

Border Tax Adjustment
Gary Clyde Hufbauer

Toward an Asia Pacific Economic Community?
Gary Clyde Hufbauer and Jeffrey J. Schott

The Economics of Korean Unification
Marcus Noland

The Case for Trade: A Modern Reconsideration
J. David Richardson

The Future of the World Trading System
John Whalley, in collaboration with Colleen Hamilton

Standards and APEC: An Action Agenda
John S. Wilson

For orders outside the US and Canada please contact:
Longman Group UK Ltd.   Telephone Orders: 0279 623923
PO Box 88   Fax: 0279 453450
Fourth Avenue   Telex: 81259
Harlow, Essex CM 19 5SR   UK

Canadian customers can order from the Institute or from either:
RENOUF BOOKSTORE   LA LIBERTÉ
1294 Algoma Road   3020 chemin Sainte-Foy
Ottawa, Ontario K1B 3W8   Quebec G1X 3V6
Telephone: (613) 741-4333   Telephone: (418) 658-3763
Fax: (613) 741-5439   Fax: (800) 567-5449